DATE DUE			

The Catholic Tradition:
The Church, Vol. 1

The Catholic Tradition

REV. CHARLES J. DOLLEN
DR. JAMES K. McGOWAN
DR. JAMES J. MEGIVERN
EDITORS

The Catholic Tradition

The Church
Volume 1

A Consortium Book

Library of Congress Card Catalog Number: 79-1977
ISBN: 0-8434-0726-3
ISBN; 0-8434-0725-5 series

The publisher gratefully acknowledges permission to quote from the
following copyrighted sources. In cases where those properties contain
scholarly apparatus such as footnotes, such footnotes have been omitted
in the interest of the general reader.

GEORGE BELL & SONS
Bede's Ecclesiastical History of the English Nation, edited by J. A.
Giles, D.C.L., 1907.

THE CATHOLIC UNIVERSITY OF AMERICA PRESS, INC.
"The Unity of the Catholic Church" from *The Fathers of the Church*,
Volume 36, *St. Cyprian: Treatises*, translated and edited by Roy J.
Deferrari, copyright ©1958; Selections from *The Fathers of the Church*,
Volume 19, *Eusebius Pamphile: Ecclesiastical History*, Books 1-5,
translated by Roy J. Deferrari, copyright 1953 and Volume 29, *Eusebius
Pamphile: Ecclesiastical History*, Books 6-10, translated by Roy J.
Deferrari, copyright ©1955; Selections from *The Fathers of the Church*,
Volume 24, *St. Augustine: The City of God*, Books XVII–XXII, trans-
lated by Gerald G. Walsh, S.J. and Daniel J. Honan, copyright 1954.

THE CHRISTIAN LITERATURE COMPANY
Selections from "St. Jerome: On Famous Men" from *A Select Library of
Nicene and Post-Nicene Fathers*, translated by Philip Schaff, D.D., LL.D.
and Henry Wace, D.D., 1892.

CHARLES DOLMAN
*Symbolism: or Exposition of the Doctrinal Differences between Catho-
lics and Protestants as Evidenced by Their Symbolic Writings* by John
Adam Moehler, translated by James Burton Robertson, 1843.

EARLY ENGLISH TEXT SOCIETY
Selections from King Alfred's West-Saxon Version of *Gregory's Pastoral
Care*, 1872.

Table of Contents

Introduction

The Catholic Tradition is a 14 volume anthology of excerpts from the great Catholic writers from antiquity to the present day. *The Catholic Tradition* is intended for the armchair reader who has not studied theology or church history and has not time to struggle unassisted through 198 books. The publisher's intention is to provide such a reader with a compact home library that will permit him to familiarize himself with the great Catholic writers and their works. The works included in *The Catholic Tradition* are all religious in subject. The publisher did not include fiction or nonfiction books on secular subjects written by Catholic authors.

The Catholic Tradition arranges the writings according to religious subjects. There are seven religious subjects, each of which is covered in two volumes: The Church; Mass and the Sacraments; Sacred Scripture; The Saviour; Personal Ethics; Social Thought; and Spirituality. Within each subject, the writings are arranged in chronological order, which permits the reader to follow the development of Catholic thought across 2000 years.

Each excerpt in *The Catholic Tradition* is preceded by a brief biographical and explanatory introduction to help the reader understand the world in which the writer lived and wrote, and the problems with which he was dealing.

The selection of the excerpts and the writing of the introductions has been a long and difficult process. The task of making the final selections was particularly arduous (as such choices always are); the most modern authors, about whose writing there is yet no final judgment provoking the most debate. The selection of authors was made originally in the publisher's offices and then submitted to the three editors of the series who refined the selection. The editors submitted their selection to an unofficial board of scholars who very kindly made constructive comments.

The process of assembling the many hundreds of books from which to make the final selection was in itself a vast task. Many of the books under consideration were very scarce and not available in bookstores or libraries. The work of collecting the books and then making selections among them stretched over a three year period, and many books were selected for inclusion and later rejected after careful scrutiny and reflection.

The editing of *The Catholic Tradition* was a long and difficult job because the literature of Roman Catholicism is a vast and complex body. Of all the Christian denominations, the Roman Catholic Church is by far the oldest and largest. Its ranks include a tremendous number of saints and scholars, writers and thinkers, mystics and preachers: many of whom felt so strongly about their faith that they were willing to die for it. They have left an incomparably rich legacy of art and writing. Selecting from it is not simple.

The selections that we made are representative of the best of mainstream Catholic writing. Generally, they should be intelligible to a thoughtful layman. Some however, may prove more technical than others, and some of the very recent writers may seem controversial. The reader should bear in mind that some theological questions simply do not admit of facile answers, and that some of the earlier writers were considered controversial in their own days. It is also well to remember that the writings gathered here, brilliant and revered as their authors may be, are not necessarily official statements of Church policy. But they are, all of them, solidly part of the Catholic tradition.

The writers are all Catholics, many of them clergymen, some of them converts to Catholicism. They all wrote as loyal

Introduction

servants of the Church and from a Catholic point of view. When they wrote on personal ethics they proceeded from the assumption that man's goal was to imitate Christ, not simply to follow a secular set of ethical rules. When they wrote on social problems they expressed the need to solve social problems because they loved their neighbors, not for the material enrichment of society. Their writings on Christ reflect an intense struggle to bend human language to divine definition. Taken together, their writings form a literary tradition that is Roman Catholic at heart. That tradition has certain ingredients that are not present in the literary traditions of the other Christian denominations. Particularly, the heritage of liturgical ceremony and mystical contemplation have left an incomparable treasure of literature that is here presented in the volumes entitled *Mass and the Sacraments,* and *Spirituality.*

The whole corpus of Catholic thinking and writing, distilled here in *The Catholic Tradition,* is generally considered by scholars to have three important periods: the ancient, or patristic, period; the high middle-ages, which is the era of St. Thomas Aquinas and sometimes called the scholastic period; finally the time in which we live today, the last 100 years. These three epochs are golden ages of Catholic writing. They are separated from each other by the generally unproductive eras of the dark ages and the Reformation.

Through all these epochs the great Catholic writers have preserved and developed the Christian message: love God; love your fellow man. Each writer wrote conscious of the tradition behind him, conscious that he was building on the work of men before him, adapting their work to changed conditions or continuing their work on the outer edges of human speculation.

The present day writers, those of the third great era of Catholic writing, are the most important part of *The Catholic Tradition.* Here for the first time their thinking is presented along with the work of their predecessors; here can be seen the stunning achievement of today's Catholic writing, and how it follows logically from the writing of the patristic and scholastic thinkers.

The present day writers presented in *The Catholic Tradition* number 114, over half of the total number of writers chosen.

Their writing will probably prove more intelligible to the average reader because they write in today's idiom and they address contemporary problems.

Oddly enough, many if not most of the modern writers are not familiar to the average Catholic. St. Augustine, and St. Thomas Aquinas are household names, but only serious Catholic readers today are familiar with the masterful writings of Karl Rahner, Edward Schillebeeckx, Raymond Brown, and Gustavo Gutiérrez. None the less, these men are representative of a great historical flowering of Catholic writing today and their names may well echo down the ages.

THE PUBLISHER

St. Ignatius of Antioch

d. 110

Ignatius, bishop of Antioch in Syria, was sentenced to death during the reign of the Emperor Trajan (98-107 a.d.), and is thought to have died a martyr's death in Rome around 107 a.d. It is an irony of history that we know nothing of his activities in his home country before his arrest. As he was on his way under military escort from Syria to Rome, he wrote seven letters which have survived. Four were written during a stop-over in Smyrna; three of them were addressed to nearby Christian communities that had sent representatives to meet him as he passed through, those at Ephesus, Tralles, and Magnesia. The fourth was addressed to the Christians of Rome, alerting them to his coming and pleading with them to do nothing to prevent his martyrdom.

His guards then moved him on to Troas, and there he found the opportunity to write three more letters: one to the Church of Smyrna which had treated him so kindly, one to the church in Philadelphia that he had had some slight contact with earlier in the journey, and a personal one to Polycarp, bishop of Smyrna, who had apparently done all he could for Ignatius during his stay there.

We know from Polycarp that the route of Ignatius took him through Philippi, where he met with the local church, but thereupon he drops out of sight and we can only conjecture *that his end came in the Roman Coliseum, as tradition contends. His letters are of exceptional interest in that they come from a period that is not very well represented in surviving documents, and yet which must have been of special importance in the formation of the early Christian Church and its practices.*

Two things especially characterize Ignatius: his enthusiasm and his insistence on unity. He presents us with a picture of a remarkably well organized Church: a single bishop presides as God's representative, his priests form an apostolic senate around him, and the deacons perform the services of Christ. The role of the bishop in the Church has clearly evolved well beyond what is found in the New Testament.

It is tantalizing to think of how much else we could have learned from Ignatius. As leader of the pivotal Christian Church in Antioch in the half-century after Peter and Paul, he would have had access to all the major developments of that crucial period. It was a time of persecution and struggle that called for strong leadership. We can sense the voice of hard experience when he writes to Polycarp: "Stand firm like an anvil under the hammer. A great boxer will take a beating and yet win through."

What we do learn from him indirectly is that major Christian beliefs are well on their way toward the fuller expression that they will finally find in the 4th and 5th century Councils. He combines the doctrinal approaches of Paul and John, becoming an eloquent advocate of the imitation of Christ as the basis of morality. As he writes to the Philadelphians: "Be imitators of Jesus Christ, as He is of His Father." This theme is ultimately carried to the point of suffering and dying as Jesus did, the goal which he fervently hopes the Romans will not deprive him of by any plea for clemency. "I would rather die for Jesus Christ than rule the last reaches of the earth . . . The pangs of new birth are upon me."

SEVEN EPISTLES

I

TO THE EPHESIANS

Ignatius Theophorus greets the Church of Ephesus in Asia, congratulating you as you deserve and wishing you perfect joy in Jesus Christ—you who have grown in spiritual stature through the fullness of God the Father, and have been predestined from eternity to eternal abiding and unchanging glory, and have been united and chosen through a true passion by the will of the Father and of Jesus Christ, our God.

I have welcomed in God your well beloved name, which is yours by reason of your natural [sense and] goodness in accord with faith and charity in Jesus Christ, our Savior. Imitators of God as you are, with hearts warmed in the blood of God, you have done perfectly the work that fell to you to do; for you were eager to visit me when you heard that I was on my way from Syria, in chains because of our common name and hope, and longing, with the help of your prayers, to face the wild beasts in Rome and not to fail and so become a disciple. And so in God's name I received your whole community in the person of Onesimus, your bishop, in the flesh, a man whose charity is beyond all power to say. I beg of you to love him in Jesus Christ and to be like him to a man. May He be blessed who gave you the grace to have and to deserve to have such a bishop.

A word about Burrhus, my fellow worker and your deacon by the will of God, a man blessed in every way. It is my prayer that he may continue with me to your honor and that of your bishop. Crocus, too, who is worthy of God and of yourselves, I have received as an exemplar of the love you bear me. He has been a great comfort to me in every way. May the Father of Jesus Christ reward him with His grace—and not only him but Onesimus, Burrhus, Euplus and Fronto; for in them I saw the love of all of you. If only I deserve it, may I have joy in you always. And so it is right for you to glorify Jesus Christ in every way, who has given you glory so that you may be made perfect in a single obedience to your bishop and the priests and be made holy in every way.

I do not give you orders as though I were a person of importance, for I have not yet been made perfect in Jesus Christ, even though I am a prisoner for His name. But, at last, I am beginning to be His disciple and to speak to you as His disciples, too. For I have need of being trained by you in faith, counsel, endurance and long-suffering. Still, love will not let me be silent in your regard, and so I make bold to beg you to be in harmony with God's mind. For Jesus Christ, the life that cannot be taken from us, is the mind of the Father, and the bishops appointed to ends of the earth are of one mind with Jesus Christ.

Hence, it is right for you to concur, as you do, with the name of the bishop. For your priests, who are worthy of the name and worthy of God, like the strings of a lyre, are in harmony with bishops. Hence it is that in the harmony of your minds and hearts Jesus Christ is hymned. Make of yourselves a choir, so that with one voice and one mind, taking the key-note of God, you may sing in unison with one voice through Jesus Christ to the Father, and He may hear you and recognize you, in your good works, as members of His son. It is good for you, therefore, to be in perfect unity that you may at all times be partakers of God.

And if I, in a short time, have achieved such spiritual and not merely human communion with your bishop, all the more do I congratulate you who have become one with him, as the Church is one with Jesus Christ and as Jesus Christ is one with the Father, so that all things may be in harmony. Let no man be deceived. If a person is not inside the sanctuary he is deprived of the Bread [of God]. For if the prayer of one or two men has so much force, how much greater is that of the bishop and of the whole Church. Any one, therefore, who fails to assemble with the others has already shown his pride and set himself apart. For it is written: 'God resists the proud.' Let us be careful, therefore, not to oppose the bishop, so that we may be obedient to God.

And let a man respect the bishop all the more if he sees him to be a man of few words. For, whoever is sent by the Master to run His house, we ought to receive him as we would receive the Master himself. It is obvious, therefore, that we ought to regard the bishop as we would the Lord Himself. I should tell you that Onesimus himself is full of praise for your orderly, religious behavior, because all of you are living according to truth and because among you no heresy finds a home. Indeed, you do not so much as listen to anyone unless his speech is of Jesus Christ in truth.

There are some who, in guile and wickedness, have a way of bearing the Name about while behaving in a way unworthy of God. Such men you must shun as you would wild beasts; for they are mad dogs that bite when you are not on your guard. Of these you must beware, for these men are hard to heal. There is one Doctor active in both body and soul, begotten and yet unbegotten, God in man, true life in death, son of Mary and Son of God, first able to suffer and then unable to suffer, Jesus Christ, our Lord.

Let no one, therefore, deceive you as, in fact, being wholly given to God, you are not deceived. For, so long as no passion within you has an established power to torment you, you are certainly living according to God. As a cheap sacrifice in your stead I offer myself for you Ephesians, for your Church which will be remembered in every age. Carnal men can no more do the works of the spirit than those who walk in the spirit do the things of the flesh; nor can faith do the things of infidelity nor infidelity the things of faith. Since you do all things in Jesus Christ, even those things are spiritual which you do according to the flesh.

I have learned that some strangers holding bad doctrine have passed your way, but that you have not allowed them to sow their seed among you and have stopped your ears lest you should receive what they sowed. Like the stones of a temple, cut for a building of God the Father, you have been lifted up to the top by the crane of Jesus Christ, which is the Cross, and the rope of the Holy Spirit. For your faith has drawn you up and charity has been the road leading to God. You are all fellow pilgrims, carrying with you God and His temple; you are bearers

5

of Christ and of holy offerings, decked out in the command-ments of Jesus Christ. And with this letter I am able to take part in your festivity, to be of your company, to share in the joy that comes from setting your heart not on what is merely human in life, but on God.

And so do not cease to pray for all other men, for there is hope of their conversion and of their finding God. Give them the chance to be instructed, at least by the way you behave. When they are angry with you, be meek; answer their words of pride by your humility, their blasphemies by your prayers, their error by your steadfastness in faith, their bullying by your gentleness. Let us not be in a hurry to give them tit for tat, but, by our sweet reasonableness show that we are their brothers. Let us rather be eager to imitate the Lord, striving to be the first in bearing wrongs, in suffering loss, in being despised, so that no weed of the evil one may be found among you; but abide in Jesus Christ in perfect purity and temperance of body and soul.

The last days are at hand. For the rest, let us live in rever-ence and fear of the patience of God, let it turn in judgment against us. Either let us fear the wrath which is to come or else let us love the grace we have—one or the other, so long as we are found in Jesus Christ unto true life. Let nothing appeal to you apart from Him, by whose help I bear my chains about with me like spiritual pearls; and in these, with your prayers—in which I trust always to have a share—may I rise again, so that I may be found in the company of the Christian Ephesians who have always been at one with the Apostles through the power of Jesus Christ.

I know who I am and to whom I am writing. I am a con-demned man; you have received mercy. I am in danger; you are safe. You are the road for those on the way to die for God. You have shared in the sacraments with Paul who was made a saint, who died a martyr, who deserved to be blessed—in whose foot-steps may I be found when I reach God; in whose every letter there is a mention of you in Christ Jesus.

Be zealous, therefore, to assemble more frequently to ren-der thanks and praise to God. For, when you meet together frequently, the powers of Satan are destroyed and danger from him is dissolved in the harmony of your faith. There is nothing

6

better than peace in which an end is put to the warfare of things in heaven and on earth.

You are aware of all these truths if you have perfect faith and love for Jesus Christ—the beginning and end of life; for faith is the beginning and the end is love and God is the two of them brought into unity. After these comes whatever else makes up a Christian gentleman. No one commits sin who professes the faith, and no one hates who is possessed of charity. A tree is shown by its fruit, and in the same way those who profess to belong to Christ will be seen by what they do. For what is needed is not mere present profession, but perseverance to the end in the power of faith.

It is better to say nothing and be [a Christian] than to speak and not to be [one]. It is good to teach, if one practices what he preaches. There is one Teacher who spoke—and the thing was done; and even the things He did without speaking are worthy of the Father. Anyone who is really possessed of the word of Jesus can listen to His silence and so be perfect; so that he may act through his words and be known by his silence. Nothing is hidden from the Lord and even the things we hide are near Him. Let us do all that we do, therefore, as though He were dwelling within us—we as His temple and He within as our God. And so, indeed, it is, and will be clearly seen by us from the love we justly bear Him.

Make no mistake, brethren; the corrupters of families will not inherit the kingdom of God. If, then, those are dead who do these things according to the flesh, how much worse if, with bad doctrine, one should corrupt the faith of God for which Jesus Christ was crucified. Such a man, for becoming contaminated, will depart into unquenchable fire; and so will any one who listens to him.

It was for this reason that the Lord received the ointment on his head—that he might breathe the odor of incorruptibility into the Church. Be not anointed with the bad odor of the doctrine of the prince of this world, lest he lead you away captive from the life proposed to you. Why do we not all become wise by accepting the knowledge of God which is Jesus Christ? Why do we perish in our folly by being ignorant of the grace which the Lord has truly sent us?

I offer up my life as a poor substitute for the Cross, which is a stumbling block to those who have no faith, but to us salvation and eternal life. Where is the wise man? Where is the philosopher? Where is the boasting of the so-called men of prudence? For our God Jesus Christ was, according to God's dispensation, the fruit of Mary's womb, of the seed of David; He was born and baptized in order that He might make the water holy by His passion.

The maidenhood of Mary and her child-bearing and also the death of the Lord were hidden from the prince of this world—three resounding mysteries wrought in the silence of God. How, then, did He appear in time? A star, brighter than all other stars, shone in the sky, and its brightness was ineffable and the novelty of it caused astonishment. And on the rest of the stars, along with the sun and the moon, formed a choir about the star; but the light of the star by itself outshone all the rest. It was a puzzle to know the origin of this novelty unlike anything else. Thereupon all magic was dissolved, every bond of malice disappeared, ignorance was destroyed, the ancient kingdom was ruined, when God appeared in the form of man to give us newness of eternal life. What had been prepared in God now had a beginning. And, because of the plan for the abolition of death, all things were disturbed.

If, through your prayers, Jesus Christ should make me worthy and if it should be His will, and still more if the Lord should reveal it to me, in a second letter which I intend to write to you, I shall explain more fully what I have merely touched upon—the dispensation of becoming the new man Jesus Christ, who is of the race of David according to the passion and resurrection. Come together in common, one and all without exception in charity, in one faith and in one Jesus Christ, who is of the race of David according to the flesh, the son of man and Son of God, so that with undivided mind you may obey the bishop and the priests, and break one Bread which is the medicine of immortality and the antidote against death, enabling us to live for ever in Jesus Christ.

I am offering up my life for you and for those whom, to the honor of God, you sent to Smyrna; and from here I write to you, thanking the Lord and loving Polycarp as I love you. Remember me as Jesus Christ remembers you. Pray for the Church which is in Syria, from which I, the last of the faithful there, am being led away a prisoner to Rome; for so I was deemed worthy to be found to God's glory. Farewell in God the Father and in Jesus Christ our common hope.

II

TO THE MAGNESIANS

Ignatius Theophorus to the Church in Magnesia near the Maeander that is blessed with the grace of God the Father through Jesus Christ our Savior. I salute you and wish you every joy in God the Father and in Jesus Christ.

I have heard of the perfect order of your love toward God; and so it is with great joy and in the faith of Jesus Christ that I have decided to address you. Honored as I have been with a name so dear to God, I sing, in the chains I bear about with me, the praise of the Churches. And I pray that the Churches may have unity in the flesh and spirit of Jesus Christ, who is our everlasting life—a union in faith and charity that is to be preferred to all else and, especially, union with Jesus and the Father, through whom we shall reach God if only we bear with and escape from the wanton attacks of the prince of this world.

It was possible for me to see you in the persons of your devout bishop Damas and the worthy priests, Bassus and Apollonius, and my fellow worker, the deacon of Zotion. May I continue to have joy in him, since he is obedient to the bishop, as to the grace of God, and to the priests, as to the law of Jesus Christ.

It ill becomes you to treat your bishop too familiarly because of his youth. You should show him all reverence out of respect for the authority of God the Father. This, I understand, the holy priests do. They take no advantage of his youthful appearance, but they yield to him as to one who is wise in God—not, of course, merely to him, but to the Father of Jesus Chirst, who is the bishop over all. To the honor of Him who loves you, you must obey without any insincerity; for in this case one does not so much deceive a bishop who can be seen as try to outwit one who is invisible—in which case one must reckon not with a man, but with God who knows our hidden thoughts.

It is not enough to be Christians in name; it behooves us to be such in fact. So, too, there are those who invoke the name of the bishop while their actions are without any regard for him. Such men, it seems to me, are lacking in good conscience, for they do not assemble regularly as enjoined.

Seeing that all things have an end, two things are proposed to our choice—life and death; and each of us is to go to his appropriate place. As there are two currencies, the one of God, and the other of the world, each stamped in its own way, so the unbelieving have the stamp of the world; those who, in charity, believe have the stamp of God the Father through Jesus Christ. And, unless it is our choice to die, through Him, unto His passion, His life is not in us.

In the persons I have mentioned I have seen in faith, and have loved, your whole community; and so I exhort you to be careful to do all things in the harmony of God, the bishop having the primacy after the model of God and the priests after the model of the council of the Apostles, and the deacons (who are so dear to me) having entrusted to them the ministry of Jesus Christ—who from eternity was with the Father and at last appeared to us. Let all reverence one another in conformity with God's will. Let no man regard his neighbor with the eyes of the flesh, but in Jesus Christ love one another at all times. Let there be nothing among you to divide you; but be at one with the bishop and with those who are over you, thus affording a model and lesson of immortal life.

Just as the Lord, being one with the Father, did nothing, either in His own person or through the Apostles, without the Father, so you should do nothing without the bishop and the council of priests. Nor should you try to make a thing out to be reasonable, merely because it seems so to you personally; but let there be in common a single prayer, one petition, one mind, one hope, in love, in the unmixed joy which is Jesus Christ who is the best of all. Hasten all of you together as to one temple of God, to one altar, to Jesus Christ alone, who came forth from one Father in whom He is and to whom He has returned.

Do not be led astray either by new doctrines or old fables which are now useless, for, to go on observing Jewish rites is to deny that we have received grace. Remember that the holiest prophets lived according to Jesus Christ, and for this reason they were persecuted; they were inspired by His grace so that unbelievers might be fully assured that there is one God, who has manifested Himself in Jesus Christ His Son, who is His Word proceeding from silence, and who in all things was pleasing to Him who sent Him.

How, then, shall we be able to live apart from Him, seeing that the prophets were His disciples in the Spirit and expected Him as their Master, and that many who were brought up in the old order have come to the newness of hope? They no longer observe the Jewish Sabbaths, but keep holy the Lord's day, on which, through Him and through His death, our life arose; and by this mystery—though some deny Him—we have received our faith, and therefore we persevere in the hope of being found to be the disciples of Jesus Christ, our only Master; and because of this mystery He whom the prophets rightly waited for came and raised them from the dead.

And, therefore, let us not be ungrateful for His loving kindness; for, were He to act toward us as we do toward Him, we should perish. So, let us become His disciples; let us learn to live the life that Christianity calls for. No one with any other name than this can belong to God. Put away, therefore, the bad leaven which is old and stale, and be converted into the new leaven which is Jesus Christ. Be salted in Him, lest any of you lose your savor, for by your savor will you be judged. It is out of place to preach Jesus Christ and to practice Judaism. For Christianity did not believe in Judaism, but Judaism in Christianity; it was in this that men of every tongue believed and were gathered together in God.

Do not think that I have heard that any among you, my beloved, are practicing Judaism; but I say these things, small as I am in comparison with yourselves, to forewarn you against falling into the snares of an empty doctrine. I hope, rather, that you may be fully convinced of the birth and passion and the resurrection that took place during the period of the governorship of Pontius Pilate. These things were really and truly done by Jesus Christ, our hope; and from this hope may God forbid that any of you should be turned aside.

If only I am worthy, I hope I may have joy in you in every way. It is true that I am in bonds, but in comparison with any of you who are at liberty I am no one. I know that you are not vain, for you have Jesus Christ within you; and when I praise you I know that you reprove yourselves more than ever—for, it is written: 'The just man is his own accuser.'

Be eager, therefore, to be confirmed in the commandments of our Lord and His Apostles, so that 'whatever you do may prosper' in body and spirit, in faith and charity, in the Son and Father and Spirit, in the beginning and in the end, along with your most reverend bishop and the priests—the spiritual wreath that so fitly crowns him—and the deacons, who are men of God. Be obedient to your bishop and to one another, as Jesus Christ in His human nature was subject to the Father and as the Apostles were to Christ and the Father. In this way there will be union of body and spirit.

I have exhorted you briefly, because I know that you are full of God. Remember me in your prayers, so that I may reach God, and also the Church in Syria, of which, however unworthily, I am a member. I need your united prayer and love in God, if the Church in Syria is to have the grace of being bedewed by your fervent prayer.

From Smyrna, where I am writing to you, the Ephesians salute you. They are with me, like yourselves, for the glory of God, and have been an unfailing consolation to me; so, too, Polycarp, the bishop of the people of Smyrna, and all the other Churches, too, salute you in honor of Jesus Christ. Trusting that you may remain in the harmony of God, possessed of the spirit of union which is Jesus Christ, farewell.

IV

TO THE ROMANS

Ignatius Theophorus to the Church on which the majesty of the most high Father and of Jesus Christ, His only Son, has had mercy; to the Church beloved and enlightened by the faith and charity of Jesus Christ, our God, through the will of Him who has willed all things that exist—the Church in the place of the country of the Romans which holds the primacy. I salute you in the name of Jesus Christ, the Son of the Father. You are a Church worthy of God, worthy of honor, felicitation and praise, worthy of attaining to God, a Church without blemish, which holds the primacy of the community of love, obedient to Christ's law, bearing the Father's name. To you who are united, outwardly and inwardly, in the whole of His commandment and filled with grace, in union with God and with every alien stain filtered away, I wish every innocent joy in Jesus Christ, our God.

In answer to my prayer and beyond all I asked for, I have at last seen the faces I have longed to see. In chains as I am for Jesus Christ, I hope to salute you, if only it be His will to grant me grace to reach my goal. I shall know that the beginning is providential if, in the end, without hindrance, I am to obtain the inheritance. But I am afraid of your love; it may do me wrong. It is easy for you to have your way, but if you do not yield to me, it will be hard for me to reach God.

I would have you think of pleasing God—as indeed you do—rather than men. For at no later time shall I have an opportunity like this of reaching God; nor can you ever have any better deed ascribed to you—if only you remain silent. If only you will say nothing in my behalf, I shall be a word of God. But, if our love is for my body, I shall be once more a mere voice. You can do me no greater kindness than to suffer me to be sacrificed to God while the place of sacrifice is still prepared. Thus forming yourselves into a chorus of love, you may sing to the Father in Jesus Christ that God gave the bishop of Syria the grace of being transferred from the rising to the setting sun. It is good to set, leaving the world for God, and so to rise in Him.

Never have you envied anyone. You have been others' teachers. I trust that what you have taught and prescribed to others may now be applied by yourselves. Beg only that I may have inward and outward strength, not only in word but in will, that I may be a Christian not merely in the name but in fact. For, if I am one in fact, then I may be called one and be faithful long after I have vanished from the world. Nothing merely visible is good, for our God, Jesus Christ, is manifest the more now that He is hidden in God. Christianity is not the work of persuasion, but, whenever it is hated by the world, it is a work of power.

I am writing to all the Churches to tell them all that I am, with all my heart, to die for God—if only you do not prevent it. I beseech you not to indulge your benevolence at the wrong time. Please let me be thrown to the wild beasts; through them I can reach God. I am God's wheat; I am ground by the teeth of the wild beasts that I may end as the pure bread of Christ. If anything, coax the beasts on to become my sepulcher and to leave nothing of my body undevoured so that, when I am dead, I may be no bother to anyone. I shall be really a disciple of Jesus Christ if and when the world can no longer see so much as my body. Make petition, then, to the Lord for me, so that by these means I may be made a sacrifice to God. I do not command you, as Peter and Paul did. They were Apostles; I am a condemned man. They were free men; I am still a slave. Still, if I suffer, I shall be emancipated by Jesus Christ and, in my resurrection, shall be free. But now in chains I am learning to have no wishes of my own.

I am already battling with beasts on my journey from Syria to Rome. On land and at sea, by night and by day, I am in chains with ten leopards around me—or at least with a band of guards who grow more brutal the better they are treated. However, the wrongs they do me make me a better disciple. 'But that is not where my justification lies.' May I find my joy in the beasts that have been made ready for me. My prayer is that they will be prompt in dealing with me. I shall coax them to devour me without delay and not be afraid to touch me, as has happened in some cases. And if, when I am ready, they hold back, I shall provoke them to attack me. Pardon me, but I know what is good for me. I am now beginning to be a disciple; may nothing visible or invisible prevent me from reaching Jesus Christ. Fire and cross and battling with wild beasts, [their clawing and tearing,] the breaking of bones and mangling of members, the grinding of my whole body, the wicked torments of the devil— let them all assail me, so long as I get to Jesus Christ.

Neither the kingdoms of this world nor the bounds of the universe can have any use for me. I would rather die for Jesus Christ than rule the last reaches of the earth. My search is for

Him who died for us; my love is for Him who rose for our salvation. The pangs of new birth are upon me. Forgive me, brethren. Do nothing to prevent this new life. Do not desire that I shall perish. Do not hand over to the world a man whose heart is fixed on God. Do not entice me with material things. Allow me to receive the pure light. When I reach it, I shall be fully a man. Allow me to be a follower of the passion of my God. Let those who hold Him in their hearts understand what urges me, realize what I am choosing, and share my feelings.

The prince of this world is eager to tear me to pieces, to weaken my will that is fixed on God. Let none of you who are watching the battle abet him. Come in, rather on my side, for it is the side of God. Do not let your lips be for Jesus Christ and your heart for the world. Let envy have no place among you. And even, when I am come, if I should beseech you, pay no attention to what I say; believe, rather, what I am writing to you now. For alive as I am at this moment of writing, my longing is for death. Desire within me has been nailed to the cross and no flame of material longing is left. Only the living water speaks within me saying: Hasten to the Father. I have no taste for the food that perishes nor for the pleasures of this life. I want the Bread of God which is the Flesh of Christ, who was of the seed of David; and for drink I desire His blood which is love that cannot be destroyed.

I desire no longer to live a purely human life; and this desire can be fulfilled if you consent. Make this your choice, if you yourselves would be chosen. I make my petition in a few words. Please believe me; Jesus Christ will make it clear to you that I speak the truth, for He was the mouth without deceit through which the Father truly spoke. Beg for me that, through the Holy Spirit, I may not fail. I have not written to you after the manner of men, but according to the mind of God. If I die, it will prove you loved me; if I am rejected, it will be because you hated me.

Remember in your prayers that Church of Syria, which now, in place of me, has God for its pastor. Jesus Christ, along with your love, will be its only bishop. For myself, I am ashamed to be called one of them, for I am not worthy, being the last among them and, as it were, born out of due time. If I reach

God, I shall be some one only by His mercy. My spirit salutes you—and with it the love of the Churches which welcomed me in the name of Jesus Christ. They treated me as more than a passing pilgrim; for even the communities that did not lie along the route I was taking conducted me from city to city.

I am writing this letter to you from Smyrna by the hands of the Ephesians, who deserve all praise. Among many others who are with me there is my dear friend Crocus. I trust you have come to know those who went ahead of me from Syria to Rome for the glory of God. Please tell them that I am not far away. All of them are worthy of God and of yourselves. You will do well to help them in every way. The date of this writing is the ninth day before the calends of September. Farewell, and persevere to the end in Jesus Christ.

V

TO THE PHILADELPHIANS

Ignatius Theophorus to the Church of God the Father and of Jesus Christ in Philadelphia in Asia. You have felt God's mercy and are firmly established in union with God and with unduring joy in the passion of our Lord, through abundant mercy you have been given full assurance of His resurrection. I greet you in the blood of Jesus Christ. Your Church is to me a cause of unending and unbroken joy. It will be even more so, if all continue to be at one with the bishop and with his priests and with the deacons, who have been appointed according to the mind of Jesus Christ. All these are men after His own will and He has confirmed them in stability through His Holy Spirit.

I know that your bishop has been given his ministry for the common good, not by any effort of his own or of others nor out of vain glory, but through the love of God the Father and of the Lord Jesus Christ. I am full of admiration for the sweet reasonableness of a man who can do more by his silence than others by speaking. He has been attuned to the commandments like a harp with its strings. And so my soul blesses his determination which is fixed on God. I know how virtuous and perfect it is, how unperturbable and calm, how modeled his life is on the sweet reasonableness of God.

You are children of truth; shun schisms and heresies. Follow, as sheep do, wherever the shepherd leads. There are many wolves plausible enough to ensnare the pilgrims of God by evil pleasure. However, the harmony among you will leave no place for them.

Keep away from the poisonous weeds which grow where Jesus Christ does not till the soil, for they are not of the planting of the Father. Not that I have found any division among you—except the filtering away of impure elements. For, all who belong to God and Jesus Christ are with the bishop. And those, too, will belong to God who have returned, repentant, to the unity of the Church so as to live in accordance with Jesus Christ. Make no mistake, brethren. No one who follows another into schism inherits the Kingdom of God. No one who follows heretical doctrine is on the side of the passion.

Be zealous, then, in the observance of one Eucharist. For there is one flesh of our Lord, Jesus Christ, and one chalice that brings union in His blood. There is one altar, as there is one bishop with the priests and deacons, who are my fellow workers. And so, whatever you do, let it be done in the name of God.

Dear brothers, my love for you is full and overflowing, and with immense joy I give you whatever assurance I can; and yet not I, but Jesus Christ for whom I am in chains—for I am more and more afraid that I am far from perfection. However, your prayer to God will make me perfect, so that I may gain the inheritance that God's mercy has assigned me, if only I take refuge in the Gospel as in the body of Jesus and in the Apostles as the priests of the Church. Let us likewise love the prophets, for it was they who foretold the Gospel and hoped in Him and looked for His coming. By their faith and union with Jesus Christ they were saved. They are worthy of love and admiration for their holiness. They were approved by Jesus Christ and numbered with us in the good news of our common hope.

Still, if anyone preaches a Judaizing system to you, do yot listen to him. It is better to listen to Christianity preached by one who is circumcized than to Judaism preached by one who is not. Both alike, if they fail to preach Jesus Christ, are for me tombstones and graves inscribed merely with the names of men. Beware of the tricks and traps of the prince of this world, else you will succumb to his wiles and grow languid in love. Assemble

17

together, all of you in oneness of heart. I thank God that my conscience is clear, for there is not one among you who can claim, covertly or openly, that I have been burdensome to him in any matter, great or small. I pray that nothing that I have said may be taken in evidence against any to whom I have spoken.

There may be some who outwardly sought to deceive me, but the spirit, which is from God, is not deceived. He knows whence it comes and whither it goes; and He makes clear what is hidden. I cried out in your midst and I spoke with a loud voice—the voice of God: Give heed to the bishop, the priests and the deacons. When I said this, there were those who suspected that I knew ahead of time of the schism of some among you. But He is my witness, for whom I am in chains, that I knew of this from no human lips. It was the Spirit that proclaimed these words: Apart from the bishop let nothing be done. Guard your flesh as a temple of God. Love unity. Shun schisms. Be imitators of Jesus Christ, as He is of His Father.

As for me, I played my part, like a mediator appointed to bring about unity. For, wherever there is division or anger, God has no place. Now God forgives all who repent, so long as their repentance turns to union with God and to communion with the bishop. I have faith in the grace of Jesus Christ; He will break all your bonds. I beseech you to do all in the light of Christ's teaching and nothing in a party spirit. There are some whom I heard to say: Unless I find it in the documents, I do not believe in what is preached. When I said: It is the written word, they replied: That is what is in question. For me, Jesus Christ is the written word, His cross and death and resurrection and faith through Him make up the untampered documents. Through these, with the help of your prayers, I desire to be justified.

The priests were good; but still better is the High Priest to whom the Holy of Holies was committed, to whom alone the mysteries of God were committed. He is the door of the Father through which Abraham and Isaac and Jacob and the prophets, the Apostles and the Church all enter. All these enter into the unity of God. But what distinguishes the Gospel is that it contains the coming of the Savior, Our Lord Jesus Christ, His passion, His resurrection. The preaching of the beloved prophets

18

had Him in view. The Gospel is the perfection of Eternal Life. Taken together, all these things are good so long as your faith is alive with chastity.

The news has reached me that, thanks to your prayer and the sympathy you showed in Christ Jesus, the Church of Antioch in Syria is enjoying peace. I feel that you ought, as a Church of God, to choose a deacon to go there as an ambassador of God, for the glory of the Name and to congratulate them when they assemble together. Blessed in Jesus Christ is the man who is to be found worthy of this ministry. All praise to you, too, who send him. You can do this for the Name of God if only you choose to; just as the Churches which are near neighbors sent deacons or priests and, some of them, bishops.

The deacon, Philo of Cilicia, a man of good name who is now ministering to me in the word of God, and Rhaius Agathopus, an outstanding person of Syria who gave up his present occupations to follow me, join in speaking highly of you. I give thanks to God for your kindness in receiving them with the kindness which the Lord shows you. But may the grace of Jesus Christ forgive those who treated them with scant respect. The love of the brethren in Troas salutes you. I am writing from here by the hand of Burrhus, who was sent by the Ephesians and Smyrnaeans to accompany me as a token of respect. The Lord Jesus Christ will reward them who hope in Him in the body, soul and spirit, in faith, and love and concord. Farewell in Christ Jesus, our common hope.

St. Cyprian
200-258

Cyprian was born in Africa in the first decade of the third century, probably in Carthage. His family was well-off and he received a classical education. He became a Christian, probably in 246, and soon after was ordained a priest; by 249 he was elected Bishop of Carthage by the people. Within a year the new emperor Decius began his harsh persecution of Christians. Cyprian went into hiding at this time, and thereafter he constantly had to defend himself against the charge that he had fled out of cowardice and lack of concern for his flock.

In 251, after returning from exile, Cyprian wrote two documents dealing with problems that had arisen during the persecution. One, On the Lapsed, dealt with the question of how to treat Christians who had renounced their faith, at least externally, under duress. The other, On the Unity of the Church, is the selection that follows.

Of the early Latin writers Cyprian is second only to Tertullian, whom he referred to as his master. His career as a Christian lasted only a dozen years, since he was martyred during the Valerian persecution in 258. Those years were obviously filled with conflict and turmoil, yet his writings convey a calmness and equanimity that led to their being used as models for centuries.

The "pamphlet" that follows is both the best and the best-known of Cyprian's works, for it deals directly with the theme that was central to his thought. He is the theologian of the unity of the Church, a subject he never tires of elaborating. As he says in chapter 5, "This unity we ought to hold firmly and defend, especially we bishops who watch over the Church, that we may provide that also the episcopate itself is one and undivided."

As in the case of Ignatius of Antioch, Cyprian's insistence on unity had autobiographical roots. He saw the splintering of Christians into various factions as scandalous, an intolerable violation of God's plan. In search for solutions to the fragmentation problem, he concluded that the bishop was the key. This famous work was probably read by Cyprian to the synod that gathered in Carthage in the spring of 251 to deal with a schism that had a significant following. Occasional passages illustrate the limpid power of the Latin language at its best, as in chapter 23: "God is one and Christ one and His Church one and the faith one and the people one joined together by the tie of concord into a solid unity of body. The unity cannot be torn asunder..."

The prestige of Cyprian in later ages was enhanced by a highly idealized account, the oldest known Christian biography. Even though it lacks historical value, it serves to illustrate that the place of Cyprian in Christian annals is secure. He was the first African bishop to die as a martyr, witnessing to the unity of Christ's Church.

ON THE
UNITY OF THE CHURCH

CHAPTER 1

Since the Lord warns us in these words: 'Ye are the salt of the earth,' and since He bids us to be simple unto harmlessness, and yet to be prudent with our simplicity, what else, most beloved brethren, befits us than to have foresight and watching with an anxious heart alike to perceive the snares of the crafty enemy and to beware lest we, who have put on Christ the wisdom of God the Father, seem to be wise in guarding our salvation. For persecution alone is not to be feared, nor the advances which are made in open attack to overwhelm and cast down the servants of God. To be cautious is easier when the object of fear is manifest, and the soul is prepared for the contest beforehand, when the adversary declares himself. The enemy is more to be feared and guarded against when he creeps up secretly, when deceiving us under the appearance of peace he steals forward by hidden approaches, from which too he receives the name of serpent (creeper, crawler, stealer). This is always his cunning; this is his blind and dark deceit for circumventing men. Thus from the very beginning of the world did he deceive and, flattering with lying words, mislead the inexperienced soul with its reckless incredulity. Thus trying to tempt the Lord himself, as if he would creep up again and deceive, he approaches secretly. Yet he was understood and driven back and so cast down, because he was discovered and unmasked.

CHAPTER 2

In this an example has been given us to flee the way of the old man; to walk in the footsteps of the conquering Christ, that we may not heedlessly be turned back again unto the snare of death, but that, on guard against the danger, we may receive and possess immortality. But how can we possess immortality, unless we keep those commandments of Christ by which death is overcome and conquered, He Himself warning us in these words: 'If thou wilt enter into life, keep the commandments,' and again: 'If you do what I command you, I no longer call you servant but friends.' These, finally, He calls strong and steadfast, these grounded upon a rock of firm foundation, these firmly established against all the tempests and storms of the world with an unmoveable and unshaken firmness. 'He who hears my words,' He says, 'and does them, I shall liken him to a wise man who built his house upon a rock. The rain descended and the floods came, the winds blew and beat upon that house, but it did not fall, for it was founded upon a rock.' Therefore, we ought to stand firm upon His words, and to learn and do whatever He taught and did. But how does he say that he believes in Christ who does not do what Christ ordered him to do? Or, whence shall he attain the reward of faith, who does not keep the faith of the commandment? He will necessarily waver and wander, and caught up by the breath of error will be blown as the dust which the wind stirs up, nor will he make any advance in his walk toward salvation, who does not hold to the truth of the saving way.

CHAPTER 3

But not only must we guard against things which are open and manifest but also against those which deceive with the subtlety of clever fraud. Now what is more clever, or what more subtle than that the enemy, detected and cast down by the coming of Christ, after light had come to the Gentiles, and the saving splendor had shone forth for the preservation of man, that the deaf might receive the hearing of spiritual grace, the blind open their eyes to the Lord, the weak grow strong with eternal health, the lame run to the church, the dumb supplicate with clear voices and prayers, seeing the idols abandoned and his shrines and temples deserted because of the great populace of believers, devise a new fraud, under the very title of Christian name to deceive the incautious? He invented heresies and schisms with which to overthrow the faith, to corrupt the truth, to divide unity. Those whom he cannot hold in the blindness of the old way, he circumvents and deceives by the error of a new way. He snatches men from the Church itself, and, while they seem to themselves to have already approached the light and to

24

have escaped the night of the world, he again pours forth other shadows upon the unsuspecting, so that, although they do not stand with the Gospel of Christ and with the observation of Him and with the law, they call themselves Christians, and, although they walk in darkness, they think that they have light, while the adversary cajoles and deceives, who, as the Apostle says, transform himself into an angel of light, and adorns his ministers as those of justice who offer night for day, death for salvation, despair under the offer of hope, perfidy under the pretext of faith, antichrist under the name of Christ, so that while they tell plausible lies, they frustrate the truth by their subtlety. This happens, most beloved brethren, because there is no return to the source of truth, and the Head is not sought, and the doctrine of the heavenly Master is not kept.

CHAPTER 4

If anyone considers and examines these things, there is no need of a lengthy discussion and arguments. Proof for faith is easy in a brief statement of the truth. The Lord speaks to Peter: 'I say to thee,' He says, 'thou art Peter, and upon this rock I will build my church, and the gates of hell shall not prevail against it. And I will give thee the keys of the kingdom of heaven; and whatever thou shalt bind on earth shall be bound also in heaven, and whatever thou shalt loose on earth shall be loosed also in heaven.' Upon him, being one, He builds His Church, and although after His resurrection He bestows equal power upon all the Apostles, and says: 'As the Father has sent me, I also send you. Receive ye the Holy Spirit: if you forgive the sins of anyone, they will be forgiven him; if you retain the sins of anyone, they will be retained,' yet that He might display unity, He established by His authority the origin of the same unity as beginning from one. Surely the rest of the Apostles also were that which Peter was, endowed with an equal partnership of office and of power, but the beginning proceeds from unity, that the Church of Christ may be shown to be one. This one Church, also, the Holy Spirit in the Canticle of Canticles designates in the person of the Lord and says: 'One is my dove, my perfect one is but one, she is the only one of her mother, the chosen one of her that bore her.' Does he who does not hold this unity think that he holds the faith? Does he who strives against the Church and resists her think that he is in the Church, when too the blessed Apostle Paul teaches this same thing and sets forth the sacrament of unity saying: 'One body and one Spirit, one hope of your calling, one Lord, one faith, one baptism, one God'?

CHAPTER 5

This unity we ought to hold firmly and defend, especially we bishops who watch over the Church, that we may prove that also the episcopate itself is one and undivided. Let no one deceive the brotherhood by lying; let no one corrupt the faith by a perfidious prevarication of the truth. The episcopate is one, the parts of which are held together by the individual bishops. The Church is one which with increasing fecundity extend far and wide into the multitude, just as the rays of the sun are many but the light is one, and the branches of the tree are many but the strength is one founded in its tenacious root, and, when many streams flow from one source, although a multiplicity of waters seems to have been diffused from the abundance of the overflowing supply nevertheless unity is preserved in their origin. Take away a ray of light from the body of the sun, its unity does not take on any division of its light; break a branch from a tree, the branch thus broken will not be able to bud; cut off a stream from its source, the stream thus cut off dries up. Thus too the Church bathed in the light of the Lord projects its rays over the whole world, yet there is one light which is diffused everywhere, and the unity of the body is not separated. She extends her branches over the whole earth in fruitful abundance; she extends her richly flowing streams far and wide; yet her head is one, and her source is one, and she is the one mother copious in the results of her fruitfulness. By her womb we are born; by her milk we are nourished; by her spirit we are animated.

CHAPTER 6

The spouse of Christ cannot be defiled; she is uncorrupted and chaste. She knows one home, with chaste modesty she guards the sanctity of one couch. She keeps us for God; she assigns the children whom she has created to the kingdom. Whoever is separated from the Church and is joined with an adulteress is separated from the promises of the Church, nor will he who has abandoned the Church arrive at the rewards of Christ. He is a stranger; he is profane; he is an enemy. He cannot have God as a father who does not have the Church as a mother. If whoever was outside the ark of Noe was able to escape, he too who is outside the Church escapes. The Lord warns, saying: 'He who is not with me is against me, and who does not gather with me, scatters.' He who breaks the peace and concord of Christ acts against Christ; he who gathers somewhere outside the Church scatters the Church of Christ. The Lord says: 'I and the Father are one.' And again of the Father and Son and the Holy Spirit it is written: 'And these three are one.' Does anyone believe that this unity which comes from divine strength, which is closely connected with the divine sacraments, can be broken asunder in the Church and be separated by the divisions of colliding wills? He who does not hold this unity, does not hold the law of God, does not hold the faith of the Father and the Son, does not hold life and salvation.

CHAPTER 7

This sacrament of unity, this bond of concord inseparably connected is shown, when in the Gospel the tunic of the Lord Jesus Christ is not at all divided and is not torn, but by those who cast lots for the garment of Christ, who rather might have put on Christ, a sound garment is received, and an undamaged and undivided tunic is possessed. Divine Scripture speaks and says: 'Now of the tunic, since it was woven throughout from the upper part without seam, they said to one another: "Let us not tear it, but let us cast lots for it, whose it shall be." He bore the unity that came down from the upper part, that is, that came down from heaven and the Father, which could not all be torn by him who received and possessed it, but he obtained it whole once for all and a firmness inseparably solid. He cannot possess the garment of Christ who tears and divides the Church of Christ. Then on the other hand when at the death of Solomon his kingdom and people were torn asunder, Ahias the prophet met King Jeroboam in the field and tore his garment into twelve pieces, saying: 'Take to thee ten pieces, for thus saith the Lord: "Behold I rend the kingdom out of the hand of Solomon, and will give thee ten sceptres, but two sceptres shall remain to him for the sake of my servant David and for the sake of Jerusalem the city which I have chosen, that I may place my name there." When the twelve tribes of Israel were torn asunder, the prophet Ahias rent his garment. But because the people of Christ cannot be torn asunder, His tunic woven and united throughout was not divided by those who possessed it. Undivided, joined, connected it shows the coherent concord of us who have put on Christ. By the sacrament and sign of His garment, He has declared the unity of the Church.

CHAPTER 8

Who then is so profane and lacking in faith, who so insane by the fury of discord as either to believe that the unity of God, the garment of the Lord, the Church of Christ, can be torn asunder or dare to do so? He Himself warns us in His Gospel, and teaches saying: 'And there shall be one flock and one shepherd.' And does anyone think that there can be either many shepherds or many flocks in one place? Likewise the Apostle Paul insinuating this same unity upon us beseeches and urges us in these words: 'I beseech you, brethren,' he says, 'by the name of our Lord Jesus Christ, that you all say the same thing, and that there be no dissensions among you: but that you be perfectly united in the same mind and in the same judgment.' And again he says: 'Bearing with one another in love, careful to preserve the unity of the Spirit, in the bond of peace.' Do you think that you can stand and live, withdrawing from the Church, and building for yourself other abodes and different dwellings, when it was said to Rhaab, in whom the Church was prefigured: 'You shall gather your father and your mother and your brethren and the entire house of your father to your own self in your house, and it will be that everyone who goes out of the door of your house shall be his own accuser'; likeise, when the sacrament of the Passover contains nothing else in the law of the Exodus than that the lamb which is slain in the figure of Christ be eaten in one house? God speaks, saying: 'In one house it shall be eaten, you shall not carry the flesh outside of the house.' The flesh of Christ and the holy of the Lord cannot be carried outside, and there is no other house for believers except the one

28

Church. This house, this hospice of unanimity the Holy Spirit designates and proclaims, when He says: 'God who makes those of one mind to dwell in his house.' In the house of God, in the Church of Christ, those of one mind dwell; they persevere in concord and simplicity.

CHAPTER 9

So the Holy Spirit came in a dove. It is a simple and happy animal, not bitter with gall, not cruel with its bites, not violent with lacerating claws; it loves the hospitalities of men; when they give birth they bring forth their offspring together; when they go and come they cling together; they spend their lives in mutual intercourse; they recognize the concord of peace by the kiss of the beak; they fulfill the law of unanimity in all things. This is the simplicity which ought to be known in the Church; this the charity to be attained, that the love of the brethren imitate the doves, that their gentleness and tenderness equal that of the lambs and the sheep. What is the savagery of wolves doing in the breast of a Christian, and the madness of dogs and the lethal poison of snakes and the bloody cruelties of beasts? Congratulations are due, when such as these are separated from the Church, lest they prey upon the doves and sheep with their cruel and venemous contagion. Bitterness cannot cling and join with sweetness, darkness with light, rains with clear weather, fighting with peace, sterility with fecundity, drought with running waters, storm with calm. Let no one think that the good can depart from the Church; the wind does not ravage the wheat, nor does the storm overturn the tree strongly and solidly rooted; the light straws are tossed about by the tempest; the feeble trees are thrown down by the onrush of the whirlwind. The Apostle Paul execrates and strikes at these, when he says: 'They have gone forth from us, but they were not of us. For if they had been of us, they would have continued with us.'

CHAPTER 10

Hence heresies have both frequently arisen and are arising, while the perverse mind has no peace, while discordant perfidy does not maintain unity. Indeed the Lord permits and suffers these things to happen, while the choice of one's own liberty

29

remains, so that, while the norm of truth examines our hearts and minds, the sound faith of those who are approved may become manifest in a clear light. Through the Apostle the Holy Spirit forewarns and says: 'For there must be factions, so that those who are approved among you may be made manifest.' Thus the faithful are approved; thus the perfidious are disclosed; thus also before the day of judgment, already here too the souls of the just and the **unjust** are divided and the chaff is separated from the wheat. From **these** are those who of their own accord set themselves over daring strangers without divine appointment, who establish themselves as prelates without any law of ordina- tion, who assume the name of bishop for themselves, although no one gives them the episcopacy; whom the Holy Spirit in the psalms designates as sitting in the chair of pestilence, the plague and disease of the faith, deceiving with a serpent's tongue and masters in corrupting truth, vomiting lethal poisons from their pestilential tongues, whose speech creeps about like cancer, whose discussions inject a deadly virus within the breast and heart of everyone.

CHAPTER 11

Against such people the Lord cries out; from these He restrains and recalls His wandering people saying: 'Hearken not to the words of false prophets, since the visions of their hearts frustrate them. They speak, but not from the mouth of the Lord. They say to them who reject the word of God: Peace shall be to you and to all who walk in their own desires. To everyone who walks in the errors of his own heart [they say] : 'Evil shall not come upon you.' I have not spoken to them, yet they have prophesied. If they had stood in my counsel and had heard my words, and if they had taught my people, I would have turned them from their evil thoughts.' These same people does the Lord again designate and point out, when He says: 'They have aban- doned me to the fountain of living water, and have dug for themselves broken cisterns which cannot hold water.' Although there cannot be another baptism than the one, they think that they baptize; although the fountain of life has been deserted, they promise the grace of the life-giving and saving water. There men are not washed but rather are made foul, nor are their sins purged but on the contrary piled high. That nativity generates sons not for God but for the devil. Being born through a lie they do not obtain the promises of truth; begotten of perfidy they lose the grace of faith. They cannot arrive at the reward of peace who have broken the peace of the Lord by the madness of discord.

CHAPTER 12

Let not certain ones deceive themselves by an empty interpretation of what the Lord has said: 'Whenever two or three have gathered together in my name, I am with them.' Corrupters and false interpreters of the Gospel quote the last words and pass over earlier ones, being mindful of part and craftily suppressing part. As they themselves have been cut off from the Church, so they cut off a sentence of one chapter. For when the Lord urged unanimity and peace upon His disciples, He said: 'I say to you that if two of you agree upon earth concerning anything whatsoever that you shall ask, it shall be granted you by my Father who is in heaven. For wherever two or three have gathered together in my name, I am with them,' showing that the most is granted not to the multitude but to the unanimity of those that pray. 'If two of you,' He says, 'agree upon earth'; He placed unanimity first; He set the concord of peace first; He taught that we should agree faithfully and firmly. But how can he agree with anyone, who does not agree with the body of the Church herself and with the universal brotherhood? How can two or three be gathered in the name of Christ, who it is clear are separated from Christ and His gospel? For we did not withdraw from them, but they from us, and when thereafter heresies and schisms arose, while they were establishing diverse meeting places for themselves, they abandoned the source and origin of truth. The Lord, moreover, is speaking of His Church, and He is speaking to those who are in the Church, that if they are in agreement, if, according to what He has commanded and admonished, although two or three are gathered together, they pray with unanimity, although they are two or three, they can obtain from the majesty of God, what they demand. 'Wherever two or three have gathered, I,' He said, 'am with them,' namely, with the simple and the peaceful, with those who fear God and keep

the commandments of God. He said that He was with these although two or three, just as also He was with the three children
in the fiery furnace, and, because they remain simple toward
God and in unanimity among themselves, He animated them in
the midst of flames with the breath of dew; just as he was present with the two apostles shut up in prison, because they were
simple, because they were of one mind, He opened the doors of
the prison and returned them again to the market-place that
they might pass on the word to the multitude which they were
faithfully preaching. When then He lays it down in His commandments and says: 'Where there are two or three, I am with
them,' He who established and made the Church did not separate
men from the Church, but rebuking the faithless for their discord
and commanding peace to the faithful by His word, He shows
that He is with two or three who pray with one mind rather
than with a great many who are in disagreement, and that more
can be obtained by the harmonious prayer of a few than by the
discordant supplication of many.

CHAPTER 13

So too when He gave the law of prayer, He added, saying:
'And when you stand up to pray, forgive whatever you have
against anyone, that your Father also who is in heaven may forgive you your offenses.' And He calls back from the altar one
who comes to the sacrifice with dissension, and He orders Him
first to be reconciled with his brother and then return with peace
and offer his gift to God, because God did not look with favor
upon the gifts of Cain; for he could not have God at peace with
him, who through envious discord did not have peace with his
brother. What peace then do the enemies of the brethren promise
themselves? What sacrifices do the imitators of priests believe
that they celebrate? Do they who are gathered together outside
the Church of Christ think that Christ is with them when they
have been gathered together?

CHAPTER 14

Even if such men are slain in confession of the Name that
stain is not washed away by blood; the inexpiable and serious
fault of discord is purged not even by martyrdom. He cannot

be a martyr who is not in the Church. He will not be able to arrive in the kingdom who deserted her who is to rule. Christ gave us peace; He ordered us to be in agreement and of one mind; He commanded us to keep the bonds of love and charity uncorrupted and inviolate. He cannot display himself a martyr who has not maintained fraternal charity. The Apostle Paul teaches and bears witness to this when he says: 'If I have faith so that I remove mountains, but not so that I have charity, I am nothing; and if I distribute all my goods for food, and if I hand over my body so that I am burned, but not so that I have charity, I accomplish nothing. Charity is noble, charity is kind, charity envieth not, is not puffed up, is not provoked; does not act perversely, thinks no evil, loves all things, believes all things, hopes all things, bears all things. Charity never will fall away.' 'Never,' he says, 'will charity fall away.' For she will always be in the kingdom and will endure forever in the unity of the brotherhood clinging to it. Discord cannot come to the kingdom of heaven; to the rewards of Christ who said: 'This is my commandment that you love one another, even as I have loved you.' He will not be able to attain it who has violated the love of Christ by perfidious dissension. He who does not have charity does not have God. The words of the blessed Apostle John are: 'God,' he says, 'is love, and he who abides in love, abides in God and God abides in him.' They cannot abide with God who have been unwilling to be of one mind in God's Church. Although they burn when given over to flames and fire, or lay down their lives when thrown to the beasts, that crown of faith will not be theirs, but the punishment of perfidy, and no glorious ending of religious valor but the destruction of desperation. Such a man can be slain; he cannot be crowned. Thus he professes himself to be a Christian, just as the devil often falsely declares himself to be even Christ, although the Lord forewarned of this saying: 'Many will come in my name saying: "I am the Christ," and will deceive many.' Just as He is not Christ, although he deceives in His name, so he cannot seem a Christian who does not abide in His Gospel and in the true faith.

CHAPTER 15

For both to prophesy and to drive out demons, and to perform great miracles on earth is certainly a sublime and admirable thing, yet whoever is found in all this does not attain the kingdom of heaven unless he walk in the observance of the right and just way. The Lord gives warning and says: 'Many will say to me in that day: "Lord, Lord, have we not prophesied in Thy name and cast out devils in thy name and worked great miracles in thy name?" And then I will say to them: "I never knew you. Depart from me ye workers of iniquity." There is need of righteousness that one may deserve well of God as judge; His precepts and admonitions must be obeyed that our merits may receive their reward. The Lord in the Gospel, when he was directing the way of our hope and faith, in a brief summary said: 'The Lord thy God is one Lord,' and 'Thou shalt love the Lord thy God with thy whole heart, and with thy whole soul and with thy whole strength. This is the first, and the second is like unto it: Thou shalt love thy neighbor as thyself. On these two commandments depend the whole law and the prophets. He taught at the same time unity and love by the authority of His teaching; He included all the prophets and the law in two commandments. But what unity does he preserve, what love does he guard or consider, who mad with the fury of discord splits the Church, destroys the faith, disturbs the peace, dissipates charity, profanes the sacrament?

CHAPTER 16

This evil, most faithful brethren, began long ago, but now the dangerous destruction of the same evil has increased, and the venemous plague of heretical perversity and schisms has begun to rise and to spread more, because even so it was to be at the decline of the world, for the Holy Spirit proclaimed it to us and forewarned us through the Apostle: 'In the last days,' he says, 'dangerous times will come, men will be lovers of self, haughty, proud, covetous, blasphemous, disobedient to parents, ungrateful, impious, without affection, without law, slanderers, incontinent, merciless, not loving the good, treacherous, stubborn, puffed up with pride, loving pleasure more than God, having a semblance of piety, but denying its power. Of such are they who make their way into houses and captivate silly women who are sin-laden and led away by various lusts; ever learning, yet never attaining knowledge of the truth. Just as Jannes and Mambres resisted Moses, so these resist the truth. But they will make no further progress, for their folly will be obvious to all, as was that of those others.' Whatever things were foretold are being fulfilled and, as the end of the world now approaches, have come with the testing of men and the times alike. More and more, as the adversary raves, error deceives, stupidity raises its head, envy inflames, covetousness blinds, impiety depraves, pride puffs up, discord exasperates, anger rushes headlong.

CHAPTER 17

Yet let not the extreme and precipitous perfidy of many move or disturb us, but rather let it strengthen our faith by the truth of things foretold. As certain ones begin to be such, because these things were predicted beforehand, thus let other brethren beware of matters of a similar sort, because these also were predicted, as the Lord instructed us saying: 'Be on your guard therefore; behold I have told you all things beforehand.' I beseech you, avoid men of this sort, and ward off from your side and from your hearing their pernicious conversation as the contagion of death, as it is written: 'Hedge in thy ears with thorns, and hear not a wicked tongue.' And again: 'Evil communications corrupt good manners.' The Lord teaches and admonishes that we must withdraw from such. 'They are blind guides,' He says, 'of the blind. But if a blind man guide a blind man, both shall fall into a pit.' Such a one is to be turned away from, and whoever has separated himself from the Church is to be shunned. Such a man is perverted and sins and is condemned by his very self. Does he seem to himself to be with Christ, who acts contrary to the priests of Christ, who separates himself from association with His clergy and His people? That man bears arms against the Church; he fights against God's plan. An enemy of the altar, a rebel against the sacrifice of Christ, for the faith faithless, for religion sacrilegious, a disobedient servant, an impious son, a hostile brother, despising the bishops and abandoning the priests of God, he dares to set up another altar, to compose another prayer with unauthorized words, to profane the truth of the Lord's offering by false sacrifices, and not to know that he who struggles against God's plan on account of his rash daring is punished by divine censure.

CHAPTER 18

Thus Core, Dathan, and Abiron, who tried to assume for themselves in opposition to Moses and Aaron the freedom to sacrifice, immediately paid the penalty for their efforts. The earth, breaking its bonds, opened up into a deep chasm, and the opening of the receding ground swallowed up the standing and the living, and not only did the anger of the indignant God strike those who had been the authors [of the revolt], but fire that went out from the Lord in speedy revenge also consumed two hundred and fifty others, participants and sharers in the same madness, who had been joined together with them in the daring, clearly warning and showing that whatever the wicked attempt by human will to destroy God's plan is done against God. Thus Ozias the king also, when, carrying the censer and violently assuming to himself the right to sacrifice contrary to the law of God, although Azarias, the priest, resisted him, he was unwilling to give way and obey, was confounded by the divine indignation and was polluted on his forehead by the spot of leprosy, being marked for his offense against the Lord where they are signed who merited well of the Lord. And the sons of Aaron, who place a strange fire on the altar, which the Lord had not ordered, were immediately extinguished in the sight of the avenging Lord.

CHAPTER 19

These, certainly, they imitate and follow, who despise God's tradition and seek after strange doctrines and introduce teachings of human disposition. These the Lord rebukes and reproves in His Gospel when He says: 'You reject the commandment of God that you may establish your own tradition.' This crime is worse than that which the lapsed seem to have committed, who while established in penance for their crime beseech God with full satisfactions. Here the Church is sought and entreated, there the Church is resisted; here there can have been necessity, there the will is held in wickedness; here he who lapsed harmed only himself, there he who tried to cause a heresy or schism deceived many by dragging them with him; here there is the loss of one soul, there danger to a great many. Certainly this one knows that he has sinned and bewails and laments; that one swelling in his sin and taking pleasure in his very crimes separates children from their Mother, entices sheep from their shepherd, and disturbs the sacraments of God. And whereas the lapsed has sinned once, the former sins daily. Finally, the lapsed later, after achieving martyrdom, can receive the promises of the kingdom; the former, if he is killed outside the Church, cannot arrive at the rewards of the Church.

CHAPTER 20

Let no one marvel, most beloved brethren, that even certain of the confessors proceed to these lengths, that some also sin so wickedly and so grievously. For neither does confession [of Christ] make one immune from the snares of the devil, nor does it defend him who is still placed in the world, with a perpetual security against worldly temptations and dangers and onsets and attacks; otherwise never might we have seen afterwards among the confessors the deceptions and debaucheries and adulteries which now with groaning and sorrow we see among some. Whoever that confessor is, he is not greater or better or dearer to God than Solomon, who, however, as long as he walked in the ways of the Lord, so long retained the grace which he had received from the Lord; after he had abandoned the way of the Lord, he lost also the grace of the Lord. And so it is written: 'Hold what you have, lest another receive thy crown.' Surely the Lord would not make this threat, that the crown of righteousness can be taken away, unless, when righteousness departs, the crown also must depart.

CHAPTER 21

Confession is the beginning of glory, not already the merit of the crown; nor does it achieve praise, but it initiates dignity, and, since it is written; 'He that shall persevere to end, he shall be saved,' whatever has taken place before the end is a step by which the ascent is made to the summit of salvation, not the end by which the topmost point is held secure. He is a confessor, but after the confession the danger is greater, because the adversary is the more provoked. He is a confessor; for this reason he ought to stand with the Gospel of the Lord, for by the Gospel he has obtained glory from the Lord. 'To whom much is given, of him much is required'; and to whom the more dignity is allotted, from him the more service is demanded. Let no one perish through the example of a confessor, let no one learn injustice, no one insolence, no one perfidy from the habits of a confessor. He is a confessor; let him be humble and quiet, in his actions let him be modest with discipline, so that he who is called a confessor of Christ may imitate the Christ whom he confesses. For since he says: 'Everyone that exalts himself shall be humbled, and everyone that humbles himself shall be exalted,' and since he himself has been exalted by the Father, because He, the Word and the Power and the Wisdom of God the Father humbled Himself on earth, how can He love pride who even by His law enjoined humility upon us and Himself received from the Father the highest name as the reward of humility? He is a confessor of Christ, but only if afterwards the majesty and dignity of Christ be not blasphemed by him. Let not the tongue which has confessed Christ be abusive nor boisterous; let it not be heard resounding with insults and contentions; let it not after words of praise shoot forth a serpent's poisons against the brethren and priests of God. But if he later become blameworthy and abominable, if he dissipates his confession by evil conversation, if he pollutes his life with unseemly foulness, if, finally, abandoning the Church where he became a confessor and breaking the concord of its unity, he change his first faith for a later faithlessness, he cannot flatter himself by reason of his confession as if elected to the reward of glory, when by this very fact the merits of punishment have grown the more.

CHAPTER 22

For the Lord chose even Judas among the Apostles, and yet later Judas betrayed the Lord. Nevertheless, the firmness and faith of the Apostles did not on this account fall, because the traitor Judas defected from their fellowship. So also in this case the sanctity and dignity of the confessors was not immediately diminished, because the faith of some of them was broken.

The blessed Apostle speaks in his letter saying: 'For what if some of them have fallen away from the faith? Has their infidelity made of no effect the faith of God? God forbid. For God is true, but every man a liar.' The greater and better part of the confessors stand firm in the strength of their faith and in the truth of the Lord's law and teaching, neither do they depart from the peace of the Church, who remember that they have obtained grace in the Church from God's esteem, and by this very fact do they obtain greater praise for their faith, that they separated themselves from the perfidy of those who had been joined with them in the fellowship of confession, and withdrew from the contagion of their crime. Moreover, illumined by the light of the Gospel, shining with the pure white light of the Lord, they are as praiseworthy in preserving the peace of Christ as they were victorious in their encounter with the devil.

CHAPTER 23

Indeed, I desire, most beloved brethren, and I likewise advise and entreat, that, if it can be done, no one of the brethren perish, and that our rejoicing Mother enclose in her bosom one body of people in agreement. If, however, saving counsel cannot recall certain leaders of schisms and authors of dissensions who persist in their blind and obstinate madness to the way of salvation, yet the rest of you either taken by your simplicity, or induced by error, or deceived by some craftiness of misleading cunning, free yourselves from the snare of deceit, liberate your wandering steps from errors, recognized the right way of the heavenly road. The words of the Apostle giving testimony are: 'We charge you in the name of the Lord Jesus Christ that you withdraw from all brethren who walk disorderly and not according to the tradition which they received from us.' And again he says: 'Let no one deceive you with vain words; for because of these things comes the wrath of God upon the children of disobedience. Be ye not, therefore, partakers with them.' We must withdraw, rather flee from those who fall away, lest, while one is joined with them as they walk wickedly, and passes over the paths of error and crime, wandering apart from the way of the true road, he himself also be caught in a like crime. God is one and Christ one and His Church one and the faith one and the people one joined together by the tie of concord into a solid unity of body. The unity cannot be torn asunder, nor can the one body be separated by a division of its structure, nor torn into bits by the wrenching asunder of its entrails by laceration. Whatever departs from the parent-stem will not be able to breathe and live apart; it loses the substance of health.

CHAPTER 24

The Holy Spirit warns us, saying: 'Who is the man that desireth life; who loveth to see the best days? Keep thy tongue from evil, and thy lips from speaking guile. Turn away from evil and do good; seek after peace, and pursue it.' The son of peace ought to seek and follow peace; he who knows and loves the bond of charity ought to restrain his tongue from the evil of dissension. Among his divine commands and salutary instructions the Lord now very near His passion added the following: 'Peace I leave you, my peace I give you.' This inheritance He gave us, all the gifts and rewards of His promise He assured us in the conservation of peace. If we are heirs of Christ, let us remain in the peace of Christ; if we are sons of God, we ought to be peace-makers. 'Blessed,' He said, 'are the peace-makers, for they shall be called the sons of God.' The sons of God should be peace-makers, gentle in heart, simple in speech, harmonious in affection, clinging to one another faithfully in the bonds of unanimity.

CHAPTER 25

This unanimity existed of old among the Apostles; thus the new assembly of believers, guarding the commandments of the Lord, maintained their charity. Scripture proves this in the following words: 'But the multitude of those who believed acted with one soul and one mind.' And again, 'And all were persevering with one mind in prayer with the women and Mary the mother of Jesus and His brethren.' Thus they prayed with efficacious prayers; thus they were able with confidence to obtain whatever they asked of God's mercy.

CHAPTER 26

But with us unanimity has been so diminished that even the liberality of our good works has been lessened. Then they sold their homes and estates, and, laying up treasures for themselves in heaven, they offered to the Apostles the proceeds to be distributed for use among the poor. But now we do not even give a tenth of our patrimony, and, although the Lord orders us to sell, we rather buy and increase. So has the vigor of faith withered in us; so has the strength of believers languished. And therefore the Lord, looking upon our times, says in His Gospel: 'When the Son of man comes, do you think that He will find faith on the earth?' We see that what he foretold is coming to pass. There is no faith in the fear of God, in the law of justice, in love, in works. No one considers fear of the future; no one thinks of the day of the Lord and the anger of God and the punishments to come upon unbelievers and the eternal torments decreed for the faithless. Whatever our conscience would fear, if it believed, because it does not believe, it does not fear at all. But if it did believe, it would also be on guard; if it were on guard, it would also escape.

CHAPTER 27

Let us rouse ourselves in so far as we can, most beloved brethren, and, breaking the sleep of old inertia let us awake to the observing and keeping of the Lord's precepts. Let us be such as He Himself ordered us to be when He said: 'Let your loins be girt, and your lamps brightly burning, and you yourself like to men waiting for their Lord, when He shall come from the wedding, that when He comes and knocks, they may open to Him. Blessed are those servants whom the Lord, when He comes, shall find watching.' We ought to be girt, lest, when the day of departure come, it finds us burdened and entangled. Let our light shine forth in good works and glow, so that it may lead us from the night of this world to the light of eternal brightness. Let us always with solicitude and caution await the sudden coming of the Lord, so that, when He knocks, our faith may be vigilant, ready to receive from the Lord the reward of its vigilance. If these mandates are kept, if these warnings and precepts are maintained, we cannot be overtaken while sleeping by the deceit of the devil; we will reign as vigilant servants with Christ our Lord.

Eusebius of Caesarea
260-339

Eusebius of Caesarea is a peculiar figure in the early Church. As a man he seems not to have been of any special note in either sanctity or intelligence. He is not remembered for any theological contribution; indeed, he was on the wrong side in the great controversies of the day. It has even been said that there were very good reasons for forgetting him. Yet his time and place in history were such that he was to make an irreplaceable contribution.

Eusebius personally saw the appalling sufferings and deaths of many fellow Christians in the East. He saw his best friend and master, Pamphilus, arrested, tortured, and jailed. He worked with him in prison for two years, then watched his martyrdom in 310 a.d. Then suddenly the nightmare was over and the new emperor, Constantine, committed himself to advance the cause of Christianity. At the same time Eusebius was named bishop of Caesarea and enjoyed the friendship of the Emperor.

This incredible turnaround in events deeply impressed Eusebius, giving him a theological perspective that was to be the hallmark of all his works. His was a straightforward view that was convinced that God's plan was evident in history. The spread of the Roman Empire from the time of Augustus was part of the providential fulfillment of God's ancient promise to Abraham. The recent persecutions were punishment for letting worldly ambition make its way into the Church, but with the conversion of Constantine, one of the most important moments of history, the Church was at last in a position to achieve its mission. Constantine was obviously God's instrument, the man chosen to rule the earthly life of God's people.

This simplistic view is understandable in the euphoria of its day, but within a century events would force Augustine to replace it with a much more sophisticated analysis of the relationship of Empire and Church in his City of God. *But despite all his shortcomings Eusebius performed a service that has put all subsequent generations in his debt. His* Ecclesiastical History *is a collection of facts, documents, and excerpts from other authors that trace the life of the Church from Apostolic times down to Constantine's victory (313) in nine books, of which the first five chapters of the first book are presented in the following section. A tenth book, written later, traced the story another decade to the defeat of Licinius that assured the sole rulership of Constantine (323). The last five chapters of that book are also included here.*

One of the maddening things about this work of Eusebius from a contemporary viewpoint is the feeling which it leaves that, despite the great value of its contents, the author should have been able to do much better. It is little more than a literary chronicle with an utterly chaotic plan. In acknowledging our gratitude for what he gives us, we must also note surprising gaps in his account. As the first effort at any kind of a systematic Church history, it is of inestimable importance, a pioneering work for which there were no models. He offers a wealth of information that would otherwise have been lost. But there is a frustrating lack of commentary or interpretation, which has raised the question as to just how much Eusebius himself understood of what was going on around him.

Despite all the reservations expressed about the stature of Eusebius himself, his Ecclesiastical History *is valuable beyond all calculation as our only source-book for various early Christian documents and events. However much he may be criticized, the simple fact remains that he has no competition; no one else of his day attempted to do what he did, so his contribution will always be appreciated by Christians everywhere.*

ECCLESIASTICAL HISTORY

BOOK ONE

CHAPTER 1

Since it is my purpose to hand down a written account of the successions of the holy Apostles as well as of the times extending from our Saviour to ourselves; the number and nature of the events which are said to have been treated in ecclesiastical history; the number of those who were her illustrious guides and leaders in especially prominent dioceses; the number of those who in each generation by word of mouth or by writings served as ambassadors of the word of God; the names, the number, and the times of those who out of a desire for innovation launched into an extremity of error and proclaimed themselves the introducers of knowledge falsely so called, mercilessly ravaging the flock of Christ like ravening wolves; and besides this what straightway befell the entire Jewish race as the result of its plot against our Saviour; furthermore, the number, and times of the war waged by the Gentiles against the divine Word; and the character of those who on various occasions have passed through the contest of blood and tortures in His behalf; and, in addition to this, the martyrdoms of our times and with them all the gracious and kindly succor of our Saviour; [in view of all this] I shall begin with the first dispensation of God in our Saviour and Lord, Jesus Christ.

But at this point my account asks for the indulgence of the reasonable, for I confess that it is beyond my power to fulfill the promise completely and perfectly, since we are the first to enter upon the undertaking, attempting, as it were, to travel a deserted and untrodden road, praying that we may have God as our guide and the power of the Lord as our co-worker, being unable to discover anywhere even the bare tracks of those who traveled the same path before us, except only for the brief remarks through which in one way or another they have left us partial accounts of the times in which they lived, raising their voices like torches from afar and crying out from on high as from a distant and lofty watch tower, bidding us how we must walk and keep straight the course of our story without error and danger. So, having gathered from what they have mentioned here and there such matters as we think will be useful for the subject that lies before us, and having culled appropriate passages from the ancient writers, as if, as it were, from intellectual meadows, we shall endeavor to consolidate them in an historical narrative, happy if we succeed in rescuing the successions, if not of all, then at least of the most renowned of the Apostles of our Saviour in those Churches which even today are accounted pre-eminent. I am of the opinion that it is most necessary for me to labor on this subject because I am unaware that any one of the ecclesiastical writers has up to now given serious attention to this kind of writing, and I hope that it will appear very useful to those who are interested in historical research. Now, I have already composed a summary of this material in the *Chronological Canons* which I have drawn up; nevertheless, in the present work I have undertaken to make the narrative as full as possible.

My work, as I have said, will begin with the dispensation conceived in relation to Christ and the divinity ascribed to Him, loftier and greater than human conception. For, he who intends to hand down in writing the story of the Church's leadership would have to begin with the very origin of Christ's dispensation itself, more divine than it seems to most, since we have laid claim to our name from Him.

CHAPTER 2

Since His nature is twofold—on the one hand like the head of the body whereby He is recognized as God; on the other, comparable to the feet whereby He put on man of like passions with ourselves for the sake of our own salvation—our account of subsequent events therefore would be complete [only] if we should begin with the story of the most capital and lordly events of His entire history. In this way, furthermore, will both the genuine antiquity and the divine majesty of the Christian religion be shown to those who assume that it is recent and foreign, having put in its appearance no earlier than yesterday. Now, no language would be sufficient for a description of the origin and the dignity and the very substance and nature of Christ, just as, indeed, the Holy Spirit says in the prophecies: 'Who shall declare his generation?' for no one knows the Father except the Son, nor in turn does anyone ever know the Son worthily except the Father alone who begot Him. And who except the Father could clearly conceive the Light that existed before the world and the wisdom that was intellectual and essential before the ages, the living Word who was in the beginning God by the side of the Father, the first and only offspring of God before all creation and making both visible and invisible, the commander-in-chief of the rational and immortal host of heaven, the angel of great counsel, the promoter of the ineffable plan, together with the Father the maker of all things, the second cause of the universe after the Father, the true and only-begotten Son of God, the Lord and God and King of all things begotten, who has received at once lordship and power with divinity itself and might and honor from the Father, for, according to the mystical passages of the Scriptures which deal with His divinity: 'In the beginning was the Word, and the Word was with God; and the Word was God; all things were made through him, and without him was made nothing'? This, indeed, the great Moses also teaches, as the most ancient of all Prophets, when, under the influence of the Holy Spirit, he describes the creation and arrangement of the universe, that the Creator and Maker of all things yielded to Christ Himself, and to no other than to His own clearly divine and first-born Word the making of subordinate things, and communed with Him regarding the creation of man. 'For,' he says, 'God said, "Let us make man to our image and likeness." ' And another of the Prophets confirms this statement, speaking of His divine nature somewhat like this: 'He spoke, and they were made: He commanded and they were created,' introducing the Father and Maker as Ruler of all, commanding with a royal nod, and second to Him the divine Word, no other than He who is proclaimed by us as carrying out His Father's commands. Him, too, all who from the origin of man are said to have excelled in righteousness and in the virtue of piety, the great servant Moses and his followers and before

47

him the first Abraham and his children and as many righteous
men and Prophets as appeared thereafter, contemplated with
the pure eyes of the mind and recognized, and they gave Him
the worship befitting the Son of God; and He Himself, never becoming indifferent to the worship of the Father, was established
as teacher of the knowledge of the Father to all men. Thus the
Lord God is said to have appeared as a common man to Abraham while seated by the oak of Mambre, but he straightway
falling down, although he saw a man with his eyes, worshiped
Him as God, besought Him as Lord, and confessed that he was
not ignorant who He was, using these very words: 'O Lord who
judgest all the earth, wilt thou not make judgment?' For, if it
should be unreasonable to suppose that the unbegotten and
immutable substance of God the Almighty was changed into the
form of man and, in turn, that the eyes of the beholders were
deceived by the phantasm of something created and that such
things were falsely invented by the Scripture, who else could
be proclaimed God and the Lord who judges all the earth and
makes judgment, appearing in the shape of a man—if it be not
proper to call Him the first cause of all things—than His pre-
existent word alone? And concerning Him it was also said in the
Psalms: 'He sent his word, and healed them: and delivered them
from their destructions.' Of Him Moses very clearly speaks,
calling Him a second Lord after the Father, when he says: 'The
Lord rained upon Sodom and Gomorrha brimstone and fire
from the Lord.' Him, too, the divine Scripture calls God, when
He again appeared to Jacob in the form of a man, saying to
Jacob: 'Thy name shall not be called Jacob, but Israel shall
be thy name, because thou hast been strong with God,' when
also 'he called the name of the place "the Vision of God," '
saying: 'For I have seen God face to face, and my soul has
been saved.' Nor is it at all proper to suppose that the the-
ophanies described above were of subordinate angels and
ministers of God, since whenever one of these appears to men
the Scripture does not conceal the fact, calling them precisely
by name not God nor indeed Lord, but angels, as it is easy to
prove by countless references. Him, too, Josue, the successor of
Moses, calls the leader of the heavenly angels and archangels
and of the supernal powers and as if he were the power and

wisdom of the Father, entrusted with the second rank of sovereignty and rule over all, 'prince of the host of the Lord,' although he saw Him only in the form and shape of a man. At any rate, it is written: 'And it came to pass, when Josue was in the field of the city of Jericho, he lifted up his eyes, and saw a man standing over against him, holding a drawn sword, and he went to him and said: "Art thou one of ours, or of our adversaries?" ' 'And he said to him, "I am prince of the host of the Lord and now I am come." ' 'And Josue fell on his face to the ground and said to him, "What commandeth my Lord to his servant?" ' 'And the prince of the Lord said to Josue, "Loose thy shoe from off they feet, for the place whereon thou standest is a holy place." ' Here, too, you will perceive from the identity of words that this is no other than he who also spoke to Moses, for Scripture says with the very words and with reference to this very person: 'And when the Lord saw that he went forward to see, the Lord called to him out of the midst of the bush, and said, Moses, Moses. And he said, What is it? And he said, Come not nigh thither, put off the shoe from thy feet: for the place whereon thou standest is holy ground. And he said to him, I am the God of thy father, the God of Abraham, the God of Isaac, and the God of Jacob.'

And that there really is a certain substance living and subsisting before the world, who ministered to the Father and God of the universe for the making of all created things called the Word and Wisdom of God, can be learned not only by the preceding proofs but from the very person of Wisdom herself, who through Solomon somewhat thus reveals the mysteries concerning herself: 'I wisdom dwell in counsel, and am present in learned thoughts. By me kings reign, and the mighty decree justice; by me great men are magnified, and princes rule the earth by me.' And to this she adds: 'The Lord created me in the beginning of his ways for his works; before the world he set me up; in the beginning before making the earth, before the fountain of waters sprang out, before the mountains had been established, and before all the hills he brought me forth. When he prepared the heavens, I was present with him, and when he made safe the fountains under the heavens, I was with him disposing them. I was she in whom he was delighted every day, and I was delighted before him at all times, when he re-joiced that he had completed the world.' So, let this be our proof in brief that the divine Word pre-existed and appeared to some, if not to all, men.

Now, why this announcement was not made long before to all men and to all nations, as it is now, would appear evident from the following. The life of men in the past was not yet able to receive the all-wise and all-virtuous teaching of Christ. Immediately in the beginning, after the first life in blessed-ness, the first man, despising God's command, fell into this mortal and perishable life and exchanged his former life of luxury with God for this curse-laden earth; and those who populated this entire world of ours after him were manifestly much worse, with the exception of one here and there, and chose a brutish manner of living and an intolerable life. They gave no thought to city or state, to the arts or sciences, and, besides, were unacquainted even with the name of laws and ordinances, virtue and philosophy; like nomads in a desert, they lived like savage and cruel creatures, destroying natural reason and the germs of thought and civilization in man's soul by the excess of their self-chosen wickedness, giving themselves over entirely to all manner of iniquity, so as at one time to corrupt one another, at another to kill one another, and again to eat human flesh, to venture on battles with God and on battles with giants celebrated among all men, even to plan to fortify the earth against heaven, and by the madness of a per-verted mind to prepare war against the supreme God Himself. While they were leading this manner of life, God, the Guardian of all, pursued them with floods and conflagrations, as if they had been a wild forest spread over the whole earth, and with successive famines and plagues and wars in turn and with thunderbolts from on high He cut them down, as if checking some terrible and quite obstinate disease of their souls with more severe punishments. Then, when the stupor of wickedness, as of a terrible intoxication, was spread widely over almost everyone, over shadowing and beclouding the souls of nearly all, the first-born and first-created wisdom of God, namely, the pre-existent Word himself, because of His exceeding love of man, appeared to His subjects now in visions of angels, now also to one or two of the ancients beloved of God in person, as a saving power of God, in no other than human form, for in no other way was it possible for them [to perceive Him].

When the seeds of true religion now had been cast by them upon a multitude of men, and a whole nation of Hebraic origin existed on earth persevering in true religion, He handed down to them through the Prophet Moses, as to multitudes still corrupted by their ancient ways, images and symbols of a certain mystical sabbath and of circumcision and instructions in other spiritual principles, but not unveiled initiations into the mysteries themselves. But when their law became celebrated and like a fragrant breeze was spread among all men, then, indeed, under their influence the minds of most of the Gentiles were softened by the law-givers and philosophers everywhere, and their wild and savage brutality was so changed to mildness that they possessed deep peace, friendships, and social intercourse. Even at that time, at the beginning of the Roman Empire, there appeared again to all men and to the Gentiles throughout the world, as if previously assisted and now actually ready for the reception of the knowledge of the Father, that same teacher of the virtues, the assistant of the Father in all good things, the divine and heavenly Word of God, in a human body in no way differing in substance from our own nature. And he performed and suffered such things as were in accord with the prophecies which foretold that One who was both man and God would come to dwell in the world, as the performer of miraculous deeds, and that He would be made manifest to all the Gentiles as the teacher of the worship of the Father, and that the marvel of His birth and His new teaching and the wonder of His deeds, and, in addition to these, the manner of His death and resurrection from the dead, and, above all, His divine ascension into heaven would also be made manifest. Thus Daniel the Prophet, under the influence of the divine Spirit, saw His kingdom in the end and was inspired thus to describe the vision of God in human fashion: 'For I beheld,' he says, 'till thrones were placed, and the Ancient of days sat: his garment was white as snow, and the hair of his head like clean wool: his throne like flames of fire: the wheels of it like a burning fire. A swift stream of fire issued forth from before him: thousands of thousands ministered to him, and ten thousand times a hundred thousand stood before him: the judgment sat, and the books were opened.' And next he says: 'I beheld, and lo, one like the son of man came with the clouds of heaven, and he came even to the Ancient of days; and he was presented before him. And to him was given power, and glory, and a kingdom, and all peoples, tribes, and tongues shall serve him. His power is an everlasting power that shall not pass away: and his kingdom shall not be destroyed.' These words clearly could apply to none other than to our Saviour, the God-Word, who in the beginning was with God, called 'son of man' because of His final Incarnation. But, since we have collected in special commentaries the prophetic utterances regarding our Saviour Jesus Christ, and in others have given a fuller demonstration of what is revealed concerning Him, we shall be satisfied for the present with what has been said [thus far].

CHAPTER 3

It is now time to show that the very name of Jesus, and especially that of Christ had already been honored by the ancient God-loving Prophets. Moses himself, having been the first to make known the name of Christ as being especially revered and glorious, having handed down the types and symbols of heavenly things and the mysterious images according to the oracle which said to him: 'See that thou make all things according to the pattern which was shown thee on the mount,' and having consecrated a man High Priest of God, in so far as it was at all possible, calls this man Christ; that is, to this dignity of the High Priesthood which with him surpassed all pre-eminence among men, for additional honor and glory he attaches the name of Christ. Thus, then, he indeed knew Christ as a Being divine. And the same [Moses] by divine inspiration foresaw the name Jesus very clearly, and again also endowed this with special privilege. The name of Jesus, which had never been uttered among men before it was made known to Moses, Moses applied first to this One alone, who, he knew, again as a type and a symbol, would receive the rule over all after his death. His successor, at any rate, who had never before used the title 'Jesus,' but had been called by another name, 'Auses,' which his parents had bestowed upon him, he himself proclaims Jesus, as a privilege of honor far greater than a royal crown, giving him the name because Jesus, the son of Nave, himself bore a resemblance to our Saviour, who alone, after Moses and the completion of the symbolic workship transmitted by him, received the rule of the true and pure religion. And in this way Moses bestowed the name of our Saviour Jesus Christ, as a mark of the greatest honor, upon the two men who in his time surpassed all the rest of the people in virtue and glory—the high priest and him who would rule after him. And the Prophets of succeeding times also clearly foretold Christ by name, giving testimony beforehand both to the intrigue of the people of the Jews which was destined to arise against Him and to the calling of the Gentiles through Him. At one time, Jeremias bears testimony in words somewhat as follows: 'The breath of our mouth, Christ the Lord, is taken in their sins, to whom we said: Under his shadow we shall live among the Gentiles.' At another time, David speaks in perplexity thus: 'Why have the Gentiles raged, and the people devised vain things? The kings of the earth stood up, and the princes met together, against the Lord, and against his Christ,' to which he later adds in the person of Christ Himself: 'The Lord hath said to me: Thou art my son, this day have I begotten thee. Ask of me, and I will give thee the Gentiles for thy inheritance, and the utmost parts of the earth for thy possession.' Now, the name of Christ adorned not only those among the Hebrews who were honored with the prepared oil as a symbol, but also the kings whom the Prophets at the bidding of God anointed and, as it were, constituted typical Christs, since they also bore in themselves the types of the royal and sovereign power of the only and true Christ, the divine Word who ruleth over all. We have also learned through tradition that some of the Prophets themselves had already through anointing become Christs in type, so that all these have reference to the true Christ, the divine and heavenly Word, who really is the only High Priest of all, the only King of all creation, and the Father's only Archprophet of the Prophets. And the proof of this is that no one of those symbolically anointed of old, either of priests or of kings or indeed of Prophets, possessed so great a power of divine virtue as was displayed by our Saviour and Lord Jesus, the only true Christ. No one of them, indeed, although they were renowned for dignity and honor among their own peoples for very many generations, ever called their subjects Christians from the symbolical application of the name of Christ to themselves. Moreover, no one of them received the honor of veneration from their subjects, nor after death was there any such disposition among their subjects as to be ready to die in behalf of him who was honored. And never throughout the world of nations did so great a commotion arise over any person of that day, since the power of the symbol was unable to create such an effect among them as the presence of reality which was exhibited by our Saviour. For He received the symbol and types of the High Priesthood from no one, and He did not derive His earthly origin from a race of priests, and He was not elevated to a kingdom by armed forces of men, and He was not a prophet like those of old, and He obtained no honor nor any pre-eminence among the Jews, yet with all, even if without symbols but with the truth itself, He was adorned. Though He did not then obtain honors like those which we have mentioned above, yet He was called Christ more than any of them, and as the only true Christ of God Himself He filled the whole world with Christians, His truly reverend and holy name, handing down to them no longer types or images but the uncovered virtues themselves and the heavenly life in the very doctrines of truth, and He has received the chrism, not that prepared with material substances but the very divine anointing itself with the spirit of God, by sharing in the unbegotten divinity of the Father. And Isaias again teaches this very truth, exclaiming in one place as if from Christ Himself: 'The Spirit of the Lord is upon me. Wherefore he hath anointed me; to preach the gospel to the poor, he hath sent me, to announce deliverance to captives and sight to the blind.' And not only Isaias, but also David, proclaims to His Person, saying: 'Thy throne, O God, is forever and ever: the sceptre of thy kingdom is a sceptre of uprightness. Thou hast loved justice, and hated iniquity: therefore God, thy God, hath anointed thee with the oil of gladness above thy fellows.' In these passages the text calls Him God in the first verse, and in the second honors Him with a royal sceptre; then, in turn, going on, after royal and divine power, represents Him in the third place as having become Christ, anointed not with oil of material substances but with the divine 'oil of gladness.' In this way, moreover, it points out His special distinction and great superiority over and difference from those of old who as types were anointed more materially. Elsewhere, the same David makes his statements about Him, speaking clearly somewhat as follows: 'The Lord said to my Lord: Sit thou at my right hand: Until I make thy enemies the footstool of thy feet,' and 'From the womb before the day star I begot thee. The Lord hath sworn, and he will not repent: Thou art a priest forever according to the order of Melchisedek.' Melchisedek is introduced in the Holy Scriptures of the most high God, not consecrated by any materially prepared oil, and not even as belonging by racial descent to the priesthood of the Hebrews. Thus, according to His order and not that of others who received symbols and types, our Saviour has been called Christ and priest with an appeal to an oath. Thus, also, the narrative does not tell us that He was anointed corporeally by the Jews or that He was of a tribe that held the priesthood, but that He came into being from God himself before the day star, that is, before the establishment of the world, and that He possesses an immortal and ageless priesthood to boundless eternity. A great and clear proof of the immaterial and divine anointing that took place upon Him is that He alone of all those who have ever existed up to this time is called Christ by all men throughout the whole world, and is confessed and borne witness to under this name by all, and is so commemorated by Greeks and barbarians and up to this day is honored as a king by His worshipers throughout the world, and is admired as more than a Prophet, and is glorified as the only and true High Priest of God, and, above all this, as the pre-existent Word of God, who came into being before all ages and received the honor of worship from the Father, is worshiped as God. Yet, most wonderful of all, we who have consecrated ourselves to Him honor Him not only with our voices and with the sound of words but also with the entire disposition of our soul, so as to prefer giving testimony to Him rather than saving our own lives.

CHAPTER 4

Let these remarks suffice at this point as a necessary preface to my history, that no one may regard our Lord and Saviour, Jesus Christ, as one recently come into being because of the time of His ministry in the flesh. But, that no one may suppose His teaching to be new and strange as if composed by a youth and one differing in no respect from the rest of men, come, let us also discuss this point briefly. For, when the presence of our Saviour, Jesus Christ, recently shone forth upon all men, an admittedly new nation appeared in such numbers in accord with the inscrutable prophecies of the time, not small and not weak and not dwelling somewhere in a corner of the earth, but the most populous of all the nations and the most pious, indestructible and unconquerable in that it always obtains help from God, the nation that has been honored by all with the name of Christ. When one of the Prophets foresaw with the eye of the Divine Spirit what this nation was destined to be he was so amazed as to exclaim: 'Who hath ever heard such a thing? and who hath spoken thus? hath the earth brought forth in one day? and hath a nation been brought forth at once?' And the same Prophet also indicates in a manner its future name, when he says: 'And a new name shall be applied to those who serve me, which shall be blessed on the earth.' But, even if we are clearly new and this truly recent name of Christians has lately been known among all nations, our life and manner of conduct in accordance with the very teachings of our religion have not been recently fashioned by us, but, as it were, from the first creation of man have been established by the natural concepts of the God-favored men of old, as we shall somehow show as follows. The nation of Hebrews is really not new, but a nation held in high esteem for its antiquity by all men, and is itself known to all. Now, stories and writings among this nation include ancient men, to be sure rare and few in number, yet distinguished for piety and righteousness and every other virtue, some remarkable before the flood, others after it; of the children and descendants of Noe, for example, Abraham, whom the children of the Hebrews proudly proclaim as their own founder and progenitor. If anyone should tell us, going back from

Abraham to the first man, that all those who have had the testimony of righteousness were Christians in fact if not in name, he would strike not far from the truth. For, as the name professes to show, that the Christian man through the knowledge of Christ and His teachings excels in sobriety and righteousness and patience of life and manliness of virtue and in the pious confession of the one and only God over all, all this was zealously practiced by them no less than by us. They did not care about bodily circumcision, as we do not; nor about the observance of Sabbaths, as we do not; nor about the avoidness of certain foods nor about making a distinction in the others, such as Moses, first of all, in the beginning handed down to his successors to be observed as symbols, just as such things are of no concern to Christians today. But they clearly knew Him, the Christ of God, since it has already been shown that He was seen by Abraham, deliberated with Isaac, spoke to Israel, and conversed with Moses and the Prophets thereafter. Hence you would find that those God-favored men were deemed worthy even of the name of Christ according to the words which say regarding them: 'Touch ye not my anointed [Christs]: and do no evil to my prophets.' Hence it is clear that the religion which was recently proclaimed to all the Gentiles through the teaching of Christ must be considered the first and most ancient of all and the oldest discovery of religion by those God-favored men of the age of Abraham. If now it is said that Abraham received the command of circumcision much later, nevertheless he is said to have received before this command the testimony of justice through faith, as the divine Scripture so says somewhere: 'Abraham believed God, and it was reputed to him unto justice.' And to Abraham, as he was before circumcision, a prophecy was given by God, who revealed Himself to him (and this was Christ Himself, the Word of God) regarding those who in later times were to be justified in a manner similar to himself, in these very words: 'And in thee shall all the kindred of the earth be blessed,' and 'He shall become a great and mighty nation, and in him all the nations of the earth shall be blessed.' We may also believe this as having been fulfilled in us. For he was justified by faith in the Word of God, the Christ, who was revealed to him, after he had renounced the superstitions of his fathers and the former errors of his life, and had confessed the God, who is over all, as one and had served this God by deeds of virtue and not by worship of the law of Moses which was later, and to him, as he was then, it was said that all the tribes and all the nations of the earth will be blessed in him; and by deeds more manifest than words is that manner of religion of Abraham shown to be practiced at present among Christians alone throughout the whole earth. What, then, would prevent us, who are of Christ, from confessing that our manner of life and religion and that of the God-beloved men of old is one and the same? So we demonstrate that the correct practice of religion which was handed down to us by the teaching of Christ is not new and strange, but, if we must speak truthfully, is the very first and the only true religion. Let this discussion suffice for the subject.

CHAPTER 5

Now, then, after the necessary introduction to our proposed history of the Church, it remains for us to continue on our course as if upon a journey, from the appearance of our Saviour in the flesh, after invoking God, the Father of the Word, and Jesus Christ Himself, our revealed Saviour and Lord, the heavenly Word of God to assist us and to co-operate in the attaining of truth in our narrative. It was the forty-second year of the reign of Augustus, and the twenty-eighth after the subjection of Egypt and the death of Antony and Cleopatra, with the latter of whom the dynasty of the Ptolemies in Egypt came to an end, when our Saviour and Lord, Jesus Christ, at the time of the first census, while Cyrenius was Governor of Syria, in accord with the prophecies concerning Him, was born in Bethlehem of Judaea. Flavius Josephus, the most famous of the historians among the Hebrews, also makes mention of this census in the time of Cyrenius, adding another account about the sect of Galileans which arose at about the same time, of which Luke, among our writers, has made mention in the Acts, saying: 'After him rose up Judas the Galilean in the days of the census and drew some people after him; he too perished, and all his followers were scattered abroad.' The writer mentioned above in agreement with this provides the following by way of explanation in Book 18 of his *Antiquities*: 'And Cyrenius, one of those summoned to the Senate, a man who had held other offices and had passed through all to become consul, and a person of great dignity in other respects, came to Syria with a small force, having been sent by Caesar with judicial power over the people and to make an evaluation of their property.' And a little later he says: 'But Judas, a Gaulonite, of a city by the name of Gamala, taking Sadduchus, a Pharisee, with him, instigated a revolt, saying that the valuation led to nothing else than downright slavery, and calling upon the people to defend their liberty.' And in Book 2 of the *History of the Jewish War* he writes as follows about the same man: 'At this time a certain Galilean, Judas by name, incited the inhabitants to revolt, calling them cowards, if they submitted to the payment of tribute to the Romans, and if they endured, besides God, mortal masters.' So much for Josephus.

BOOK TEN

CHAPTER 5

Come now, let us finally quote also the imperial decrees of Constantine and Licinius as translated from the Latin.

A copy of the imperial ordinances as translated from the Latin tongue.

'When watching long ago that freedom of worship should not be denied, but that, according to the mind and purpose of each one, authority should be given of caring for divine things according to his choice, we had issued orders to the Christians . . . to guard the faith of their own sect and worship; but since many different conditions seemed clearly to have been set forth in that decree, in which such authority was granted to the same persons, it seems likely that some of them after a while were repelled from such observance.

'When under happy auspices I, Constantine Augustus, and I, Licinius Augustus, had come to Milan and held an inquiry about all matters such as pertain to the common advantage and good, these things along with the others that seemed to benefit the many, or rather, first and foremost, we resolved to issue decrees by which esteem and reverence for the Deity might be procured, that is, that we might give all Christians freedom of choice to follow the ritual which they wished, so that whatever is of the nature of the divine and heavenly might be propitious to us and to all those living under our authority. Accordingly, with sound and most correct reasoning we decided upon this our plan: that authority is to be refused no one at all to follow and to choose the observance or the form of worship of the Christians, and that authority be given to each one to devote his mind to that form of worship which he himself considers to be adapted to himself, in order that the Deity may be able in all things to provide for us His accustomed care and goodness. And so it was natural for us to send a rescript that this is pleasing to us, in order that, when those conditions had been altogether removed which were contained in our former letters sent to your Devotion concerning the Christians, those things, also, which seemed to be very unfavorable and foreign to our clemency might be removed, and that now each one of those who had the same inclination to observe the ritual of the Christians might without any hindrance engage in this very observance freely and simply. And we resolved to present these matters in the fullest measure to your Grace, that you may know that we have granted to the same Christians free and unlimited authority to look after their own ritual. And when you observe that we have granted this unlimited authority to them, your Devotion will see that authority has been given to others, also, who wish to continue their own observance and ritual, a condition which is clearly accommodated to the peacefulness of our times, so that each one may have authority to choose and to observe whatever ritual his spiritual inclination wishes. This, then, we have done, so that we may seem to have detracted nothing from any honorable ritual.

'And this, also, besides the rest, we resolve with respect to the Christians: that their places at which they were formerly accustomed to assemble, concerning which, also, in the former letter sent to your Devotion a definite ordinance had been laid down for that time, to the effect that if some had manifestly bought these places either out of our own treasury or from some other source, be returned to the same Christians without payment or any other demand for compensation, putting aside all negligence and ambiguity; furthermore, if any perchance have received them as gifts, that they should restore them as quickly as possible to the same Christians, with the understanding that, if either those who have bought these same places or those who have acquired them as gifts demand something from our generosity, they go to the prefect of the district, in order that thought may be taken through our beneficence in their behalf, also. All these things must be handed over to the body of Christians immediately and without any delay.

'And since the same Christians had not only those places in which they used to assemble, but are known to have had others, also, which belonged not to individuals among them, but to the rightful claim of their whole body, that is, of the Christians, all these, in accordance with the law which we have just mentioned, you are to order to be restored without delay to the same Christians, that is, to their group and to each assembly, guarding clearly the aforementioned statement, that whoever restore the same places without compensation, even as we have already said, may hope for indemnification from our own generosity.

'In all these matters you should exercise the utmost care for the aforementioned group of Christians, so that our order may be carried out as quickly as possible, and that also in this forethought may be exercised through our beneficence for the common and public peace. For by this means, as has been mentioned before, the divine zeal in our behalf, which we have already experienced in many things, will remain steadfast forever. And that the scope of this our decree and generosity may be brought to the knowledge of all, it is fitting that these matters as decreed by us be declared everywhere, and brought to the knowledge of all by being published at your order, so that the decree of this our generosity may escape the notice of no one.'

Copy of another imperial decree which he also made, pointing out that the favors have been made to the Catholic Church alone.

'Greetings, Anulinus, our most honorable Sir. This is the manner of our benevolence, to will that those things which belong to another by right not only suffer no harm but even be restored, most honorable Anulinus. Wherefore, we wish that

61

when you receive this letter, if any of those things which belonged to the Catholic Church of the Christians in the several cities, or even in other places, should now be possessed either by citizens or by any others, you should have them restored immediately to these same churches, since we have determined that these things which these same churches formerly possessed should be restored to them as their right. Since, then, your Devotion sees that the order of this our command is most clear, make haste to restore to them as quickly as possible all things, whether gardens or buildings or whatever belonged by right to these same churches, so that we may learn that you have rendered most careful obedience to this order of ours. Farewell, Anulinus, our most honored and beloved friend.'

Copy of an imperial letter, in which he commands that a synod of bishops be held at Rome in behalf of the unity and harmony of the churches.

'Constantine Augustus to Miltiades, Bishop of Rome, and to Mark. Since such documents and many of them from Anulinus, the most illustrious proconsul of Africa, have been dispatched to me, in which it is clear that Caecilian, Bishop of the city of Carthage, is censured on many counts by some of his colleagues in Africa, and since this seems to me a very serious matter in these provinces, which Divine Providence has freely entrusted to my Devotedness, and where there is a great multitude of people, the many are found set upon the worse course, splitting up into two parties, as it were, and the bishops at odds among themselves, I resolved that Caecilian himself, with ten bishops of those who seem to censure him, and ten of the others whom he himself may consider necessary to his cause, should set sail for Rome, so that these in the presence of you and, moreover, of Reticius and Maternus and Marinus, your colleagues, whom I have ordered to hasten to Rome for this purpose, may hear him as you may judge to be in harmony with the most sacred law. Yet, in order that you may have the fullest knowledge of all these matters, I have attached to my letter copies of the documents sent to me by Anulinus, and have sent them to your colleagues previously mentioned. And when your Constancy reads these, he will determine in what manner it is necessary to carry on a most careful investigation of the case mentioned above, and to reach a decision in keeping with justice, since it does not escape the notice of your Grace that I give such respect to the lawful Catholic Church, as to wish to leave behind no schism or division in any place. May the divinity of the great God protect you for many years, most honored Sir.'

Copy of an imperial letter, by which he orders a second synod to be held for the purpose of removing every dissension among the bishops.

'Constantine Augustus to Cherstus, Bishop of Syracuse. Already on a former occasion, when some basely and perversely had begun to cause divisions concerning the form of worship of the holy and heavenly Power and the Catholic faith, wishing to cut off such rivalries among them, I had issued orders that certain of the bishops be sent from Gaul, and, indeed, that those be called from Africa who were of opposite sides contending so stubbornly and so persistently that, with the Bishop of Rome present, this problem which seemed to have been raised might by their presence receive a proper and careful examination. But when, as it happens, some, forgetting even their own salvation and the reverence due their most holy religion, even now still do not cease to continue their personal enmities, being unwilling to abide by the decisions already rendered, and affirming that even then it was a few who had rendered their opinions and decisions, or even that they hurried to pass a quick and a sharp judgment without first examining everything that ought to have been investigated carefully, and as a result of all this it comes about that these very ones, who ought to be of one mind in brotherly love, are rather shamefully separated from one another, and furnish for the men who have souls foreign to this most holy religion the occasion for scoffing; wherefore it has become a matter of conscience with me to insist that what should have ceased by voluntary agreement after the judgment had been rendered, even now may possibly be ended in the presence of so many. Since, therefore, we have ordered that very many bishops from diverse and numberless places come to the city of Arles by the first of August, we have thought to write you also to obtain from the very brilliant Latronianus, the "corrector" of Sicily, a public vehicle, and to add to your group any two of the second rank, whomever you yourself decide to choose, and also to take along three servants who shall be able to serve you along the way, and be present on the same day at the place mentioned above, so that both by your Constancy and by the complete agreement of mind and soul of the rest who assemble, even this dissension which until now has kept up a disgraceful existence, when all has been heard that likely will be said by those now at variance with one another, whom we have likewise ordered to be on hand, may possibly be recalled, even if slowly, to a due condition of religion and to brotherly faith and harmony. May Almighty God keep you in good health for many years.'

CHAPTER 6

Copy of an imperial letter in which money is granted to the churches.

'Constantine Augustus to Caecilian, Bishop of Carthage. Since it has indeed given pleasure among all the provinces, that is, the African, the Numidian, and the Muretanian, that a contribution be made to certain specified ministers of the lawful and holy Catholic religion for expenses, I have given a letter to Ursus, the most distinguished finance minister of Africa, and I have indicated to him that he exercise care to pay to your Constancy 3,000 folles. Do you, then, when you have received the aforesaid sum of money, order it to be distributed to all those mentioned above according to the plan sent you by Hosius. But if you now should discover some lack for fulfilling this my desire as regards them all, you should ask unhesitatingly whatever you discover is necessary from Heraclides the administrator of our possessions. For, when he was here, I truly issued orders to him that, if your Constancy asked of him any money, he deem it wise to pay it to you without any hesitancy. And since I learned that some people, who, perchance, are not of sound mind, wish to turn astray the people of the holy and Catholic Church by some vile deceit, know that I have given such orders as these to Anulinus, the proconsul, and to Patricius, also, the vicar of the prefects, when they were here, to the effect that in all remaining matters and especially in this they bestow fitting attention, and not allow such an event to be disregarded. Wherefore, if you should observe that some such men are continuing in this madness, without any hesitation proceed to the above-mentioned judges and bring this matter before them, so that they (as I ordered them when they were here) may turn these people from their error. May the divinity of the great God protect you for many years.'

CHAPTER 7

Copy of an imperial letter in which he commands that the presidents of the churches be relieved of all services to the State.

'Greeting, Anulinus, our most honorable Sir. Since from very many circumstances it appears that religious worship, in which the highest reverence for the most holy and heavenly [Power] is preserved, when once disregarded, has brought the gravest dangers to public affairs, and that this, when once it has been lawfully restored and preserved, has brought the greatest good fortune on the Roman name and exceptional prosperity on all the affairs of men (for Divine Providence bestows this), it has seemed good that those men who, with fitting holiness and constant observance of this law, provide their services for the ritual of divine worship, receive the rewards of their individual efforts, most honored Anulinus. For this reason I wish that those within the province which is under your guidance in the Catholic Church, over which Caecilian has been placed, who bestow their services on this holy worship, and whom they call clerics, be held once and for all completely exempt from all the public services, so that they may not be drawn away by any error or sacrilegious lapse from the worship due to the Divinity, but, rather, may without any hindrance devote themselves entirely to their own law. For, while rendering the greatest service to the Deity, they seem to render a correspondingly great service to the common good. Farewell, Anulinus, our most honored and very dear friend.

CHAPTER 8

Such gifts, then, did the divine and heavenly grace of the appearance of our Saviour bestow upon us, and such abundance of blessings for all men was procured by our peace. And thus were our affairs fulfilled in rejoicing and in festive assemblies. But the sight of what was seen was not bearable to the envy that hates good and to the demon who loves evil, just as the events that befell the aforementioned tyrants were not sufficient to bring Licinius to sound reason. He who was deemed worthy of sharing the rule and held the second position of honor to the great Emperor Constantine, and was related by marriage and was of the noblest kinship with him, abandoned the imitation of the good and eagerly sought the evil manners and the wickedness of the impious tyrants; and he chose to follow the judgment of those whose destruction he had witnessed with his very eyes rather than to abide with the friendship and association of the nobler man. Filled, indeed, with envy of the common benefactor, he carried on against him an impious and very dreadful war, with no regard for the laws of nature, unmindful of oaths and of ties of blood and of agreements. Constantine, the wholly good emperor, furnishing him with the tokens of true good will, did not envy him kinship with himself, and did not deny him the enjoyment of an illustrious marriage with his sister; instead, he deemed him worthy to become a partaker of the nobility of his fathers and of his imperial blood and origin, and provided the right of enjoying the supreme rule as a brother-in-law and joint-emperor, favoring him with the direction and administration of no inferior part of the peoples under the rule of the Romans, while Licinius, to the contrary, was engaged in the opposite conduct, contriving daily all sorts of schemes against Constantine, and meditating all manner of plots that he might reward his benefactor with evils. At first, then, while trying to conceal his intrigue, he feigned friendship, and hoped that by frequently resorting to trickery and deceit he might most easily attain his expectations. But, for Constantine, God was Friend, Protector, and Guardian, who brought to light for him the plots devised in secret and darkness, and reproved them. Of such power is the great weapon of godliness to ward off the attack of the enemy, and to strengthen the protection of its own safety. Armed then with this, our emperor, most beloved of God, escaped the plots of this hateful one. And Licinius, when he saw that his covert scheme was by no means progressing as he wished (for God exposed to the emperor, whom He loved, every trickery and wickedness), since he no longer was able to conceal himself, chose open warfare. Thereupon, intending to war at close quarters with Constantine, even now he was hastening to array himself against the God of all, whom he knew Constantine worshiped; and so he set about to attack his pious subjects quietly and in silence, although they had never at any time done any harm to his rule. And he did this, being forced by his innate wickedness into a terrible blindness. Thus, he placed before his eyes neither the memory of those who persecuted Christians before him nor of those whom he himself murdered and punished for the impious deeds they had performed, but turned aside from sound reasoning, and, becoming quite mad, determined to war on God Himself, as the Helper of Constantine, instead of on him who was being helped.

First, he expelled every Christian from his house; thus he himself deprived himself, wretched man, of the prayers to God in his behalf, which they were taught by their ancestral custom to make for all men. And then he gave orders that the soldiers in the cities be singled out and deprived of their rank of honor unless they chose to sacrifice to demons.

These matters were yet small when judged by comparison with more serious actions. But why is it necessary to mention separately and distinctly the things done by this God-hater, namely, how this most lawless man invented laws devoid of law? Indeed, he laid down a law that no one should treat humanely those who were suffering in prison by distributing food among them, that no one should take pity on those perishing from hunger in bonds, and that no one should be kindly at all or do them any kindly service, even when drawn on by a natural sympathy for their neighbors. And of his laws this one, at any rate, was most openly shameless and most severe in disregarding every gentle impulse, according to which punishment was even placed upon those showing mercy, that they suffer equally with the ones being shown mercy, and that they be delivered over to bonds and imprisonment, and that those ministering humane acts suffer punishment equally with those undergoing it. Such were the decrees of Licinius. Why is

67

it necessary to enumerate his new regulations pertaining to marriage, or his revolutionary changes with regard to those who were departing this life, in which he dared to annul the ancient laws of the Romans, which were established well and wisely, and introduce in their stead certain barbarous and crude regulations, lawless laws that were really contrary to law; and the countless injunctions he devised against his subject peoples, and all sorts of taxes of gold and silver, and revaluation of land, and the harmful exactions from men in the country districts no longer living but long since departed? And what banishments this man-hater invented for those who had done no wrong, what arrests of noble and highly esteemed men, whose wedded wives he separated from them and gave over to certain lewd characters of his household for insult; and with how many married women and unmarried girls this drunken old sot satisfied the unbridled lust of his soul, why should one dwell upon these things, when the excesses of his last deeds prove the first to be of small and of no account?

At any rate, in the final course of his madness he went against the bishops, and, deeming them the servants of the God of all, and opposed to what he was doing, he plotted against them not yet openly, to be sure, from fear of his superior, but again secretly and craftily, and he destroyed the most highly respected among them through the connivance of the governors. And the manner of their death was strange, such as was never known before. For instance, what was done at Amasea and the other cities of the Pontus exceeds every excess of cruelty. There some of the churches of God were torn apart from top to bottom; others they closed, so that none of the accustomed worshipers might gather or return to God the services due Him. For he did not think that the prayers were being offered up for him (this being the reckoning of an evil conscience), but he had been persuaded that we did everything and appeased God in behalf of the God-beloved emperor. Therefore he set forth to vent his wrath upon us. Indeed, the flatterers among the governors, being convinced that they were doing what pleased the impious man, inflicted on some of the bishops in the usual manner the penalties of evil-doers, and those who had done no wrong were led away and punished without disguise like murderers. And some now endured a novel death, their bodies being cut into many pieces, and, after this cruel and most frightening spectacle, being hurled into the depths of the sea as food for fishes. Thereupon, flight became the watchword of God-fearing men, and again the fields, again the deserts and valleys and mountains received the servants of Christ. And when the impious man thus made progress in these measures, he cast about in his mind the idea of stirring up the persecution against all. He would have succeeded in his purpose, and there would have been nothing to stop him from attaining his aim, had not God, the Champion of souls of His own, very quickly foreseen what would take place, and caused to shine forth immediately, as if in deep darkness and gloomy night, a great luminary and savior for all, guiding into those regions with a mighty hand, His servant Constantine.

CHAPTER 9

To him, accordingly, from heaven above as the worthy fruit of piety did He grant the trophies of victory over the impious ones, but the guilty one with all his counselors and friends He threw down prone under the feet of Constantine.

When Licinius had carried his madness to the last extreme against him, the emperor, the friend of God, thinking that he was no longer to be endured, summoned his prudent reasoning, and, tempering the firm manner of justice with benevolence, decided to aid those in sore distress under the tyrant, and hastened to save the greater part of the human race by putting insignificant spoilers out of the way. When he employed benevolence alone during the time before this and showed mercy on him who was unworthy of any sympathy, nothing further came of it, because Licinius did not give up his evil ways, but rather increased his madness against the subject peoples; while for those who were being ill treated, no hope of safety was left, as they were being oppressed by a tyrannical wild beast. Wherefore, mingling his hatred of evil with his love of good, the defender of the good went forth together with his son Crispus, a most benevolent emperor, extending his saving right hand to all who were perishing. Thereupon, with the aid of God, the universal King and the Son of God, the Saviour of all, as guide and ally, the father and son encircled the array of the haters of God, and easily bore off the victory, for everything in the attack was made smooth for them by God in accordance with His plan. Indeed, suddenly and sooner than it can be spoken, those who yesterday and the day before were breathing out slaughter and threatenings were no more, nor was there any remembrance of their names, and their pictures and honors received the disgrace that they deserved, and the things that Licinius had seen with his own eyes happen to the impious tyrants of old, these he himself similarly suffered, since he neither received instruction himself nor did he acquire wisdom from the strokes that befell his neighbors, but he continued along the same road of impiety as they did, and justly was hurled over the same precipice.

Thus, then, was Licinius cast down and laid prostrate; but Constantine, the greatest conqueror, excelling in every virtue that comes from godliness, with his son Crispus, an emperor most dear to God and in every way like his father, recovered their own East, and rendered as one united realm the Empire of the Romans, as of old, bringing under their peace all of it from the rising of the sun on both sides of the inhabited earth, north and south, even to the farthest limits of the declining day. Thus, then, men were relieved of all fear of those who formerly oppressed them, and they set about celebrating with bright and festive days of feasting, and all things were filled with light, and with smiling countenances and gleaming eyes; those who formerly looked at each other with downcast expressions now danced and sang throughout the cities and countryside alike, honoring first of all God, the universal King, for so they had been instructed, and then the devout emperor with his sons dear to God; thus, there was oblivion of past evils, and a forgetfulness of every impious deed, and an enjoyment of present blessings and expectation of those yet to come. Thus, then, were put forth in every place from the hand of the victorious emperor decrees full of benevolence and laws that provided evidence of munificence and true piety. Thus, in truth, when every vestige of tyranny had been cleansed away, the foundation of their rightful kingdom was kept secure and without reproach for Constantine and his sons alone. And when they, as the first of all their actions, cleansed the world of hatred for God, mindful of the blessings bestowed on them by God, they manifested their love of virtue and love of God and their piety and gratitude with respect to the Deity by the deeds which they performed openly in the sight of all men.

St. Jerome
348-420

Jerome was born in Stridon in Dalmatia and went to Rome where he studied the Greek and Latin classics with a passionate interest. He was baptized by Pope Liberius around 365, then went to Trier where he took up theology and resolved to become a monk. He went to the East and lived for several years as a hermit in the Syrian desert. He was ordained a priest and went to Constantinople where he studied the Bible for two years under Gregory Nazianzen. He then went to Rome where he was secretary and counselor to Pope Damasus for three years. When the pope died, Jerome went to Palestine and settled in Bethlehem where he spent the remaining thirty years of his life, chiefly engaged in prayer, the instruction of his fellow monks, and his great work of revising, translating, and commenting upon the Scriptures. The Latin "Vulgate" translation of the Bible is, of course, his greatest and best known achievement.

Jerome was certainly one of the best educated of the Fathers and showed remarkable versatility. His knowledge of languages, flair for style, and capacity for work put him in a class by himself. He had his faults, but the contributions that he made, especially to the Latin-speaking world, were quite simply beyond measure.

On Famous Men has been called the first "History of Christian Literature." It is incomplete, contains errors, and is often inexact, but, like the Ecclesiastical History *of Eusebius, its greatest importance stems from the simple fact that there is nothing else like it in existence. If it had not been written and preserved, we would all have been impoverished. It is an encyclopedic list, giving information on Christian writers from the authors of the New Testament down to Jerome himself, numbering altogether 135.*

There is an apologetic intent behind the composition. In Jerome's day there were still those who viewed Christianity as a shallow religion, devoid of any great classical tradition, unworthy of those who wished to live the life of the mind. Such were the sentiments of many of its more educated enemies: Symmachus, Celsus, Porphyry, Julian. The followers of Jesus were boors, numbskulls, and ignoramuses. If there was anyone who had a right to object to such allegations, it was the tremendously talented and cultivated Jerome, but he set out in this work to catalogue all earlier Christians whom he knew of whose achievements in writing belied the stereotype.

The selection that follows is from the first half of On Famous Men, *the first and second century examples down to Origen. One interesting note is the fact that Jerome includes Philo, Seneca, and Josephus, none of whom were Christians but all of whom were in a significant way related to the development of early Christianity. As a pioneer he included many figures who turned out to be mediocre and forgettable. He underrated the stature of Chrysostom, Basil, and Ambrose. He exaggerated the importance of Origen. But on the whole the work stands as a landmark to a "Church come of age," no longer intimidated by pagan learning, proud of the accomplishments of its own members, and ready to employ intelligence fully in the service of the Gospel.*

ON FAMOUS MEN

CHAPTER I

Simon Peter the son of John, from the village of Bethsaida in the province of Galilee, brother of Andrew the apostle, and himself chief of the apostles, after having been bishop of the church of Antioch and having preached to the Dispersion—the believers in circumcision, in Pontus, Galatia, Cappadocia, Asia and Bithynia—pushed on to Rome in the second year of Claudius to overthrow Simon Magus, and held the sacerdotal chair there for twenty-five years until the last, that is the fourteenth, year of Nero. At his hands he received the crown of martyrdom being nailed to the cross with his head towards the ground and his feet raised on high, asserting that he was unworthy to be crucified in the same manner as his Lord. He wrote two epistles which are called Catholic, the second of which, on account of its difference from the first in style, is considered by many not to be by him. Then too the Gospel according to Mark, who was his disciple and interpreter, is ascribed to him. On the other hand, the books, of which one is entitled his Acts, another his Gospel, a third his Preaching, a fourth his Revelation, a fifth his "Judgment" are rejected as apocryphal.

Buried at Rome in the Vatican near the triumphal way he is venerated by the whole world.

CHAPTER II

James, who is called the brother of the Lord, surnamed the Just, the son of Joseph by another wife, as some think, but, as appears to me, the son of Mary sister of the mother of our Lord of whom John makes mention in his book, after our Lord's passion at once ordained by the apostles bishop of Jerusalem, wrote a single epistle, which is reckoned among the seven Catholic Epistles and even this is claimed by some to have been published by some one else under his name, and gradually, as time went on, to have gained authority. Hegesippus who lived near the apostolic age, in the fifth book of his Commentaries, writing of James, says "After the apostles, James the brother of the Lord surnamed the Just was made head of the Church at Jerusalem. Many indeed are called James. This one was holy from his mother's womb. He drank neither wine nor strong drink, ate no flesh, never shaved or anointed himself with ointment or bathed. He alone had the privilege of entering the Holy of Holies, since indeed he did not use woolen vestments but linen and went alone into the temple and prayed in behalf of the people, insomuch that his knees were reputed to have acquired the hardness of camels' knees." He says also many other things, too numerous to mention. Josephus also in the 20th book of his Antiquities, and Clement in the 7th of his Outlines mention that on the death of Festus who reigned over Judea, Albinus was sent by Nero as his successor. Before he had reached his province, Ananias the high priest, the youthful son of Ananus of the priestly class taking advantage of the state of anarchy, assembled a council and publicly tried to force James to deny that Christ is the son of God. When he refused Ananius ordered him to be stoned. Cast down from a pinnacle of the temple, his legs broken, but still half alive, raising his hands to heaven he said, "Lord forgive them for they know not what they do." Then struck on the head by the club of a fuller such a club as fullers are accustomed to wring out garments with—he died. This same Josephus records the tradition that this James was of so great sanctity and reputation among the people that the downfall of Jerusalem was believed to be on account of his death. He it is of whom the apostle Paul writes to the Galatians that "No one else of the apostles did I see except James the brother of the Lord," and shortly after the event the Acts of the apostles bear witness to the matter. The Gospel also which is called the Gospel according to the Hebrews, and which I have recently translated into Greek and Latin and which also Origen often makes use of, after the account of the resurrection of the Saviour says, "but the Lord, after he had given his grave clothes to the servant of the priest, appeared to James (for James had sworn that he would not eat bread from that hour in which he drank the cup of the Lord until he should see him

76

rising again from among those that sleep)" and again, a little later, it says "'Bring a table and bread,' said the Lord." And immediately it is added, "He brought bread and blessed and brake and gave to James the Just and said to him, 'my brother eat thy bread, for the son of man is risen from among those that sleep.'" And so he ruled the church of Jerusalem thirty years, that is until the seventh year of Nero, and was buried near the temple from which he had been cast down. His tombstone with its inscription was well known until the siege of Titus and the end of Hadrian's reign. Some of our writers think he was buried in Mount Olivet, but they are mistaken.

CHAPTER III

Matthew, also called Levi, apostle and aforetimes publican, composed a gospel of Christ at first published in Judea in Hebrew for the sake of those of the circumcision who believed, but this was afterwards translated into Greek though by what author is uncertain. The Hebrew itself has been preserved until the present day in the library at Caesarea which Pamphilus so diligently gathered. I have also had the opportunity of having the volume described to me by the Nazarenes of Beroea, a city of Syria, who use it. In this it is to be noted that wherever the Evangelist, whether on his own account or in the person of our Lord the Saviour quotes the testimony of the Old Testament he does not follow the authority of the translators of the Septuagint but the Hebrew. Wherefore these two forms exist "Out of Egypt have I called my son," and "for he shall be called a Nazarene."

CHAPTER IV

Jude the brother of James, left a short epistle which is reckoned among the seven catholic epistles, and because in it he quotes from the apocryphal book of Enoch it is rejected by many. Nevertheless by age and use it has gained authority and is reckoned among the Holy Scriptures.

CHAPTER V

Paul, formerly called Saul, an apostle outside the number of the twelve apostles, was of the tribe of Benjamin and the town of Giscalis in Judea. When this was taken by the Romans he removed with his parents to Tarsus in Cilicia. Sent by them to Jerusalem to study **law** he was educated by Gamaliel a most learned man whom **Luke** mentions. But after he had been present at the death of the martyr Stephen and had received letters from the high priest of the temple for the persecution of those who believed in Christ, he proceeded to Damascus, where constrained to faith by a revelation, as it is written in the Acts of the apostles, he was transformed from a persecutor into an elect vessel. As Sergius Palus Proconsul of Cyprus was the first to believe on his preaching, he took his name from him because he had subdued him to faith in Christ, and having been joined by Barnabas, after traversing many cities, he returned to Jerusalem and was ordained apostle to the Gentiles by Peter, James and John. And because a full account of his life is given in the Acts of the Apostles, I only say this, that the twenty-fifth year after our Lord's passion, that is the second of Nero, at the time when Festus Procurator of Judea succeeded Felix, he was sent bound to Rome, and remaining for two years in free custody, disputed daily with the Jews concerning the advent of Christ. It ought to be said that at the first defence, the power of Nero having not yet been confirmed, nor his wickedness broken forth to such a degree as the histories relate concerning him, Paul was dismissed by Nero, that the gospel of Christ might be preached also in the West. As he himself writes in the second epistle to Timothy, at the time when he was about to be put to death dictating his epistle as he did while in chains; "At my first defence no one took my part, but all forsook me: may it not be laid to their account. But the Lord stood by me and strengthened me; that through me the message might be fully proclaimed and that all the Gentiles might hear, and I was delivered out of the mouth of the lion"—clearly indicating Nero as lion on account of his cruelty. And directly following he says "The Lord delivered me from the mouth of the lion" and again shortly "The Lord delivered me from every evil work and saved me unto his heavenly kingdom," for indeed he felt within himself that his martyrdom was near at hand, for in the same epistle he announced "for I am already being offered and the time of my departure is at hand." He

78

then, in the fourteenth year of Nero on the same day with Peter, was beheaded at Rome for Christ's sake and was buried in the Ostian way, the twenty seventh year after our Lord's passion. He wrote nine epistles to seven churches: *To the Romans* one, *To the Corinthians* two, *To the Galatians* one, *To the Ephesians* one, *To the Philippians* one, *To the Colossians* one, *To the Thessalonians* two; and besides these to his disciples, *To Timothy* two, *To Titus* one, *To Philemon* one. The epistle which is called the *Epistle to the Hebrews* is not considered his, on account of its difference from the others in style and language, but it is reckoned, either according to Tertullian to be the work of Barnabas, or according to others, to be by Luke the Evangelist or Clement afterwards bishop of the church at Rome, who, they say, arranged and adorned the ideas of Paul in his own language, though to be sure, since Paul was writing to Hebrews and was in disrepute among them he may have omitted his name from the salutation on this account. He being a Hebrew wrote Hebrew, that is his own tongue and most fluently while the things which were eloquently written in Hebrew were more eloquently turned into Greek and this is the reason why it seems to differ from other epistles of Paul. Some read one also to the Laodiceans but it is rejected by everyone.

CHAPTER VI

Barnabas the Cyprian, also called Joseph the Levite, ordained apostle to the Gentiles with Paul, wrote one *Epistle,* valuable for the edification of the church, which is reckoned among the apocryphal writings. He afterwards separated from Paul on account of John, a disciple also called Mark, none the less exercised the work laid upon him of preaching the Gospel.

CHAPTER VII

Luke a physician of Antioch, as his writings indicate, was not unskilled in the Greek language. An adherent of the apostle Paul, and companion of all his journeying, he wrote a *Gospel,* concerning which the same Paul says, "We send with him a brother whose praise in the gospel is among all the churches" and to the Colossians "Luke the beloved physician salutes you," and to Timothy "Luke only is with me." He also wrote another excellent volume to which he prefixed the title *Acts of the Apostles,* a history which extends to the second year of Paul's sojourn at Rome, that is to the fourth year of Nero, from which we learn that the book was composed in that same city. Therefore the *Acts of Paul and Thecla* and all the fable about the lion baptized by him we reckon among the apocryphal writings, for how is it possible that the inseparable companion of the apostle in his other affairs, alone should have been ignorant of this thing. Moreover Tertullian who lived near those times, mentions a certain presbyter in Asia, an adherent of the apostle Paul, who was convicted by John of having been the author of the book, and who, confessing that he did this for love of Paul, resigned his office of presbyter. Some suppose that whenever Paul in his epistle says "according to my gospel" he means the book of Luke and that Luke not only was taught the gospel history by the apostle Paul who was not with the Lord in the flesh, but also by other apostles. This he too at the beginning of his work declares, saying "Even as they delivered unto us, which from the beginning were eyewitnesses and ministers of the word." So he wrote the gospel as he had heard it, but composed the Acts of the apostles as he himself had seen. He was buried at Constantinople to which city, in the twentieth year of Constantius, his bones together with the remains of Andrew the apostle were transferred.

CHAPTER VIII

Mark the disciple and interpreter of Peter wrote a short gospel at the request of the brethren at Rome embodying what he had heard Peter tell. When Peter had heard this, he approved it and published it to the churches to be read by his authority as Clemens in the sixth book of his Hypotyposes and Papias, bishop of Hierapolis, record. Peter also mentions this Mark in his first epistle, figuratively indicating Rome under the name of Babylon "She who is in Babylon elect together with you saluteth you and so doth Mark my son." So, taking the gospel which he himself composed, he went to Egypt and first preaching Christ at Alexandria he formed a church so admirable in doctrine and continence of living that he constrained all followers of Christ to his example. Philo most learned of the Jews seeing the first church at Alexandria still Jewish in a degree, wrote a book on their manner of life as something creditable to his nation telling how, as Luke says, the believers had all things in common at Jerusalem, so he recorded that he saw was done at Alexandria, under the learned Mark. He died in the eighth year of Nero and was buried at Alexandria, Annianus succeeding him.

CHAPTER IX

John, the apostle whom Jesus most loved, the son of Zebedee and brother of James, the apostle whom Herod, after our Lord's passion, beheaded, most recently of all the evangelists wrote a *Gospel*, at the request of the bishops of Asia, against Cerinthus and other heretics and especially against the then growing dogma of the Ebionites, who assert that Christ did not exist before Mary. On this account he was compelled to maintain His divine nativity. But there is said to be yet another reason for this work, in that when he had read Matthew, Mark, and Luke, he approved indeed the substance of the history and declared that the things they said were true, but that they had given the history of only one year, the one, that is, which follows the imprisonment of John and in which he was put to death. So passing by this year the events of which had been set forth by these, he related the events of the earlier period before John was shut up in prison, so that it might be manifest to those who should diligently read the volumes of the four Evangelists. This also takes away the discrepancy which there seems to be between John and the others. He wrote also one *Epistle* which begins as follows "That which was from the beginning, that which we have heard, that which we have seen with our eyes and our hands handled concerning the word of life" which is esteemed of by all men who are interested in the church or in learning. The other two of which the first is "The elder to the elect lady and her children" and the other "The elder unto Gaius the beloved whom I love in truth," are said to be the work of John the presbyter to the memory of whom another sepulchre is shown at Ephesus to the present day, though some think that there are two memorials of this same John the evangelist. We shall treat of this matter in its turn when we come to Papias his disciple. In the fourteenth year then after Nero, Domitian having raised a second persecution he was banished to the island of Patmos, and wrote the *Apocalypse*, on which Justin Martyr and Irenæus afterwards wrote commentaries. But Domitian having been put to death and his acts, on account of his excessive cruelty, having been annulled by the senate, he returned to Ephesus under Pertinax and continuing there until the time of the emperor Trajan, founded and built churches throughout all Asia, and, worn out by old age, died in the sixty-eighth year after our Lord's passion and was buried near the same city.

CHAPTER X

Hermas whom the apostle Paul mentions in writing to the Romans "Salute Phlegon, Hermes, Patrobas, Hermas and the brethren that are with them" is reputed to be the author of the book which is called *Pastor* and which is also read publicly in some churches of Greece. It is in fact a useful book and many of the ancient writers quote from it as authority, but among the Latins it is almost unknown.

CHAPTER XI

Philo the Jew, an Alexandrian of the priestly class, is placed by us among the ecclesiastical writers on the ground that, writing a book concerning the first church of Mark the evangelist at Alexandria, he writes to our praise, declaring not only that they were there, but also that they were in many provinces and calling their habitations monasteries. From this it appears that the church of those that believed in Christ at first, was such as now the monks desire to imitate, that is, such that nothing is the peculiar property of any one of them, none of them rich, none poor, that patrimonies are divided among the needy, that they have leisure for prayer and psalms, for doctrine also and ascetic practice, that they were in fact as Luke declares believers were at first at Jerusalem. They say that under Caius Caligula he ventured to Rome, whither he had been sent as legate of his nation, and that when a second time he had come to Claudius, he spoke in the same city with the apostle Peter and enjoyed his friendship, and for this reason also adorned the adherents of Mark, Peter's disciple at Alexandria, with his praises. There are distinguished and innumerable works by this man: *On the five books of Moses,* one book *Concerning the confusion of tongues,* one book *On nature and invention,* one book *On the things which our senses desire and we detest,* one book *On learning,* one book *On the heir of divine things,* one book *On the division of equals and contraries,* one book *On the three virtues,* one book *On why in Scripture the names of many persons are changed,* two books *On covenants,* one book *On the life of a wise man,* one book *Concerning giants,* five books *That dreams are sent by God,* five books of *Questions and answers on Exodus,* four books *On the tabernacle and the Decalogue,* as well as books *On victims and promises or curses, On Providence, On the Fews, On the manner of one's life, On Alexander,* and *That dumb beasts have right reason,* and *That every fool should be a slave,* and *On the lives of the Christians,* of which we spoke above, that is, lives of apostolic men, which also he entitled, *On those who practice the divine life,* because in truth they contemplate divine things and ever pray to God, also under other categories, two *On agriculture,* two *On drunkenness.* There are other monuments of his genius which have not come to our hands. Concerning him there is a proverb among the Greeks "Either Plato philonized, or Philo platonized," that is, either Plato followed Philo, or Philo, Plato, so great is the similarity of ideas and language.

CHAPTER XII

Lucius Annæus Seneca of Cordova, disciple of the Stoic Sotion and uncle of Lucan the Poet, was a man of most continent life, whom I should not place in the category of saints were it not that those *Epistles of Paul to Seneca and Seneca to Paul,* which are read by many, provoke me. In these, written when he was tutor of Nero and the most powerful man of that time, he says that he would like to hold such a place among his countrymen as Paul held among Christians. He was put to death by Nero two years before Peter and Paul were crowned with martyrdom.

CHAPTER XIII

Josephus, the son of Matthias, priest of Jerusalem, taken prison by Vespasian and his son Titus, was banished. Coming to Rome he presented to the emperors, father and son, seven books *On the captivity of the Jews,* which were deposited in the public library and, on account of his genius, was found worthy of a statue at Rome. He wrote also twenty books of *Antiquities,* from the beginning of the world until the fourteenth year of Domitian Caesar, and two of *Antiquities against Appion,* the grammarian of Alexandria who, under Caligula, sent as legate on the part of the Gentiles against Philo, wrote also a book containing a vituperation of the Jewish nation. Another book of his entitled, *On allruling wisdom,* in which the martyr deaths of the Maccabeans are related is highly esteemed. In the eighth book of his *Antiquities* he most openly acknowledges that Christ was slain by the Pharisees on account of the greatness of his miracles, that John the Baptist was truly a prophet, and that Jerusalem was destroyed because of the murder of James the apostle. He wrote also concerning the Lord after this fashion: "In this same time was Jesus, a wise man, if indeed it be lawful to call him man. For he was a worker of wonderful miracles, and a teacher of those who freely receive the truth. He had very many adherents also, both of the Jews and of the Gentiles, and was believed to be Christ, and when through the envy of our chief men Pilate had crucified him, nevertheless those who had loved him at first continued to the end, for he appeared to them the third day alive. Many things, both these and other wonderful things are in the songs of the prophets who prophesied concerning him and the sect of Christians, so named from Him, exists to the present day."

CHAPTER XIV

Justus, of Tiberias of the province of Galilee, also attempted to write a *History of Jewish affairs* and certain brief *Commentaries* on the Scriptures but Josephus convicts him of falsehood. It is known that he wrote at the same time as Josephus himself.

CHAPTER XV

Clement, of whom the apostle Paul writing to the Philippians says "With Clement and others of my fellow-workers whose names are written in the book of life," the fourth bishop of Rome after Peter, if indeed the second was Linus and the third Anacletus, although most of the Latins think that Clement was second after the apostle. He wrote, on the part of the church of Rome, an especially valuable *Letter to the church of the Corinthians,* which in some places is publicly read, and which seems to me to agree in style with the epistle to the Hebrews which passes under the name of Paul but it differs from this same epistle, not only in many of its ideas, but also in respect of the order of words, and its likeness in either respect is not very great. There is also a second *Epistle* under his name which is rejected by earlier writers, and a *Disputation between Peter and Appion* written out at length, which Eusebius in the third book of his Church history rejects. He died in the third year of Trajan and a church built at Rome preserves the memory of his name unto this day.

CHAPTER XVI

Ignatius, third bishop of the church of Antioch after Peter the apostle, condemned to the wild beasts during the persecution of Trajan, was sent bound to Rome, and when he had come on his voyage as far as Smyrna, where Polycarp the pupil of John was bishop, he wrote one epistle *To the Magnesians* a third *To the Trallians* a fourth *To the Romans,* and going thence, he wrote *To the Philadelphians* and *To the Smyrneans* and especially *To Polycarp,* commending to him the church at Antioch. In this last he bore witness to the Gospel which I have recently translated, in respect of the person of Christ saying, "I indeed saw him in the flesh after the resurrection and I believe that he is," and when he came to Peter and those who were with Peter, he said to them "Behold! touch me and see me how that I am not an incorporeal spirit" and straightway they touched him and believed. Moreover it seems worth while inasmuch as we have made mention of such a man and of the *Epistle* which he wrote *to the Romans,* to give a few "quotations": "From Syria even unto Rome I fight with wild beasts, by land and by sea, by night and by day, being bound amidst ten leopards, that is to say soldiers who guard me and who only become worse when they are well treated. Their wrong doing, however, is my schoolmaster, but I am not thereby justified. May I have joy of the beasts that are prepared for me; and I pray that I may find them ready; I will even coax them to devour me quickly that they may not treat me as they have some whom they have refused to touch through fear. And if they are unwilling, I will compel them to devour me. Forgive me my children, I know what is expedient for me. Now do I begin to be a disciple, and desire none of the things visible that I may attain unto Jesus Christ. Let fire and cross and attacks of wild beasts, let wrenching of bones, cutting apart of limbs, crushing of the whole body, tortures of the devil,—let all these come upon me if only I may attain unto the joy which is in Christ."

When he had been condemned to the wild beasts and with zeal for martyrdom heard the lions roaring, he said "I am the grain of Christ. I am ground by the teeth of the wild beasts that I may be found the bread of the world." He was put to death the eleventh year of Trajan and the remains of his body lie in Antioch outside the Daphnitic gate in the cemetery.

CHAPTER XVII

Polycarp disciple of the apostle John and by him ordained bishop of Smyrna was chief of all Asia, where he saw and had as teachers some of the apostles and of those who had seen the Lord. He, on account of certain questions concerning the day of the Passover, went to Rome in the time of the emperor Antoninus Pius while Anicetus ruled the church in that city. There he led back to the faith many of the believers who had been deceived through the persuasion of Marcion and Valentinus, and when Marcion met him by chance and said "Do you know us" he replied, "I know the firstborn of the devil." Afterwards during the reign of Marcus Antoninus and Lucius Aurelius Commodus in the fourth persecution after Nero, in the presence of the proconsul holding court at Smyrna and all the people crying out against him in the Amphitheater, he was burned. He wrote a very valuable *Epistle to the Philippians* which is read to the present day in the meetings in Asia.

CHAPTER XVIII

Papias, the pupil of John, bishop of Hierapolis in Asia, wrote only five volumes, which he entitled *Exposition of the words of our Lord,* in which, when he had asserted in his preface that he did not follow various opinions but had the apostles for authority, he said "I considered what Andrew and Peter said, what Philip, what Thomas, what James, what John, what Matthew or any one else among the disciples of our Lord, what also Aristion and the elder John, disciples of the Lord had said, not so much that I have their books to read, as that their living voice is heard until the present day in the authors themselves." It appears through this catalogue of names that the John who is placed among the disciples is not the same as the elder John whom he places after Aristion in his enumeration. This we say moreover because of the opinion mentioned above, where we record that it is declared by many that the last two epistles of John are the work not of the apostle but of the presbyter.

He is said to have published a *Second coming of Our Lord or Millennium.* Irenæus and Apollinaris and others who say that after the resurrection the Lord will reign in the flesh with the saints, follow him. Tertullian also in his work *On the hope of the faithful,* Victorinus of Petau and Lactantius follow this view.

CHAPTER XIX

Quadratus disciple of the apostles, after Publius bishop of Athens had been crowned with martyrdom on account of his faith in Christ, was substituted in his place, and by his faith and industry gathered the church scattered by reason of its great fear. And when Hadrian passed the winter at Athens to witness the Eleusinian mysteries and was initiated into almost all the sacred mysteries of Greece, those who hated the Christians took opportunity without instructions from the Emperor to harass the believers. At this time he presented to Hadrian a work composed in behalf of our religion, indispensable, full of sound argument and faith and worthy of the apostolic teaching. In which, illustrating the antiquity of his period, he says that he has seen many who, oppressed by various ills, were healed by the Lord in Judea as well as some who had been raised from the dead.

CHAPTER XX

Aristides a most eloquent Athenian philosopher, and a disciple of Christ while yet retaining his philosopher's garb, presented a work to Hadrian at the same time that Quadratus presented his. The work contained a systematic statement of our doctrine, that is, an *Apology* for the Christians, which is still extant and is regarded by philologians as a monument to his genius.

CHAPTER XXI

Agrippa surnamed Castor, a man of great learning, wrote a strong refutation of the twenty-four volumes which Basilides the heretic had written against the Gospel, disclosing all his mysteries and enumerating the prophets Barcabbas and Barchob and all the other barbarous names which terrify the hearers, and his most high God Abraxas, whose name was supposed to contain the year according to the reckoning of the Greeks. Basilides died at Alexandria in the reign of Hadrian, and from him the Gnostic sects arose. In this tempestuous time also, Cochebas leader of the Jewish faction put Christians to death with various tortures.

CHAPTER XXII

Hegesippus who lived at a period not far from the Apostolic age, writing a *History* of all ecclesiastical events from the passion of our Lord, down to his own period, and gathering many things useful to the reader, composed five volumes in simple style, trying to represent the style of speaking of those whose lives he treated. He says that he went to Rome in the time of Anicetus, the tenth bishop after Peter, and continued there till the time of Eleutherius, bishop of the same city, who had been formerly deacon under Anicetus. Moreover, arguing against idols, he wrote a history, showing from what error they had first arisen, and this work indicates in what age he flourished. He says, "They built monuments and temples to their dead as we see up to the present day, such as the one to Antinous, servant to the Emperor Hadrian, in whose honour also games were celebrated, and a city founded bearing his name, and a temple with priests established." The Emperor Hadiran is said to have been enamoured of Antinous.

CHAPTER XXIII

Justin, a philosopher, and wearing the garb of philosopher, a citizen of Neapolis, a city of Palestine, and the son of Priscus Bacchius, laboured strenuously in behalf of the religion of Christ, insomuch that he delivered to Antoninus Pius and his sons and the senate, a work written *Against the nations,* and did not shun the ignominy of the cross. He addressed another book also to the successors of this Antoninus, Marcus Antoninus Verus and Lucius Aurelius Commodus. Another volume of his *Against the nations,* is also extant, where he discusses the nature of demons, and a fourth against the nations which he entitled, *Refutation* and yet another *On the sovereignty of God,* and another book which he entitled, *Psaltes,* and another *On the Soul,* the *Dialogue against the Jews,* which he held against Trypho, the leader of the Jews, and also notable volumes *Against Marcion,* which Irenaeus also mentions in the fourth book *Against heresies,* also another book *Against all heresies* which he mentions in the *Apology* which is addressed to Antoninus Pius. He, when he had held διατριβάς in the city of Rome, and had convicted Crescens the cynic, who said many blasphemous things against the Christians, of gluttony and fear of death, and had proved him devoted to luxury and lusts, at last, accused of being a Christian, through the efforts and wiles of Crescens, he shed his blood for Christ.

* * * * *

CHAPTER XXXV

Irenaeus, a presbyter under Pothinus the bishop who ruled the church of Lyons in Gaul, being sent to Rome as legate by the martyrs of this place, on account of certain ecclesiastical questions, presented to Bishop Eleutherius certain letters under his own name which are worthy of honour. Afterwards when Pothinus, nearly ninety years of age, received the crown of martyrdom for Christ, he was put in his place. It is certain too that he was a disciple of Polycarp, the priest and martyr, whom we mentioned above. He wrote five books *Against heresies* and a short volume, *Against the nations* and another *On discipline,* a letter to Marcianus his brother *On apostolical preaching,* a book of *Various treatises;* also to Blastus, *On schism,* to Florinus *On monarchy* or *That God is not the author of evil,* also an excellent *Commentary on the Ogdoad* at the end of which indicating that he was near the apostolic period he wrote "I adjure thee whosoever shall transcribe this book, by our Lord Jesus Christ and by his glorious advent at which He shall judge the quick and the dead, that you diligently compare, after you have transcribed, and amend it according to the copy from which you have transcribed it and also that you shall similarly transcribe this adjuration as you find it in your pattern." Other works of his are in circulation to wit: to Victor the Roman bishop *On the Paschal controversy* in which he warns him not lightly to break the unity of the fraternity, if indeed Victor believed that the many bishops of Asia and the East, who with the Jews celebrated the passover, on the fourteenth day of the new moon, were to be condemned. But even those who differed from them did not support Victor in his opinion. He flourished chiefly in the reign of the Emperor Commodus, who succeeded Marcus Antonius Verus in power.

* * * * *

CHAPTER XXXVIII

Clemens, presbyter of the Alexandrian church, and a pupil of the Pantaenus mentioned above, led the theological school at Alexandria after the death of his master and was teacher of the Catechetes. He is the author of notable volumes, full of eloquence and learning, both in sacred Scripture and in secular literature; among these are the *Stromata,* eight books, *Hypotyposes* eight books, *Against the nations* one book, *On pedagogy,* three books, *On the Passover, Disquisition on fasting* and another book entitled, *What rich man is saved?* one book *On*

Calumny, On ecclesiastical canons and against those who follow the error of the Fews one book which he addressed to Alexander bishop of Jerusalem. He also mentions in his volumes of *Stromata* the work of Tatian *Against the nations* which we mentioned above and a *Chronography* of one Cassianus, a work which I have not been able to find. He also mentioned certain Jewish writers against the nations, one Aristobulus and Demetrius and Eupolemus who after the example of Josephus asserted the primacy of Moses and the Jewish people. There is a letter of Alexander the bishop of Jerusalem who afterwards ruled the church with Narcissus, on the ordination of Asclepiades the confessor, addressed to the Antiochians congratulating them, at the end of which he says "these writings honoured brethren I have sent to you by the blessed presbyter Clement, a man illustrious and approved, whom you also know and with whom now you will become better acquainted a man who, when he had come hither by the special providence of God, strengthened and enlarged the church of God." Origen is known to have been his disciple. He flourished moreover during the reigns of Severus and his son Antoninus.

* * * * *

CHAPTER LII

Judas, discussed at length the seventy weeks mentioned in Daniel and wrote a *Chronography* of former times which he brought up to the tenth year of Severus. He is convicted of error in respect of this work in that he prophesied that the advent of Anti-Christ would be about his period, but this was because the greatness of the persecutions seemed to forebode the end of the world.

* * * * *

CHAPTER LIV

Origen, surnamed Adamantius, a persecution having been raised against the Christians in the tenth year of Severus Pertinax, and his father Leonidas having received the crown of martyrdom for Christ, was left at the age of about seventeen, with his six brothers and widowed mother, in poverty, for their property had been confiscated because of confessing Christ. When only eighteen years old, he undertook the work of instructing the Catechetes in the scattered churches of Alexandria. Afterwards appointed by Demetrius, bishop of this city, successor to the presbyter Clement, he flourished many years. When he had already reached middle life, on account of the churches of Achaia, which were torn with many heresies, he was journeying to Athens, by way of Palestine, under the authority of an ecclesiastical letter, and having been ordained presbyter by Theoctistus and Alexander, bishops of Caesarea and Jerusalem, he offended Demetrius, who was so wildly enraged at him that he wrote everywhere to injure his reputation. It is known that before he went to Caesarea, he had been at Rome, under bishop Zephyrinus. Immediately on his return to Alexandria he made Heraclas the presbyter, who continued to wear his philosopher's garb, his assistant in the school for catechetes. Heraclas became bishop of the church of Alexandria, after Demetrius. How great the glory of Origen was, appears from the fact that Firmilianus, bishop of Caesarea, with all the Cappadocian bishops, sought a visit from him, and entertained him for a long while. Sometime afterwards, going to Palestine to visit the holy places, he came to Caesarea and was instructed at length by Origen in the Holy Scriptures. It appears also from the fact that he went to Antioch, on the request of Mammaea, mother of the Emperor Alexander, and a woman religiously disposed, and was there held in great honour, and sent letters to the Emperor Philip, who was the first among the Roman rulers, to become a christian, and to his mother, letters which are still extant. Who is there, who does not also know that he was so assiduous in the study of Holy Scriptures, that contrary to the spirit of his time, and of his people, he learned the Hebrew language, and taking the Septuagint translation, he gathered the other translation also in a single work, namely, that of Aquila, of Ponticus the Proselyte, and Theodotian the Ebonite, and Symmachus an adherent of the same sect who wrote commentaries also on the gospel according to Matthew, from which he tried to establish his doctrine. And besides these, a fifth, sixth, and seventh translation, which we also have from his library, he sought out with great diligence, and compared with other editions. And since I have given a list of his works, in the volumes of letters which I have written to Paula, in a letter which I wrote against the works of Varro, I pass this by now, not failing however, to make mention of his immortal genius, how that he understood dialectics, as well as geometry, arithmetic, music, grammar, and rhetoric, and taught all the schools of philosophers, in such wise that he had also diligent students in secular literature, and lectured to them daily, and the crowds which flocked to him were marvellous. These, he received in the hope that through the instrumentality of this secular literature, he might establish them in the faith of Christ.

It is unnecessary to speak of the cruelty of that persecution which was raised against the Christians and under Decius, who was mad against the religion of Philip, whom he had slain,—the persecution in which Fabianus, bishop of the Roman church, perished at Rome, and Alexander and Babylas, Pontifs of the churches of Jerusalem and Antioch, were imprisoned for their confession of Christ. If any one wishes to know what was done in regard to the position of Origen, he can clearly learn, first indeed from his own epistles, which after the persecution, were sent to different ones, and secondly, from the sixth book of the church history of Eusebius of Caesarea, and from his six volumes in behalf of the same Origen.

He lived until the time of Gallus and Volusianus, that is, until his sixty-ninth year, and died at Tyre, in which city he also was buried.

St. Augustine
354-430

Aurelius Augustine was born of a Christian mother and a pagan father in Tagaste in North Africa. At age 16 he had to interrupt his studies due to lack of funds. The following year he was able to resume them in Carthage, thanks to a benefactor, and there engaged in a free-wheeling lifestyle that included taking a concubine and fathering a son. For nine years he was a member of the sect of the Manichees, during most of which time he taught school in Carthage.

Augustine was baptized in Milan in 387, returned to Africa, sold his property, gave the money to the poor, and took up a monastic way of life with some friends. In 395 he became Bishop of Hippo, the position he held for the remaining 35 years of his life. During that time two great controversies required much of his attention. From 400 to 420 Donatism had to be dealt with, but from 412 on he was also confronted with Pelagianism. He died in 430 as the Vandals were besieging the gates of Hippo.

The preaching of St. Ambrose, the discovery of Neoplatonism, and the reading of St. Paul have been described as the three factors contributing to Augustine's conversion.

The impact of Augustine's thought on Western Christianity was so comprehensive as to be immeasurable. His City of God is his masterpiece, written in the course of the years 413 to 427.

It is a vast synthesis of knowledge of all sorts. It consists of 22 books, of which the first ten are his reply to the charge that Christian other-worldliness was the cause of the decline of the Roman Empire. In book ten he begins his contrast of the pagan worldview with the Christian, but it is only in book eleven that he finally gets down to his main thesis in terms of the "two cities" in human history.

Part Three, (books 11 to 14) deals with the origin of the two cities, Part Four (books 15 to 18) describes the development of the cities, and Part Five (books 19 to 22) presents the ends of the cities. This monumental panorama gives perennial testimony to the genius of Augustine. Thomas Merton said of it in 1950: "The City of God is the autobiography of the Church written by the most Catholic of her great saints. . . . for those who can understand it, [it] contains the secret of death and life, war and peace, hell and heaven."

The selection that follows is from Part Four, Book 18. It contains the whole of chapters 46 through 54, surveying the New Testament events in the context of world history. These few pages are a prime example of his theological vision of the Church. This vision of the providential flow of history, written over fifteen centuries ago, was itself a most important determinant in the actual history of those subsequent centuries. It has been said that Augustine's City of God provided "a blueprint for the Middle Ages," yet his influence has extended well beyond any particular period. The case can easily be made that as long as the Church of Christ continues in the Western world it will always have something of an Augustinian dimension, so great was this visionary's imprint upon it.

THE CITY OF GOD

According to prophecy, Christ was born in Bethlehem of Juda, at the time, as I said, when Herod was king in Judea. At Rome, the republic had given way to the empire, and the Emperor Caesar Augustus had established a world-wide peace.

Christ was born a visible man of a human virgin mother, but he was a hidden God because God was His Father. So the Prophet had foretold: 'Behold the virgin shall be with child, and shall bring forth a son; and they shall call his name Emmanuel, which is, interpreted, God with us.' To prove that He was God, Christ worked many miracles, some of which—as many as seemed necessary to establish His claim—are recorded in the Gospels. Of these miracles the very first was the marvelous manner of His birth; the very last, His ascension into heaven in His body risen from the dead.

Despite all, the Jews who refused to believe that He was destined to die and to rise from the dead slew Him and were ravaged by the Romans worse than before, torn from their fatherland where foreigners were already lording it over them, and scattered over the whole earth—for they are now everywhere. And it is their own Scriptures that bear witness that it is not we who are the inventors of the prophecies touching Christ. That is why many of them, who pondered these prophecies before His passion and more especially after His Resurrection, have come to believe in Him, as was foretold: 'For if thy people, O Israel, shall be as the sand of the sea, a remnant of them shall be converted.' But the rest have been blinded, as was also foretold: 'Let their table become as a snare before them, and a recompense, and a stumbling-block. Let their eyes be darkened that they see not; and their back bend thou down

THE CATHOLIC TRADITION: The Church

always.' That is why when they refuse to believe in our Scriptures and read their own like blind men, they are fulfilling what their own Prophets foretold.

However, some of them may object that we Christians made up the non-Jewish prophecies concerning Christ which are circulating under the name of the Sibyl—or others under any other names. My answer is that we have no need of any others than the ones in our opponents' books, precisely because these enemies, who are scattered over the whole earth wherever the Church is expanding and who possess and preserve these books, are living witnesses, however, reluctant, to the truth of our position. For, in the very psalms which they read there is a prophecy to this effect: 'He is my God. His mercy shall help me. My God has shown this to me in the midst of my enemies. Slay them not lest they forget thy law. Scatter them in thy power.' God has shown the grace of His mercy to His Church 'in the midst of her enemies,' for, as St. Paul says: 'By their offense salvation has come to the Gentiles.'

Although they were conquered and oppressed by the Romans, God did not 'slay' them, that is, He did not destroy them as Jews. For, in that case, they would have forgotten and would have been useless as witnesses to what I am speaking of. Consequently, the first part of the prophecy, 'Slay them not lest they forget thy law,' is of small import without the rest, 'Scatter them.' For, if the Jews had remained bottled up in their own land with the evidence of their Scriptures and if they were not to be found everywhere, as the Church is, the Church would not then have them as ubiquitous witnesses of the ancient prophecies concerning Christ.

CHAPTER 47

So much, then, for the Jewish Prophets who have spoken of Christ. If there are any prophets, already known or likely to be discovered, who are outside of the Jewish race and whose prophecies are not reckoned canonical, anything I should have to say would be superfluous. However, the fact that there may be such prophets is worth mentioning, since it is not unreasonable to believe that there may have been men among other races to whom the mystery of Christ was revealed and who felt an impulse to proclaim what they knew. Such men need not have shared in the same grace which inspired the Hebrew Prophets, since their knowledge could have come through those bad angels who, as we know, openly avowed Christ Incarnate even when the Jews failed to recognize Him.

I think that not even the Jews themselves will presume to maintain that no one saved the descendants of Israel (after his older brother became reprobate) ever belonged to God. It is true, of course, that there was never any other people properly called God's people except their own. But they cannot deny that in other races there have been some who belonged to the true Israelites, citizens of the supernal fatherland, one with them in a heavenly, if not in an earthly, communion. If they should deny this, there is a very simple refutation at hand in the person of that wonderful, holy man, Job. He was neither a native Jew, nor a proselyte, that is, an alien adopted into the people of Israel. He was descended of Idumean stock; he was born in Idumea; he died there; yet, Holy Writ accords him the praise of saying that no one of his contemporaries matched him for justice and piety. Although the Chronicles do not inform us just when he lived, we can gather from his book that it was three generations later than Israel. Because of its unique importance, the Jews have adopted his book into their authoritative canon.

There is no doubt in my mind that Divine Providence gave us Job as an example to make us understand that there may have been other men among the pagan nations who lived according to God's law, pleased Him, and so belonged to the spiritual Jerusalem. Nevertheless, we must believe that no man received such graces save one to whom the one Mediator between God and man, the man Jesus Christ, was made known by heavenly revelation. His Incarnation was revealed to those ancient saints before the event, as it has been announced to us after the event, so that one and the same faith may bring all the predestined through Him into the City of God, into the house and temple of God, to God Himself.

Yet, it will still be objected that Christians have made up all other prophecies (except the Jewish ones) which concern the grace of God as given through Jesus Christ. Hence, the only cogent way that is left for refuting any non-Christians who may argue this point (and for converting them, if they will do some straight thinking) is to produce the divinely inspired prophecies of Christ which are contained in the books of the Jews—the people who were torn away from their ancestral home and scattered over the whole earth and have thus furnished a witness to help the Church in its universal expansion.

CHAPTER 48

The house of God, the Church, is more glorious by far than was that first house, the Temple, built of wood, stone, precious metals, and other costly materials. And this is why the reconstruction of the Temple did not make good the prophecy of Aggeus. Indeed, the facts I reviewed just a moment ago bear witness that the Temple was never so glorious after its glory was overcast, first, by the cessation of all prophecy, and, secondly, by the gigantic calamities which befell the Jews themselves, including that final wholesale destruction of the city at the hands of the Romans.

Surely, the glory of the House of the New Testament is greater than that of the Old because it was built of better materials, namely, those living stones which are human beings renewed by faith and grace. Yet, precisely because Solomon's Temple was renovated—was made new—it was a prophetic symbol of the second Testament which is called New. Accordingly, we must understand the words God spoke by Aggeus' mouth, 'And I will give peace in that place,' as referring to the place for which the Temple stood. Since the restored Temple signified the Church which Christ was to build, those words can mean only: 'I will give peace in that place (the Church) which this place (the rebuilt Temple) forefigures.' (All symbols seem in some way to personify the realities of which they are symbols. So, St. Paul says, 'The rock was Christ,' because the rock in question symbolized Christ.)

Not, however, until the House of the New Testament receives its final consecration will its greater glory in relation to the house of the Old Testament be made perfectly clear. This will take place at the second coming of Him whom the Hebrew text calls 'The Desired of all nations.' Obviously, His first coming was not desired of all nations, for unbelievers did not even know whom they should desire to come. In the end, too, as the Septuagint puts it with equal prophetic meaning: 'The chosen of the Lord shall come from all nations.' Then, truly, only the chosen shall come, those of whom St. Paul says: Even 'as he chose us in him before the foundation of the world.'

I mean that the Master Builder who said: 'Many are called but few are chosen' is not going to say that His House was built of those who were called, but who had to be cast out from the feast, but only of His chosen ones—and this House will fear no ruin. While time lasts, the reprobates, too, help to crowd our churches, but the winnowing fan will separate them from the elect on judgment's threshing-floor. It is their presence which prevents the glory of this House from shining as brightly as it will when all those who dwell in it are to dwell there forever.

CHAPTER 49

In this unfriendly world, in evil days like these, the Church through the lowliness she now endures is winning the sublime station she is to have in heaven. Meanwhile, the sting of fears and ache of tears, the vexatious toil and hazardous temptations, teach her to rejoice only in the healthy joy of hope. With so many sinners mingled with the saints, all caught in the single fishing net the Gospel mentions, this life on earth is like a sea in which good and bad fishes caught in a net swim about indistinguishably until the net is beached, and the bad ones are separated from the good. Only then does God so reign in the good, as in His temple, that he may be all in all.

Accordingly, we recognize the fulfillment now of the Psalmist's words: 'I have declared and I have spoken, they are multiplied beyond numbering.' This has been going on ever since Christ declared and spoke, first, by the lips of His precursor, John, and subsequently by His own: 'Do penance, for the kingdom of heaven is at hand.' He chose disciples, whom He called Apostles, men of humble birth, undistinguished, unschooled in letters, so that, however great they might become in character and accomplishment, He would be their holiness and their success. Among them He had one bad man, of whom He made good use to carry out the purposes of His passion and to set an example for His Church, how she should bear with bad men, too. To the degree that His physical presence was required, He sowed the seed of the holy Gospel, then suffered, died, and rose from the dead. Quite apart from the profound mystery of His blood shed for the remission of sins, He taught us by His passion what we should suffer for the Truth, and by His resurrection what we should hope for in eternity. He passed forty days on earth with His disciples, ascended into heaven, before their very eyes, and ten days later sent down the Holy Spirit.

When the promised Holy Spirit came down upon the faithful, each one of them was empowered to speak the languages of all nations—a very great miracle and a very greatly necessary one—to show that the Catholic Church was to be one throughout all nations and was so destined to speak in the tongues of all.

CHAPTER 50

The Church expanded from Jerusalem out, in accordance with the well-known prophecy: 'The Lord's commands shall go out from Sion, his word from Jerusalem,' and with what our Lord said to His disciples who were marveling over His Resurrection from the dead: 'He opened their minds that they might understand the Scriptures, and said to them: Thus is it written; and thus the Christ should suffer, and should rise again from the dead on the third day; and that repentance and remission of sins should be preached in his name to all the nations, beginning from Jerusalem.' This prediction was repeated when He answered their question about His second coming by saying: 'It is not for you to know the times or dates which the Father has fixed by his own authority; but you shall receive power when the Holy Spirit comes upon you, and you shall be witnesses for me in Jerusalem, and in all Judea and Samaria and even to the very ends of the earth.'

It was only after many in Judea and Samaria had believed that the disciples went out to other peoples to preach the Gospel, like lamps which the Lord had equipped with the wick of His word and lit with the light of the Holy Spirit. For He had told them: 'Do not be afraid of those who kill the body but cannot kill the soul.' But they were so hotly fired with love that they did not feel this chilling fear. In this spirit the Gospel was preached throughout the whole world—to the accompaniment of horrendous persecutions, manifold torturings, and death of martyrs—by men who had seen and heard Christ before His passion and after His resurrection and by those who carried on where they left off. Meanwhile, God gave them solemn attestation by signs and wonders and various prodigies; and by the gifts of the Holy Spirit, too.

As a result, the Gentiles believed in Him who had died for their redemption and began, with Christian tenderness, to venerate the martyrs' blood—the very blood they had spilled in diabolical fury. Even the kings whose laws had depopulated the Church came to bow down before that saving Name, which their earlier savagery had tried to abolish from the earth, and even undertook to drive out the false gods for whose sake they had persecuted the worshipers of the true God.

CHAPTER 51

When the Devil saw the human race abandoning the temples of demons and marching happily forward in the name of the freedom-giving Mediator, he inspired heretics to oppose Christian teaching under cover of the Christian name as though their presence in the City of God could go unchallenged like the presence, in the city of confusion, of philosophers with wholly different and even contradictory opinions!

Heretics are those who entertain in Christ's Church unsound and distorted ideas and stubbornly refuse, even when warned, to return to what is sound and right, to correct their contagious and death-dealing doctrines, but go on defending them. When they leave the Church they are ranked as enemies who try her patience. Even so, their evil-doing profits the loyal Catholic members of Christ's Body, for God makes good use of bad men, while 'for those who love God all things work together unto good.' Actually, all foes of the Church, whether blinded by error or moved by malice, subserve her in some fashion. If they have power to do her physical harm, they develop her power to suffer; if they oppose her intellectually, they bring out her wisdom; since she must love even her enemies, her loving kindness is made manifest; and whether she has to deal with them in the persuasiveness of argument or the chastisement of law, they bring into play her power to do good.

So it is that the diabolical prince of the ungodly city is not allowed to harm the pilgrim City of God, even when he stirs up his tools and dupes against her. Beyond all doubt, Divine Providence sees to it that she has both some solace of prosperity that she may not be broken by adversity and some testing of adversity that she may not be weakened by prosperity. Thus, the one balances the other, as one can see from the words of the psalm, 'According to the multitude of sorrows in my heart, so thy consolations have gladdened my soul,' and those of St. Paul: 'Rejoicing in hope, being patient in tribulation.'

St. Paul also says: 'All who want to live piously in Christ Jesus will suffer persecution.' Persecution, therefore, will never be lacking. For, when our enemies from without leave off raging and there ensues a span of tranquility—even of genuine tranquility and great consolation at least to the weak—we are not without enemies within, the many whose scandalous lives wound the hearts of the devout. These people bring discredit upon the Christian and Catholic name—a name so dear to 'all who want to live piously in Christ Jesus'—that they grieve bitterly to see their own brethren love it less than pious people should. There is that other heartache of seeing heretics, too, using the name and sacraments, the Scriptures and the Creed of genuine Christians. They realize how many would-be converts are driven into perplexed hesitancy because of heretical dissension, while the foul-mouthed find in heretics further pretext for cursing the Christian name, since these heretics at least call themselves Christian.

So it is that those who want to live piously in Christ must suffer the spiritual persecution of these and other aberrations in thought and morals, even when they are free from physical violence and vexation. This explains the verse: 'According to the multitude of sorrows in my heart'—there is no mention of the body. On the other hand, they recall the unchangeable, divine promise that no one of them can be lost. As St. Paul says: 'The Lord knows who are his,' and 'For those whom he has foreknown he has also predestined to become conformed to the image of his son.' And the psalm just cited goes on: 'Thy consolations have gladdened my soul.'

Yet, even the mental suffering which the devout undergo because of the lives of bad or pretended Christians is a source of spiritual profit because it flows from their charity, in virtue of which they would not have sinners be lost or go on blocking the salvation of others. Besides, the devout experience immense consolation when conversions flood the souls with a joy as great as the previous anguish on their account was excruciating.

So it falls out that in this world, in evil days like these, the Church walks onward like a wayfarer stricken by the world's hostility, but comforted by the mercy of God. Nor does this state of affairs date only from the days of Christ's and His Apostles' presence on earth. It was never any different from the days when the first just man, Abel, was slain by his ungodly brother. So it shall be until this world is no more.

CHAPTER 52

Consequently, I think that no one should rashly say or believe, as some have done or do, that the Church will undergo no more than the ten persecutions she has suffered, except the very last of all, Antichrist's, which will be number eleven. These ten persecutions are numbred as follows: first, Nero's, then those of Domitian, Trajan, Antoninus, Severus, Maximinus, Decius, Valerian, Aurelian, and, tenth, that of Diocletian and Maximian. The theory is that the ten plagues of the Egyptians which occurred before the beginning of the exodus of God's people must be correlated with these ten Christian persecutions, and that the eleventh, namely, Antichrist's, is foreshadowed by the eleventh plague, namely, the drowning of the Egyptians in the Red Sea when they were hot on the trail of the Hebrews who passed over as if it were dry land.

I do not think, however, that what happened in Egypt was a prophetic prefiguration of the persecutions. I say this—despite the fact that those who think otherwise seem to have matched them, each with each, so nicely and ingeniously—because I can see here no prophetic spirit but mere human guesswork, which occasionally hits the truth and just as often misses.

What, for instance, are those who hold this theory going to say about our Lord's crucifixion? Was that not a persecution and, if so, what number will they give it? If they answer that we should omit this one, since it was only the singling out and slaying of the Head, and should begin counting with the persecutions leveled against the Body, then what do they plan to do with the persecution launched, after our Lord's Ascension, in Jerusalem: in which Stephen was stoned; John's brother, James, beheaded; Peter, imprisoned, sentenced to death, and then freed by an angel; the brethren, scattered in flight from Jerusalem; and Saul, later on the Apostle Paul, violently attacked the Church? What are they going to say about St. Paul's own sufferings, in Judea and wherever he preached Christ so fervently? For, in preaching the faith he had formerly fought, he received in return something of what he had dealt out to others.

Why, too, must they begin counting with Nero, since the Church grew and survived up to Nero's day only in the midst of frightful persecutions which I need not here recall? Possibly they think that we should include only royal persecutions? In such an arrangement, what about Herod? He was a king, and he let loose a mighty persecution—after the Ascension, too. What about Julian the Apostate? His persecution is not included among the ten. Would they contend that his disqualifying of all Christian teachers and students engaged in liberal education was not a form of persecution? It was under Julian that Valentinian the Elder, who was next but one in the imperial succession, was stripped of his military rank for professing the Christian faith. Or take just one detail of the projected persecution in Antioch. A great many Christians were seized for the torture. The first, a young man of great faith and courage, was tortured for a whole day. When Julian heard him singing while being torn with claws and other instruments of torture, he was so staggered by this free and merry spirit that his hair fairly stood on end, and he feared the even more unregal embarrassment the others might cause him.

Further, in our own day, Valens, the Arian brother of the Valentinian just mentioned, laid waste the Church in the East in a great persecution. What kind of thinking is it, anyhow, which loses sight of the fact that, as the Church grows and flourishes throughout the world, she may be hounded by some rulers in certain sections while other sections are at peace? Or, possibly, we should not count the brutal persecution visited upon Gothic Christians in their own land by their own king, since the people were all Catholics, several of whom won the martyr's crown? I have heard about this one from some of the brethren who were children there at the time and who can recall without hesitation all the details of which they were witnesses.

What about conditions in Persia in our time? Did not the Christians there have such a raging persecution (if, indeed, it is over yet) that many of them fled as refugees even as far as the Roman towns? The more I ponder facts like these, the more I think we should abstain from trying to define the number of persecutions destined for the Church. And I think it no less rash to attempt fortelling what further persecutions may come from rulers. The only one that will come with absolute certainty is the very last, that of Antichrist, on which subject no Christian can entertain any doubt. So, I leave this question of future persecutions in a state of neutral indecision, neither building up nor tearing down either side, content to remind all to refrain from venturesome presumption.

CHAPTER 53

This much is certain, that, with His second coming, Jesus Himself will quench the fires of that final persecution which will be Antichrist's. For it is written: 'He will slay him with the breath of His mouth, and He will destroy him with the brightness of His coming.'

At this point people usually inquire: When will all this happen? A most unreasonable question, for, if it were good for us to know the answer, the Master, God Himself, would have told us His disciples when they asked Him. When they had Him face to face, they did not receive such news in silence, either, but plainly asked Him: 'Lord, wilt thou at this time restore the kingdom to Israel?' And He replied: 'It is not for you to know the times or dates which the Father has fixed by his own authority'—an answer, it should be noted, given to men who had not sought to know the exact hour, or day, or year, but only the general time of this fulfillment. Obviously, then, it is a waste of effort for us to attempt counting the precise number of years which this world has yet to go, since we know from the mouth of Truth that it is none of our business.

Not to be put off, however, some men have presumed to say that the complement of years between our Lord's Ascension and His second coming will be 400, others, 500, others, as high as 1,000. It would be both a lengthy and pointless task to show how each one tries to bolster up his opinion. They fall back on human guesswork, you may be sure, for the canonical Scriptures afford them nothing clearcut in the way of supporting evidence.

Suffice it to say that the fingers of all such calculators were slackened by Him who imposed silence with the words: 'It is not for you to know the times or dates which the Father has fixed by his own authority.'

This text, being taken from the New Testament, has, of course, done nothing to stop the votaries of the false gods from pretending to define, on the basis of responses from the demon gods whom they adore, just how long the Christian religion was destined to endure. When these people had to face the fact that many gigantic persecutions, instead of destroying the faith, had made it grow beyond belief, they trumped up some Greek verses or other, in the form of an oracle's effusion to a questing client, to make Christ out blameless in the propagation of this criminally sacrilegious sect. The verses added that it was Peter who contrived by black magic to have Christ's name adored, and that this farce would go on for 365 years, whereupon it would end abruptly.

O these learned men! O these cultivated intelligences! They refuse to believe in Christ, yet gladly believe in such preposterous things about Christ as that, while He was not the master magician to his pupil Peter and was guileless while Peter alone was the villain, Peter yet chose to promote the worship of Christ's name rather than of his own, and did this by means of the dark arts he knew, the efforts he made, the perils he underwent and, even, the shedding of his own blood! If Peter made the world love Christ by means of magic, by what innocent means did Christ make Peter love Him to this extent?

Let them answer this question in their own hearts. And let them understand, also, if they can, that heavenly grace alone made the world love Christ, for the sake of everlasting life, the very same grace which made Peter, too, love Christ and, looking to Him for everlasting life, suffer for His name's sake the brief death of the body.

And, by the way, what kind of gods are these that can foretell things, yet cannot prevent their happening? Do they have to collapse completely in the face of one magician and his one act of black magic in killing, as they claim a year-old body, cutting him up and then burying him with abominable ceremonies so as to persuade the god to allow a religion hostile to them to wax big and strong over so long a period, triumph over the horrendous savagery of so many persecutions—and not by resisting, but by suffering them—and, finally, achieve the overthrow of their own statues, temples, rites, and oracles? What kind of god was it—certainly not ours—who was so drawn or driven by Peter's monstrous crime as to grant all this success? For, so the verses say, Peter's magic imposed this on a god, not on any demon. Well, that is the kind of god people have who refuse to have Christ!

CHAPTER 54

I would produce a great deal more in the way of refutation had not the fatal year, foretold by fraudulent prophecy, and taken on faith by the empty-headed, already elapsed. Several years ago, the religion of Christ, which was established by Himself and His Apostles, had already lasted 365 years. Why, then, seek any further for arguments to scotch that pagan lie? Not to take Christ's birth as the starting point (because in infancy and boyhood He had no disciples), Christian faith and worship certainly became public knowledge when He personally appeared and began to have disciples, after He was baptized by John in the Jordan. This, in fact, is what is referred to in the prophecy concerning Him: 'He shall rule from sea to sea, and from the river to the ends of the earth.'

However, for the sake of this debate, it is best to begin with the Resurrection. He was to suffer, die, and rise from the dead before the content of faith could receive its definitive form. This is what St. Paul had in mind when he said to the Athenians: 'He calls upon all men everywhere to repent; inasmuch as he had fixed a day on which he will judge the world with justice by a man whom he has appointed, in whom he had *defined* faith for all by raising him from the dead.' It was after the Resurrection, too, that the Holy Spirit was to be given in that city from which, as has been ordained, the second Law, the New Testament, was first to be proclaimed. The first Law, the Old Testament, had come out of Mount Sinai by the lips of Moses; but of the Law Christ came to give it was foretold: The law shall come forth from Sion, and the word of the Lord from Jerusalem.' This explains why Christ ordered repentance to be preached in His name among all peoples, but beginning in Jerusalem. It was there that the worship of this name arose when men were called upon to believe in Jesus Christ crucified and risen from the dead. It was there that this faith had such an electrifying introduction that several thousands of men turned to Christ with astonishing enthusiasm, sold what they had to give to the poor, embraced voluntary poverty with holy determination and burning love, and steeled themselves, in the midst of enraged and bloodthirsty Jews, to battle unto death for the truth—not with weapons of war, but with the more potent weapon of patient suffering. If this was the result of divine power, rather than of black magic, why should anyone hesitate to believe that the same divine power may have operated in the same way throughout the rest of the world? If, on the other hand, one persists in maintaining that Peter must already have performed his act of sorcery for so many men in Jerusalem to have been stirred to worship Christ's name—men who had either caught and crucified Him or had derided Him when He was crucified—then the year of these conversions is the proper starting point, and we must ask when the 365 years were up.

Very well. Now, Christ died in the year when the Gemini were consuls, on the twenty-fifth day of March. He rose from the dead on the third day, as the Apostles could prove from the witness with their own eyes. After forty days He ascended into heaven. Ten days later, on the fiftieth day after His resurrection, he sent down the Holy Spirit. On that day 3,000 men believed when the Apostles preached to them. It was on that day that the Christian religion began, and it was by the efficacy of the Holy Spirit, as we believe and the facts prove, and not by means of Peter's black magic, as impious foolishness has thought or feigned to think. A short time afterwards, 5,000 more men were converted upon the occasion of Peter's working a miracle upon a beggar, lame from birth, who used to be carried to the temple gate to get alms. In the name of Jesus Christ this man leaped to his feet cured. And so, as time went by, the Church grew by one influx after another of believers.

Thus, we can establish the very day on which the first year of Christianity began, namely, the fifteenth of May, the day when the Holy Spirit came down. Starting there and counting the consuls, we find that the 365 years were over on May 15, during the consulate of Honorius and Eutychianus.

Now, in the following year, during the consulate of Manlius Theodorus, when, according to that demonic oracle or human fabrication, there ought to have been no Christianity left, I need not investigate how things were faring in other parts of the world, but I do know what happened in the illustrious city of Carthage in Africa. There, on March 31, Gaudentius and Jovius, officers of the Emperor Honorius, destroyed the temples of the false gods and smashed their statues.

Almost thirty years have gone by since that day and anyone can see how Christianity has grown, especially by the conversion of those who were held back from the faith because they took that prophecy to be true. When the fated number of years had elapsed, however, they realized how senseless and ridiculous it was.

We who are Christians in name and in deed do not believe in Peter, but in Him in whom Peter believed; we have been drawn to Christ by Peter's exhortations, not drugged by his incantations; we have been helped by his services, not hoodwinked by his sorceries. Christ was Peter's teacher in that faith which leads to everlasting life. The same Christ is our teacher, too.

Let me, at long last, end this Book. I have described in such detail as I judged adequate the historical course of the two cities, the heavenly and earthly, intermingled as they have been from the beginning and are to be until the end of time. The earthly one has made for herself, according to her heart's desire, false gods out of any sources at all, even out of human beings, that she might adore them with sacrifices. The heavenly one, on the other hand, living like a wayfarer in this world, makes no false gods for herself. On the contrary, she herself is made by the true God that she may be herself a true sacrifice to Him.

Both of these cities alike make use of temporal goods and both are equally afflicted by temporal ills—but how different they are in faith, how dissimilar in hope, how unlike in love! This will go on until they are to be separated in the Last Judgment, when each shall achieve its appointed end—an end which will have no end.

I must undertake now to treat of those ends.

Pope St. Gregory the Great

540-604

Gregory was a native Roman who entered the civil service and became prefect of his home city around 570. About five years later he decided to become a monk and converted his family home into a monastery. But before long he was prevailed upon to reenter public life, this time in the service of the Church. In 579 he was sent to Constantinople as papal representative at the Byzantine court, where he continued his monastic lifestyle. He was recalled to Rome around 586, and in 590 during a terrible epidemic in which Pope Pelagius II died, Gregory was elected pope.

When the emperor in Constantinople and the exarch in Ravenna failed to do anything about the Lombard invasions, Gregory assumed the responsibility and personally saved Rome by working out a truce. This led to the people recognizing the pope as their true protector and de facto civil ruler, and was thus an important stage on the way to the Papal States. Gregory's administrative ability was of such breadth that he was able to enter into significant and fruitful relations with the Church in the East, in Africa, in Spain, in Gaul, and in England. He decided to use monks as missionaries to the latter, sending Augustine of Canterbury with 40 monks to evangelize the Anglo-Saxons (597).

In an age of decline Gregory served chiefly as a bridge to pass on the heritage lest it be lost in the upheavals of the day. His longest work, The Book of Morals, *an exposition of Job, began as conferences to his monks in Constantinople and grew to 35 books. It is a veritable summa, a storehouse of earlier Christian theology.*

The selection that follows, however, is from his Pastoral Care, *written in his first year as pope (590). Written in Latin, it was translated into Greek during his lifetime, and three centuries later King Alfred the Great had it translated into West Saxon (Old English). Throughout the Middle Ages it served as guidebook for bishops and priests, thereby wielding tremendous influence on the understanding of Christian ministry and its appropriate exercise.*

Pastoral Care *is divided into four books. Only the first is excerpted here to give an idea of the style and outlook that marks it. That book explores the question of the ideal pastor: what type person should he be, and what sort of motives should lead him to the ministry? The second book takes up the virtues that ought to be found in him once he assumes that ministry. Book three takes up preaching, especially how it is to be accommodated to different audiences, and book four shows the need for a habit of examining one's conscience; otherwise, who is to care for the shepherds? Care for others ought not to be allowed to lead to neglect in caring for oneself.*

Modern tastes will certainly find Gregory too moralistic, but in all fairness, to appreciate the magnitude of his contribution, the needs of his age, the state of education, the chaotic social shifts taking place, the uncertainties concerning the future, all these must be calculated into the picture to realize his importance and achievement.

PASTORAL CARE

I. That the unlearned are not to presume to undertake
the office of teacher.

Since no art can be taught by him who has not diligently learnt it before, why are the unlearned ever so
rash as to undertake the care of teaching, when the art
of teaching is the art of all arts? Who does not know that the
wounds of the mind are more obscure than the wounds of the
body? And yet worldly physicians are ashamed of undertaking
to cure wounds which they cannot see, especially if they
neither understand the disease nor the herbs which are to be
employed. And sometimes those who are to be physicians of
the mind, although they cannot understand anything of the
spiritual precepts, are not ashamed of taking upon themselves
to be physicians of the mind. But since now all the honour of
this world is turned by the grace of God to the honour of the
pious, so that now the most pious are in greatest estimation,
many pretend to be pious teachers because they desire great
worldly honour. On which subject Christ himself exclaimed,
and said thus: "They desire to be greeted first, and honoured
in market-places and at banquets, and to recline first at suppers,
and they seek the most honourable seat in assemblies." Since
with pride and vainglory they thus arrive at the honour of pastoral care, they are unable properly to fulfil the duties of their
ministration and to become teachers of humility; but their
exhortation in teaching is disgraced, when they teach one thing,
having learnt another. Such men God chided through the prophet, and reproached them with such doings, when he said: "They
reigned, but not by my will; they were princes, and I knew
them not." Those who so rule, rule through their own power,
not through that of the highest Judge, since they are not
supported on any foundation of the divine power, nor chosen
for any excellence, but they are inflamed by their own desire,
so as to seize on so high an office rather than obtain it by their

deserts. And the eternal and unseen Judge exalts them as if he
knew them not, and suffers it without interfering, as an example of patience. But though they perform many wonders
in their office, when they come to him he says, "Depart from
me, ye evildoers; I know not what ye are." Again, he rebuked
them through the prophet for their want of learning, when he
said, "The shepherds had not understanding; they had my law,
and knew me not." He who knows not God's commands is
not acknowledged by God. The same said St. Paul: "He who
knows not God, God knows not him." Foolish teachers come
for the people's sins. Therefore often through the teacher's
folly the disciples come to grief, and often through the teacher's
wisdom foolish disciples are preserved. If, then, both are foolish,
we must consider what Christ himself said in his Gospel, he
said: "If the blind lead the blind, they will both fall into a
pit." On the same subject the Psalmist spoke:—May their eyes
be dimmed that they may not see, and their back always bent."
He did not say this because he wished or desired it to befall
any man, but he prophesied how it was to happen. For the eyes
are the teachers, and the back the disciples; because the eyes are
in the front and upper part of the body, and the back comes
after everything; and in the same way the teachers go before the
people, and the people after. When the eyes of the teacher's
mind are dimmed, which ought to go before with good examples, the people bend their backs under many heavy burdens.

    II. Nor, again, let the learned, who are not willing to live as
        they have learnt in books, undertake the dignity of
        teaching.

Many wise teachers also fight with their behaviour against
the spiritual precepts which they teach with words, when they
live in one way and teach in another. Often when the shepherd
goes by dangerous ways, the flock, which is too unwary, falls.
Of such shepherds the prophet spoke: "Ye trod down the grass
of God's sheep, and ye defiled their water with your feet,
though ye drank it before undefiled." Thus the teachers drink
very pure water when they learn the divine wisdom, and also
when they teach it; but they defile it with their own vices, and
set an example to the people by their vices, not by their in-

struction. Though the people thirst for instruction, they cannot drink it, but it is defiled by the teachers doing one thing and teaching another. Of whom again God spoke through the prophet: "Bad priests are the people's fall." No man injures more the holy assembly than those who assume the name and order of the holy office, and then pervert it; for no man dare admonish them if they do wrong, and sins become very widely extended, since they are so much honoured. But they would of their own accord flee the burden of so great a sin, being unworthy of it, if they would hear with the ears of their heart, and carefully consider the words of Christ, when he said, "He who deceives one of these little ones, it were better for him to have a millstone tied to his neck, and so to be thrown to the bottom of the sea." By the mill is signified the circuit of this world, and also of man's life, and their toil, and by the bottom of the sea their end and the last judgment. The mill is turned when the man is ended; the great mill is turned when this world is ended. He who attains holy orders, and with bad examples, either of words or of works, leads others astray, it were better for him to end his life in a humbler station and in earthly works; for if he do well in them he will have a good reward for it, if he do ill he will suffer less torment in hell if he arrive there alone, than if he bring another with him.

III. Of the burden of rule, and how he is to despise all toils, and how afraid he must be of every luxury.

We have said thus much in few words, because we wished to show how great is the burden of teaching, lest any one dare undertake it who is unworthy of it, lest he through desire of worldly honour undertake the guidance of perdition. Very justly the apostle James forbade it when he said, "Brothers, let there not be too many masters among you." Therefore the mediator himself between God and men, that is Christ, shunned undertaking earthly rule. He who surpasses all the wisdom of the higher spirits, and reigned in heaven before the world was, it is written in the Gospel that the Jews came and wished to make him king by force. When the Saviour perceived it, he dismissed them and hid himself. Who could easier rule men without sin than he who created them? He did not shun supremacy because any man was worthier of it, but he wished to set us an example of not coveting it too much; and also wished to suffer for us. He wished not to be king, yet of his own free will he came to the cross. He shunned the honour of reigning, and chose the punishment of the most ignominious death, that we who are his members might learn from him to shun the seductions of this world; and also that we might not dread its fear and terror, and for the sake of truth, love toil and dread luxury, and therefore avoid it. For through luxury men are often inflated with pride, while hardships through pain and sorrow purify and humble them. In prosperity the heart is puffed up; in adversity, even if it were formerly puffed up, it is humbled. In prosperity men forget themselves; in adversity they must remember themselves, even if they are unwilling. In prosperity they often lose the good they formerly did; in adversity they often repair the evil they long ago did. Often a man is subjected to the instruction of adversity, although before he would not follow the moral example and instruction of his teacher. But although schooled and taught by adversity, soon, if he attain to power, through the homage of the people he becomes proud and accustomed to presumption. As king Saul at first declined the throne, and deemed himself quite unworthy of it. But as soon as he obtained the rule of the kingdom, he became proud, and was angry with that same Samuel who formerly brought him to the throne, and consecrated him, because he told him of his faults before the people, since he could not control him before with their approval; and when he wished to depart from him, he seized him, and tore his clothes, and insulted him. So also David, who pleased God in nearly everything, as soon as he had not the burden of so many troubles, he was wounded with pride, and showed it very cruelly in the murder of Uriah, his own faithful servant, for the shameless desire of his wife. The same one who formerly spared him who had sinned against him with so many evils, became so immoderately eager for the death of the virtuous Uriah, without any crime or offence against himself. The same David who forbore injuring the king who brought him into such painful exile, and drove him from his country, when he had him completely in his power in the cave, took a lappet of his coat as a sign of having had him in his power, and yet let him escape for his former allegiance. The same David exposed his own army to great danger, and caused many to perish, when he laid snares for his faithful and innocent servant. The sin would have removed him very far from the number of all the saints, had not his toils and troubles come to his help again.

VIII. Of those who wish to become bishops, how they seize on the words of the apostle Paul to excuse their desire.

But those who wish to seize on such authority excuse their desire with the words of St. Paul: "He who desires to be a bishop, desires a good work." If he praised and encouraged, again he forbade the desire, saying, "A bishop should be blameless." It is besides said what kind of man he must be to be blameless. With the one speech he encouraged, with the other he dissuaded, as if he had openly said: "I praise your desire, but learn to know what it is, and if ye neglect to estimate yourselves at your real worth, the higher the authority ye attain to, the more manifest and notorious will ye make your unfitness." Thus the great craftsman incites and encourages his disciples, and sternly rebukes their pride by blaming them, that he may bring them to life. We must also reflect that at the time when the office of bishop was in such high estimation, he who accepted it accepted marytrdom. At that time it was praiseworthy for a man to desire to become a bishop, for there was no doubt that through it he would arrive at a cruel martyrdom. It is a proof of a bishop's holding his office well for him to end it with good works. Therefore it is said: "He who desires the office of bishop, desires a good work." He, therefore, who does not aspire to that office from the desire of such works, is his own witness that he desires his own vainglory; he not only does wrong in not loving the holy ministration, but altogether slights it; and when he aspires to the honour of rule, his heart is nourished with the contemplation of the desire of having other men subject to him, and his own exaltation, and rejoices in being praised. Hence he is puffed up in spirit, and rejoices in the possession of abundant wealth. He simulates humility, and through it seeks the possessions of this world. Under the pretence of mortifying his pride he increases it. Instead of distributing his property he accumulates it. When the mind thinks to make humility a pretext for pride, that which he displays openly he perverts in secret.

> IX. How the mind that desires to be above others deceives itself, when it thinks to perform many good works, and simulates it before other men, if he has worldly honour, and wishes to neglect it when he has it.

But when he wishes to undertake honour and rule, he thinks on the surface of his heart that he will do many good works in his office, and acknowledges in his inmost heart that he desires it out of pride and conceit of authority, but ponders and considers in the back of his mind that he will perform many good works, but in the pith is something else hid. On the surface of his mind he is deceived about himself as to the good works; he pretends to love that which he loves not: he loves the glory of this world, and pretends to shun and dread it. When he desires in his heart to rule, he is very timid and cautious; when he has what he wished to have, he is very bold. While he is aspiring to it he dreads not attaining it, and when he attains the honour he thinks he who granted him the honour was bound to grant it of necessity, and enjoys the divine honour in a worldly spirit, and very soon forgets his former pious resolutions. How can it otherwise happen but that the mind which was formerly diverted from its usual routine through the desire of worldly honour returns thereto when it has attained its desire? And the eyes of the mind soon return to its former works. But let every man consider before how useful and obedient he is to those he is bound to obey in his actions, and by his performance under these circumstances he can judge whether, if he is to have higher authority, he is able to carry out his former intentions, for men seldom learn humility in a high station if they were proud and reckless in a humbler one. How can he avoid praise and vainglory when he is exalted, who formerly desired them when he was without power? How can he be without covetousness when he has to consult the interests of many, if formerly he would not avoid it when he had to consult his own interests alone? Let him beware of allowing himself to be deceived with his own imagination, lest he believe that he will do well in that station when he would not in the lesser; for in a higher station men oftener lose good habits than learn them there, if they had them not in a humbler station and in greater leisure. An untaught steersman can very easily steer straight enough on a smooth sea, but the skilled steersman does not trust him on a rough sea and in great storms. And what is sovereignty and rule but the mind's storm, which ever tosses the ship of the heart with the waves of the thoughts, and is driven hither and thither in very narrow straits of words and works, as if it were wrecked amongst great and many rocks? What need is there to say more about this, except that he who is known to possess the above-mentioned qualities is to undertake it if he is obliged, and he who is not fit is not to approach it, even if compelled? And let him who is gifted with such qualities and merits as we have mentioned above, and too obstinately refuses the supremacy, be careful not to tie up the money he has received in the napkin mentioned by Christ in his Gospel; that is, let him not tie up the divine gifts he has received, both in virtues and in riches, in the cloth of his sloth, and through his laziness hide it, lest he be reproached for it afterwards. Let those who are devoid of such gifts, and yet wish for supremacy, beware lest they seduce with their bad example those who are going the right way to the kingdom of heaven, as the Pharisees did: they neither cared to go the right way themselves, nor to suffer others. Such things are to be considered and meditated on, because he who understakes the office of bishop undertakes the charge of the people's health, and he must traverse the country like a physician, and visit the houses of sick men. If he has not yet given up his own vices, how can he doctor the minds of other men, while he has in his own mind many open wounds? The doctor is much too bold and shameless who visits the houses of other men, undertaking to cure them, and has on his own face an open wound unhealed.

X. What kind of a man he is to be who is to rule.

But every effort is to be made to induce him to undertake the office of bishop who mortifies his body with many hardships, and lives spiritually, and regards not the pleasures of this world, nor dreads any worldly trouble, but loves the will of God alone. It is befitting for such a disposition, not for weakness of body or mere worldly reproach to decline the supremacy, nor to be greedy of other men's property, but liberal with his own, and his heart is to be always inclined to forgiveness for piety's sake, yet never more so than is befitting for righteousness. He must not do anything unlawful, but he must bewail the unlawful deeds of others as if they were his own sins; and he must sympathize with their weakness in his heart, and rejoice in the prosperity of his neighbours as his own. His works must make him worthy of being imitated by other men. He must strive to live so as to moisten the dried-up heart with the flowing waves of his instruction. He must learn to accustom himself to incessant prayer, until he sees he can obtain from God what he requires, as if it were said to him, "Thou hast called me; here I am." What thinkest thou, now, if a criminal comes to one of us, and prays him to lead him to a man in power who is angry with him, and intercede for him? If he is not known to me, or any man of his household, I shall very soon answer him and say: "I cannot undertake such an errand: I am not familiar enough with him." If we are ashamed to speak so to strangers, how dare we speak so to God? Or how can he presume to undertake the office of mediator between God and other men, who is not sure of being himself intimate with God through the merits of his life, or to intercede for other men while he knows not whether he himself has been interceded for? He has reason to fear arousing greater anger because of his own sins. We all know that among men he who prays a man to intercede for him with another, who is angry with the interceder also, irritates the angry mind and arouses worse anger. Let those consider this who still desire this world, and avoid arousing with their intercessions more violent anger of the severe Judge, lest, when they covet so great authority, they lead their disciples into destruction. But let every one carefully examine himself, lest he presume to undertake the office of instruction whilst any vice prevail within him. Let him not desire to intercede for the sins of others who is disgraced with his own.

XI. What kind of man is not to attain thereto.

About which the sublime voice commanded Moses to tell Aaron be also a staff to support with: let there be also love, yet not too effeminate; let there be also vigour, but not too severe; let there be also zeal, but not too excessively fierce; let there be also kindness, yet not more scrupulous than is fitting; that when righteousness and mercy are associated in the ruler's authority, he may, while soothing the hearts of his subjects, inspire them with reverence, and, whilst correcting, soothe them.

> XVIII. How the teacher is not to diminish his care of inner things for outer occupations, nor neglect outer things for the inner.

Let not the ruler forsake the inner care of the divine ministration for the occupation of outer works, nor let him diminish his care of inner government for outward occupations; lest he be hampered by the outer or engaged exclusively in the inner occupations, so that he cannot accomplish the exterior duties which he owes to his neighbours. Many, however, will not consider that they are set over other brothers to superintend them in divine things; but with the desire of their entire heart exercise worldly care, and rejoice that they have it to exercise; and when they have it not, they strive day and night to obtain it, and are greatly grieved in spirit when they are without that which they would like to have. And when they happen to be again without authority they are more troubled in mind because of the want; since it was his desire to be allowed to toil therein, and it seems to him a hardship to be without worldly troubles. And so it happens, when he rejoices in being occupied with worldly matters, that he ought to teach. Therefore the subjects become indifferent to righteous life when they wish to live spiritually, through the evil example set by their superior. Then they become rebellious, and thus are led astray. As when the head is unsound all the members are useless, even if they are sound, and as the army which is ready to attack another nation is useless if the general goes wrong; so also when the bishop is engaged in the ministrations which properly belong to earthly judges, no one incites or encourages the minds of the subjects to spiritual works, nor does any one correct their faults, but the shepherd is useless who ought to watch over the flock. Therefore the subjects cannot obtain the light of truth, because the desire of earthly things occupies the understanding and blinds the mind's eyes of the people with temptation, as dust does the eyes of the body in summer in a high wind. Therefore the Redeemer of mankind spoke very rightly dissuading us from gluttony: "Beware dulling your hearts with gluttony and drunkenness and manifold worldly cares." He also added fear when he said: "Lest the terrible day of judgment come on you." He showed what was to be the coming of this day when he said: "It shall come as a snare on all dwellers on the earth." And again he said: "No man can obey two masters." Paul also said, wishing to divert the mind of pious men from the companionship of this world, and charged them very straitly when he said: "Let no servant of God be too much engaged in worldly matters, lest he offend him to whom he formerly rendered himself." When he directed that the servants of the Church were to have quietness in their ministrations, he also directed that they were to keep themselves free from other occupations; he said: "If ye have to deliver judgment in worldly things, take those who are least esteemed in the household, and appoint them judges, that they may rule and arrange about earthly things who are not so greatly honoured with divine gifts." As if he had openly said: "Make them useful in the one pursuit if they cannot be so in the other." Therefore Moses, who was in such honour with God that he often spoke to him, was once reproved by his father-in-law Jethro, although he was a heathen and foreigner, who said that he occupied himself foolishly with the earthly service of the people, and advised him to appoint others to decide for him the differences among the people, that he might have the more leisure to understand secret and spiritual matters, so as to be able to teach the people more wisely and prudently; because lords and rulers ought to meditate on the loftiest subjects, and the subjects discharge humbler duties. The rulers ought to be before the people as a man's eye before his body, to see his path and steps. So it is necessary that the eye of the

ruler be not obscured by the dust of earthly cares, because
all those in authority are heads of the subjects, and the head
has to guide the feet and make them step in the right path; the
head above must take care not to let the feet slip in their
course, for, if the feet fail, the whole body is inclined, and the
head comes to the ground. How, then, can the bishop properly
enjoy the pastoral dignity, if he is himself engaged in those
earthly occupations which he ought to blame in others? Therefore God justly requited them by reproving them through the
prophet when he said: "As the people are, such is the priest."
The priest is the same as the people, when he does the same as
they do, and has the same aspirations as they. Jeremiah the
prophet perceived it, when he wept very sorely, and spoke
as if the temple were altogether destroyed, he said: "Alas, why
is the gold dimmed, and why is the noblest colour changed?
The stones of the temple are scattered, and lie at the end of
every street." What signifies the gold, which is so precious
above all substances, but the excellence of holiness? Or what
signifies the noble colour but the reverence of piety, which is
to be loved by all? What signify also the stones of the holy
edifice but the office of holy ordination? What also signifies
the wide street but the wide road of this present life? Of the
wide road Truth, that is Christ himself, spoke: "It is a very
spacious and wide road which leads to destruction." The gold
is blackened when the sanctity of a man's life is stained with
earthly works. The noblest hue is changed when the possession
of the good deeds he formerly accomplished is diminished,
since he was formerly thought to live virtuously. When any one,
after obtaining the holy office, is busily engaged in earthly
works, it is as if the fair hue of the gold were changed and it
were dulled and despised in the eyes of men. And the gems of
the sanctuaries lie scattered at the end of the streets. The
gems of the sanctuaries lie scattered along the streets when
the men, who ought to keep themselves unoccupied for the
adornment of the church in the secret ministrations of the
temple, desire the wide roads of this world outside. For the
gems of the sanctuaries were made in order to shine on the robe
of the highest priest among the holiest holinesses. But when the

priests do not incite their subjects to virtue and reverence of our Redeemer with the merits of their life, their gems of the holiest holinesses are not in the ornaments of the bishop's robe, but lie scattered up and down the streets, when the offices of holy ordination are left to the wide roads of their own desires and are tied to earthly occupations. We must also know that he did not say that the gems were scattered along the streets, but at the ends of the streets; because although they live in a worldly manner they desire to be considered the best, and, although they go in the wide road of their own will and desires, they wish to be considered the best and holiest. And yet, in cases of need, earthly occupations are sometimes to be tolerated, yet never to be loved too much, lest they oppress the mind of the man who loves them too much, so that he is oppressed and overcome with the burden, and depressed from the highest to the lowest. Yet many undertake ministration, and wish to be free and unoccupied, so as to devote themselves to divine works, and would not concern themselves at all with earthly things. These, when they entirely neglect the care of worldly things, do not at all help their subjects in their need. Therefore their instruction is often despised when they blame and hate the faults of their subjects, and do them no other good in this world; for the word of instruction cannot penetrate the heart of the poor man unless he be encouraged with kindness. But the seed of words grows very well when the humanity of the teacher softens and moistens the breast of the hearer. Therefore it is necessary for the ruler to be able and know how to irrigate and water the minds of others, and also to provide for their outer wants. The pastors are to be fervidly zealous about the inner wants of their subjects, without neglecting the care of their outer wants. The spirit of the subjects is necessarily broke if the teacher and shepherd neglect helping them outwardly. About which the first shepherd, St. Peter, earnestly admonished us, and said: "I, your fellow-servant and witness of Christ's suffering, entreat you to feed God's flock which is under your care." Soon after he showed whether he meant food of the mind or of the body, when he said: "Without compulsion, of your own freewill, ye must provide for your flock for the love of God, not for base gain." With these words he fully warned and taught us, lest, after replenishing and bettering the wants of their subjects, they themselves should be slain with the sword of avarice, lest, while their neighbours are refreshed and aided by them, they themselves abstain from the bread of righteousness. This same zeal of the shepherds St. Paul aroused, saying: "He who cares not for those that are his, and especially God's, servants, is an apostate and infidel." Yet, with all this, it is always to be feared and due care taken, lest, while they perform outer duties, they be not estranged from inner contemplation; because the minds of rulers, as we have remarked above, when occupied with these transitory things and inconsiderately devoted to them, often let the inner love grow cold, and are not afraid of forgetting that they have received the control of men's souls. But it is necessary that their solicitude about the outer wants of their subjects be kept within due bounds. Concerning which it was well said to the prophet Ezekiel that the priests were not to shave their heads with razors, nor, on the other hand, let their locks grow, but clip them with scissors. Priests are very properly called *sacerds*, that is in English "cleansers," because they are to act as guides of believers and govern them. The hair on their head signifies outer thoughts, for it grows and flourishes over the brain and yet no one feels it; which signifies the cares of this present life. Our thoughts often proceed from us so carelessly that we no more feel it than a man can feel his hair above the skin, because we often meditate on improper subjects. Yet all those who are to be above others must be careful of outer things, and yet must not be too much hampered by them. The priest was with good reason forbidden to shave his head, or let his hair grow; that is, that he is not to cut away from his mind all the thoughts which he ought to preserve for the benefit of his subjects, nor yet let them grow too rankly so as to be useless and evil. About which it was well said that the cutter was to cut his hair; in other words, that he is to be as zealous as is needful in the care of transitory things, and yet so as easily to be able to clip them without pain to prevent their growing too luxuriantly; lest, while the bodily life is protected, the thoughts of the heart be tied down through the excessive care of outer things; the priest must preserve his locks so as to cover the skin, and yet clip them before they fall into his eyes.

XLVI. That the peaceful are to be admonished in one way, in another the quarrelsome.

The peaceful are to be admonished in one way, in another the quarrelsome. The quarrelsome are to be admonished to know certainly that they do not possess so many good qualities, as ever to be able to be spiritual, if through strife they neglect to live properly and virtuously on good terms with others. It is written in the books of St. Paul, that the fruit of the Spirit is love, and joy, and righteous peace. He, then, who does not care to keep peace, rejects the fruit of his spirit. Again, St. Paul said: "When there are among you evil spirit and strife, are ye not then carnal?" And again, he said: "Seek peace and goodness with all men, without which no man can see God." And again he admonished, saying: "Zealously unite yourselves with concord and peace, that ye may be of like mind as ye are of like body, as ye are all called to the same hope." To the summons of that hope no man can come, unless he run thither with concord towards his neighbour. And yet very many receive a special gift, and then presumptuously relinquish the gift which is greater, that is concord; as many do who bridle their greediness an subdue their bodies, so as to be able to fast better than others, and then through that good quality lose that which is better than abstinence, that is concord. Let him who wishes to separate abstinence from concord consider the words of the Psalmist; he said: "Praise God with the timbrel and in the dance." The timbrel is made of dry hide, which sounds when struck; and in the dance a number of men are assembled to sing something with the same words and voice. He, therefore, who mortifies his body, and neglects to live in concord with his neighbour, praises the Lord with the timbrel, but will not do so with the dance. Often also, when any one is exalted above others by greater wisdom, he wishes to separate himself from the society of others; and the more he knows, and the wiser he is than others, the more foolish he becomes, and the more he opposes the virtue of concord. But they should hear the words of Truth itself, saying: "Have salt in you, and have peace among you." He mentioned salt instead of wisdom, because he wished us to have both peace and wisdom; for it is

no excellence or virtue to have wisdom, and not to care for
peace, because the more he knows, the worse his guilt, and the
greater the injury he inflicts on himself with the deceit. He is
the less able to excuse himself from deserving punishment, the
more able he was with his wisdom carefully to avoid sin, if he
would. But it was very rightly said to him through the apostle
James; he said: "If ye have a bad spirit among you, and con-
tumely and strife in your hearts, boast not nor rejoice thereat,
and strive not with your falsehoods against the truth; for that
wisdom has not descended from heaven, but is earthly and
animal, and also devilish. But that which comes from God is of
good will and peaceful." Being of pure and good will, is purely
and righteously understanding what he understands. Being
peaceful consists in not exalting himself at all above his equals,
nor separating himself from their society. The quarrelsome are
to be told to know, that as long as they keep aloof from the
love of their neighbours, and are at variance with them, they
cannot bring anything good to please God. Of which is written
in the books of Christ: "If thou wilt bring thine offering to the
altar, and there remember well something that thy neighbour
has done against thee, leave thine offering before the altar, and
go first after him; reconcile thyself with him before thou
bring thine offering; then bring thine offering." That is, that he
is to go in quest of his neighbour, and give him the chance of
returning to what is right. From this precept we can judge how
intolerable an evil discord is, when offerings are refused because
of it. Since every evil can be neutralized with good, it is too
great a sin which causes no good to be acceptable, unless the
evil be relinquished beforehand. The quarrelsome are to be
admonished, if they will not open their bodily ears to hear the
divine instruction, to open their mental eyes, and observe these
earthly creatures; how birds of one and the same kind fly so
peacefully, and how seldom they care to desert their family;
and also how the dumb cattle gather together in herds, and feed
together. Now we can understand from the peacefulness of
irrational animals, how great a sin the rational race of man commits in being quarrelsome, when with their rational intellect
they neglect what the dumb animals preserve in their kind.
The peaceful, on the other hand, are to be admonished, when

they love the peace that they have here more than they ought, and do not desire to attain to eternal peace. But the tranquillity they desire often injures their minds very severely, because, the more this tranquillity and ease please them, the less they are pleased with that to which they are called, and the more they desire this present, the less they aspire to the eternal life. Of this same Christ spoke through himself, when he distinguished between this earthly and the heavenly peace, and diverted his apostles from the present to the eternal peace, saying: "My peace I give to you, and my peace I leave with you." As if he had said: "I lend you this transitory, and give you the lasting peace." If, then, the mind and love of man are entirely devoted to the transitory peace, he can never attain to the one which is given to him. But we are to have this present peace in such a way as to love, and yet despise it, lest the mind of him who loves it fall into sin, if he love it too immoderately. The peaceful are also to be admonished not to desire peace too excessively, lest, through desire of this earthly peace, they leave unblamed the bad vices of others, and so alienate themselves from the peace of their Creator by conniving at unrighteousness; lest, when they fear discord outwardly, they be inwardly cut off from the society of the internal Judge. What else is this transitory peace but, as it were, a footprint of the eternal peace? What can be more foolish than to love the trace of anything in the dust, and not to love that which made the trace? Of which David spoke, when he entirely joined the society of internal peace, and proclaimed that he would have no concord with the wicked, saying: "How, do I not hate all those, O Lord, who hate thee? Before thy foes my spirit shrank, and I hated them with perfect hatred, because they were also my foes." We ought to hate God's enemies so perfectly as to love what they are, and hate what they do. We must help their lives by blaming their faults. But how can we think how great a sin it is to tire of blaming the bad, and make peace with the worst, when the prophet brought it as a gift and offering to God, that he excited the hostility of the wicked against himself for the love of God? Therefore it was that the tribe of Levi grasped their swords, and went out through the host, slaying the sinful; and therefore it is written that their hands were hallowed to God, because they spared not the sinful, but slew them. Therefore, also, Phineas despised the friendship of his neighbours, when he slew his own companion because he lay with the Midianitish woman, and slew the harlot also; and so with his anger he appeased the anger of God. And again, Christ said through himself: "Think not that I came on earth to send peace on the earth, but a sword." Because, when we incautiously associate ourselves in friendship with wicked men, we bind ourselves to their sins. From this same cause Jehosaphat, who before was praiseworthy in all the deeds of his life, very nearly perished entirely through the friendship of Ahab. He was rebuked by God, when it was said to him through the prophet: "Thou helpedst the wicked man, and mingledst thy friendship with him who hated God, and therefore thou hast merited the anger of God, because the good works were not formerly found in thee; that was, that thou didst remove the groves from the land of Judah." From which we can hear, that the more we associate and agree in the friendship of the wicked, the farther we are separated from the highest righteousness. The peaceful are also to be admonished not to fear to disturb this transitory peace with themselves by severity, when they have to speak. And again, those who outwardly trouble them with severity are to be admonished to preserve peace entire within themselves notwithstanding. Both of which David said that he very carefully observed, saying: "I love those who hated peace; and when I chid them, they attacked me without cause." They attacked him because of the quarrel, and yet he was their friend; he did not tire of blaming the foolish, and although they blamed him, he loved them. Of this same St. Paul spoke again: "I would, if it could be so, that ye had peace with every man, as far as is in your power." He said "if it could be so," and he also said "as far as is in your power," because he knew that it is very difficult to do both, to chide him him who does evil, and to preserve peace with him. But it is very necessary for us, although this transitory peace be disturbed by our quarrel in the minds of the wicked, that it be entirely preserved in ours. Therefore he said of peace, "as far as is in your power," because peace ought properly to be in the heart both of the chider and of him who suffers himself to be chid. If, then, it depart from the heart of the one, let it remain in the other's. About which the same Paul admonished his disciples in another place, and spoke thus: "If any one will not listen to our words and letters, let it be made known to us, and have no intercourse with him, that he may be ashamed." And again, he said afterwards: "Ye must not treat him as an enemy, but remonstrate with him like a brother." As if he had openly said: "Relinquish the outer peace, and hold fast to the inner, that your enmity may humble the sinner's heart, yet so that peace may not depart from your heart, although it is not regarded."

Venerable St. Bede
673-735

Bede was born in the English kingdom of Northumbria in 673 on land which was donated the following year for the foundation of two monasteries, Wearmouth and Jarrow. He entered the monastery in his youth and spent his entire life there. He was ordained deacon in 691 and priest in 702. Known as the "Venerable," Bede is the first Englishman of whom it is possible to form a clear personal picture.

Bede lived in the darkest hour of European civilization. Roman organization was gone and Europe was caught in a pincer movement with the advance of Islam on both Eastern and Western fronts. Yet his own life was remarkably uneventful. He never traveled far from his monastery and was never involved in the courts of the mighty, but he is remembered while his contemporaries are forgotten.

Vital to Bede's achievement was the fact that the first abbot had taken care to collect a respectable library, probably some two hundred books making up the substance of the Western heritage. With this collection Bede made himself the most learned man in Europe. He taught himself to write Latin with accuracy and fluency, and then wrote commentaries on the Gospels that ranked with those of St. Augustine and St. Gregory the Great. He also mastered mathematics and astronomy and wrote two books on chronology that became the classical authority for centuries. It was he who made fashionable the dating of years according to their relation to the birth of Christ (a.d./b.c.).

But his real fame and importance stem from his Ecclesiastical History of the English People *a work that makes him "the father of English history." He has been compared to Herodotus for his reverence for the past, his excellence in narrative and anecdote and his patriotism. Completed in 732, the work truly represents a decisive moment in the development of the art and science of historiography. It is not merely chronicle but also conscious interpretation.*

The Ecclesiastical History *is a continuous narrative made up of five books and spans a period of almost eight centuries, from the invasion of Britain by Julius Caesar to the last years of Bede himself. It is one of those few works that has been read constantly since its production. More than 150 manuscript copies of it survive.*

The first book starts with Caesar's invasion and in 34 chapters carries the story down to 603 a.d. The second picks up with the death of Pope Gregory (604) and goes to 633, in 20 chapters. Book three has 30 chapters and covers from 633 to 665; book four contains 32 chapters, going from 665 to 687. The final book with 24 chapters covers from 687 to 731.

The selection that follows gives the first nine chapters of Book One, to show Bede's style of using earlier historians, especially the Romans, to set the scene for his own work. Then we skip ahead to chapter 23 of the same Book to see his narrative of the "British mission," following the story through to the middle of chapter 27. A third segment, telling of the death of Augustine of Canterbury concludes the piece. It is drawn from Book Two, chapter three.

The genius of Bede is that he recognized the significance of what he was involved in. He realized that a new day was dawning in the life of the Church and that all those who had contributed to making it possible ought to be remembered in records for posterity. In doing so he has made later Christian generations more aware of the eternal dimension in the temporal.

THE ECCLESIASTICAL HISTORY
OF THE ENGLISH NATION

BOOK I

PREFACE

I formerly, at your request, most readily transmitted to you the Ecclesiastical History of the English Nation, which I had newly published, for you to read, and give it your approbation; and I now send it again to be transcribed, and more fully considered at your leisure. And I cannot but commend the sincerity and zeal, with which you not only diligently give ear to hear the words of the Holy Scripture, but also industriously take care to become acquainted with the actions and sayings of former men of renown, especially of our own nation. For if history relates good things of good men, the attentive hearer is excited to imitate that which is good; or if it mentions evil things of wicked persons, nevertheless the religious and pious hearer or reader, shunning that which is hurtful and perverse, is the more earnestly excited to perform those things which he knows to be good, and worthy of God. Of which you also being deeply sensible, are desirous that the said history should be more fully made familiar to yourself, and to those over whom the Divine Authority has appointed you governor, from your great regard to their general welfare. But to the end that I may remove all occasion of doubting what I have written, both from yourself and other readers or hearers of this history, I will take care briefly to intimate from what authors I chiefly learned the same.

My principal authority and aid in this work was the learned and reverend Abbot Albinus; who, educated in the Church of Canterbury by those venerable and learned men, Archbishop Theodore of blessed memory, and the Abbot Adrian, transmitted to me by Nothelm, the pious priest of the Church of London, either in writing, or by word of mouth of the same Nothelm, all that he thought worthy of memory, that had been done in the province of Kent, or the adjacent parts, by the disciples of the blessed Pope Gregory, as he had learned the same either from written records, or the traditions of his ancestors. The same Nothelm, afterwards going to Rome, having, with leave of the present Pope Gregory, searched into the archives of the holy Roman Church, found there some epistles of the blessed Pope Gregory, and other popes; and returning home, by the advice of the aforesaid most reverend father Albinus, brought them to me, to be inserted in my history. Thus, from the beginning of this volume to the time when the English nation received the faith of Christ, have we collected the writings of our predecessors, and from them gathered matter for our history; but from that time till the present, what was transacted in the Church of Canterbury, by the disciples of St. Gregory or their successors, and under what kings the same happened, has been conveyed to us by Nothelm through the industry of the aforesaid Abbot Albinus. They also partly informed me by what bishops and under what kings the provinces of the East and West Saxons, as also of the East Angles, and of the Northumbrians, received the faith of Christ. In short I was chiefly encouraged to undertake this work by the persuasions of the same Albinus. In like manner, Daniel, the most reverend Bishop of the West Saxons, who is still living, communicated to me in writing some things relating to the Ecclesiastical History of that province, and the next adjoining to it of the South Saxons, as also of the Isle of Wight. But how, by the pious ministry of Cedd and Ceadda, the province of the Mercians was brought to the faith of Christ, which they knew not before, and how that of the East Saxons recovered the same, after having expelled it, and how those fathers lived and died, we learned from the brethren of the monastery, which was built by them, and is called Lastingham. What ecclesiastical transactions took place in the province of the East Angles, was partly made known to us from the writings and tradition of our ancestors, and partly by relation of the most reverend Abbot Esius. What was done towards promoting the faith, and what was the sacerdotal succession in the province of Lindsey, we had either from the letters of the most reverend prelate Cunebert, or by word of mouth from other persons of good credit. But what was done in the

Church throughout the province of the Northumbrians, from the time when they received the faith of Christ till this present, I received not from any particular author, but by the faithful testimony of innumerable witnesses, who might know or remember the same; besides what I had of my own knowledge. Wherein it is to be observed, that what I have written concerning our most holy father, Bishop Cuthbert, either in this volume, or in my treatise on his life and actions, I partly took and faithfully copied from what I found written of him by the brethren of the Church of Lindisfarne; but at the same time took care to add such things as I could myself have knowledge of by the faithful testimony of such as knew him. And I humbly entreat the reader, that if he shall in this that we have written find anything not delivered according to the truth, he will not impute the same to me, who, as the true rule of history requires, have laboured sincerely to commit to writing such things as I could gather from common report, for the instruction of posterity.

Moreover, I beseech all men who shall hear or read this history of our nation, that for my manifold informities both of mind and body, they will offer up frequent supplications to the throne of Grace. And I further pray, that in recompense for the labour wherewith I have recorded in the several countries and cities those events which were most worthy of note, and most grateful to the ears of their inhabitants, I may for my reward have the benefit of their pious prayers.

CHAPTER I

Britain, an island in the ocean, formerly called Albion, is situated between the north and west, facing, though at a considerable distance, the coasts of Germany, France, and Spain, which form the greatest part of Europe. It extends 800 miles in length towards the north, and is 200 miles in breadth, except where several promontories extend further in breadth, by which its compass is made to be 3675 miles. To the south, as you pass along the nearest shore of the Belgic Gaul, the first place in Britain which opens to the eye, is the city of Rutubi Portus, by the English corrupted into Reptacestir. The distance from hence across the sea to Gessoriacum, the nearest shore of the Morini, is fifty miles, or as some writers say, 450 furlongs. On the back of the island, where it opens upon the boundless ocean, it has the islands called Orcades. Britain excels for grain and trees, and is well adapted for feeding cattle and beasts of burden. It also produces vines in some places, and has plenty of land and water-fowls of several sorts; it is remarkable also for rivers abounding in fish, and plentiful springs. It has the greatest plenty of salmon and eels; seals are also frequently taken, and dolphins, as also whales; besides many sorts of shell-fish, such as muscles, in which are often found excellent pearls of all colours, red, purple, violet, and green, but mostly white. There is also a great abundance of cockles, of which the scarlet dye is made; a most beautiful colour, which never fades with the heat of the sun or the washing of the rain; but the older it is, the more beautiful it becomes. It has both salt and hot springs, and from them flow rivers which furnish hot baths, proper for all ages and sexes, and arranged according. For water, as St. Basil says, receives the heating quality, when it runs along certain metals, and becomes not only hot but scalding. Britain has also many veins of metals, as copper, iron, lead, and silver; it has much and excellent jet, which is black and sparkling, glittering at the fire, and when heated, drives away serpents; being warmed with rubbing, it holds fast whatever is applied to it, like amber. The island was formerly embellished with twenty-eight noble cities, besides innumerable castles, which were all strongly secured with walls, towers, gates, and locks. And, from its lying almost under the North Pole, the nights are light in summer, so that at midnight the beholders are often in doubt whether the evening twilight still continues, or that of the morning is coming on; for the sun, in the night, returns under the earth, through the northern regions at no great distance from them. For this reason the days are of a great length in summer, as, on the contrary, the nights are in winter, for the sun then withdraws into the southern parts, so that the nights are eighteen hours long. Thus the nights are extraordinarily short in summer, and the days in winter, that is, of only six equinoctial hours. Whereas, in Armenia, Macedonia, Italy, and other countries of the same latitude, the longest day or night extends but to fifteen hours, and the shortest to nine.

This island at present, following the number of the books in which the Divine law was written, contains five nations, the English, Britons, Scots, Picts, and Latins, each in its own peculiar dialect cultivating the sublime study of Divine truth. The Latin tongue is, by the study of the Scriptures, become common to all the rest. At first this island had no other inhabitants but the Britons, from whom it derived its name, and who, coming over into Britain, as is reported, from Armorica, possessed themselves of the southern parts thereof. When they, beginning at the south, had made themselves masters of the greatest part of the island, it happened, that the nation of the Picts, from Scythia, as is reported, putting to sea, in a few long ships, were driven by the winds beyond the shores of Britain, and arrived on the northern coasts of Ireland, where, finding the nation of the Scots, they begged to be allowed to settle among them, but could not succeed in obtaining their request. Ireland is the greatest island next to Britain, and lies to the west of it; but as it is shorter than Britain to the north, so, on the other hand, it runs out far beyond it to the south, opposite to the northern parts of Spain, though a spacious sea lies between them. The Picts, as has been said, arriving in this island by sea, desired to have a place granted them in which they might settle. The Scots answered that the island could not contain them both; but "We can give you good advice," said they, "what to do; we know there is another island, not far from ours, to the eastward, which we often see at a distance, when the days are clear. If you will go thither, you will obtain settlements; or, if they should oppose you, you shall have our assistance." The Picts, accordingly, sailing over into Britain, began to inhabit the northern parts thereof, for the Britons were possessed of the southern. Now the Picts had no wives, and asked them of the Scots; who would not consent to grant them upon any other terms, than that when any difficulty should arise, they should choose a king from the female royal race rather than from the male which custom, as is well know, has been observed among the Picts to this day. In process of time, Britain, besides the Britons and the Picts, received a third nation, the Scots, who, migrating from Ireland under their leader, Reuda, either by fair means, or by force of arms, secured to themselves those settlements among the Picts which they still possess. From the name of their commander, they are to this day called Dalreudins; for, in their language, Dal signifies a part.

Ireland, in breadth, and for wholesomeness and serenity of climate, far surpasses Britain; for the snow scarcely ever lies there above three days: no man makes hay in the summer for winter's provision, or builds stables for his beasts of burden. No reptiles are found there, and no snake can live there; for though often carried thither out of Britain, as soon as the ship comes near the shore, and the scent of the air reaches them, they die. On the contrary, almost all things in the island are good against poison. In short, we have known that when some persons have been bitten by serpents, the scrapings of leaves of books that were brought out of Ireland, being put into water, and given them to drink, have immediately expelled the spreading poison, and assuaged the swelling. The island abounds in milk and honey, nor is there any want of vines, fish, or fowl; and it is remarkable for deer and goats. It is properly the country of the Scots, who, migrating from thence, as has been said, added a third nation in Britain to the Britons and the Picts. There is a very large gulf of the sea, which formerly divided the nation of the Picts from the Britons; which gulf runs from the west very far into the land, where, to this day, stands the strong city of the Britons, called Alcluith. The Scots, arriving on the north side of this bay, settled themselves there.

CHAPTER II

Britain had never been visited by the Romans, and was, indeed, entirely unknown to them before the time of Caius Julius Cæsar, who, in the year 693 after the building of Rome, but the sixtieth year before the incarnation of our Lord, was consul with Lucius Bibulus, and afterwards while he made war upon the Germans and the Gauls, which were divided only by the river Rhine, came into the province of the Morini, from whence is the nearest and shortest passage into Britain. Here, having provided about eighty ships of burden and vessels with oars, he sailed over into Britain; where, being first roughly handled in a battle, and then meeting with a violent storm, he lost a considerable part of his fleet, no small number of soldiers, and almost all his horses. Returning into Gaul, he put his legions into winter-quarters, and gave orders for building six hundred sail of both sorts. With these he again passed over early in spring into Britain, but, whilst he was marching with a large army towards the enemy, the ships, riding at anchor, were, by a tempest either dashed one against another, or driven upon the sands and wrecked. Forty of them perished, the rest were, with much difficulty, repaired. Cæsar's cavalry was at the first charge, defeated by the Britons, and Labienus, the tribune, slain. In the second engagement, he, with great hazard to his men, put the Britons to flight. Thence he proceeded to the river Thames, where an immense multitude of the enemy had posted themselves on the farthest side of the river, under the command of Cassibellaun, and fenced the bank of the river and almost all the ford under water with sharp stakes: the remains of these are to be seen to this day, apparently about the thickness of a man's thigh, and being cased with lead, remain fixed immovably in the bottom of the river. This, being perceived and avoided by the Romans, the barbarians, not able to stand the shock of the legions, hid themselves in the woods, whence they grievously galled the Romans with repeated sallies. In the meantime, the strong city of Trinovantum, with its commander Androgeus, surrendered to Cæsar, giving him forty hostages. Many other cities, following their example, made a treaty with the Romans. By their assistance, Cæsar at length, with much difficulty, took Cassibellaun's town, situated between two marshes, fortified by the adjacent woods, and plentifully furnished with all necessaries. After this, Cæsar returned into Gaul, but he had no sooner put his legions into winter-quarters, than he was suddenly beset and distracted with wars and tumults raised against him on every side.

CHAPTER III

In the year of Rome 798, Claudius, fourth emperor from Augustus, being desirous to approve himself a beneficial prince to the republic, and eagerly bent upon war and conquest, undertook an expedition into Britain, which seemed to be stirred up to rebellion by the refusal of the Romans to give up certain deserters. He was the only one, either before or after Julius

Cæsar, who had dared to land upon the island; yet, within a very few days, without any fight or bloodshed, the greatest part of the island was surrendered into his hands. He also added to the Roman empire the Orcades, which lie in the ocean beyond Britain, and then, returning to Rome the sixth month after his departure, he gave his son the title of Britannicus. This war he concluded in the fourth year of his empire, which is the forty-sixth from the incarnation of our Lord. In which year there happened a most grievous famine in Syria, which, in the Acts of the Apostles is recorded to have been foretold by the prophet Agabus. Vespasian, who was emperor after Nero, being sent into Britain by the same Claudius, brought also under the Roman dominion the Isle of Wight, which is next to Britain on the south, and is about thirty miles in length from east to west, and twelve from north to south; being six miles distant from the southern coast of Britain at the east end, and three only at the west. Nero, succeeding Claudius in the empire, attempted nothing in martial affairs; and, therefore, among other innumerable detriments brought upon the Roman state, he almost lost Britain; for under him two most noble towns were there taken and destroyed.

CHAPTER IV

In the year of our Lord's incarnation 156, Marcus Antoninus Verus, the fourteenth from Augustus, was made emperor, together with his brother, Aurelius Commodus. In their time, whilst Eleutherus, a holy man, presided over the Roman church, Lucius, king of the Britons, sent a letter to him, entreating that by his command he might be made a Christian. He soon obtained his pious request, and the Britons preserved the faith, which they had received, uncorrupted and entire, in peace and tranquillity until the time of the Emperor Diocletian.

CHAPTER V

In the year of our Lord 189, Severus, an African, born at Leptis, in the province of Tripolis, received the imperial purple. He was the seventeenth from Augustus, and reigned seventeen years. Being naturally stern, and engaged in many wars, he governed the state vigorously, but with much trouble. Having been victorious in all the grievous civil wars which happened in his time, he was drawn into Britain by the revolt of almost all the confederate tribes; and, after many great and dangerous battles, he thought fit to divide that part of the island, which he had recovered from the other unconquered nations, not with a wall, as some imagine, but with a rampart. For a wall is made of stones, but a rampart, with which camps are fortified to repel the assaults of enemies, is made of sods, cut out of the earth, and raised above the ground all round like a wall, having in front of it the ditch whence the sods were taken, and strong stakes of wood fixed upon its top. Thus Severus drew a great ditch and strong rampart, fortified with several towers, from sea to sea; and was afterwards taken sick and died at York, leaving two sons, Bassianus and Geta; of whom Geta died, adjudged a public enemy; but Bassianus, having taken the surname of Antoninus, obtained the empire.

CHAPTER VI

In the year of our Lord's incarnation 286, Diocletian, the thirty-third from Augustus, and chosen emperor by the army, reigned twenty years, and created Maximian, surnamed Herculius, his colleague in the empire. In their time, one Carausius, of very mean birth, but an expert and able soldier, being appointed to guard the sea-coasts, then infested by the Franks and Saxons, acted more to the prejudice than to the advantage of the commonwealth; and from his not rest ring to its owners the booty taken from the robbers, but keeping all to himself, it was suspected that by intentional neglect he suffered the enemy to infest the frontiers. Hearing, therefore, that an order was sent by Maximian that he should be put to death, he took upon him the imperial robes, and possessed himself of Britain, and having most valiantly retained it for the space of seven years, he was at length put to death by the treachery of his associate, Allectus. The usurper, having thus got the island from Carausius, held it three years, and was then vanquished by Asclepiodotus, the captain of the Prætorian bands, who thus at the end of ten years restored Britain to the Roman empire. Meanwhile, Diocletian in the east, and Maximian Herculius in the west, commanded the churches to be destroyed, and the Christians to be slain. This persecution was the tenth since the reign of Nero, and was more lasting and bloody than all the others before it; for it was carried on incessantly for the space of ten years, with burning of churches, outlawing of innocent persons, and the slaughter of martyrs. At length, it reached Britain also, and many persons, with the constancy of martyrs, died in the confession of their faith.

CHAPTER VII

At that time suffered St. Alban, of whom the priest Fortunatus, in the Praise of Virgins, where he makes mention of the blessed martyrs that came to the Lord from all parts of the world, says—

In Britain's isle was holy Alban born.

This Alban, being yet a pagan, at the time when the cruelties of wicked princes were raging against Christians, gave entertainment in his house to a certain clergyman, flying from the persecutors. This man he observed to be engaged in continual prayer and watching day and night; when on a sudden the Divine grace shining on him, he began to imitate the example of faith and piety which was set before him, and being gradually instructed by his wholesome admonitions, he cast off the darkness of idolatry, and became a Christian in all sincerity of heart. The aforesaid clergyman having been some days entertained by him, it came to the ears of the wicked prince, that this holy confessor of Christ, whose time of martyrdom had not yet come, was concealed at Alban's house. Whereupon he sent some soldiers to make a strict search after him. When they came to the martyr's house, St. Alban immediately presented himself to the soldiers, instead of his guest and master, in the habit or long coat which he wore, and was led bound before the judge.

It happened that the judge, at the time when Alban was carried before him, was standing at the altar, and offering sacrifice to devils. When he saw Alban, being much enraged that he should thus, of his own accord, put himself into the hands of the soldiers, and incur such danger in behalf of his guest, he commanded him to be dragged up to the images of the devils, before which he stood, saying, "Because you have chosen to conceal a rebellious and sacrilegious person, rather than to deliver him up to the soldiers, that his contempt of the gods might meet with the penalty due to such blasphemy, you shall undergo all the punishment that was due to him if you abandon the worship of our religion." But St. Alban, who had voluntarily declared himself a Christian to the persecutors of the faith, was not at all daunted at the prince's threats, but putting on the armour of spiritual warfare, publicly declared that he would not obey the command. Then said the judge, "Of what family or race are you?"—"What does it concern you," answered Alban, "of what stock I am? If you desire to hear the truth of my religion, be it known to you, that I am now a Christian, and bound by Christian duties."—"I ask your name," said the judge; "tell me it immediately."—"I am called Alban by my parents," replied he; "and I worship and adore the true and living God, who created all things." Then the judge, inflamed with anger, said, "If you will enjoy the happiness of eternal life, do not delay to offer sacrifice to the great gods." Alban rejoined, "These sacrifices, which by you are offered to devils, neither can avail the subjects, nor answer the wishes or desires of those that offer up their supplications to them. On the contrary, whosoever shall offer sacrifice to these images, shall receive the everlasting pains of hell for his reward."

The judge, hearing these words, and being much incensed, ordered this holy confessor of God to be scourged by the executioners, believing he might by stripes shake that constancy of heart, on which he could not prevail by words. He, being most cruelly tortued, bore the same patiently, or rather joyfully, for our Lord's sake. When the judge perceived that he was not to be overcome by tortures, or withdrawn from the exercise of the Christian religion, he ordered him to be put to death. Being led to execution, he came to a river, which, with a most rapid course, ran between the wall of the town and the arena where he was to be executed. He there saw a multitude of persons of both sexes, and of several ages and conditions, who were doubtlessly assembled by Divine instinct, to attend the blessed confessor and martyr, and had so taken up the bridge on the river, that he could scarce pass over that evening. In short, almost all had gone out, so that the judge remained in the city without attendance. St. Alban, therefore, urged by an ardent and devout wish to arrive quickly at martyrdom, drew near to the stream, and on lifting up his eyes to heaven, the channel was immediately dried up, and he perceived that the water had departed and made way for him to pass. Among the rest, the executioner, who was to have put him to death, observed this, and moved by Divine inspiration hastened to meet him at the place of execution, and casting down the sword which he had carried ready drawn, fell at his feet, praying that he might rather suffer with the martyr, whom he was ordered to execute, or, if possible, instead of him.

Whilst he thus from a persecutor was become a companion in the faith, and the other executioners hesitated to take up the sword which was lying on the ground, the reverend confessor, accompanied by the multitude, ascended a hill, about 500 paces from the place, adorned, or rather clothed with all kinds of flowers, having its sides neither perpendicular, nor even craggy, but sloping down into a most beautiful plain, worthy from its lovely appearance to be the scene of a martyr's sufferings. On the top of this hill, St. Alban prayed that God would give him water, and immediately a living spring broke out before his feet, the course being continued, so that all men perceived that the river also had been dried up in consequence of the martyr's presence. Nor was it likely that the martyr, who had left no water remaining in the river, should want some on the top of the hill, unless he thought it suitable to the occasion. The river having performed the holy service, returned to its natural course, leaving a testimony of its obedience. Here, therefore, the head of our most courageous martyr was struck off, and here he received the crown of life, which God has promised to those who love him. But he who gave the wicked stroke, was not permitted to rejoice over the deceased; for his eyes dropped upon the ground together with the blessed martyr's head.

At the same time was also beheaded the soldier, who before, through the Divine admonition, refused to give the stroke to the holy confessor. Of whom it is apparent, that though he was not regenerated by baptism, yet he was cleansed by the washing of his own blood, and rendered worthy to enter the kingdom of heaven. Then the judge, astonished at the novelty of so many heavenly miracles, ordered the persecution to cease immediately, beginning to honour the death of the saints, by which he before thought they might have been diverted from the Christian faith. The blessed Alban suffered death on the twenty-second day of June, near the city of Verulam, which is now by the English nation called Verlamacestir, or Varlingacestir, where afterwards, when peaceable Christian times were restored, a church of wonderful workmanship, and suitable to his martyrdom, was erected. In which place, there ceases not to this day the cure of sick persons, and the frequent working of wonders.

At the same time suffered Aaron and Julius, citizens of Chester, and many more of both sexes in several places; who, when they had endured sundry torments, and their limbs had been torn after an unheard-of manner, yielded their souls up, to enjoy in the heavenly city a reward for the sufferings which they had passed through.

CHAPTER VIII

When the storm of persecution ceased, the faithful Christians, who, during the time of danger, had hidden themselves in woods and deserts, and secret caves, appearing in public, rebuilt the churches which had been levelled with the ground; founded, erected, and finished the temples of the holy martyrs, and, as it were, displayed their conquering ensigns in all places; they celebrated festivals, and performed their sacred rites with clean hearts and mouths. This peace continued in the churches of Britain until the time of the Arian madness, which, having corrupted the whole world, infected this island also, so far removed from the rest of the globe, with the poison of its arrows; and when the plague was thus conveyed across the sea, all the venom of every heresy immediately rushed into the island, ever fond of something new, and never holding firm to any thing.

At this time, Constantius, who, whilst Diocletian was alive, governed Gaul and Spain, a man of extraordinary meekness and courtesy, died in Britain. This man left his son Constantine, born of Helen his concubine, emperor of the Gauls. Eutropius writes, that Constantine, being created emperor in Britain, succeeded his father in the sovereignty. In his time the Arian heresy broke out, and although it was detected and condemned in the Council of Nice, yet it nevertheless infected not only all the churches of the continent, but even those of the islands, with its pestilent and fatal doctrines.

CHAPTER IX

In the year of our Lord's incarnation 377, Gratian, the fortieth from Augustus, held the empire six years after the death of Valens; though he had long before reigned with his uncle Valens, and his brother Valentinian. Finding the state of the commonwealth much impaired, and almost gone to ruin, he looked around for some one whose abilities might remedy the existing evils; and his choice fell on Theodosius, a Spaniard. Him he invested at Sirmium with the royal robes, and made him emperor of Thrace and the Eastern provinces. At which time, Maximus, a man of valour and probity, and worthy to be an emperor, if he had not broken the oath of allegiance which he had taken, was made emperor by the army, passed over into Gaul, and there by treachery slew the Emperor Gratian, who was in a consternation at his sudden invasion, and attempting to escape into Italy. His brother, Valentinian, expelled from Italy, fled into the East, where he was entertained by Theodosius with fatherly affection, and soon restored to the empire. Maximus the tyrant, being shut up in Aquileia, was there taken and put to death.

CHAPTER XXIII

In the year of our Lord 582, Maurice, the fifty-fourth from Augustus, ascended the throne, and reigned twenty-one years. In the tenth year of his reign, Gregory, a man renowned for learning and behaviour, was promoted to the apostolical see of Rome, and presided over it thirteen years, six months and ten days. He, being moved by Divine inspiration, in the fourteenth year of the same emperor, and about the one hundred and fiftieth after the coming of the English into Britain, sent the servant of God, Augustine, and with him several other monks, who feared the Lord, to preach the word of God to the English nation. They having, in obedience to the pope's commands, undertaken that work, were, on their journey, seized with a sudden fear, and began to think of returning home, rather than proceed to a barbarous, fierce, and unbelieving nation, to whose very language they were stranger; and this they unanimously agreed was the safest course. In short, they sent back Augustine, who had been appointed to be consecrated bishop in case they were received by the English, that he might, by humble entreaty, obtain of the holy Gregory, that they should not be compelled to undertake so dangerous, toilsome, and uncertain a journey. The pope, in reply, sent them a hortatory epistle, persuading them to proceed in the work of the Divine word, and rely on the assistance of the Almighty. The purport of which letter was as follows:—

"Gregory, the servant of the servants of God, to the servants of our Lord. Forasmuch as it had been better not to begin a good work, than to think of desisting from that which has been begun, it behoves you, my beloved sons, to fulfil the good work, which, by the help of our Lord, you have undertaken. Let not, therefore, the toil of the journey, nor the tongues of evil speaking men, deter you; but with all possible earnestness and zeal perform that which, by God's direction, you have undertaken; being assured, that much labour is followed by an eternal reward. When Augustine, your chief, returns, whom we also constitute your abbat, humbly obey him in all things; knowing, that whatsoever you shall do by his direction, will, in all respects, be available to your souls. Almighty God protect you with his grace, and grant that I may, in the heavenly country, see the fruits of your labour. Inasmuch as, though I cannot labour with you, I shall partake in the joy of the reward, because I am willing to labour. God keep you in safety, my most beloved sons. Dated the 23rd of July, in the fourteenth year of the reign of our pious and most august lord, Mauritius Tiberius, the thirteenth year after the consulship of our said lord. The fourteenth indiction."

CHAPTER XXIV

The same venerable pope also sent a letter to Ætherius, bishop of Arles, exhorting him to give favourable entertainment to Augustine on his way to Britain; which letter was in these words:—

"To his most reverend and holy brother and fellow bishop Ætherius, Gregory, the servant of the servants of God. Although

religious men stand in need of no recommendation with priests who have the charity which is pleasing to God; yet as a proper opportunity is offered to write, we have thought fit to send you this our letter, to inform you, that we have directed thither, for the good of souls, the bearer of these presents, Augustine, the servant of God, of whose industry we are assured, with other servants of God, whom it is requisite that your holiness assist with priestly affection, and afford him all the comfort in your power. And to the end that you may be the more ready in your assistance, we have enjoined him particularly to inform you of the occasion of his coming; knowing, that when you are acquainted with it, you will, as the matter requires, for the sake of God, zealously afford him your relief. We also in all things recommend to your charity, Candidus, the priest, our common son, whom we have transferred to the government of a small patrimony in our church. God keep you in safety, most reverend brother. Dated the 23rd day of July, in the fourteenth year of the reign of our most pious and august lord, Mauritius Tiberius, the thirteenth year after the consulship of our lord aforesaid. The fourteenth indiction.

CHAPTER XXV

Augustine, thus strengthened by the confirmation of the blessed Father Gregory, returned to the work of the word of God, with the servants of Christ, and arrived in Britain. The powerful Ethelbert was at that time king of Kent; he had extended his dominions as far as the great river Humber, by which the Southern Saxons are divided from the Northern. On the east of Kent is the large Isle of Thanet containing according to the English way of reckoning, 600 families, divided from the other land by the river Wantsum, which is about three furlongs over, and fordable only in two places, for both ends of it run into the sea. In this island landed the servant of our Lord, Augustine, and his companions, being, as is reported, nearly forty men. They had, by order of the blessed Pope Gregory, taken interpreters of the nation of the Franks, and sending to Ethelbert, signified that they were come from Rome, and brought a joyful message, which most undoubtedly assured to all that took advantage of it everlasting joys in heaven, and a kingdom that would never end, with the living and true God. The king having heard this, ordered them to stay in that island where they had landed, and that they should be furnished with all necessaries, till he should consider what to do with them. For he had before heard of the Christian religion, having a Christian wife of the royal family of the Franks, called Bertha; whom he had received from her parents, upon condition that she should be permitted to practise her religion with the Bishop Luidhard, who was sent with her to preserve her faith. Some days after, the king came into the island, and sitting in the open air, ordered Augustine and his companions to be brought into his presence. For he had taken precaution that they should not come to him in any house, lest, according to an ancient superstition, if they practised any magical arts, they might impose upon him, and so get the better of him. But they came furnished with Divine, not with magic virtue, bearing a silver cross for their banner, and the image of our Lord and Saviour painted on a board; and singing the litany, they offered up their prayers to the Lord for the eternal salvation both of themselves and of those to whom they were come. When he had sat down, pursuant to the king's commands, and preached to him and his attendants there present, the word of life, the king answered thus:—"Your words and promises are very fair, but as they are new to us, and of uncertain import, I cannot approve of them so far as to forsake that which I have so long followed with the whole English nation. But because you are come from far into my kingdom, and, as I conceive, are desirous to impart to us those things which you believe to be true, and most beneficial, we will not molest you, but give you favourable entertainment, and take care to supply you with your necessary sustenance; nor do we forbid you to preach and gain as many as you can to your religion." Accordingly he permitted them to reside in the city of Canterbury, which was the metropolis of all his dominions, and, pursuant to his promise, besides allowing them sustenance, did not refuse them liberty to preach. It is reported that, as they drew near to the city, after their manner, with the holy cross, and the image of our sovereign Lord and King, Jesus Christ, they, in concert, sung this litany: "We beseech thee, O Lord, in all thy mercy, that thy anger and wrath be turned away from this city, and from thy holy house, because we have sinned. Hallelujah."

CHAPTER XXVI

As soon as they entered the dwelling-place assigned them, they began to imitate the course of life practised in the primitive church; applying themselves to frequent prayer, watching and fasting; preaching the word of life to as many as they could; despising all worldly things, as not belonging to them; receiving only their necessary food from those they taught; living themselves in all respects conformably to what they prescribed to others, and being always disposed to suffer any adversity, and even to die for that truth which they preached. In short, several believed and were baptized, admiring the simplicity of their innocent life, and the sweetness of their heavenly doctrine. There was on the east side of the city, a church dedicated to the honour of St. Martin, built whilst the Romans were still in the island, wherein the queen, who, as has been said before, was a Christian, used to pray. In this they first began to meet, to sing, to pray, to say mass, to preach, and to baptize, till the king, being converted to the faith, allowed them to preach openly, and build or repair churches in all places.

When he, among the rest, induced by the unspotted life of these holy men, and their delightful promises, which, by many miracles, they proved to be most certain, believed and was baptized, greater numbers began daily to flock together to hear the word, and, forsaking their heathen rites, to associate themselves, by believing, to the unity of the church of Christ. Their conversion the king so far encouraged, as that he compelled none to embrace Christianity, but only showed more affection to the believers, as to his fellow citizens in the heavenly kingdom. For he had learned from his instructors and leaders to salvation, that the service of Christ ought to be voluntary, not by compulsion. Nor was it long before he gave his teachers a settled residence in his metropolis of Canterbury, with such possessions of different kinds as were necessary for their subsistence.

CHAPTER XXVII

In the meantime, Augustine, the man of God, repaired to Arles, and, pursuant to the orders received from the holy Father Gregory, was ordained archbishop of the English nation, by Ætherius, archbishop of that city. Then returning into Britain, he sent Laurentius the priest, and Peter the monk, to Rome, to acquaint Pope Gregory, that the nation of the English had received the faith of Christ, and that he was himself made their bishop. At the same time, he desired his solution of some doubts that occurred to him. He soon received proper answers to his questions, which we have also thought fit to insert in this our history:—

The First Question of Augustine, Bishop of the Church of Canterbury.—Concerning bishops, how they are to behave themselves towards their clergy? or into how many portions the things given by the faithful to the altar are to be divided? and how the bishop is to act in the church?

Gregory, Pope of the City of Rome, answers.—Holy Writ, which no doubt you are well versed in, testifies, and particularly St. Paul's Epistle to Timothy, wherein he endeavours to instruct him how he should behave himself in the house of God; but it is the custom of the apostolic see to prescribe rules to bishops newly ordained, that all emoluments which accrue, are to be divided into four portions;—one for the bishop and his family, because of hospitality and entertainments; another for the clergy; a third for the poor; and the fourth for the repair of churches. But in regard that you, my brother, being brought up under monastic rules, are not to live apart from your clergy in the English church, which, by God's assistance, has been lately brought to the faith; you are to follow that course of life which our forefathers did in the time of the primitive church, when none of them said anything that he possessed was his own, but all things were in common among them.

But if there are any clerks not received into holy orders, who cannot live continent, they are to take wives, and receive their stipends abroad; because we know it is written, that out of the same portions above-mentioned a distribution was made to each of them according to every one's wants. Care is also to be taken of their stipends, and provision to be made, and they are to be kept under ecclesiastical rules, that they may live orderly, and attend to singing of psalms, and, by the help of God, preserve their hearts, and tongues, and bodies from all that is unlawful. But as for those that live in common, why need we say anything of making portions, or keeping hospitality and exhibiting mercy? inasmuch as all that can be spared is to be spent in pious and religious works, according to the commands of Him who is the Lord and Master of all, "Give alms of such things as you have, and behold all things are clean unto you."

Augustine's Second Question.—Whereas the faith is one and the same, why are there different customs in different churches? and why is one custom of masses observed in the holy Roman church, and another in the Gallican church?

Pope Gregory answers.—You know, my brother, the custom of the Roman church in which you remember you were bred up. But it pleases me, that if you have found anything, either in the Roman, or the Gallican, or any other church, which may be more acceptable to Almighty God, you carefully make choice of the same, and sedulously teach the church of the English, which as yet is new in the faith, whatsoever you can gather from the several churches. For things are not to be loved for the sake of places, but places for the sake of good things. Choose, therefore, from every church those things that are pious, religious, and upright, and when you have, as it were, made them up into one body, let the minds of the English be accustomed thereto.

Augustine's Third Question.—I beseech you to inform me, what punishment must be inflicted, if any one shall take anything by stealth from the church?

Gregory answers.—You may judge, my brother, by the person of the thief, in what manner he is to be corrected. For there are some, who, having substance, commit theft; and there are others, who transgress in this point through want. Wherefore it is requisite, that some be punished in their purses, others with stripes; some with more severity, and some more mildly. And when the severity is more, it is to proceed from charity, not from passion; because this is done to him who is corrected, that he may not be delivered up to hell-fire. For it behoves us to maintain discipline among the faithful, as good parents do with their carnal children, whom they punish with stripes for their faults, and yet design to make those their heirs whom they chastise; and they preserve what they possess for those whom they seem in anger to persecute. This charity is, therefore, to be kept in mind, and it dictates the measure of the punishment, so that the mind may do nothing beyond the rule of reason. You may add, that they are to restore those things which they have stolen from the church. But, God forbid, that the church should make profit from those earthly things which it seems to lose, or seek gain out of such vanities.

Augustine's Fourth Question.—Whether two brothers may marry two sisters, which are of a family far removed from them?

Gregory answers.—This may lawfully be done; for nothing is found in holy writ that seems to contradict it.

Augustine's Fifth Question.—To what degree may the faithful marry with their kindred? and whether it is lawful for men to marry their stepmothers and relations?

Gregory answers.—A certain worldly law in the Roman commonwealth allows, that the son and daughter of a brother and sister, or of two brothers, or two sisters, may be joined in matrimony; but we have found, by experience, that no offspring can come of such wedlock; and the Divine Law forbids a man to "uncover the nakedness of his kindred." Hence of necessity it must be the third or fourth generation of the faithful, that can be lawfully joined in matrimony; for the second, which we have mentioned, must altogether abstain from one another. To marry with one's stepmother is a heinous crime, because it is written in the Law, "Thou shalt not uncover the nakedness of thy father:" now the son, indeed, cannot uncover his father's nakedness; but in regard that it is written, "They shall be two in one flesh," he that presumes to uncover the nakedness of his stepmother, who was one flesh with his father, certainly uncovers the nakedness of his father. It is also prohibited to marry with a sister-in-law, because by the former union she is become the brother's flesh. For which thing also John the Baptist was beheaded, and ended his life in holy martyrdom. For, though he was not ordered to deny Christ, and indeed was killed for confessing Christ, yet in regard that the same Jesus Christ, our Lord, said, "I am the Truth," because John was killed for the truth, he also shed his blood for Christ.

But forasmuch as there are many of the English, who, whilst they were still in infidelity, are said to have been joined in this execrable matrimony, when they come to the faith they are to be admonished to abstain, and be made to know that this is a grievous sin. Let them fear the dreadful judgment of God, lest, for the gratification of their carnal appetites, they incur the torments of eternal punishment. Yet they are not on this account to be deprived of the communion of the body and blood of Christ, lest they seem to be punished for those things which they did through ignorance before they had received baptism. For at this time the Holy Church chastises some things through zeal, and tolerates some through meekness, and connives at some things through discretion, that so she may often, by this forbearance and connivance, suppress the evil which she disapproves. But all that come to the faith are to be admonished not to do such things. And if any shall be guilty of them, they are to be excluded from the communion of the body and blood of Christ. For as the offence is, in some measure, to be tolerated in those who did it through ignorance, so it is to be strenuously prosecuted in those who do not fear to sin knowingly.

Augustine's Sixth Question.—Whether a bishop may be ordained without other bishops being present, in case there be so great a distance between them, that they cannot easily come together?

Gregory answers.—As for the church of England, in which you are as yet the only bishop, you can no otherwise ordain a bishop than in the absence of other bishops; unless some bishops should come over from Gaul, that they may be present as witnesses to you in ordaining a bishop. But we would have you, my brother, to ordain bishops in such a manner, that the said bishops may not be far asunder, that when a new bishop is to be ordained, there be no difficulty, but that other bishops, and pastors also, whose presence is necessary, may easily come together. Thus, when, by the help of God, bishops shall be so constituted in places everywhere near to one another, no ordination of a bishop is to be performed without assembling three or four bishops. For, even in spiritual affairs, we may take example by the temporal, that they may be wisely and discreetly conducted. It is certain, that when marriages are celebrated in the world, some married persons are assembled, that those who went before in the way of matrimony, may also partake in the joy of the succeeding couple. Why, then, at this spiritual ordination, wherein, by means of the sacred ministry, man is joined to God, should not such persons be assembled, as may either rejoice in the advancement of the new bishop, or jointly pour forth their prayers to Almighty God for his preservation?

* * * * *

BOOK II

CHAPTER III

In the year of our Lord 604, Augustine, archbishop of Britain, ordained two bishops, viz. Mellitus and Justus; Mellitus to preach to the province of the East-Saxons, who are divided from Kent by the river Thames, and border on the Eastern sea. Their metropolis is the city of London, which is situated on the bank of the aforesaid river, and is the mart of many nations resorting to it by sea and land. At that time, Sabert, nephew to Ethelbert by his sister Ricula, reigned over the nation, though he was under subjection to Ethelbert, who, as has been said above, had command over all the nations of the English as far as the river Humber. But when this province also received the word of truth, by the preaching of Mellitus, King Ethelbert built the church of St. Paul, in the city of London, where he and his successors should have their episcopal see. As for Justus, Augustine ordained him bishop in Kent, at the city which the English nation named Rhofescestir, from one that was formerly the chief man of it, called Rhof. It was almost twenty-four miles distant from the city of Canterbury to the westward, and contains a church dedicated to St. Andrew, the apostle. King Ethelbert, who built it, bestowed many gifts on the bishops of both those churches, as well as on that of Canterbury, adding lands and possessions for the use of those who were with the bishops.

After this, the beloved of God, Father Augustine, died, and his body was deposited without, close by the church of the apostles, Peter and Paul, above spoken of, by reason that the same was not yet finished, nor consecrated, but as soon as it was dedicated, the body was brought in, and decently buried in the north porch thereof; wherein also were interred the bodies of all the succeeding archbishops, except two only, Theodorus and Berthwald, whose bodies are within that church, because the aforesaid porch could contain no more. Almost in the midst of this church is an altar dedicated in honour of the blessed Pope Gregory, at which every Saturday their service is solemnly performed by the priest of that place. On the tomb of the said Augustine is written this epitaph:—

"Here rests the Lord Augustine, first archbishop of Canterbury, who, being formerly sent hither by the blessed Gregory, bishop of the city of Rome, and by God's assistance supported with miracles, reduced King Ethelbert and his nation from the worship of idols to the faith of Christ, and having ended the days of his office in peace, died the 26th day of May, in the reign of the same king."

St. Peter Damian
1007-1072

Peter was born in Ravenna of poor parents, both of whom died while he was very young. His elder brother Damian cared for and educated him, so Peter later adopted his name as a sign of affection. After his studies he stayed on as a teacher in the local school until 1035 when he entered the monastery of Fonte Avellana. His austerity, learning, and eloquence all assured a prominent future for him in that community, and in 1042 he was made prior. This involved him in the public life of the day and Pope Stephen IX named him cardinal-bishop of Ostia in 1058 over his strenuous protests.

Ostia was a decaying seaport that did not require a great deal of his time. It was intended rather as a base from which Popes Nicholas II and Alexander II over the next twelve years would send him as papal legate to mediate various crises. His personal integrity and strength of character made him singularly successful in this capacity of ecclesiastical statesman.

As an eleventh-century ascetic Peter gives us some interesting insights into the Church of the time. Ever since the early days when Christianity had everything to fear from pagan philosophy there has been a stream of tradition reflecting intellectual dualism. Mistrust of "worldly" wisdom was kept alive especially in the ascetic tradition. Thus Peter spurns Plato and Pythagoras, renounces Euclid, and blocks his ears to Cicero *and Demosthenes. Why? "Let the simplicity of Christ instruct me, and the true humility of the wise loose me from the chains of doubt." He would thus deny that this is anti-intellectualism and insist that it is anti-pride, anti-"wisdom of the flesh," and that it is necessary if one is to discover and accept the foolishness of the Cross.*

Besides this interesting knowledge/ignorance dialectic, there is also a fascinating individual/community tension. This too is at the very heart of the monastic tradition. Solitude is seen as essential, yet one must belong to a community of brothers. The work that follows is addressed to one form of that problem. The Church is a community and therefore its public prayer is always in the plural and in responsorial form. What was the monk to do when he prayed the Divine Office in solitude? Peter's theology comes through very clearly: "let him not be ashamed to utter the words of the Church when he is alone . . . let him fulfill the duty of his universality bravely . . . rather than to concern himself with the suitability of what he is saying."

From a contemporary perspective one may sense some particular dangers in this outlook, especially concerning its implications for the Liturgy, but there is no denying the power and dignity contained therein, for it implies a deep and realistic faith. Later he expresses it this way: ". . . each of the faithful is a little Church, since without any violation of the mystery of her inward unity each man receives all the sacraments of human redemption which are divinely given to the whole Church." All in all, this is an intriguing glimpse into the thought of a fiery Christian personality who viewed church membership as something that went to the very depths of the soul.

BOOK OF
THE LORD BE WITH YOU

To the lord Leo, who, for love of divine liberty, has become a recluse, from Peter the sinful monk, his servant and son.

You know well, most dear father, that I do not regard you just as a colleague or a friend, but as a father, a teacher, a master, a lord, and one who is dearer to me than any other; it is to your prayers that I look to gain me a hearing from the merciful God, and a place in Heaven. What more shall I say? I have always held you to be my guardian angel, and the advice which you have given me in any doubtful matter which was causing me hesitation and difficulty has been accepted as if it had been proclaimed by a messenger from Heaven. So, whenever a crisis of conscience or thought seizes me, before coming to consult you, I beseech the Lord in His mercy to make you the instrument of His will, that through your lips He may decree the course I must take. Now, following my usual custom, I seek to learn from you the answer to a question which many inquirers have asked of me.

Many of the brethren, followers of the eremitic life, have asked me whether, since they live alone in their cells, it is right for them to say *Dominus vobiscum, Jube, domne, benedicere,* and the like; and whether, despite the fact that they are by themselves, they should say the responses, as the custom of the Church demands. Some of them argue the matter within themselves in this way: 'Are we to ask a blessing of the stones and furnishings of our cells, or say to them, "The Lord be with you?" ' Others fear that if they depart in any way from the prescribed order of the Church they are guilty of sin, in so far as they are diminishing their duty of divine service. And when they come to me for a solution, my foolish wit is driven to make inquiry. Since, then, these difficulties hem me in, I fly to you along the well-worn path which leads to the spring, not of Ciceronian eloquence, but of Divine wisdom.

CHAPTER ONE

I spurn Plato, the searcher into the hidden things of nature, who set a measure to the movements of the planets, and calculated the courses of the stars; Pythagoras, who divided the round world into its regions with his mathematician's rod, means nothing to me; I renounce the much-thumbed books of Nichomachus, and Euclid too, round-shouldered from pouring over his complex geometrical problems; the rhetoricians with their syllogisms and the cavillings of the sophists are useless in this matter. Let the gymnasts shiver in their nakedness for love of wisdom, and the peripatetics seek truth at the bottom of a well.

For I seek from you the Highest Truth, not that which lies ignobly hidden in a well, but that which rose from the earth, and, made manifest to all the world, reigns in eternal majesty in Heaven. What are the inventions of crazy poets to me? What do I care for the melodramatic adventures of pompous tragedians? Let the comedians put an end to the poisoned stream of scurrilities flowing from their noisy lips, and the satirists cease to burden their audiences with bitter banquets of insidious slander. The Ciceronians shall not sway me with their smooth speech, nor the followers of Demosthenes convince me by skilled argument or captious persuasion. Back to you shades, you whom worldly wisdom has defiled! Those blinded by the sulphurous flames of the teachings of darkness can give me nothing. Let the simplicity of Christ instruct me, and the true humility of the wise loose me from the chains of doubt. For, as St. Paul says: 'When God showed us His wisdom, the world, with all its wisdom, could not find its way to God; and now God would use a foolish thing, our preaching, to save those who will believe in it.'

Away, then, with the letter which kills; let the life-giving spirit come to our aid. For the wisdom of the flesh brings death, but that of the spirit brings life and peace, since the wisdom of the flesh is the enemy of God; it is not subject to God's law, nor can it be. And since the wisdom of the flesh is unable to bear the yoke of God's law, it cannot look upon it either, for its eyes are clouded with the smoke of pride. Loosen this knot for me, father, and do not suffer the disciple of Christ's lowliness to be deceived by the mouthings of proud philosophers. Teach me that of which the unskilled throng of dialecticians knows nothing; let wise folly tell me that which foolish wisdom cannot understand.

CHAPTER TWO

But perhaps you will ask me first to propound my own solution, and give me your judgment afterwards, as do the masters in the schools, who first ask their pupils' opinion concerning a particular problem in the proposition under discussion, so that by drawing them out they may discover their abilities. At your command I will tell you what I think of this problem, so that by your authority I may be corrected if I am mistaken, or have my opinion confirmed if I am right. It is not irrelevant to try to point out the origins of these liturgical customs before we endeavour, by God's grace, to give an answer to these questions of the brethren. The man who is to read the gospel is so humble that he does not ask to be blessed by the priest but by whomever the priest may appoint, saying: 'Pray, lord, a blessing.' But the priest, to show an equal humility, does not delegate the task of blessing to any of his ministers; he does not even presume to give the blessing; but he asks that God, who is above all things, may bestow a blessing.

CHAPTER THREE

The phrase *Dominus vobiscum* is the priest's greeting to the people; he prays that the Lord may be with them, in accordance with the words spoken by the Prophet: 'I shall dwell within them', and with those spoken by our Saviour to His disciples and all the faithful: 'Behold, I am with you.' This form of greeting, then, is no mere innovation instituted by human authority; it has the sanction of the ancient authority of the Scriptures. Anyone who examines the holy writings carefully will find many examples of its use, both in the singular and the plural. Did not the angel say to the blessed Mother of God: 'The Lord is with thee'? And to Gideon likewise: 'The Lord is with thee, thou mightiest of men'? In the book of Ruth, too, we read that Boaz greeted his harvesters with the words: 'The Lord be with you.' And in the Book of Chronicles we find that the prophet sent by God hailed Asa King of Juda and his army as they were returning in triumph from battle with these words: 'The Lord be with you, for you were with the Lord.'

When the Church receives the salutary greeting of the priest, she greets him in return, and in doing so prays that, as he has desired that the Lord may be with them, so He may deign to be with him. 'And with thy spirit', she replies, meaning: 'May almighty God be with your soul, so that you may worthily pray to Him for our salvation.' Notice that she says not 'with thee', but 'with thy spirit'; this is to remind us that all things concerned with the services of the Church must be performed in a spiritual manner. And certainly God must prefer to be with a man's spirit, for it is the soul of a reasonable man that is made in God's image and likeness; it alone is capable of receiving divine grace and illumination.

And the greeting which the bishop gives his people: 'Peace be with you' or 'Peace to you', also has its roots in the authority of Holy Writ, and is not just the product of man's mind. For we read in the Old Testament that the angel said to Daniel 'Peace be to you'; and in the New Testament the Lord almost always greets His disciples with the words 'Peace to you.' And He commended the same form of greeting to His disciples, saying: 'Into whatsoever house you shall enter, salute it, saying: "Peace to this house." ' So it is fitting that the rulers of the Church, who are the successors of the Apostles, should use this form of greeting; for they salute the household of God in which it is right that all men should be the sons of peace, so that the greeting of peace which rests upon them may be advantageous both to the givers of the greeting and to its receivers.

CHAPTER FOUR

Now it is clear from the premisses which I have stated that just as the prophetic writings, the poetry of the psalms and the grace of the gospel have been handed down to us by divine inspiration, so the phrase 'The Lord be with you' comes down to us not through any human choosing, but by the authority of the Old and New Testaments. We do not take away from or add to the authority of the Holy Scriptures because of changing circumstances, because the customs of the Church are preserved in them; so it is wrong for any reason whatever to utter this priestly greeting sometimes and to pass it over in silence at others; for it is unlawful to alter the established custom of the Church even if not more than one person is present.

CHAPTER FIVE

Indeed, the Church of Christ is united in all her parts by such a bond of love that her several members form a single body and in each one the whole Church is mystically present; so that the whole Church universal may rightly be called the one bride of Christ, and on the other hand every single soul can, because of the mystical effect of the sacrament, be regarded as the whole Church. Certainly Isaac with his prophetic nostrils could detect the presence of the whole Church when he said concerning one of his sons: 'See, the smell of my son is as the smell of a field.' And that widow who was in debt and who at Elisha's command scattered her too small quantity of oil like seed and soon reaped a rich harvest when it overflowed her vessels was undoubtedly a symbol of the Church.

If we look carefully through the fields of the Holy Scriptures we will find that one man or one woman often represents the Church. For though because of the multitude of her peoples the Church seems to be of many parts, yet she is nevertheless one and simple in the mystical unity of one faith and one divine baptism. And although the seven women had a single husband, a single virgin was said to be espoused to the heavenly bridegroom. Of her the apostle says: 'I have espoused you to one husband, that I may present you as a chaste virgin to Christ.'

Now it can be clearly deduced from all this, as I said before, that since the whole Church is represented in the person of one man, and because of this is called a single virgin, holy Church is one in all her members, and complete in each of them; her many members form a single whole in the unity of faith, and her many parts are united in each member by the bond of charity and the various gifts of grace, since all of these proceed from one source.

CHAPTER SIX

For indeed, although holy Church is divided in the multiplicity of her members, yet she is fused into unity by the fire of the Holy Spirit; and so even if she seems, as far as her situation in the world is concerned, to be scattered, yet the mystery of her inward unity can never be marred in its integrity. 'The love of God is shed abroad in our hearts by the Holy Ghost which is given unto us.' This Spirit is indeed without doubt both one and manifold; one in the essence of His greatness, and manifold in the diverse gifts of His grace, and He gives to holy Church, which He fills, this power: that all her parts shall form a single whole, and that each part shall contain the whole. This mystery of undivided unity was asked for by Truth Himself when He said to His Father concerning His disciples: 'I do not pray for these alone, but for them also who shall believe in Me through their word; that they may all be one; as Thou, Father, art in Me and I in Thee, that they also may be one in us: that the world may believe that Thou hast sent Me. And the glory which Thou gavest Me I have given them; that they may be one, even as we are one.'

If, therefore, those who believe in Christ are one, then wherever we find a member according to outward appearances, there, by the mystery of the sacrament, the whole body is present. And so whatever belongs to the whole applies in some measure to the part; so that there is no absurdity in one man saying by himself anything which the body of the Church as a whole may utter, and in the same way many may fittingly give voice to that which is properly said by one person. Hence, when we are all assembled together we can rightly say: 'Bow down thine ear O Lord and hear me: for I am poor and needy. Preserve my soul, for I am holy.' And when we are by ourselves, there is no incongruity in our singing: 'Sing aloud unto God our strength: make a joyful noise unto the God of Jacob.' And it is not irrelevant that many of us say together: 'I will bless the Lord at all times: his praise shall continually be in my mouth'; or that often when we are alone we sing with many tongues: 'O magnify the Lord with me, and let us exalt his name together' and other things of this kind. For on the one hand the solitariness of a single person does no harm to the words of many; and on the other the vast number of the faithful does not prejudice their unity since by the power of the Holy Spirit who is in each of us and fills the whole our solitude is manifold and our multiplicity singular.

CHAPTER SEVEN

But now let those who say 'Are we to ask a blessing of the stones and planks of our cells, or ask that the Lord be with them?' tell me why, when they are alone in their cells they say: 'O come, let us sing unto the Lord.' I pray you tell me, brothers, if I may speak with your good leave, whom do you exhort? Whom do you summon to the night-office of divine praise when you say 'Come let us sing unto the Lord' or 'Come let us adore the Lord King of martyrs'? These verses are called invitatories because by their means the congregation of the faithful is summoned to give praise to God. If then there is really no one to hear you, whom do you urge to sing to the Lord by these words of exhortation?

Come, I say, brethren and tell me whether you are not concerned with the mystery of the unity of the Church but rather with the number of those present in the flesh when you say: 'Arising in the night let us all keep watch' or 'Our limbs being rested by sleep, let us arise swiftly.' Why do you not either pass over in silence or put into the singular number all those hymns and prayers which the holy fathers composed in the plural?

Since you consider it wrong to ask or to give a blessing when there is no one else present, why, when you come to the lessons, do you read the homilies of the Fathers and the sermons of preachers, which by the very nature of the act of reading appear to be addressed to the people; so that all your words are directed, as it seems, to another person or to an audience. To take the very words of these homilies, to whom, may I ask, do you say: 'Listen, dearly beloved brethren' and so on, when no brethren are present? If you wish to adapt all these things by means of your protesting pen to your solitary state, you will find that it is impossible; and so you will have to leave them out and new ones will have to be composed for you. Why, when you come to the prayers, do you say 'Let us pray' when there is no one there to pray with you? If you can see no one, whom are you summoning to share in your prayer? Why when you have finished reciting the office do you follow the custom of saying: 'Let us bless the Lord' when there is no one at hand who will bless the Lord with you?

Consider carefully, therefore, all these things and those others which are too numerous to mention, and be punctilious in your observance of the laws of ecclesiastical custom whether you are alone or with others. For if the doctors of the Church had deemed it necessary, they would have given us one version of the offices of the Church for the use of solitaries and another for the use of communities; but by being content to compose one only, without any variation, they taught us to hold to this one order with inviolable respect. For they perceived that whatever is reverently offered up in God's service by any member of the Church is sustained by the faith and devotion of the whole body, since the Spirit of the Church, which gives life to the whole body which is preserved by Christ its Head, is one. The whole Church is composed of the joining together of its different members; but it is certainly a single body, established on the firm foundation of a single faith and filled with the power of one life-giving Spirit. This is why the Apostle says: 'There is one body and one Spirit, even as ye are called in one hope of your calling.' And so it is good that whatever action in the holy offices is performed by any one section of the faithful should be regarded as the common act of the whole Church, joined in the unity of faith and the love of charity.

CHAPTER EIGHT

Now this is why, when in offering the Mass we say: 'Be mindful, O Lord, of Thy servants and handmaids', we add a little later 'For whom we offer, or who offer up to Thee, this sacrifice of praise'. These words make it quite plain that the sacrifice of praise is offered by all the faithful, women as well as men, even though it appears to be offered by the priest alone; for that which he performs with his hands in offering sacrifices to God is rendered pleasing by the earnest piety in the souls of the multitude of the faithful. This is made clear by another passage: 'We beseech Thee therefore, O Lord, graciously to accept this oblation of our service and that of Thy whole family.' These words make it even clearer that the sacrifice which is placed upon the holy altar by the priest is offered up by the whole of God's family. This unity of the Church was clearly proclaimed by the Apostle when he said: 'For we being many are one bread and one body.' For so great is the unity of the Church in Christ that throughout the whole world there is but one bread which is the Body of Christ and one chalice which is the Chalice of His Blood. Just as the divinity of the Word of God is one and fills the whole world, so although that Body is consecrated in many places and on many days, yet there are not many bodies but the one Body of Christ. And just as this bread and wine are truly changed into the Body of Christ, so all those who worthily partake of it in the Church are made into the one Body of Christ, as He Himself bore witness when He said: 'He that eateth My flesh and drinketh My blood dwelleth in Me and I in him.'

If, therefore, we are all one body in Christ and we who dwell in Him cannot be separated from one another in spirit even though we are separated in the flesh, I can see no harm in our observing, when we are alone, the common custom of the Church, since by the mystery of our undivided unity we are never apart from her. When I in my solitude utter the common words of the Church I show that I am one with her and that by the indwelling of the Spirit I truly dwell in her: and if I am truly a member of her it is not unfitting that I fulfil my universal duty.

CHAPTER NINE

Moreover the eyes, tongue, feet and hands each have their own particular function in the human body; yet the hands do not touch, the feet do not walk, the tongue does not speak nor the eyes see of themselves and for their own sake; the special function of each part of the body can be attributed to the whole. And those functions which belong to a particular member by virtue of its nature can be said to be performed by the body which is the whole, so that the whole may properly be said to manifest the activity of its parts and the part that of the

169

whole. That is why St. Paul's tongue could truthfully say: 'I suffer trouble in Christ's gospel even unto bonds', although his tongue was not itself in chains; and he goes on to say: 'The word of God is not bound.' Peter and John ran to Christ's sepulchre, although it was only their feet which performed the act of running; Stephen saw the heavens opened, although seeing is the special function of the eyes. Isaac touched and felt his son Jacob, yet the power of touching and feeling belongs particularly to the hands. And so it is clear that any action of an individual member is the work of the whole body; and conversely each of the parts participates in the action of the body as a whole.

CHAPTER TEN

What cause for astonishment, then, is there in the fact that a priest, who is certainly a member of the ecclesiastical body, should when he is alone represent the whole Church in giving greeting and replying, saying 'The Lord be with you' and answering 'And with thy spirit'; or that he should afterwards both ask and give a blessing? For by the mystery of her inward unity the whole Church is spiritually present in the person of each human being who has a share in her faith and her brotherly love. Truly, the fact of aloneness cannot make the unity of faith a solitary thing, nor can the presence of many cause it to be divided. What harm does it do for many voices to come from one mouth if the faith they express is one? For, as I have already said, the whole Church forms a single body. The Apostle bears witness to this: 'For as the body is one, and hath many members, and all the members of that one body, being many, are one body; so also is Christ. For by one Spirit are we all baptized into one body'; and again: 'Christ's body, which is the Church.'

If, then, the whole Church is the one body of Christ and we are members of the Church why should we not, since we are truly united to her, use when we are alone the words of the Church which is our body? Indeed, if we who are many are one in Christ, each of us possesses in Him the whole; and so although in our bodily solitude we seem to be far from the Church, yet we are most immediately present in her through the inviolable mystery of unity. And so it is that that which belongs to all belongs to each, and conversely that which is particular to some is also common to all in the unity of faith and love. So the people have a right to cry: 'Have mercy on me, O God, have mercy on me' and 'Make haste, O God, to deliver me; make haste to help me, O Lord'; and an individual man to say: 'God be merciful unto us and bless us.' Our holy fathers decided that this fellowship and communion of Christ's faithful ought to be a matter so certain that they made it an article of the creed of the Catholic faith and commanded us to observe it as one of the basic precepts of the Christian religion. For as soon as we have said 'I believe in the Holy Ghost and the holy Catholic Church' we add 'The communion of saints'; so that when we give witness to God of our faith we speak also of the fellowship of the Church which is one with Him. Now the communion of the saints in the unity of faith consists in this: they believe in one God, are reborn in one baptism, strengthened by one Holy Spirit, and admitted into the same eternal life by the grace of adoption.

Now just as the Greeks call man a microcosm, that is to say a little world, because his body is comprised of the same four elements as the universe itself, so each of the faithful is a little Church, since without any violation of the mystery of her inward unity each man receives all the sacraments of human redemption which are divinely given to the whole Church. If one man, then, can be said to receive the sacraments which are common to the whole Church, why should he be prevented, when alone, from uttering the words common to the whole Church, for the sacraments are so much more important than any words.

CHAPTER ELEVEN

In case there is still some perverter of our arguments who says: 'Those things which were instituted for the whole assembly of the faithful must under no circumstances be used by solitary individuals,' we will now give an example which has the authority of the Holy Scriptures themselves, so that he may be convinced by reason rather than by words. The book of Joshua tells us something which is well known; namely that the children of

171

Reuben and Gad, and half the tribe of Manasseh, departing from the children of Israel out of Shiloh so that they might enter the country of Gilead, the land of their possession, built a great altar in the land of Canaan. The people of Israel were very angry and took up arms against them, asking why they had dared so rashly to build an altar other than the altar of the Lord. They answered that they had not done this as a transgression, but to secure a witness for the future; 'lest', they said, 'in time to come your children might speak unto our children, saying: What have ye to do with the Lord God of Israel? For the Lord hath made Jordan a border between us and you, ye children of Reuben and children of Gad; ye shall have no part in the Lord. So shall your children make our children cease from fearing the Lord.'

If there is anyone to whom it is not already clear, let me explain briefly why I have brought in this part of the story. It is to show that some of the brethren might, in their simplicity, be disturbed by the thought that they were in some way cut off from the body of the faithful if they did not dare, in their solitude, to use the common words of the Church in their prayers. And so they use these words that they may show that they still form part of the ecclesiastical body, and those same words bring peace to their unquiet souls by bearing witness to the spiritual presence of the faithful. For indeed the children of Reuben and of Gad built an altar, not for the offering of libations, but as an emblem of their unity with the people of Israel; and these others now say, as if they were their children: 'Behold the altar of the Lord, which our fathers made, not for burnt-offerings nor for sacrifices; but as a witness between us and you.' They did what they did as a witness of the fellowship of Israel, and we say what we say as a symbol of the true unity of the Church; they lest they be looked down upon by their brethren and we lest we be tormented by our thoughts. They built the likeness of an earthly altar; we declare the truth of spiritual unity; they for a witness to their children, and we to maintain the inviolable mystery of our new birth and the fellowship of our brethren.

CHAPTER TWELVE

Some of the things which the Church does seem unnecessary as far as human reasoning is concerned; but if we look at the mystery of their inward virtue we will see that they are divine. Who has not been amazed by the fact that canon law decrees that no man who has been married twice may ever be raised to the priesthood, and yet allows a priest who has committed fornication to be restored to his former office when he has done penance? What the Apostle thinks about fornication is perfectly clear: 'Neither fornicators nor idolaters nor adulterers shall inherit the kingdom of God.' But of those who marry a second time he says: 'The wife is bound by the law as long as her husband liveth; but if her husband be dead she is at liberty to be married to whom she will; only in the Lord.' It is perfectly plain from these words that those who marry twice do not transgress the law of God; and that fornicators are cut off from the kingdom of God because of the excesses of the flesh.

What is the meaning of this, then? Why are those who have committed no sin deprived of all hope of the priesthood, while others whose guilt has cut them off from God's kingdom are not, provided they worthily do penance, deprived of the assurance of ecclesiastical rank? Unless for this reason: that second marriages, although not sinful, affect in some way the mystery of the Church. For just as Christ, the high-priest of the good things to come, a true priest according to the order of Melchisedech, who on the altar of the Cross offered to God the Father the lamb of His own body for the world's salvation, is the husband of one bride, Holy Church, who is certainly a virgin since she keeps inviolate the unity of faith, so every priest is commanded to be the husband of one wife, so that he may bear the likeness of the great Bridegroom.

Thus, as far as those who have married twice are concerned, it is not the degree of sin but the nature of the sacrament which is important; they are rejected so that the mystical pattern of true priesthood may be preserved, not as a punishment for their sins. Otherwise the apostle would have numbered among the sins that which he permits to be done. And the holy canons number those who condemn second marriages among the Novatian heretics. We will, if we have not already said enough to maintain the mystery of ecclesiastical unity, proceed still further.

CHAPTER THIRTEEN

I ask you now in all charity, brethren, whether if two brothers are together one of them may rightly say to the other 'The Lord be with you'. Is he not speaking in the plural to a single person, and setting aside literal meaning in observing the custom of the Church? For, according to the rules of speech, when he is speaking to an individual he should say: 'with thee', not 'with you'. And if it is wrong for him to address one man in the plural, he should always use the singular 'The Lord be with thee'. No one who has frequented the threshold of the Apostles can fail to know how inconsistent this is with the law of the Church. For there is no doubt that neither the most blessed bishop of the Holy See, when he is saying his private Mass with a single server, nor any bishop or priest of the Catholic Church uses this form of words in the singular.

If, then, we can approve the custom of the holy priests; if one man has the right to say to another 'The Lord be with you' without discord or contravention of the rules of ecclesiastical order, is there any reason why a single man by himself should not use this form of words, since as far as the literal meaning of the words goes there is little to choose in incongruity between saying it to oneself and saying it to one other person? Since, then, the authority of ecclesiastical custom is such that all the power of polished eloquence yields to it humbly; since it is far less concerned with words than with meaning, if the rules of grammar may be ignored when there are two men present, it follows that one man alone can set them aside without blame. Therefore, as the Church's authority permits the use of the phrase 'The Lord be with you' when only two are present, one man alone has the right to use the same phrase without going against her authority.

The same is true of the response 'And with thy spirit' and of the asking and giving of a blessing by and to the reader when one is alone. It is not the number of persons with which we are

174

concerned, but rather the mystical unity of the Church, whose unity does not exclude a multiplicity of members and whose numerousness does not destroy her unity, since her one body includes many members and her many members make up a single body; neither is the wholeness of the body destroyed by the number of her members.

CHAPTER FOURTEEN

It is not surprising that Holy Church is said to be many in one and one in many when you remember that the people of the earthly Israel, because they were related by birth, maintained among themselves this same pattern of unity. Moses sent messengers to the king of Edom, saying: 'Thus saith thy brother Israel.' And again, when King Arad the Canaanite waged war against Israel and triumphed over them, having taken some of them prisoners, Israel vowed a vow to the Lord, saying: 'If thou wilt deliver this people into my hands, then I will utterly destroy their cities.' We find another clear example in the Book of Kings, when the people of Israel said to the people of Judah, on David's return to his kingdom: 'I have ten parts in the King, and I have also more right in David than thee: why then didst thou despise me, that my advice should not be first had in bringing back my king?'

If that people could speak as one person because they all sprang from one stock, or rather, because they all worshipped one God, and thus show themselves to be one in many, how much more may holy Church, since she is made holy and governed by the one Spirit of God, filled with the mysteries of one faith and baptism, and called by the grace of adoption to take possession of one inheritance, have such a fellowship within herself that each member may use the words of all and all may use the words of each. And so it happens that when we are saying the Divine Office we often sing, in honour of a single saint, words which we know apply to the whole Church; this will be quite clear to you if you read the hymns to the Blessed Mother of God and the other saints carefully.

CHAPTER FIFTEEN

Indeed the Church of Christ, which is an immovable pillar, to whom the keys of the kingdom of heaven were given, is not the slave of case and number, but binds under her own laws all the modes of speech. She is concerned with souls, not words, so she takes little notice of the presence of bodies or the moments of time, but considers the devotion and unity of souls. 'She judgeth all things, yet herself is judged of no man.' This is why we say, when we are celebrating the holy solemnities of Easter: 'O God, who on this day through Thine only-begotten Son hast overcome death and opened unto us the gate of everlasting life', when we all know very well that that Pasch of the Jews, during which the Lord suffered and rose again, is past, and that the light of Paschal rejoicing shines upon us on the nearest Sunday. In the same way we say on the feast of the Ascension and at Whitsun 'today', since the time of their occurrence is determined according to the Easter reckoning. And we celebrate the beheading of John the Baptist in the month of August, although it is almost certain that he was slain by Herod about the time of the Lord's Passion.

The same is true of the feast of St. James, and that of St. Peter-in-Chains. We read in the Acts of the Apostles: 'Herod, after he had killed James the brother of John with the sword, because he saw that it pleased the Jews proceeded to take Peter also.' It goes on: 'Then were the days of the unleavened bread' and adds soon afterwards 'And when he had apprehended him, he put him in prison, and delivered him to four quaternions of soldiers to keep him, intending after Easter to bring him forth to the people'. It is clear from this that the actual events took place at one time of year and the festivals which celebrate them are instituted at quite another. For these feasts, as you know, are celebrated at the end of July, and however you search through the Old Testament you will not find that the Jews celebrated either their Pasch or the days of unleavened bread at that time. But since these feasts could not be celebrated properly during the Easter solemnities, the Church appointed another time for their observance.

176

I have given this short account of certain great feast-days so that you may clearly understand that Holy Church is not bound by the laws of time; rather, she governs the changes of time according to her pleasure. Nor does she serve the elements; it is they who are subject to and obey her. This is why the teacher of the Gentiles says: 'All things are yours, whether Paul or Apollos or Cephas, or the world, or life, or death, or things present or things to come; all are yours; and ye are Christ's, and Christ is God's.' And in order to show how Holy Church excels in the greatness of her authority he says again to these same Corinthians: 'Do ye not know that the saints shall judge the world? and if the world shall be judged by you, are ye unworthy to judge the smallest matters? Know ye not that we shall judge angels? how much more things that pertain to this life.'

CHAPTER SIXTEEN

But, to return to the matter in hand, is it surprising that holy Church, to whom God has committed such power, should so change the words which serve her according to her wishes that individual men may utter the words of many, and the many those of individuals? Is there any reason why those words which are specially suited to some men should not be said by others? We know that when children are baptized, the priest says: 'What dost thou ask?' And not the child itself, but another, answers on its behalf: 'Faith,' etc. That which is the child's own reply is said by another. If one person may utter the words of another even in his holy sacrament of our regeneration, which is the source of all human salvation, why should not one man make answer for another when it is a question of an ecclesiastical greeting or the asking of a blessing? It is no innovation of modern foolhardiness to claim that one man may make the responses on behalf of another in the Church; it has the sanction of apostolic authority; for St. Paul said to the Corinthians: 'Otherwise, when thou shalt bless with the spirit, who shall occupy the place of the unlearned?'

It comes to this, that if any man is afraid to say: 'The Lord be with you' because he is alone, or even to reply 'And with thy spirit', then he must fear to say 'Let us pray'. He must

177

say 'Let me pray' lest he should seem to summon to prayer those who are not there. He who thinks it sacrilege to ask a blessing when there is no one by, or to give one, must be careful not to say, after the reading: 'Do thou, O Lord, have mercy on us'; he must say: 'Have mercy on me.' If this seems ridiculous and stupid to him, then let him not be ashamed to utter the words of the Church when he is alone, since he knows that in mind and spirit he is never separated from her. Let him not declare by his words that he is separated from that body whose member he particularly professes to be; but, because the Church of Christ is truly one, let him fulfil the duty of his universality bravely; he must strive to maintain the power of the mystical body, rather than to concern himself with the suitability of what he is saying.

CHAPTER SEVENTEEN

Now as I have said before, there is much in the customs of the Church which seems on the surface to be worthless and trivial; but when we look at it more carefully we find that it is sustained by the weight of great worth. To take but a few examples: who, to look at the vestments of a priest, would think there was anything in them worthy of admiration, unless he realized what they symbolized? But if he sees them by the light of spiritual understanding, he knows why clerics' sandals have complete soles but only partial uppers. He reflects carefully upon the reason why the alb reaches to the heels and the amice is always made of linen; he ponders the meaning of the girdle and the stole; in the same way he wonders why the dalmatic is divided into four like a cross; why the chasuble is put on over all the other vestments and why the maniple is worn on the left arm; he will understand when the rheum has been removed from the eyes and nostrils of the spirit, not the flesh.

He will realize that there is a reason why the deacon, when he is not wearing a dalmatic, should wear a chasuble when he reads; and why the said dalmatic has a fringe on the left side. Nor does he foolishly make light of the custom that pontiffs wear a pallium over their vestments, just as a plate of gold was placed upon the forehead of the high-priest of old, for his honour and glory; on this plate the name of the Lord was engraved in a tetragram which meant 'Holiness to the Lord'; there were few letters, but they contained in themselves the power of a mighty understanding. But why do we go on indefinitely? Whatever is done in God's service, whether under the old dispensation or the new, is done by symbolic figures and allegories. The building of the tabernacle, the number of the Levites, the ceremonies of the priests, and indeed the rites of holy Church today demand that we should seek in them the virtue of their spiritual meaning. And so we may say that there is a mystery hidden in the ministry since the hidden mystery of allegoric meaning is explained by the outward forms of worship.

CHAPTER EIGHTEEN

Let us unfold here briefly the matter which we took in hand so that it may be made more clear and plain, leaving out those things which have been conveniently set forth elsewhere by learned commentators. Now the vice of arrogance is not unknown to some readers, especially to those who possess grace of speech; when their unbridled tongues run through the open fields of the Scriptures the spirit of pride invades their hearts, which love to be in favour with the multitude. While they guide others along the right road they themselves hasten down the by-ways of confusion and error. That is why it is customary to say to refectory readers: 'May the Lord remove from thee the spirit of pride.' And the reader asks a blessing with such submissiveness that it is not the priest but someone whom he appoints who blesses the man who is about to read; this is done so that at the very beginning of the reading humility may be brought in to counteract any feeling of pride which might arise.

The reason why the priest utters a greeting in church is this: that he may show that he is at peace with the whole assembly of the faithful. Our Lord commanded this in the Gospel, when he said: 'When ye stand praying, forgive, if ye have ought against any: that your Father also which is in heaven may forgive you your trespasses'; and again: 'If thou bring thy gift to the altar, and there rememberest that thy brother hath ought against thee, leave there thy gift before the altar and go thy way; first be reconciled to thy brother, and then come and offer thy gift.' And so the priest before he offers sacrifice and prayers to God shows by this mutual greeting that he is bound to the faithful by the bond of brotherly love; he does this so that he may make this commandment of the Lord clear by his outward actions, as well as keeping it in his heart. Because of this, he sees as present with the eyes of the spirit all those for whom he prays, whether or not they are actually there in the flesh; he knows that all who are praying with him are present in spiritual communion. And so the eye of faith directs the words of his greeting and he realizes the spiritual presence of those whom he knows to be near at hand. Therefore let no brother who lives alone in a cell be afraid to utter the words which are common to the whole Church; for although he is separated in space from the congregation of the faithful yet he is bound together with them all by love in the unity of faith; although they are absent in the flesh, they are near at hand in the mystical unity of the Church.

CHAPTER NINETEEN

But now I would like to say a little about the merits of the solitary life and to give you some idea of what I feel about the heights of that life by my praises rather than by my arguments. The solitary life is indeed a school of heavenly learning, a training in divine arts. There all that we learn is God; He is the way by which we proceed and through which we come to a knowledge of the highest truth. The hermitage is a paradise of delight where the fragrant scents of the virtues are breathed forth like sweet sap or glowing spice-flowers. There the roses of charity blaze in crimson flame and the lilies of purity shine in snowy beauty, and with them the humble violets whom no winds assault because they are content with lowly places; there the myrrh of perfect penance perfumes the air and the incense of constant prayer rises unceasingly.

But why should I call to mind these in particular? For the lovely buds of all the holy virtues glow there many-coloured and graces flourish in an undying greenness beyond the power of words to describe. O hermitage! delight of holy souls, unfailing in your inner sweetness. You are like the Chaldean

furnace in which holy young men check the raging fire by the
power of their prayers and put out the thronging, crackling
flames by the ardour of their faith; where their bonds are burnt
and yet their limbs do not feel the fire; for they are loosed from
their sins and their souls are stirred up to sing hymns in God's
praise, saying: 'Thou hast loosed, O Lord, my bonds; I will
offer to thee the sacrifice of thanksgiving.' You are the kiln in
which the vessels of the Eternal King are shaped; where they
are beaten to an everlasting brightness by the hammer of
penance and polished with the file of wholesome chastisement;
where the rust of the worn-out soul is destroyed and the rough
dross of sin is cast aside. 'The furnace proves the potter's
vessel; and trial and tribulation prove righteous men.'

O warehouse of heavenly merchants, in which are found
the best of those wares for whom the land of the living is prepared! Happy market-place, where earthly goods are exchanged
for those of heaven, and things eternal substituted for those
which pass away! Blessed market, where life everlasting is set
out for sale and may be bought by any man, however little he
possesses; where a little bodily suffering can purchase the company of heaven and a few sparse tears procure everlasting
gladness; where we cast aside worldly possessions and enter
into the patrimony of our eternal inheritance! You, O solitary
cell, are the wonderful workshop of spiritual labour, in which
the human soul restores to itself the likeness of its Creator and
returns to its pristine purity, where the blunted senses regain
their keenness and subtlety, and tainted natures are renewed in
sincerity by unleavened bread. The gifts you bestow are these:
that while the countenance seems pale with fasting the soul
is nourished with the fatness of God's grace; that he who was
once so wrapped in darkness that he did not know himself can
with a pure heart behold God. You lead man back to his be-
ginnings and recall him from banishment to the heights of his
ancient dignity. You make it possible for man to see, from the
citadel of his mind, all earthly things flowing away beneath
him and himself passing away in the stream of perishable
things. You, O hermitage, are the tent of the holy army, the
battlefield of the victorious host, God's fortress, 'the tower of
David builded for an armoury, whereon there hang a thousand

bucklers, all shields of mighty men.' You are the battlefield of God, the arena of spiritual strife, the angels' amphitheatre, the wrestling-school of strong combatants, where the spirit struggles with the flesh and the strong is not overthrown by the weak. You are a rampart to those hastening to the fight, a bulwark for the strong, a protection for those fighters who never yield. Let the barbarian host which surrounds you rage; let them bring up their mantlets, hurl their fiery weapons and increase the number of brandished swords; those who dwell within your walls, armed with the breastplate of faith, rejoice in the invincible protection of their leader and are triumphant in the certainty that their enemies will be overthrown. It was said to them: 'The Lord shall fight for you, and ye shall hold your peace'; and to each singly: 'Fear not; for they that be with us are more than they that be with them.' You, O solitary life, are the death of vice and the life and kindler of virtue. The law exalts you; the prophets admire you; all men who have reached the heights of perfection have recognized your worth. It is to you that Moses owes his receiving of the Decalogue, because of you that Elijah saw the Lord's passing, through you that Elisha was clothed in a double portion of his master's spirit.

What more shall I say? The Redeemer of the world, at the very beginning of the work of redemption, made His herald a dweller in the desert, so that in the dawn of the new world the morning star of truth might rise from you, after whom was to come the full sun who was to bring light to the world's darkness by the glory of His splendour. You are Jacob's ladder, conveying men to heaven, and bringing angels to our aid. You are the golden highway leading men back to their native land, the racecourse which carries those who have run well onward to receive their crown. O eremitic life, you are the soul's bath, the death of evildoing, the cleanser of filth; you make clean the hidden places of the soul, wash away the foulness of sin and make souls shine with angelic purity. The hermit's cell is the meeting-place of God and man, a cross-roads for those who dwell in the flesh and heavenly things. For there the citizens of heaven hold intercourse with men, not in the language of the flesh, but by being made manifest, without any clamour of tongues, to the rich and secret places of the soul.

The cell knows those hidden counsels which God gives to men.
How fair a thing it is to see a brother in his cell pass all the
night in singing psalms, keeping watch, as it were, over God's
fortress; as he watches the stars move through their heavenly
courses the psalms proceed in order from his lips. And as the
earlier and later stars come to light alternating in their courses,
so the psalms which proceed from his lips as from a day-spring
come to an end as if keeping pace with the movement of the
stars. He is carrying out the duty of his calling, and they are per-
forming the task appointed to them; he in his chanting is reaching out inwardly towards the unapproachable light while they,
one after the other, refresh his bodily eyes with visible light.
And although each hastens towards his end by a different
path, yet the heavenly bodies are in harmony with God's
servant in their mutual obedience.

The hermit's cell sees when a heart is burning with the
fire of divine love, and knows whether a man seeks the face of
God with the constancy of perfect devotion. It knows when
his soul is sprinkled with the dew of heavenly grace and when
remorse waters it with flowing streams of tears; even if tears
do not spring from the eyes of the flesh, yet the sorrowing
heart is not far from floods of tears, for that which cannot be
plucked from the branch of outward observation is nevertheless
always preserved at the root of the moist and verdant heart. If
the soul cannot be always weeping, it is enough that it should
be sorrowful. The cell is a prison-house where precious stones
are polished so that they may be used afterwards to adorn the
temple without any wound of hammering.

You, O hermitage, are like the Lord's sepulchre; you receive those whom sin has slain and bring them again to life in
God by the breath of the Holy Spirit. You are a sepulchre from
the confusion and trouble of this life, but you open the way to
the life of heaven. Those who escape from the shipwreck of
this stormy world find in you a haven of peace; those who
were wounded in battle and flee from the enemy's hands see
in you the dwelling-place of a skilful doctor. For as soon as
they retire with a perfect heart into the shadow of your peak
the bruises of their hurt souls and the wounds of their inner
man are healed. It was of you that Jeremiah said: 'It is good

183

that a man should quietly wait for the salvation of the Lord. It is good for a man that he bear the yoke in his youth. He sitteth alone and keepeth silence because he hath borne it upon him.' He who dwells within you is lifted up above himself, for the soul which hungers for God raises itself above the sights of earth and stands upon the citadel of divine contemplation; it holds itself apart from the world's doings and soars on high on the wings of heavenly longing; when he is concerned with beholding Him who is above all things, man transcends himself as well as the rest of the lowliness of the valley of this world. The hermitage is indeed a spiritual dwelling-place, which makes proud men humble, gluttons sober, cruel men kind, wrathful men meek and those who hate burn with brotherly love. It bridles idle tongues and girds lustful loins with the girdle of shining chastity. You, O hermitage, cause light-minded men to be serious and jesters to cease uttering scurrilities; you make prattlers constrain themselves under the discipline of silence. You are the nurse of fastings and vigils, the guardian of patience, the teacher of purest simplicity; to you deceit and guild are unknown. You hold the wanderer in the chains of Christ, and make men of undisciplined behaviour repress their evildoing. You know how to bring men to the peak of perfection and raise them to the height of perfect holiness. You make them smooth and polished, marred by no roughness; you make of them squared stones, fit for building the walls of the heavenly Jerusalem; they will not be shifted by the inconstancy of their behaviour but will remain immovable in their serious following of holy religion. You make them strangers to themselves; you make the vessels of vice blossom with virtue. You are black but comely, like the tents of Kedar or the curtains of Solomon. You are the bath in which the shorn sheep are washed. You are like the fishpools of Heshbon. Your eyes are as the eyes of doves by the rivers of waters, washed with milk and fitly set. Indeed you are the mirror of souls where the human soul can behold itself clearly, supplying what is lacking, removing what is unnecessary, straightening what is crooked and rebuilding what is misshapen. You are the bridal couch on which a dowry is paid to the Holy Spirit and the happy soul is united to its heavenly spouse. Righteous men love you, and those who flee

from you, deprived of the light of truth, do not know where
to set their feet. 'If I do not remember thee let my tongue
cleave to the roof of my mouth, if I prefer not thee above my
chief joy.' Let us sing of you with cheerful voice in the words
of David: 'This is my rest for ever: here will I dwell, for I have
desired it. How fair and how pleasant art thou, O love, for
delights.' The beauty which adorned Rachel's countenance and
that better part which Mary chose, which shall never be taken
away from her, are both symbols of you. You are a garden of
spices, the fountain of gardens, a pomegranate. Although your
bark seems bitter to those who know you not, how lovely is that
which is hidden within, how sweet is your marrow! Hermitage,
you are an escape from the persecuting world, rest for the
labourer, comforter of the sorrowful, a cool refuge from the
world's heat, the rejector of sin and the freedom of souls.
David sought you when he was suffering from the world's evils
and endured the weariness of a dark and tormented heart: 'Lo,
then would I wander far off and remain in the wilderness.'

What shall I say of the others? The very Redeemer of mankind deigned to visit you and sanctify you by His presence at
the beginning of His work. For after He had been washed in
the water of baptism, as the Gospel tells us, immediately the
Spirit drove Him into the wilderness: 'And he was there in the
wilderness forty days and forty nights, tempted of Satan; and
was with the wild beasts.' Let the world recognize that it is in
your debt, since it was from you that God came to embark
upon his work of preaching and miracles. How terrible you are,
O hermitage, to the evil spirits; there the monks' cells are raised
like rows of tents in a camp, like the towers of Sion and the
ramparts of Jerusalem against the Assyrians and against Damascus, for in these cells divers tasks are carried out in a common
spirit; some sing psalms, other pray, some write and others
toil at various manual labours. Are not those divine words:
'How goodly are thy tents, O Jacob, and thy tabernacles, O
Israel! As valleys are they spread forth, as gardens by the river's
side, as the trees of aloes which the Lord hath planted, and as
cedar trees beside the waters' applicable to you? What more
shall I say of you, O solitary life, blessed life, pleasure-garden
of souls, holy life, angelic life, hall of heavenly jewels, court

of the senators of heaven? Your fragrance excels the fragrance of all spices, your taste is sweeter to the tongue of the enlightened heart than the dripping honeycomb or any honey. Whatever is said of you cannot do justice to your worth and merit, for the fleshly tongue cannot express what the spirit knows of you; no bodily organ of speech has ever revealed the sweetness of your inward savour at the heart's core. Those who know you love you; those who have rested in the delight of your loving embrace know the merits of your praise.

As for those who do not know these things, they can never know you. I know that I am unworthy to praise you; but I also most certainly know this, O blessed life, and have no hesitation in saying it: any man who strives to remain constant in the desire for your love dwells in you, and God dwells in him. Satan and his wiles are subject to him, and the devil groans to see him approaching that place from which he himself was banished. And having won a victory over the demons such a man is made the companion of the angels; an exile from the world, he is the heir of paradise; denying himself, he becomes Christ's follower. And he who follows in His footsteps now will certainly, when he comes to the end of his journey, be raised to the glory of His fellowship. I say with all confidence that he who remains in the solitary life to the end of his days for the love of God will, when he quits this mortal dwelling, come to that glorious building, the house not made with hands, his eternal home in heaven.

CHAPTER TWENTY

See, beloved father, I have given you a problem to solve, impelled thereto by the inquiries of the brethren; and have not hesitated in the meanwhile to say what I myself thought. I did not do this, however, that I might usurp the authority of a teacher and venture to instruct others, but rather that I might make clear to you what I myself think in my inexperience. Thus, whatever is to be found in the foregoing arguments is simply set out for your inspection; it is not a categorical assertion or a definitive statement but a disquisition supported by reasons. Therefore, dearly beloved, I beg you to look carefully at all that I have written; if my assumptions are false, obliterate them with a sharp knife, but if, as a result of your teaching, they are consonant with sound doctrine, then strengthen them with the force of your own authority. I could have said what I had to say more briefly, but I must confess that it gave me pleasure to prolong my speaking to your sweet self while I had the opportunity. We are happy to spend a long time in pounding spices, especially when he in whose service they are to be used has himself so sweet a fragrance.

May .almighty God command His servant Leo by secret inspiration to shed three tears or utter three sighs each day for me who am so wretched.

St. Thomas Aquinas
1225-1274

Thomas Aquinas was born in Roccasecca, Italy, and received his early education in the Benedictine abbey of Monte Cassino. He went to Naples in 1239 and it was at the university there that he was introduced to Aristotelianism. He was also attracted to the Dominicans and received the habit in 1244. After considerable opposition from his family he was finally allowed to pursue his vocation and set out for Paris in 1245 or 1246. For the next couple of years he studied under St. Albert the Great, either at Paris or Cologne, but from 1248 to 1252 he was definitely Albert's pupil in Cologne. It was there that he was ordained a priest.

Thomas began his teaching career in 1252 at the University of Paris and was elevated to the chair of master in 1256. In 1259 he returned to Italy and for the next nine years taught in Anagni, Orvieto, Rome, and Viterbo. It was while in Rome in 1265 that he is thought to have conceived the plan for his Summa Theologica *and begun working on the first part. Then in 1268 or 1269 he returned for his second professorship in Paris. He was at the height of his powers and worked prodigiously in these years so that his literary activity was staggering. He went back to Italy in 1272 and continued his teaching and writing in Naples until December 6, 1273. On that day something happened that brought his productivity to an end. When his companion*

Reginald asked why he had given up his work, Thomas replied: "I cannot go on . . . All that I have written seems to me like so much straw compared to what I have seen and what has been revealed to me." He died the next year in the Cistercian abbey of Fossanuova while journeying to France for the second Council of Lyon.

There is no need to insist upon the gigantic stature of Aquinas. As Augustine among the Fathers, so Thomas among the Scholastics represents the finest achievement of his age. The academic character of his greatest works tends to limit the audience which they reach. It also can distort one's realization of the breadth of activities he engaged in. The halls of learning were not the only places that benefited from his brilliance. He did, after all, belong to the Order of Preachers and there is every indication that he took that ministry seriously and performed it well.

The selection that follows is therefore drawn from his preaching rather than from his formal theological writings. This material was preached in the evening to the students and towns-folk of Naples during the Lent of 1273, the year before he died. They were probably given in the local dialect and recorded in Latin by Reginald, his faithful "secretary." They are included in the original, official list of the works of Aquinas which the General Chapter of the Dominicans commissioned Reginald to draw up shortly after the death of the saint. These "conferences" (collationes) convey an awareness of the importance of theology in Christian life. The Creed is explained not as a formula calling for empty endorsement but as the substance of a lifestyle, a way of looking at and acting in the world. They might be sub-titled "the Church-in-action according to Thomas Aquinas."

Nine of the twelve articles are given here.

EXPOSITION ON
THE APOSTLES' CREED

I BELIEVE IN GOD THE FATHER ALMIGHTY, CREATOR OF
HEAVEN AND EARTH

The first thing that a Christian needs is faith, without which no man is a faithful Christian. Now faith confers four boons.

(1) Faith unites the soul to God: because by faith the Christian soul is in a sense wedded to God: *I will espouse thee to myself in faith* (Osee ii, 20). For this reason, when we are baptized, we begin by confessing our faith when we are asked: *Dost thou believe in God?* for baptism is the first of the sacraments of faith. Hence our Lord said (Mark xvi, 16): *He that shall believe and shall be baptized shall be saved*; in as much as without faith baptism is of no avail. Consequently we must realise that without faith no man is acceptable to God: *Without faith it is impossible to please God* (Heb. xi, 6). Wherefore Augustine commenting on Rom. xiv, 23, *All that is not of faith is sin*, says: *Without the recognition of the eternal and unchangeable truth all virtue is but a sham even in the best of men.*

(2) Faith introduces into us a beginning of eternal life: since eternal life is nothing else than to know God: thus our Lord said (John xvii, 3): *This is eternal life, to know thee, the only true God.* This knowledge of God begins in us by faith, and is perfected in the life to come, when we shall know Him as He is: *Faith is the substance of the things to be hoped for* (Heb. xi, 1); wherefore no man can obtain the happiness of Heaven, which is the true knowledge of God, unless he know Him first by faith: *Blessed are they that have not seen, and have believed* (John xx, 29).

(3) Faith is our guide in the present life: since in order to lead a good life a man needs to know what is necessary in order to live well: and if in order to discover all that is necessary for

that purpose he had to rely on his own efforts, either he would never discover them all or he would only do so after a long time. Now faith teaches us all that is necessary for leading a good life: since we learn thereby that there is one God who is the rewarder of the good and the punisher of the wicked: and that there is another life besides this; and other like truths whereby we are sufficiently enticed to do good and avoid evil: *The just man liveth by faith* (Hab. ii, 4). This is also shown from the fact that before the coming of Christ none of the philosophers was able, however great his effort, to know as much about God or about the means necessary for obtaining eternal life, as any old woman knows by faith since Christ came down upon earth: *The earth is filled with knowledge of God* (Isa. xi, 9).

(4) By faith we overcome temptations: *The saints by faith have conquered kingdoms* (Heb. xi, 33). The reason is that all temptation is from either the devil, or the world, or the flesh. The devil tempts thee to disobey God and to refuse to be subject to Him: and this is removed by faith, in as much as it teaches us that He is the Lord of all, wherefore we must obey Him: *Your adversary the devil goeth about seeking whom he may devour: whom resist ye strong in faith.*—The world tempts us either by the attractions of prosperity or by fear of adversity: and these we overcome by faith because it teaches us that there is a better life than this, so that we despise the good things of this world and fear not its afflictions: *This is the victory that overcometh the world, our faith* (I John v, 4); and also because it teaches us that there are evils still greater, those, namely, of hell.—The flesh tempts us by drawing us to the passing pleasures of this life: while faith teaches us that if we seek them unduly we shall forfeit eternal happiness: *In all things putting on the shield of faith* (Eph. vi, 16). Hence we gather how profitable it is to have faith.

But someone will object that it is foolish to believe what one cannot see, and that one ought not to believe what one sees not.—I reply in the first place that this difficulty disappears if we consider the imperfection of our intelligence: for if a man were able by himself to know perfectly all things, visible and invisible, it would be foolish for us to believe what we do not see: whereas our knowledge is so imperfect that no philosopher has ever been able to discover perfectly the nature of a single fly. Thus we are told that a certain philosopher spent thirty years in solitude in the endeavour to know the nature of the bee. If, then, our intelligence is so weak, is it not foolish to refuse to believe anything about God, except such things alone which we are able to find out by ourselves? In fact, this is condemned by the words of Job (xxxvi, 26): *Behold God is great and surpasseth our knowledge.*—Another solution is that supposing a master were to make a statement in his own particular branch of knowledge, an ignoramus would be accounted no small fool if he were to contradict him for no other reason but that he could not understand what the master said. Now without doubt the intelligence of an angel surpasses that of the greatest philosopher far more than the intelligence of the latter surpasses that of an ignoramus. Wherefore the philosopher is a fool to disbelieve what an angel says, and a much greater fool if he disbelieves what God says: for he is condemned in the words of Ecclus. iii, 25: *Many things are shown to thee above the understanding of men.*—Yet a third solution is that life in this world would be altogether impossible if one were only to believe what one sees. How can one live without believing others? How is a man to believe that So-and-so is his father? Hence man must needs believe others in matters that he cannot know perfectly by himself. Now no one is to be believed as much as God is: wherefore those who will not believe the statements of faith are not wise, but foolish and proud. Thus the Apostle says (I Tim. vi, 4): *He is proud, knowing nothing*: and (2 Tim. i, 12): *I know in whom I have believed; and I am certain*: and (Ecclus. ii, 8) it is written: *Ye who fear God, believe in him.*—Fourthly, we may reply that God proves the truth of the things which faith teaches. Thus if a king sends a letter to which he has attached his seal, none will dare say that this letter was not written by the king's orders. Now it is plain that whatsoever the saints have belived and handed down to us concerning Christ's faith is confirmed by God's seal, which is to be seen in those works which no mere creature is able to do, namely, the miracles whereby Christ confirmed the doctrine of the Apostles and of other saints.

And if anyone say that nobody has seen those miracles done, I reply that it is a well-known fact, related in Pagan histories, that the whole world worshipped idols and persecuted the faith of Christ; yet now behold all, the wise, the noble, the rich, and the powerful and the great have been converted at the words of a few simple poor men who preached Christ. Now was this a miracle or was it not? If it was, then you have what you asked for: if you say it was not a miracle, then I say that you could not have a greater miracle than the conversion of the whole world without miracles, and we need to seek no further.

Accordingly no one should doubt about the faith, and we should believe what is of faith even more than the things that we see: since man's sight may be deceived, whereas God's knowledge is never at fault.

I believe in one God. The first of all the articles of faith is that the faithful must believe in one God.

It will be well to consider what is meant by this word *God*, for it signifies the governor and provider of all things: wherefore to believe that there is a God is to believe in one whose government and providence extend to all things: whereas one who believes that all things happen by chance does not believe that there is a God. No one, however, is so foolish as not to believe that the things of the physical world are subject to someone's government, providence and disposition; seeing that they are regulated according to a certain order and time. Thus we see the sun, the moon, and the stars and other parts of the physical world all holding a certain course, which would not happen if they were the sport of chance: and therefore a man would be a fool not to believe in God: *The fool hath said within his heart: There is no God* (Ps. xiii, 1). Some there are, however, who, although they believe that nature is governed and ordained by God, deny that human actions come under His providence, who believe, in fact, that human actions are not disposed by God. Their reason is that they see that in this world the good suffer and the wicked prosper, which would seem to argue against God's providence in regard to mankind: wherefore it is said in their person (Job xxii, 14): *He walks about the poles of the earth; nor does he consider our things.* But this is very foolish: for they behave like one who knows nothing about medicine, and who, seeing the physician prescribing water for one invalid and wine for another, according to the requirements of the medical art, believes this to be done at haphazard; whereas it is the medical art which with good reason prescribes water for the one and wine for the other. It is so with God: who with good cause and by His providence disposes such things as are necessary to man: and thus He afflicts some good men, and allows certain wicked men to prosper. Wherefore anyone who believes this to be the result of hazard is, and is reputed, a fool: since the only cause of his believing thus is because he knows not the art and the reason of the divine dispositon: *Would that he might show thee the secrets of wisdom, and that his law is manifold* (Job xi, 6).

We must, therefore, firmly believe that God governs and disposes not only the things of nature, but also the acts of men: *And they have said: The Lord shall not see; neither shall the God of Jacob understand. Understand, ye senseless among the people; and, ye fools, be wise at last. He that planted the ear, shall he not hear? Or he that formed the eye, shall he not consider? . . . The Lord knoweth the thoughts of men* (Ps. xciii, 7-11). Therefore, He sees all things, our thoughts and the secrets of our will. For this reason men are placed under a special obligation of doing good, since all their thoughts and deeds are manifest to the all-seeing God: hence the Apostle says: *All things are naked and open to his eyes* (Heb. iv, 13).

Moreover, we must believe that this God who disposes and rules all things is but one God. The reason of this is because human affairs are found to be rightly disposed when many things are subject to the disposition and government of one. A multitude of heads often produces dissension among the subjects; wherefore since the divine government surpasses human government it is evident that the world must be governed not by many gods, but by one only.

There are four motives which led men to believe in many gods. (1) The first is the weakness of human intelligence, the result being that through inability to transcend the corporeal world, men did not believe that there was any nature besides that of sensible bodies: and consequently they held that the world is disposed and ruled by those bodies which they observed to surpass all others in beauty and nobility: to which accordingly they attributed and paid divine worship: and these were the sun, the moon, and the stars. It was with these men as it would be with one who, going to court in order to see the king, thinks anyone that is well dressed or exercises an office to be the king. Of such men it is said (Wisd. xiii, 2): *They have imagined . . . the sun and moon . . . or the circle of the stars to be the gods that rule the world*: and (Isa. li, 6): *Lift up your eyes to heaven and look down to the earth beneath; for the heavens shall vanish like smoke, and the earth shall be worn away like a garment, and the inhabitants thereof shall perish in like manner. But my salvation shall be for ever, and my justice shall not fail.*

(2) The second motive was human flattery: since some men with the desire to flatter their masters and sovereigns, gave them the honour due to God, by obeying them and subjecting themselves to them, even so as to make gods of them when they were dead, or even while yet in life: *Let every nation know that Nabuchodonosor is god upon the earth, and beside him is no other* (Judith v, 29).

(3) The third motive was carnal affection for their children and kindred: thus some, through an excessive love for their own relatives, raised statues to them after they had died, the result being that they paid divine honour to these statues. Of these it is said (Wisd. xiv, 21): *Men serving either their affection or their kings gave the incommunicable name to stones and wood.*

(4) The fourth cause was the wickedness of the devil. For he it was who from the beginning desired to be equal to God: thus he says (Isa. xiv, 13): *I will place my throne in the North; I will ascend into heaven; I will be like the most High.* This desire he has never put aside; wherefore he strives his utmost to be worshipped by men and to have sacrifice offered to himself: not that he is pleased in the dog or cat that is offered to him, but in being paid the reverence due to God. Hence he said to Christ (Matt. iv, 9): *All these things will I give thee if falling down thou wilt adore me.* With this purpose the demons entered idols, and answered when questioned, that they might be reverenced as gods: *All the gods of the gentiles are demons* (Ps. cxv, 5). Thus the Apostle says (I Cor. x, 20): *The things which the heathen sacrifice, they sacrifice to devils and not to God.*

Now although all this is horrible, yet from time to time there have been some to whom these four causes apply: and who

196

though neither in word nor thought, nevertheless in deed show that they believe in many gods. Thus those who believe that the heavenly bodies can influence the human will, and who choose certain seasons for their actions, made gods and rulers of the heavenly bodies, and cast horoscopes: *Be not afraid of the signs from heaven which the heathens fear, for the laws of the people are vain* (Jer. x, 2).—Again, all those who obey kings rather than God, in matters wherein they ought not to obey them, make them their gods: *We ought to obey God rather than men* (Acts v, 29).—Again, those who love their children or their kindred more than God, imply by their deeds that there are many gods.—Or again, those who love the pleasures of the table more than God, and of whom the Apostle says (Phil. iii, 19): *Whose God is their belly.*—Again, all those who practise sorcery and incantations, treat the demons as though they were gods, inasmuch as they seek to obtain from the demons that which God alone can give, namely the knowledge of the occult and the truth about future events. We must, therefore, believe that there is but one God.

The Father almighty, Creator of heaven and earth.

As stated above, the first thing that we must believe is that there is but one God: now, the second is that this God is the Creator and Maker of heaven and earth, *of things visible and invisible.* Without having recourse to subtle explanations, it is enough for our present purpose to illustrate by means of a homely example the fact that all things were created and made by God. Supposing a man on entering a house were to feel heat in the porch, and on going further in to feel the heat increasing, and all the more as he penetrated further within, without doubt he would believe that there was a fire in the house, even though he saw it not, that must be the cause of all this heat: and the same will happen to anyone who considers this world in detail. For he will observe that all things are arranged according to their degrees of beauty and excellence, and that the nearer they are to God the more beautiful and the better they are. Hence the heavenly bodies are more beautiful and more noble than the bodies of the lower world, and invisible things than visible: wherefore we must believe that all these things come from one God who gives each thing its being and excellence: *All men are vain in whom there is not the knowledge of God; and who by these good things that are seen could not understand him that is; neither by attending to the works have acknowledged who was the workman* (Wisd. xiii, 1); and further on (verse 5); *By the greatness of the beauty and of the creature the Creator of them may be seen so as to be known thereby.* We must, therefore, take it as clearly demonstrated that all the things that are in the world comes from God.

In connection with this matter three errors are to be avoided. The first is that of the Manicheans, who say that all things visible were created by the devil: wherefore they assert that God created only invisible things. The reason for their falling into this error was that while asserting that God is the sovereign good, which is true, they said that whatsoever comes from good is itself good: so that through not knowing how to discern what is good and what is evil, they believed that whatsoever is in any way evil, is altogether evil; for instance, they said that fire, because it burns, and water, because it suffocates, are evils simply, and so on. Wherefore seeing that none of these sensible things is good simply, but is in some way evil and defective, they asserted that all visible things were made, not by the good God, but by an evil god. Arguing against these, Augustine employs the following example. If a man were to enter a smith's forge and injure himself by colliding with the smith's tools, and then blame the smith for his wickedness in possessing such tools, he would be a fool, since the smith has those tools for his work; even so is it foolish to say that a creature is evil because in some way it is harmful: since what is harmful to one is useful to another. This error is contrary to the Church's faith, and therefore we say: *Of all things visible and invisible.—In the beginning God created heaven and earth* (Gen. i, 1).—*All things were made by him* (John i, 3).

The second is the error of those who say that the world has existed from eternity: in reference to which Peter says (2 Pet. iii, 4): *Since the time that the fathers slept, all things continue as they were from the beginning of the creation.* They were led into this error through not knowing how to imagine the world as having had a beginning. Referring to these, Rabbi Moses says that they are like a man placed on an island immediately after his birth, and remaining in ignorance of the manner of child-bearing and child-birth, who, on someone telling him after he has grown up how man is conceived, carried in the womb, and born into the world, refuses to believe his informant because he deems it impossible for a man to be in his mother's womb. Even so these, in view of the present state of the world, believe not that it had a beginning. This also is contrary to the Church's faith: and, therefore, to remove this we say: *Maker of heaven and earth,* since if they were made it goes without saying that they did not always exist; hence we read in the psalm (Ps. cxlviii, 5): *He spake and they were made.*

The third is the error of those who asserted that God made the world from prejacent matter. They were led to their position, through wishing to measure God's power by our own power; and, therefore, seeing that man can make nothing without prejacent matter, they believed that it is the same with God; and consequently they said that in producing things God had prejacent matter at His disposal. But this is not true, because man is unable to make anything without prejacent matter in as much as he is a particular maker, and can only introduce this or that form into this or that matter which is presupposed from another source. The reason for this is that a man's power is confined to the form only, and consequently his causality is confined to the production of this or that form. On the other hand God is the universal cause of all things, and creates not only the form, but also the matter; so that He made all things out of nothing: wherefore to remove this positon we say: *Creator of heaven and earth.* For to create and to make differ in that the former is to make something out of nothing; and consequently, if God made something out of nothing we must needs believe that He can re-make all things if they happen to be destroyed: so that He can give sight to the blind, raise the dead to life, and work other similar miracles: *For thy power is at hand when thou wilt* (Wisd. xii, 18).

These thoughts afford us five fruits. (1) In the first place they lead us to knowledge of the divine majesty, in as much as the maker is greater than the things he makes. Therefore, since God is the maker of all things, it follows that He is greater than all things: *With whose beauty if they being delighted took them to be gods, let them know how much the Lord of them is more beautiful than they. . . . Or if they admired their power and their effects, let them understand by them that he who made them is mightier than they* (Wisd. xiii, 3, 4). Thus think or imagine whatsoever we will, it is less than God: *Behold, God is great, exceeding our knowledge* (Job xxxvi, 26).

(2) Secondly, we are led to give thanks to God, because seeing that God is the Creator of all things, it is certain that all that we are, and all that we have come from God: hence the Apostle says (I Cor. iv, 7): *What hast thou that thou hast not received?—The earth is the Lord's and the fulness thereof, the world and all they that dwell therein* (Ps. xxiii, 1). For which reason we owe Him thanksgiving: *What shall I render unto the Lord for all the things that he has rendered to me?* (Ps. cxv, 12).

(3) Thirdly, we are encouraged to be patient in adversity. For though all creatures come from God and therefore are good as regards their nature, yet if in any way they be harmful and penal to us, we must believe that what is penal is from God: but. not that which is sinful: because no evil comes from God except in so far as it is directed to a good; and consequently, if all the pains that a man suffers come from God, he must bear them patiently. For by pain sins are cleansed, the guilty are humbled and the good are urged on to the love of God: *If we have received good things at the Lord's hand, why should we not receive evil?* (Job ii, 10).

(4) Fourthly, we are persuaded to make a good use of creatures, since we ought to employ creatures for the purpose to which God made them. Now this purpose is twofold: namely, for the glory of God, since *the Lord hath made all things for himself* (Prov. xvi, 4), i.e. for His own glory; and for our profit: *Which the Lord thy God created for the service of all the nations* (Deut. iv, 19). We must, therefore, make use of things for God's glory, in such wise as thereby to please God, and to profit ourselves, i.e., so as to avoid sin in using them: *All things are thine; and we have given thee what we have received from thy hand* (I Par. xxix, 14). Hence whatsoever thou hast, be it knowledge or beauty, thou must refer all and use all for the glory of God.

(5) Fifthly, we are led to acknowledge man's dignity. For God made all things for man's sake: *Thou hast subjected all things under his feet* (Ps. viii, 8): moreover, after the angels,

man of all creatures is most like God: *Let us make man to our own image and likeness* (Gen. i, 26). He did not say this of the heaven or of the stars, but of man; not, indeed, as regards man's body, but as regards his soul which is endowed with a free will and is incorruptible, wherein he resembles God more than other creatures do. We must, therefore, realise that after the angels man excels all other creatures, and that in no way must we forfeit our dignity on account of sin or for the sake of an inordinate desire for corporeal things which are beneath us and made to serve us: and we must conduct ourselves according to the purpose for which God made us; seeing that He made man to preside over all things on earth and to be subject to Himself. Accordingly, we must rule and hold dominion over the things of the earth, but we must be subject to God by obeying and serving Him, and thus we shall attain to the enjoyment of God. May He grant that this be so.

SECOND ARTICLE

AND IN JESUS CHRIST HIS ONLY SON, OUR LORD

Not only must Christians believe in one God and that He is the Creator of heaven and earth and of all things, but they must also believe that God is the Father, of whom Christ is the True Son. As the blessed Peter says in his second canonical Epistle (i, 16), this is no fable, but an ascertained fact proved by the voice on the mountain: *For we have not by following artificial fables made known to you the power and the presence of our Lord Jesus Christ, but we were eye-witnesses of his greatness. For he received from God the Father honour and glory, the voice coming down to him from the excellent glory; 'This is my beloved Son, in whom I am well pleased. Hear ye him.' And this voice we heard brought from heaven when we were with him in the holy mount.* Moreover, on the several occasions Jesus Christ called God His Father, and Himself the Son of God: and the apostles and holy fathers reckoned this among the articles of faith, saying: *And* (I believe) *in Jesus Christ, his,* i.e. God's, *only Son.*

There were heretics, however, who believed this in a distorted sense. Thus Photinus asserted that Christ is the Son of

God in the same way as any other good men, who, by leading a good life, merit to be called God's sons by adoption through doing God's will: and so Christ who led a good life and did the will of God merited to be called a Son of God. He pretended, in fact, that Christ did not exist before the Blessed Virgin, and that He began to exist when He was conceived of her. Accordingly he erred in two ways: first by denying that He was the Son of God by nature: secondly, by asserting that with regard to His whole being, Christ began to exist in time: whereas our faith holds that He is the Son of God by nature, and that He is from eternity. Now Holy Scripture explicitly contradicts him on both counts. Against the first it is stated not only that He is the Son, but also that He is the only begotten Son: *The only begotten Son who is in the bosom of the Father, he hath declared him* (John i, 18).—Against the second: *Before Abraham was, I am* (John viii, 58): and it is undeniable that Abraham existed before the Blessed Virgin. For this reason the holy Fathers added in another Creed, against the first error, *The only begotten Son of God*; and against the second, *And born of the Father before all ages.*

Sabellius, although he said that Christ was before the Blessed Virgin, denied the distinction between the Person of the Father and the Person of the Son, and said that the Father Himself became incarnate, so that the Person of the Father is the same as that of Christ. But this is erroneous, since it removes the Trinity of Persons, contrary to the words of John viii, 16: *I am not alone, but I and the Father who sent me*; and it is plain that no one is sent by himself. Accordingly Sabellius lied, and therefore in the Creed of the Fathers, it was added, *God of God, Light of Light*; in other words, we must believe in God the Son of God the Father, and the Son who is the Light of the Father who is Light.

Arius, while admitting that Christ was before the Blessed Virgin, and that the Person of the Father was distinct from that of the Son, nevertheless attributed to Christ three things. First, that the Son of God is a creature: second, that He is the highest of all creatures made by God, not from eternity, but in the course of time: third, that God the Son was not of the same nature as God the Father, and that therefore He was not truly God. But this again is erroneous and contrary to the authority of Holy Scripture. For it is said (John x, 30): *I and the Father are one*, namely, in nature: and consequently as the Father always was, so also was the Son; and as the Father is true God, so also is the Son. Accordingly whereas Arius asserted that Christ was a creature, it is said by the Fathers in the Creed: *True God of true God*; and whereas he said that Christ was not from eternity but from time, on the contrary it is said in the Creed: *Begotten, not made*; and against his assertion that Christ was not of the same nature as the Father, it was added in the Creed, *Consubstantial with the Father.*

It is clear then that we must believe that Christ is the only begotten of God, and the true Son of God; that He has always existed together with the Father; that the Person of the Son is distinct from the Person of the Father; and that He is of one nature with the Father. This, however, in the present life we believe by faith, but we shall know it by perfect vision in eternal life: and accordingly for our own consolation we shall make a few observations on this point.

We must observe then that various things have various ways of generating: while in God generation is other than the generation of other things: wherefore we cannot obtain a notion of divine generation except from the generation of that creature which approaches nearest to a likeness to God. Now nothing is so like God as the human soul, as we have stated. And the manner of generation in the soul is that a man by his soul excog‚itates something which is called the concept of the intellect: which concept proceeds from the soul as its father, and is called the word of the mind or of man. Accordingly the soul by thought generates its word: and thus the Son of God is nothing else but the Word of God, not like the word that is uttered externally, for this is transitory, but as the word conceived inwardly. Therefore this same Word of God is of one nature with God and equal to God. Thus the Blessed John in speaking of the Word of God destroyed three heresies. Firstly, the heresy of Photinus, when he says (i. 1), *In the beginning was the Word*; secondly, that of Sabellius, when he says, *And the Word was with God*; thirdly, that of Arius, when he says, *And the Word was God.*

Now a word is not in us in the same way as it is in God. In us our own word is accidental: whereas in Him, the Word of God is the same as God Himself, since there is nothing in God that is not the divine essence. Yet none can say that God has not a Word, for it would follow that God is most foolish: and therefore, just as God always was, so also His Word always was. Now, even as a craftsman makes all things by means of the form or word which he has preconceived in his mind, so, too, God makes all things by His Word as by His art: *All things were made by him* (John i, 3). If, then, God's Word is His Son, and all His words bear a certain likeness to that Word, we ought in the first place to be willing, to hear God's words; since it is a sign that we love God, if we willingly hear His words.—Secondly, we ought to believe the words of God, since thereby the Word of God, i.e. Christ who is God's Word, dwells in us, or to quote the Apostle (Eph. iii, 17): *That Christ may dwell in your hearts by faith.—You have not his word abiding in you* (John v, 38).— Thirdly, the Word of God abiding in us should be continually in our thoughts: since not only should we believe in Him, but also meditate upon Him: else we would derive no profit from His presence: in fact, meditation of this kind is of great assistance against sin: *In my heart I have hidden thy words that I may not sin against thee* (Ps. cxviii, 11). Again, it is said of the just man (Ps. i, 2): *Day and night he shall meditate on His law.* Thus it is said of the Blessed Virgin (Luke ii, 19) that she *kept all these words, pondering on them in her heart.—*Fourthly, we ought to communicate God's Word to others, by admonishing them, preaching to them, inflaming their hearts: thus the Apostle wrote to the Ephesians (iv, 29): *Let no evil speech proceed from your mouth, but that which is good unto edification;* and to the Colossians (iii, 16): *Let the word of Christ dwell in you abundantly: in all wisdom teaching and admonishing one another*; and again to Timothy (2, iv, 2): *Preach the word, be insistent in season and out of season, reprove, entreat, rebuke in all patience and doctrine.—*Lastly, we ought to put the words of God into practice: *Be ye doers of the word and not bearers only, deceiving yourselves* (Jas. i, 22).

These five were observed by the Blessed Virgin in their order when she begot the Word of God. First she *heard:* 'The

Holy Ghost shall come upon thee' (Luke i, 35): then she con-
sented by faith: *'Behold the handmaid of the Lord'* (ibid., 38):
thirdly, she held and bore Him in her womb: fourthly, she
brought Him forth and gave birth to Him: fifthly, she nourished
and fed Him. Hence the Church sings: *The Virgin alone gave her
heaven-filled breast to the king of angels.*

THIRD ARTICLE

WHO WAS CONCEIVED BY THE HOLY GHOST, BORN OF THE VIRGIN MARY

As we have shown, a Christian must believe not only that
Christ is the Son of God, but also that He became man. Wherefore the blessed John having said many subtle things about the
Word of God that are hard to understand, goes on to tell us of
the incarnation, by saying (i, 14): *And the Word was made flesh.*
In order to throw some light on this subject, I shall illustrate it
by means of two examples.

In the first place, without doubt, nothing is more like the
Word of God than the unvoiced word that is conceived in man's
heart. Now the word conceived in the heart is unknown to all
save the one who conceived it: and it is first known to others
when the voice gives utterance to it. Thus the Word of God while
yet in the bosom of the Father was known to the Father alone;
but when He was clothed with flesh as a word is clothed with
the voice, then He was first made manifest and known: *Afterwards he was seen on earth and conversed with men* (Baruch iii,
38).—Another example lies in the fact that although the voiced
word is known by the hearing, it is not seen or touched: but
when it is written it is both seen and touched. In like manner the
Word of God became both visible and tangible when It was, as
it were, written on our flesh: and just as the parchment on which
the king's word is written is called the king's word, so the man
united to God's Word in unity of person is called the Word of
God: *Take thee a great book and write in it with a man's pen*
(Isa. viii, 1): and therefore the holy Apostles said: *Who was conceived by the Holy Ghost, born of the Virgin Mary.*

On this point there arose many errors: wherefore the holy
Fathers in another Creed, of the council of Nicea, made several
additions whereby all these errors stand condemned.

Origen said that Christ was born and came into the world in order to save the demons also: and so he asserted that all the demons would be saved at the end of the world. But this is contrary to Holy Scripture: for it is said (Matt. xxv, 41): *Depart from me, ye cursed, into everlasting fire, that was prepared for the devil and his angels.* Wherefore in order to exclude this the following clause was added: *Who for us men* (not for the demons) *and for our salvation* . . . thus stressing God's love for us.

Photinus admitted that Christ was born of the Virgin Mary, but asserted that He was a mere man, who by leading a good life, and doing God's will, merited to become a son of God, even as other holy men. And against this it is said (John vi, 38): *I came down from heaven, not to do my will, but the will of him who sent me.* Now it goes without saying that He would not have come down thence unless He had been there: and if He were a mere man He would not have been in heaven: wherefore in order to exclude this, the following words were added: *He descended from heaven.*

The Manicheans said that although the Son of God always existed, and came down from heaven, yet He had flesh not really but only apparently. But this is false: in as much as it was unbecoming for the Teacher of truth to have anything false about Him: and therefore since He had flesh ostensibly, He really had it. Thus it is said (Luke xxiv, 39): *Handle and see; for a spirit hath not flesh and bones, as you see me to have.* Wherefore in order to exclude this, they added: *And he took flesh.*

Ebion, who was of Jewish nationality, said that Christ was born of the Blessed Virgin from sexual intercourse and fecundation by the male seed. But this is false, since the Angel said (Matt. 1, 20): *For that which is conceived in her is of the Holy Ghost;* and therefore the holy Fathers excluded this by adding: *By the Holy Ghost.*

Valentine, while confessing that Christ was conceived by the Holy Ghost, taught that the Holy Ghost fashioned a heavenly body which He placed in the Virgin's womb: and this was Christ's body, so that the Blessed Virgin's co-operation was reduced to her serving as a place for Christ's body. Hence Valentine said that Christ's body passed through the Blessed Virgin as through a channel. But this is false, because the Angel said (Luke i, 35):

The Holy One that shall be born of thee shall be called the Son of God; and the Apostle (Gal. iv, 4) says: *When the fulness of time came, God sent his Son made of a woman.* For which reason they added: *Born of the Virgin Mary.*

Arius and Apollinarius said that though Christ was the Word of God born of the Virgin Mary, He had no soul but the Godhead in lieu thereof. But this is contrary to Scripture, for Christ said (John xii, 27): *Now is my soul troubled*; and again (Matt. xxvi, 38): *My soul is sorrowful even unto death.* Wherefore the holy Fathers excluded this by adding, *And was made man*: because a man is composed of a soul and a body: so that Christ had whatsoever a man can have, except sin.

In that He is said to have become man, all the aforesaid errors stand condemned, beside all possible errors, especially that of Eutyches, who maintained that the divine and human natures were mixed together so as to form one nature in Christ, that is neither purely divine nor purely human. But this is false, since in that case He would not be a man, and this would be contrary to the words, *And was made man.*

Again the error of Nestorius stands condemned, for he said that the Son of God was united to man solely by indwelling. But this is false, because then He would not be a man, but in a man; whereas that He became man is declared by the Apostle (Phil. ii, 7): *He was in habit found as a man.—Ye seek to kill me, a man who have spoken the truth to you, which I have heard of God* (John viii, 40).

From what has been said we may gather a few points for our instruction.

(1) In the first place our faith is thereby strengthened. For instance, if anyone were to tell us about a far-distant country which he had never visited, we would not believe him to the same extent as if he had been there. Accordingly before Christ came into the world, the patriarchs, prophets and John the Baptist said certain things about God; yet men did not believe them as they believe Christ who was with God, who indeed was one with God; for which reason our faith is very strong, seeing that we have received it from Christ: *No man has ever seen God, the only begotten Son, who is in the bosom of the Father, he hath declared him* (John i, 18). Hence it is that many mysteries of

faith have been made known to us after the coming of Christ, which until then were hidden.

(2) Secondly, thereby our hope is raised. Because it is evident that God's Son took our flesh and came to us, not for a trifling reason, but for our exceeding great good: wherefore He bound Himself to us, as it were, by deigning to take a human soul and body and to be born of a Virgin, in order to bestow His Godhead on us, thus becoming man that man might become God: *By whom we have access through faith into this grace wherein we stand; and glory in the hope of the glory of the sons of God* (Rom. v, 2).

(3) Thirdly, charity is inflamed thereby. Because there is no greater proof of God's love than that God the Creator became a creature, that our Lord became our brother, and that the Son of God became the Son of man: *God so loved the world that he gave his only begotten Son* (John iii, 16). The very thought of this should kindle and inflame our hearts with the love of God.

(4) Fourthly, we are encouraged to keep our souls pure: in as much as our nature was ennobled and raised through being united to God to the extent of being assumed into union with a divine Person: wherefore after the incarnation the Angel would not allow the Blessed John to worship him (Apoc. xxii, 8, 9), whereas an angel had suffered this from even the greatest patriarchs. Consequently, man ought to bear this exaltation in mind and in consideration thereof should disdain to debase himself and his nature by falling into sin. For this reason the blessed Peter (2 Peter i, 4) says: *By whom he hath given us most great and precious promises; that by these you may be made partakers of the divine nature, flying the corruption of that concupiscence which is in the world.*

(5) Thereby is inflamed our desire of going to Christ. Thus a man whose brother is king in a far-distant country will have a great longing to go to him, to be with and stay with him: wherefore seeing that Christ is our brother, we should long to be with Him and to be united to Him: *Wheresoever the body is, there will the eagles be gathered together* (Matt. xxiv, 18). The Apostle also desired *to be dissolved and to be with Christ.* This same desire increases in us when we meditate on Christ's incarnation.

FOURTH ARTICLE

SUFFERED UNDER PONTIUS PILATE, WAS CRUCIFIED, DEAD AND BURIED

Just as a Christian is required to believe in the incarnation of the Son of God; even so is it necessary that he believe in His Passion and Death, because as Augustine says: *His Birth would have profited us nothing had we not profited by His Redemption.* That Christ did indeed die for us is so hard to conceive that scarcely is our mind able to grasp it: in fact it is utterly beyond our understanding. The Apostle insinuates this when he says (Acts xiii, 41): *I work a work in your days, a work which you will not believe if any man shall tell it you.* In fact, so great is God's favour and love in our regard that He has done more for us than we are able to understand. However, we are not to believe that Christ suffered death in such wise that His Godhead died, but that His human nature died; for He died not as God, but as man. This may be illustrated by examples.

The first is in ourselves. It is clear that when a man dies, it is not the soul, but the body or the flesh that dies when body and soul are separated. Accordingly when Christ died, it was not His Godhead that died, but His human nature. But surely if the Jews did not kill His Godhead, they sinned no more than if they had killed any other man—I reply that a man who bespatters a king's robe is as guilty as though he had bespattered the king himself. Hence the Jews, though they could not slay God, yet for slaying the human nature wherewith Christ was clothed, they were punished as though they had slain the Godhead.

Again, as we have said above, the Son of God is the Word of God, and the Word of God was made flesh even as the king's word is inscribed on parchment. If, then, one were to tear the king's parchment, he would be held as guilty as if he had torn the king's word. Hence the Jews are held equally guilty as if they had slain the Word of God.

But what need was there for the Word of God to suffer for us? That the need was great may be assigned to two reasons. (1) One was the need for a remedy for sin: (2) The other was the need for an example of what we ought to do.

(1) We find a remedy in as much as Christ's Passion proves a remedy for all the evils that we incur through sin: which evils are of five kinds.

(*a*) Firstly, there is the stain of sin: because when a man sins, he defiles his soul: for just as virtue is the soul's beauty, so is sin its stain: *How happeneth it, O Israel, that thou art in thy enemies' land? . . . Thou art defiled with the dead* (Baruch iii, 10, 11). This is removed by Christ's Passion: for Christ by His Passion poured out His blood as a laver wherein sinners are cleansed: *He hath washed us from our sins in his own blood* (Apoc. i, 5). Now the soul is cleansed by Christ's blood in Baptism which from Christ's blood derives the power of regeneration; and, consequently, when a man defiles himself with sin, he does an injury to Christ, and sins more grievously than before he was baptized: *A man making void the law of Moses dieth without any mercy under two or three witnesses; how much more, think you, he deserveth worse punishments who hath trodden underfoot the Son of God and hath esteemed the blood of the testament unclean?* (Heb. x, 28, 29).

(*b*) Secondly, we incur the anger of God. For just as a carnal man loves carnal beauty, so does God love spiritual beauty, which is that of the soul. When, therefore, the soul is defiled by sin, God is offended, and the sinner becomes an object of His hatred: *To God the wicked and his wickedness are hateful* (Wisd. xiv, 9). But Christ's Passion removes this, because He atoned to God the Father for sin, for which man himself was unable to atone: whereas Christ's charity and obedience were greater than the sin and disobedience of the first man: *When we were enemies we were reconciled to God by the death of his Son* (Rom. v, 10).

(*c*) Thirdly, we incur weakness: in as much as a man thinks that if he sin once he will be able afterwards to refrain from sinning; whereas it is quite the reverse that happens: because by the first sin he is weakened and is more inclined to sin again; likewise sin has a greater power over him; and, moreover, so far as he is concerned, he puts himself in a state whence there is no escape—like a man who jumps into a well—except by the power of God. Hence after **man** had sinned, our nature was weakened and corrupt: and thus **man** was more prone to sin. But Christ diminished this weakness and infirmity, although He did not remove it altogether. And yet man is so strengthened and sin is so weakened by Christ's Passion, that sin has no longer such power over him: while man, by the help of God's grace bestowed in the Sacraments, which derive their efficacy from Christ's Passion, is able to endeavour to arise from his sins. Thus says the Apostle (Rom. vi, 6): *Our old man is crucified with him, that the body of sin may be destroyed.* Because before Christ's Passion there were few who lived without falling into mortal sin: whereas afterwards many have lived and are living without mortal sin.

(d) Fourthly, we incur the debt of punishment, because God's justice demands that whosoever sins should be punished. Now punishment is awarded according to the guilt; wherefore since the guilt of mortal sin is infinite, as being against the infinite good, namely God whose commandments the sinner holds in contempt, it follows that the punishment due to mortal sin is infinite. But Christ by His Passion delivered us from this punishment which He bore Himself: *He bore our sins*, i.e. the punishment due to our sins, *in his body* (I Peter ii, 24): because His Passion was so efficacious as to suffice to atone for all the sins of the whole world, even of a hundred thousand worlds. For this reason when a man is baptized he is released from all his sins; hence also it is that a priest forgives sins; and again that the more a man conforms to the Passion of Christ, the more is he pardoned, the more grace does he merit.

(e) Fifthly, we incur banishment from the kingdom: because those who offend their king are compelled to leave the kingdom: and thus on account of sin man is banished from paradise. For this reason immediately after he had sinned Adam was banished from paradise and the gates of Eden were closed. But Christ by His Passion opened the gates and recalled the exiles to the kingdom. For when Christ's side was pierced, the gates of paradise were opened, and by the shedding of His blood the stain of sin was deleted, God was appeased, man's weakness was removed, his punishment was expiated, the exiles were called back to the kingdom. Hence the thief received the immediate response: *This day shalt thou be with me in Paradise* (Luke xxiii, 43). This has not been said of old, not to Adam, not to Abraham, not to David: but *this day*, i.e. as soon as the gates

were opened, the thief having sought pardon, found it: *Having
. . . confidence in the entering into the holies by the blood of
Christ* (Heb. x, 19).

(2) Accordingly it is clear how profitable was Christ's
Passion as a remedy; nor is it less profitable as an example. For,
as the blessed Augustine says, Christ's Passion affords us a model
in all the circumstances of life: since whosoever wishes to lead a
perfect life needs but to despise what Christ despised on the
cross, and to desire what He desired. There is not a virtue an
example of which we do not find on the cross. If you seek an
example of charity, *greater love no man hath than that a man
lay down his life for his friends* (John xv, 13), and this Christ
did on the cross. Wherefore if He laid down His life for us, we
should not deem it a hardship to suffer any evils whatsoever for
His sake: *What shall I render unto the Lord for all the things
which he hath rendered to me?* (Ps. cxv, 12).—If anyone seek an
example of patience, he will find a most perfect example on the
cross. For a man's patience is proved to be great on two counts:
either when he suffers great evils patiently, or when he suffers
that which he is able to avoid, yet avoids not. Now Christ suffered greatly on the cross: *Oh all ye that pass by the way, attend
and see if there be any sorrow like unto my sorrow* (Lam. i, 12):
and He suffered patiently in as much *as when he suffered he
threatened not* (I Peter ii, 23). *He shall be led as a sheep to the
slaughter, and shall be dumb as a lamb before his shearer* (Isa.
liii, 7). Moreover He could have escaped, and did not escape:
*Thinkest thou that I cannot ask my Father and he will give me
presently more than twelve legions of angels?* (Matt. xxvi, 53).
Great therefore was Christ's patience on the cross: *Let us run
by patience to the fight proposed to us; looking on Jesus the
author and finisher of faith who, having joy set before him,
endured the cross, despising the shame* (Heb. xii, 1, 2).—If you
seek an example of humility, look on the Crucified: although
He was God, He chose to be judged by Pontius Pilate and to suffer death: *Thy cause hath been judged as that of the wicked* (Job
xxxvi, 17); truly 'as of the wicked': *Let us condemn him to a
most shameful death* (Wisd. ii, 20). The Master chose to die for
His servant; the Life of the Angels suffered death for man: *Made
obedient unto death* (Phil. ii, 8).—If you seek an example of

obedience, follow Him who was made obedient to the Father even unto death: *As by the disobedience of one man, many were made sinners: so also by the obedience of one, many shall be made just* (Rom. v, 19).—If you seek an example of contempt for earthly things, follow Him, the King of kings and Lord of lords, in whom are the treasures of wisdom; and see Him on the cross, despoiled, derided, spat upon, scourged, crowned with thorns, served with gall and hyssop, dead. Therefore, take no account of your apparel or of your possessions, since *they parted my garments amongst them* (Ps. xxi, 19):—nor of honours, since I suffered Myself to be jeered at and scourged,—nor of rank, since they plaited a crown of thorns and placed it on My head,— nor of pleasures, since *in my thirst they gave me vinegar to drink* (Ps. xviii, 12). Thus Augustine in commenting on Heb. xii, 2: *Who, having joy set before him, endured the cross, despising the shame,* says: *The man Christ despised all earthly things in order to teach us to despise them.*

FIFTH ARTICLE

HE DESCENDED INTO HELL, THE THIRD DAY HE ROSE AGAIN FROM THE DEAD

As we have stated, Christ's death, like that of other men, consisted in the separation of His soul from His body; while His Godhead was so inseparably united to the man Christ, that although His soul and body were separated from each other, His Godhead remained ever most perfectly united to both His soul and His body. Consequently in the tomb there was His body, together with the Son of God, who together with His soul descended into hell.

There are four reasons why Christ, together with His soul, descended into hell.

(1) The first was that He might bear the whole punishment of sin, so that thus He might wholly atone for the sin. Now the punishment of man's sin was not only the death of the body, there was also a punishment in the soul; for seeing that sin had been committed in the soul, the latter was punished by being deprived of the beatific vision, and as yet no atonement had been offered for the abolishment of this punishment. For this reason,

213

after their death and before the coming of Christ, all, even the holy patriarchs, went down into hell. Accordingly in order to bear the entire punishment due to sinners, Christ chose not only to die, but also that His soul should descend into hell. Thus it is said (Ps. lxxxvii, 5): *I am counted among them that go down into the pit: I am become as a man without help, free among the dead*: for others were there under constraint, whereas Christ was there as free.

(2) The second reason was that He might bring perfect succour to all His friends, for He had His friends not only in the world but also in hell, since one is Christ's friend by having charity; and in hell there were many who had died in charity and faith in Christ to come, such as Abraham, Isaac, Jacob, Moses, David, besides other righteous and perfect men. And since Christ had visited His friends in the world and had succoured them by His death, He wished to visit His friends who were in hell and succour them by coming to them: *I will penetrate to all the lower parts of the earth, and will behold all that sleep, and will enlighten all that hope in the Lord* (Ecclus. xxiv, 45).

(3) A third reason was that He might completely overcome the devil, for a man's triumph over another is complete when he conquers him not only in the open field, but attacks him in his stronghold and deprives him of his kingdom and even of his dwelling-place. Now Christ had triumphed over the devil and had conquered him on the cross; wherefore He said (John xii, 31): *Now is the judgement of the world, now shall the prince of this world*, i.e. the devil, *be cast out*. And, therefore, that His victory might be complete, it was His will to deprive him of his throne and imprison him in his own house, which is hell. For which reason He descended thither, deprived the devil of his own, bound him, and carried off his spoils: *Despoiling the pincipalities and powers, he hath exposed them confidently, openly triumphing over them in himself* (Col. ii, 15). Moreover, seeing that Christ had been given power and possession in Heaven and on earth, He wished to take possession of hell, so that, to quote the Apostle (Phil. ii, 10), *in the name of Jesus every knee should bow of those that are in heaven, on earth, and under the earth.— In my name they shall cast out devils* (Mark xvi, 17).

(4) The fourth and last reason was to deliver the saints who were in hell because even as Christ wished to suffer death that He might deliver the living from death, so did He wish to descend into hell in order to deliver those that were there: *Thou also by the blood of thy testament hath sent forth thy prisoners out of the pit wherein is no water* (Zach. ix, 11): *O death, I will be thy bite* (Osee xiii, 14). For although Christ destroyed death altogether, He did not altogether destroy hell, but took a piece out of it as it were, in that He did not deliver all that were there, but those only that were free from mortal as well as original sin. As regards the latter, they were freed personally therefrom by circumcision; or, before circumcision—either by the faith of their parents who were believers (as regards those who died before having the use of reason)—or by the sacrifices, and their faith in Christ to come (as regards adults). Yet all these were in hell as having contracted original sin from Adam, from which, as members of the human race, they could not be freed except by Christ. Wherefore He left there those who had gone down thither with the stain of mortal sin, as well as the uncircumcised children; and in this sense He said: *O hell, I will be thy bite*. Thus we know that Christ descended into hell, and why.

From this exposition we may gather four points for our instruction.

(1) The first is a firm hope in God, because no matter how great a man's afflictions may be, he should always hope in God's assistance and trust in Him. For nothing is so grievous as to be in hell: wherefore if Christ freed those who were in hell, anyone, provided he is a friend of God, should be confident that God will deliver him from his straits whatever they be: *She* (wisdom) *forsook not the just when he was sold . . . and went down with him into the pit, and in bands she left him not* (Wisd. x, 13, 14). And seeing that God gives special assistance to His servants, anyone who serves God should be full of confidence: *He that feareth the Lord shall tremble at nothing: he shall not be afraid, for he is his hope* (Ecclus. xxxiv, 16).

(2) Secondly, we ought to conceive fear and cast away presumption. Because although Christ suffered for sinners and descended into hell, yet He did not deliver all, but only those who were free from mortal sin, as we have said; whereas He left

those who had died in mortal sin. Consequently none who goes down thither in a state of mortal sin may hope for pardon, but he will remain in hell as long as the holy Fathers in paradise, namely, for all eternity: *These shall go into everlasting punishment: but the just into life everlasting* (Matt. xxv, 46).

(3) Thirdly, we should bear this in mind. Because as Christ descended into hell for our salvation, so we ought to take care to descend thither, by meditation on His sufferings, even as did the saintly Ezechias: *I said: In the midst of my days I shall go to the gates of hell* (Isa. xxxviii, 10). For anyone who in thought frequently goes down thither in life, is not likely to go down thither in death, because such thoughts withdraw us from sin. Thus we observe that the people of this world beware of evil doing for fear of temporal punishment: how much more then should they beware for fear of the punishment of hell, which is greater both in point of severity and in point of its manifold nature: *Remember thy last end, and thou shalt never sin* (Ecclus. vii, 40).

(4) Fourthly, we may gather an example of love. For Christ descended into hell in order to deliver His own; and consequently we ought to descend thither in order to succour our friends, in as much as they are helpless: and therefore we ought to succour those who are in purgatory. Surely he were passing cruel who would not succour his friend in an earthly prison; much more cruel, then, is he who succours not his friend in purgatory, since there is no comparison between the world's punishments and those of purgatory: *Have mercy on me, have mercy on me, at least you my friends, for the hand of the Lord hath touched me* (Job xix, 21). *It is a holy and wholesome thought to pray for the dead that they be loosed from sins* (2 Mach. xii, 46). This succour is given to them under three forms: by masses, by prayers, by alms, according to Augustine: and Gregory adds a fourth, viz. fasting. And no wonder, seeing that even in this world one friend can pay for another, but this applies only to those who are in purgatory.

The third day he rose again from the dead. Man needs to know two things, the glory of God and the punishment of hell; because through being drawn by His glory, and terrified by His punishments, men are careful on their own account, and refrain from sin. Yet these things are very difficult for a man to know; thus it is said of God's glory: *Who shall search out the things that are in heaven?* (Wisd. ix. 16). This, however, is difficult to the earthly-minded, because *he that is of the earth . . . speaketh of the earth* (John iii, 31), whereas it is not difficult for the spiritual man, since *he that cometh from heaven is above all* (ibid.). Hence God came down from Heaven and took flesh in order to teach us heavenly things. It was also difficult to know about the punishments of hell; for *no man hath been known to have returned from hell* (Wisd. ii, 1), which is said in the person of the wicked. But it cannot be said now, since just as He came down from Heaven in order to teach us heavenly things, so did He come back from hell in order to teach us about hell. Consequently we must believe not only that He became man and died, but also that He rose again from the dead. And therefore the Creed goes on: *The third day he rose again from the dead.* Now, as we are aware, there were several who rose from the dead, namely, Lazarus, the widow's son, and the daughter of the ruler of the synagogue. But Christ's resurrection differs from the resurrection of these and of others in four points. First as to the cause of resurrection, since others who came back to life arose not by their own power but either by Christ's power or at the prayer of a saint; whereas Christ arose by His own power, for He was not only man but God, and the Godhead of the Word was never separated either from His soul or from His body; and therefore whenever He chose His body could resume His soul, and His soul could resume His body: *I have power to lay down (my life) and I have power to take it up again* (John x, 18). And although He died, it was neither through weakness nor of necessity, but of power, since He chose to die. This is evident from the fact that in the moment of dying He cried out with a loud voice, which others cannot do at the moment of death, for they die from weakness. Wherefore the centurion exclaimed (Matt. xxviii, 54): *Verily this was the Son of God.* Therefore, just as by His own power He laid down His life, so by His own power He took it up again; for which reason it is said *He rose again*, and not that He was raised up as though by another: *I have slept and have taken my rest: and I have risen up* (Ps. iii, 6). Nor is this contradicted by what is said (Acts ii, 32): *This Jesus hath*

God raised again, because both the Father and the Son raised Him up, in as much as the Father's power is one and the same as the Son's.—The second difference lies in the life to which He rose again: since Christ arose to a glorious and incorruptible life: *Christ is risen from the dead through the glory of the Father* (Rom. vi, 4), whereas others rise again to the same life which they had before, as instanced in Lazarus and others.—Thirdly, they differ in fruit and efficacy, for by virtue of Christ's resurrection all rise again: *Many bodies of the saints that had slept arose* (Matt. xxviii, 52), and the Apostle (I Cor. xv, 20) declares that *Christ is risen from the dead, the first fruits of them that sleep.* And behold how Christ by His Passion attained glory: *Ought not Christ to have suffered these things and so to enter into his glory?* (Luke xxiv, 26), in order to teach us how we may be able to attain glory: *Through many tribulations we must enter into the kingdom of God* (Acts xiv, 21).—Fourthly, they differ in point of time, in as much as the resurrection of others is deferred to the end of the world, except in special cases where some have been privileged to rise again before, as, for instance, the Blessed Virgin, and, according to a pious tradition, the blessed John the Evangelist, whereas Christ rose again on the third day. The reason for this is that Christ's resurrection, death and birth were for *our salvation*, and therefore He chose to rise again at such a time as would be profitable to our salvation. Thus, had He risen again at once people would not have believed that He had died, and if He had delayed His resurrection for a long time, His disciples would not have remained faithful, and consequently His Passion would have profited no one: *What profit is there in my blood whilst I go down to corruption?* (Ps. xxix, 10). For this reason, then, He rose again the third day, that it might be believed that He died, and that the disciples might not lose faith in Him.

From the above we may gather four points for our instruction:

(1) The first is that we strive to rise again spiritually from the death of the soul which we incur by sin, to the life of righteousness, which becomes ours by repentance. Thus the Apostle (Eph. v, 14) says: *Arise, thou that sleepest, and arise from the dead, and Christ shall enlighten thee.* This is the first resurrection:

Blessed . . . is he that hath part in the first resurrection (Apoc. xx, 6).

(2) The second is that we delay not to rise again until the time of death, but that we do so quickly, seeing that Christ rose again on the third day: *Delay not to be converted to the Lord, and defer it not from day to day* (Ecclus. v, 8); for when thou art burdened with sickness thou wilt be unable to think of those things which concern thy salvation, and also because by persisting in sin thou dost forfeit a share in all the good works that are done in the Church, besides incurring many evils. Moreover, the longer the devil possesses us, as Bede says, the more loath he is to lose his hold on us.

(3) The third is that we rise again to an incorruptible life: in other words, that we so rise as not to die again, through having the purpose not to sin again: *Christ rising from the dead dieth now no more; death shall no more have dominion over him* (Rom. vi, 9).—*So do you also reckon that you are dead to sin, but alive unto God, in Christ Jesus our Lord. Let not sin therefore reign in your mortal body, so as to obey the lusts thereof: neither yield ye your members as instruments of iniquity unto sin: but present yourselves to God as those that are alive from the dead* (ibid., 11-13).

(4) The fourth point is that we rise unto a new and glorious life by avoiding whatsoever was an occasion or a cause of death and sin: *As Christ is risen from the dead by the glory of the Father, so may we also walk in the newness of life* (ibid., 4). This new life is the life of righteousness which renews the soul and brings us to the life of glory. Amen.

SIXTH ARTICLE

HE ASCENDED INTO HEAVEN, SITTETH AT THE RIGHT HAND OF GOD THE FATHER ALMIGHTY

Furthermore we must believe in Christ's ascension; in other words, we must believe that He ascended into Heaven on the fortieth day after His resurrection: hence the words, *He ascended into heaven.* In this connection we must observe three things—namely, that it was sublime, reasonable and profitable.

(1) In the first place it was sublime, since He ascended into Heaven. This is expounded in three ways:

(a) He ascended above all the corporeal heavens: *He . . . ascended above all the heavens* (Eph. iv, 10). This was realised first of all in Christ, since hitherto there was no earthly body except on earth, in fact, even Adam was in an earthly paradise.

(b) He ascended above all spiritual heavens, i.e. above spiritual natures: *Raising (Jesus) up from the dead and setting him on his right hand in the heavenly places, above all principality, and power, and virtue, and dominion, and every name that is named, not only in this world, but also in that which is to come; and he hath subjected all things under his feet* (Eph. i, 20-22).

(c) He ascended even to the Father's throne: *Lo, one like the Son of man came with the clouds of heaven; and he came even to the Ancient of days* (Dan. vii, 13). *And the Lord Jesus after he had spoken to them was taken up to heaven and sitteth on the right hand of God* (Mark xvi, 19). Right hand is not to be taken literally, but metaphorically, when we speak of God: for Christ as God is said to sit at the right hand of the Father, i.e. in equality with the Father; while as man He sits at the Father's right hand, as being next to Him in the 'highest goods.' Now this is what the devil craved for: *I will ascend into heaven: I will exalt my throne above the stars: I will sit in the mountain of the covenant, in the sides of the north. I will ascend above the height of the clouds: I will be like the most High* (Isa. xiv, 13, 14). But Christ alone arose to that height and therefore it is said that *He ascended into heaven, sitteth at the right hand of the Father.—The Lord said unto my Lord, Sit thou at my right hand* (Ps. cix, i).

(2) Secondly, Christ's ascension was reasonable, in as much as it was *into Heaven*: and this for three reasons:

(a) Firstly, because Heaven was due to Christ according to His nature: since it is natural for a thing to return to the place whence it originated. Now Christ drew His origin from God who is above all: *I came forth from the Father, and am come into the world: again I leave the world and I go to the Father* (John xvi, 28). *No man hath ascended into heaven, but he that descended from heaven, the Son of man who is in heaven* (ibid., iii, 13). And though the saints ascend to Heaven, they do not do so

as Christ did, because Christ ascended by His own power, whereas the saints are drawn up thither by Christ. *Draw me after thee.*—
Or it may be said that no man but Christ hath ascended into
Heaven, because the saints do not ascend thither except as
members of Christ, who is the head of the Church: *Wheresoever
the body shall be, there shall the eagles be gathered together*
(Matt. xxiv, 28).

(*b*) Secondly, Heaven was due to Christ on account of His
victory. Because Christ was sent into the world in order to fight
the devil; and He overcame him: therefore He merited to be
exalted above all things: *I have overcome and am set down with
my Father on his throne* (Apoc. iii, 21).

(*c*) Thirdly, it was reasonable on account of His humility.
Because there never was so great humility as Christ's who, although He was God, chose to become man, who, whereas He
was Lord, chose to take the form of a servant, being made obedient unto death (Phil. ii, 8), and descended into the depths of
hell. Therefore He merited to be exalted to the heights of Heaven,
to the very throne of God: because humility is the road to
exaltation: *He that humbleth himself shall be exalted* (Luke xiv,
11): *He that descended is the same also who ascended above all
the heavens* (Eph. iv, 10).

(3) Thirdly, Christ's ascension was profitable: and this in
three ways:

(*a*) Firstly, as our Leader: in as much as He ascended in
order to lead us thither: because whereas we knew not the way,
He showed it to us: *He shall go up that shall open the way
before them* (Mich. ii, 13)—and in order to assure us of the
possession of the heavenly kingdom: *I go to prepare a place for
you* (John xiv, 2).

(*b*) Secondly, to increase our confidence in Him: in as much
as He ascended in order to intercede for us: *(He is able . . . to
save . . . them) that come to God by him: always living to make
intercession for us* (Heb. viii, 25). *We have an advocate with the
Father, Jesus Christ the just* (I John ii, 1).

(*c*) Thirdly, in order to draw our hearts to Himself: *Wheresoever thy treasure is, there also is thy heart* (Matt. vi, 21), so
that we may despise temporal things: hence the Apostle says
(Col. iii, 1): *If you be risen with Christ, seek the things that are*

above, where Christ is sitting at the right hand of God. Mind the things that are above, not the things that are upon the earth.

SEVENTH ARTICLE

FROM THENCE HE SHALL COME TO JUDGE THE LIVING AND THE DEAD

It belongs to the office of a king and of a lord to judge: *The king that sitteth on the throne of judgement scattereth away all evil with his look* (Prov. xx, 8). Since, then, Christ ascended into Heaven and sitteth at the right hand of God, as Lord of all, it is evident that judgement belongs to Him; and for this reason in the rule of Catholic Faith we confess that *he will come to judge the living and the dead.* The same is expressed in the words of the angels (Acts i, 11): *This Jesus who is taken up from you into heaven shall so come as you have seen him going into heaven.*

Three points must be considered in connection with this judgement. (1) The first is the form of the judgement; (2) the second is that this judgement is to be feared; (3) the third is how we are to prepare for this judgement.

(1) As regards the form of the judgement, three things are to be observed: (*a*) who will be judge? (*b*) who will be judged? (*c*) concerning what will they be judged?

(*a*) The judge is Christ: *It is he who was appointed by God to be the judge of the living and the dead* (Acts x, 42), whether we take *the dead* to signify sinners, and *the living* to signify those who live aright; or *the living* to mean literally those who will then be actually alive, and *the dead* to mean those who literally will have died. And He is judged not only as God, but also as man; and this for three reasons:

Firstly, it is necessary that those to be judged should see the judge: while the Godhead is an object of so great delight, that none can see it without joy: wherefore none of the damned will be able to see it, since then he would rejoice. Hence it is necessary that He appear in the form of man so as to be seen by all: *He hath given him power to make judgement because he is the Son of man* (John v, 27).

Secondly, because He merited this position as man: because as man He was judged unjustly, for which reason God made Him judge over the whole world: *Thy cause hath been judged as*

222

that of the wicked; cause and judgement thou shalt recover (Job xxxvi, 17).

Thirdly, that men might not lose all hope if they be judged by a man: for if God alone were judge men would lose hope through terror: *They will see the Son of man coming in a cloud* (Luke xxi, 27).

All, past, present and future will be judged: thus the Apostle (2 Cor. v, 10) says: *We must all be manifested before the judgement-seat of Christ, that everyone may receive the proper things of the body according as he hath done, whether it be good or evil.* Of the wicked, some will be condemned, but not judged: namely unbelievers whose works will not be discussed, since *he that believeth not is already judged* (John iii, 18). Some will be both condemned and judged, namely the faithful who die in mortal sin: *The wages of sin is death* (Rom. vi, 23), because on account of the faith which they had they will not be excluded from the judgement. Of the good, some will be saved and will not be judged, namely those who for God's sake are poor in spirit; indeed, they will judge others: *You who have followed me, in the regeneration when the Son of man shall sit on the seat of his majesty, you also shall sit on twelve seats judging the twelve tribes of Israel* (Matt. xix, 28), which is to be referred not only to the disciples, but also to all the poor; otherwise Paul who laboured more than the others would not be of their number: and consequently we must understand these words to refer to all who follow the Apostles, and of men with an apostolic spirit. Hence the Apostle (I Cor. vi, 3) says: *Know ye not that we shall judge the angels?—The Lord will enter into judgement with the ancients of his people and its princes* (Isa. iii, 14). Some, however, will be both saved and judged, those, namely, who die in a state of righteousness: since although they died righteous, yet through being occupied with temporal matters they fell somewhat, and therefore they will be judged, yet saved; in fact, they will be judged concerning all their works both good and bad: *Walk in the ways of thy heart . . . and know that for all these God will bring thee into judgement* (Eccles. xi, 9). *All things that are done God will bring into judgement for every error, whether it be good or evil* (ibid., xii, 14). *Every idle word that men shall speak they shall render an account for it in the day of judgement* (Matt. xii, 36). Of thoughts it is said (Wisd. i, 9): *Inquisition shall be made into the thoughts of the ungodly.* Thus it is clear what will be the form of judgement.

(2) This judgement is to be feared for four reasons.

(*a*) On account of the judge's wisdom: for He knows all, thoughts, words, and deeds, since *all things are naked and open to his eyes* (Heb. iv, 13), and *all the ways of man are open to his eyes* (Prov. xvi, 2). He also knows our words: *The ear of jealousy heareth all things* (Wisd. 1, 10), as well as our thoughts: *The heart is perverse above all things and unsearchable: Who can know it? I, the Lord who search the heart and prove the reins: who give to everyone according to his way, and according to the fruit of his devices* (Jer. xvii, 9, 10). Moreover, the witnesses will be infallible, namely men's own consciences: *Their conscience bearing witness to them: and their thoughts between themselves accusing or also defending one another, in the day when God shall judge the secrets of men* (Rom. ii, 11, 16).

(*b*) On account of the judge's power, for He is almighty in Himself: *Behold the Lord God shall come with strength* (Isa. xl, 10), and also almighty in others: *The whole world shall fight with him against the unwise* (Wisd. v, 21); hence Job said (x, 7): *Whereas there is no man that can deliver out of thy hand:* and the Psalmist (cxxxviii, 8): *If I ascend into heaven thou art there: if I descend into hell thou art present.*

(*c*) Thirdly, on account of the judge's inflexible justice. Because now is the time for mercy, whereas the time to come will be the time for justice only: wherefore the present time is ours, but the future time will be God's only: *When I shall take a time I shall judge justices* (Ps. lxxiv, 3). *The jealousy and rage of the husband will not spare in the day of revenge; nor will be yield to any man's prayer; nor will he accept for satisfaction ever so many gifts* (Prov. vi, 34, 35).

(*d*) Fourthly, on account of the judge's anger. For to the just He will present a sweet and smiling countenance: *They shall see the king in his beauty* (Isa. xxxiii, 10): whereas to the wicked He will appear angry and pitiless, so that they will say to the mountains: *Fall upon us and hide us from the . . . wrath of the Lamb* (Apoc. vi, 16). This wrath does not imply disturbance of mind in God, but the effect of wrath, namely the eternal punishment inflicted on sinners. Origen says: *How straitened will the ways of sinners be at the judgement; and yet over and above the Judge will be incensed against them.*

(3) There are four remedies against this fear:

(*a*) The first is good deeds: *Wilt thou then not be afraid of the power? Do that which is good; and thou shalt have praise from the same* (Rom. xiii, 3).

(*b*) The second is confession and repentance of the evil done: and this should include three conditions, sorrow of heart, shame in confession, and rigour of satisfaction: and these atone for eternal punishment.

(*c*) The third is almsdeeds which cleanse us from all stains: *Make unto yourselves friends of the mammon of iniquity that when you shall fail they may receive you into everlasting dwellings* (Luke xvi, 9).

(*d*) The fourth is charity, namely the love of God and our neighbour: for this *charity covereth a multitude of sins* (I Pet. iv, 8; Prov. x, 12).

EIGHTH ARTICLE

I BELIEVE IN THE HOLY GHOST

As we have said above, the Word of God is the Son of God, even as man's word is a conception of man's intellect. Now man's word is sometimes a dead word; for instance, if he thinks of what he ought to do, whereas he has not the will to do it: such is faith without works, in which case faith is said to be dead (Jas. ii, 26). But God's is a living Word: *The word of God is living* (Heb. iv, 12), and therefore in God besides the Word there is will and love: hence Augustine (*De Trin.* ix, 10) says: *The Word of which we wish to speak is knowledge with love.* Now just as the Word of God is the Son of God; so is God's love the Holy Ghost: and consequently a man has the Holy Ghost when he loves God: *The charity of God is poured forth in our hearts by the Holy Ghost who is given to us* (Rom. v, 5).

Now some through entertaining a false opinion about the Holy Ghost held Him to be a creature; that He is less than the Father and the Son; and that He is God's servant and minister.

225

Wherefore in order to condemn these errors, the holy Fathers added to the second Creed five clauses about the Holy Ghost.

In the first place although there are other spirits, namely the angels, they are God's ministers: *Are they not all ministering spirits?* (Heb. i, 14): whereas the Holy Ghost is the Lord: *God is a Spirit* (John iv, 24): *The Lord is a Spirit* (2 Cor. iii, 17): and consequently *where the Spirit of the Lord is, there is liberty* (ibid.): the reason being that He makes us love God and cease to love the world. Hence the words: *I believe in the Holy Ghost, Lord.*

Secondly, the soul's life is to be united to God, in as much as God is the life of the soul, as the soul is of the body. Now the Holy Ghost unites us to God by love, for He is Himself God's love, wherefore He gives life: *It is the Spirit that quickeneth* (John vi, 64): hence they added, *and Life-giver.* The third is that the Holy Ghost is one in substance with the Father and the Son: because just as the Son is God's Word, so the Holy Ghost is the love of the Father and Son. Consequently He proceeds from both and just as God's Word is one in substance with the Father, even so God's Love is one in substance with the Father and the Son. Hence the addition, *Who proceedeth from the Father and the Son;* whence it is evident that He is not a creature.

The fourth is that He is to be worshipped equally with the Father and the Son: *True adorers shall adore the Father in spirit and in truth* (John iv, 23). *Teach all nations, baptizing them in the name of the Father and of the Son and of the Holy Ghost.* For this reason the following clause is added: *Who, together with the Father and Son, is equally adored.*

The fifth, whereby He is declared to be equal to God, is that the holy prophets spoke on behalf of God. Now it is clear that if the Holy Ghost were not God, it could not be said that the prophets spoke on His behalf: and yet Peter states (2 Pet. i, 21) that: *The holy men of God spoke inspired by the Holy Ghost.—The Lord God hath sent me, and his Spirit* (Isa. xlviii, 16), and therefore, we have this clause added: *Who spoke by the prophets.*

Hereby two errors stand condemned: the error of the Manicheans who said that the Old Testament did not come from God: and this is false since the Holy Ghost spoke by the prophets—and the error of Priscilla and Montanus who maintained that the prophets spoke not on behalf of the Holy Ghost, but as though they were out of their minds.

We derive many fruits from the Holy Ghost.

(a) The first is that He cleanses us from our sins. The reason for this is that a thing is repaired by the same one as made it. Now the soul is created by the Holy Ghost, since by Him God makes all things: in as much as it is through loving His own goodness that God is the cause of all: *Thou lovest all the things that are, and hatest none of the things that thou hast made* (Wisd. xi, 25), in which sense Dionysius (*Div. Nom.*, iv) says: *God's love did not allow him to be barren.* Consequently the human heart which is ruined by sin must needs be restored by the Holy Ghost: *Send forth thy Spirit and they shall be created, and thou shalt renew the face of the earth* (Ps. ciii, 30). Nor need we wonder that the Spirit cleanses, seeing that all sins are forgiven through love: *Many sins are forgiven her, because she hath loved much* (Luke vii, 47). *Charity coveret all sins* (Prov. x, 12). *Charity covereth a multitude of sins* (I Pet. iv, 8).

(b) Secondly, the Holy Ghost enlightens our mind, because whatsoever we know, it is through the Holy Ghost that we know it: *But the Holy Ghost, the Paraclete, whom the Father will send in my name, will himself teach you all things and will bring all things to your mind, whatsoever I shall have said to you* (John xiv, 26). *His unction teacheth you of all things* (I John ii, 27).

(c) The Holy Ghost helps us, and to a certain extent compels us, to keep the commandments. Because none can keep the commandments unless he loves God: *If any man love me, he will keep my word* (John xiv, 23). Now the Holy Ghost makes us love God; therefore He helps us to keep the commandments: *I will give you a new heart, and I will put a new spirit within you; and I will take away the stony heart out of your flesh, and I will give you a heart of flesh. And I will put my spirit in the midst of you; and I will cause you to walk in my commandments and to keep my judgements and do them* (Ezech. xxxvi, 26, 27).

(d) He strengthens our hope of eternal life, in as much as He is a kind of surety that we shall inherit it; hence the Apostle says (Eph. i, 13): *You were signed with the Holy Spirit of promise who is the pledge of our inheritance:* for He is, as it were, a token of eternal life. The reason is that eternal life is due to a man, in as much as he is made a son of God: and this is effected through his becoming like unto Christ: and a man becomes like unto Christ through having the Spirit of Christ, and this is the Holy Ghost: *For you have not received the spirit of bondage again in fear, but you have received the spirit of adoption of sons whereby we cry: Abba (Father). For the Spirit himself giveth testimony to our spirit that we are the sons of God* (Rom. vii, 15, 16). *And because you are sons, God hath sent the Spirit of his Son into your hearts crying: Abba, Father* (Gal. iv, 6).

(*e*) He counsels us when we are in doubt, and teaches us what is God's will: *He that hath an ear let him hear what the Spirit saith to the Churches* (Apoc. ii, 17). *That I may hear him as a master* (Isa. 1, 4).

NINTH ARTICLE

I BELIEVE IN THE HOLY CATHOLIC CHURCH

As in one man there is one soul and one body, yet many members withal: even so the Catholic Church is one body, having many members. The soul that quickens this body is the Holy Ghost: and therefore after confessing our belief in the Holy Ghost, we are bid to believe in the Holy Catholic Church: hence the Creed continues—*The Holy Catholic Church.*

Here be it observed that the word *Ecclesia* (Church) signifies assembly: wherefore the Holy Church signifies the assembly of the faithful, and the individual Christian is as a member of the Church, of which it is said (Ecclus. li, 31): *Draw near to me, ye unlearned, and gather yourselves together into the house of discipline.* This Holy Church has four conditions in that she is one, holy, catholic, i.e. universal, and strong, i.e. firmly established.

(1) With regard to the first, it must be noted that although various heretics have formed themselves into various sects, they do not belong to the Church, since they are so many divisions, whereas the Church is one: *One is my dove: my perfect one is but one* (Cant. vi, 8). The unity of the Church arises from three sources.—Firstly, from the unity of faith, in as much as all Christians who belong to the body of the Church have the same

belief: *I beseech you . . . that you all speak the same thing: and that there be no schisms among you* (I Cor. i, 10). *One God, one faith, one baptism* (Eph. iv, 10).—Secondly, from the unity of hope, since all are confirmed in the hope of obtaining eternal life: wherefore the Apostle says (Eph. iv, 4): *One body, and one Spirit: as you are called in one hope of your calling.*—Thirdly, from the unity of charity, in as much as all are united in loving God, and bound to one another in mutual love: *The glory which thou hast given me, I have given to them: that they may be one as we also are one* (John xvii, 22). If this love is true it is evinced in the mutual solicitude and sympathy of the members: *That we may in all things grow up in him who is the head, even Christ: from whom the whole body being compacted and fitly joined together, by what every joint supplieth, according to the operation in the measure of every part, maketh increase of the body, unto the edifying of itself in charity* (Eph. iv, 15, 16), because each one ought to be of service to his neighbour by making use of the grace that God has bestowed upon him. Therefore no man should think it of small account or allow himself to be cut off and expelled from this Church: for there is but one Church wherein men find salvation, even as outside the Ark of Noe it was not possible for anyone to be saved.

(2) With regard to the second, be it observed that there is also another assembly, that of the wicked: *I have hated the assembly of the malignant* (Ps. xxv, 5). But this is an evil assembly, whereas Christ's Church is holy: *The temple of God is holy, which ye are* (I Cor. iii, 17); hence the words, *The holy . . . Church.* In this Church the faithful are sanctified by four things.

(*a*) In the first place, just as when a church is consecrated, it is cleansed materially, even so the faithful are washed with the blood of Christ: *He hath loved us and washed us from our sins in his own blood* (Apoc. i, 5). *Jesus, that he might sanctify the people by his own blood, suffered outside the gate* (Heb. xiii, 12).

(*b*) Secondly, they are sanctified by being anointed because, just as a church is anointed, so also are the faithful anointed with a spiritual unction unto sanctification; otherwise they would not be Christians, since Christ is the same as Anointed. This unction is the grace of the Holy Ghost: *God who hath anointed us* (2 Cor. ii, 21). *Ye are sanctified . . . in the name of our Lord Jesus* (I Cor. vi, 11).

(c) Thirdly, by the indwelling Trinity, since wheresoever God dwells, that place is holy: *Verily, this place is holy* (Gen. xxviii, 16). *Holiness becometh thy house, O Lord* (Ps. xcii, 5).

(d) Fourthly, because God is invoked over them: *But thou, O Lord, art among us, and thy name hath been called upon us* (Jer. xiv, 9).

We must, therefore, beware, seeing that we are thus sanctified, lest by sin we defile our soul which is God's temple: *If any man violate the temple of God, him shall God destroy* (I Cor. iii, 17).

(3) With regard to the third, we must observe that the Church is catholic or universal—firstly, in point of place, in that it is spread throughout the whole world, contrary to the teaching of the Donatists: *Your faith is spoken of in the whole world* (Rom. i, 8). *Go ye into the whole world and preach the gospel to every creature* (Mark xvi, 15). Formerly, God was known only in Judea, whereas now He is known throughout the whole world. In this sense the Church has three parts: one is on earth, another in Heaven, the third is in Purgatory.—Secondly, the Church is universal as regards the different conditions of humanity, in as much as no exceptions are made, for it includes master and servant, male and female: *There is neither male nor female* (Gal. iii, 18).—Thirdly, it is universal in point of time. For there have been those who said that the Church was to last until a certain time; but this is false, since this Church began from the time of Abel and will endure to the end of the world: *Behold, I am with you all days, even to the consummation of the world* (Matt. xxviii, 20), and after the end of the world it will continue in Heaven.

(4) The fourth condition is that the Church is firmly established. A house is said to be firmly established when (a) it has good foundations. Now the Church's chief foundation is Christ: *Other foundation no man can lay but that which is laid, which is Christ Jesus* (I Cor. iii, 11). The Apostles and their doctrine are the Church's secondary foundation, whence she derives her stability which is described (Apoc. xxi, 14) where it is said that the city had *twelve foundations, wherein were* inscribed *the*

names of the twelve apostles. Hence the Church is called Apostolic. Moreover, it was to indicate the stability of the Church that the Blessed Peter is called the *head.*

(*b*) Secondly, a house is proved to be firmly built, if however much it be shaken, it remains standing; and the Church has ever proved indestructible. Her persecutors have failed to destroy her; in fact, it was during times of persecution that the Church grew more and more; the persecutors themselves, and those whom the Church would destroy, these it was who came to naught: *Whosoever shall fall on this stone shall be broken; but on whomsoever it shall fall, it shall grind to powder* (Matt. xxi, 44).—Again, errors have assailed her; in fact, the greater the number of errors that have arisen, the more has the truth been made manifest: *Men corrupt in mind, reprobate in faith: but they shall proceed no further* (2 Tim. iii, 8).—Nor has the Church failed before the assaults of demons: for she is like a tower of refuge to all who fight against the devil: *The name of the Lord is a strong tower* (Prov. xviii, 10). Hence the devil does his utmost to destroy the Church: but he prevails not, for our Lord said (Matt. xvi, 18) that *the gates of hell shall not prevail against it,* as though to say: 'They will war against thee, but they shall not overcome thee.' The result is that alone the Church of Peter (to whom it befel to evangelize Italy when the disciples were sent to preach) was always strong in faith; and whereas outside that Church there is either no faith at all, or it is mingled with many errors, nevertheless the Church of Peter flourishes in faith and is immune from error. Nor need we wonder at this, since the Lord said to Peter (Luke xxii, 32): *I have prayed for thee, Peter, that thy faith may not fail.*

Nicholas de Cusa
1401-1464

Nicholas was born in Kues near Trier, Germany. He studied at Heidelberg and Padua, achieving a doctorate in Canon Law in 1423. He attended the Council of Basel in 1432. In 1450 Pope Nicholas V made Cusa a cardinal and a bishop, giving him the diocese of Brixen. But before he took over he was asked to do another job as legate to Germany. His journey through the land from 1451 to 1452 was the high-point of his life. Then for five years he worked to make Brixen a model diocese until a property dispute with Duke Sigmund of Austria forced him to leave. For the last five years of his life he was an influential adviser of Pope Pius II.

Nicholas was a universal thinker who contributed to the advancement of astronomy and mathematics as well as philosophy and theology. His all-embracing spirit was something of an anomaly in his age. Complex and controversial he straddles two historical ages, not quite belonging to either. In many ways he is a forerunner of the Renaissance, but in his political thought he is thoroughly medieval. He searches for a single unifying principle; God, not man, is the beginning and end of all activity; any legitimate social order is to be based on the double authority of Peter and Caesar.

Throughout his adult life Nicholas was deeply interested in Islam. The ominous advance of the Turks on the Eastern flank of Europe was a fact of life that no one could ignore. At the Council of Basel he had procured a copy of a translation of the Koran, and when he visited Constantinople in 1437 he made a point of acquiring St. John Damascene's works against Islam. It is difficult for us to appreciate fully the shock and horror that spread through Christendom when Constantinople fell to the Turks in May of 1453. The pope organized a Crusade and in 1455 charged Nicholas with the mission to preach it throughout Germany and England, but he was detained by his dispute with Duke Sigmund.

The conflict between Christians and Muslims represented to Nicholas the much larger problem of relations between men of the many different world religions. Could a unity be found in such diversity? Was an agreement of faiths possible? Could the scandalous evil of religious wars be prevented by some kind of consensus? This is the question Nicholas ponders in De Pace Fidei, *written in 1453, shortly after the fall of Constantinople. He imagines a heavenly convention of delegates from many nations and religions to discuss the problem.*

The work brings out certain common elements implicit in all religions, but it is far from the "least-common-denominator" approach of later Deism. Among the common doctrines on which all should be able to agree are: the necessity of God's Revelation, the Trinity, the Incarnation, and the Redemption, as well as the Eucharist. Thus the work is really one of Catholic apologetics, attempting to find features in other religions that resemble or imply Catholic doctrines. In that sense it is far from the contemporary ecumenical approach, which takes doctrinal differences more seriously. But despite his excessive optimism and glossing over of quite fundamental differences, Nicholas demonstrates an openness of spirit and a willingness to give every position a hearing that was extraordinary for the time. The understanding of the Church that runs through it is a particular point of contemporary interest. The Church is "the union of the faithful and loving in Christ." It is this faith and love, not the institutional elements, that constitute the message preached by Christ. Whatever reservations one may have about this approach, it certainly takes the "catholicity" of the Church more seriously than some of the particularist polemics of the time.

UNITY AND REFORM

CHAPTER I

Due to the news of the atrocities which had recently been reported to have taken place in a most cruel fashion at Constantinople, at the hand of the king of the Turks, a certain individual, fired with the love of God, and since he had visited the aforementioned region, prayed with much weeping and besought the Creator of all that He might, out of compassion, alleviate the persecution that was raging there because of a difference of religious rites. It happened, perchance, from a long and serious meditation on this problem, that a vision appeared to this same zealous man. In this visitation it was made clear, by reason of the experience of a number of select individuals versed in the matter of religious pluralism throughout the world, how concord might be discovered and, through it, how lasting peace based on agreeable and truthful means might be established. Hence it is, so that this vision of those who were present might be known, the author, in so far as he recalls, has clearly set it forth below. After, he was lifted up to a certain intellectual height where, as though in the company of those who had already departed from life, a discussion of this matter was held in the presence of these distinguished individuals, with the Almighty presiding. The King of Heaven and Earth then related that His messengers had brought news of the groans of those oppressed in the kingdom of this world, and that many, because of religion, were warring with one another, and that they were violently forcing others to either reject the faith to which they had so long adhered, or accept death. There were many reporters of these lamentations throughout the world, and these the King ordered to report to the entire assembly of the elect. Moreover, there were also seen here all of those whom the King Himself had, at the very beginning of the world, set in charge of all the provinces and sects of the earth. Their appearance was not anthropomorphic, but they appeared rather as intellectual agents.

Then one of the prominent individuals representing all of those assembled posed this query: "O Lord, King of the Universe, what does anyone possess that you have not bestowed upon him? It has pleased you to inspire the body of man, formed out of the slime of the earth, with a rational soul, so that in him the image of your ineffable excellence may shine forth. From one person a vast multitude has been increased so that it now inhabits the entire surface of the earth. And even though that spirit of the intellect, planted in the earth and hidden in the shadows, does not perceive the light and the beginning of its origin, nonetheless, everything else that you have created is a means by which, once being perceived by his senses, he is able from time to time to lift the eyes of his mind to you, the Creator of all things. He is thereby able to be reunited with you in sublime charity, and finally to return to his source with accomplishment.

"But you are aware, O Lord, that such a vast multitude cannot exist without a great deal of diversity, and that a large portion of this multitude is forced to live a life laden with woes and misery. They live, in many cases, subject to servility and umbrage to those who rule them. As a result, it happens that very few have sufficient leisure to enable them to proceed to a knowledge of themselves by using their own freedom of judgment. Burdened and preoccupied with the cares of the body they cannot seek you, the hidden God. It is because of this that you have provided certain leaders and overseers, whom we call prophets, for your people. A number of these, acting as your vicars and legates, have in your name formulated laws and divine cults, and instructed the uneducated in their meaning and practice. These regulations they have accepted just as if it was You yourself Who personally dictated them, and their credence was in you rather than in them. At various times you have sent various prophets and teachers, now to this nation, now to that nation. Yet human nature has this weakness, that after a long passage of time certain customs are gradually accepted and defended as immutable truths. Thus it happens that not a few dissensions grow out of the fact that some communities prefer their particular beliefs to those of other groups.

"Since you alone are all powerful, come to our aid in this matter. This rivalry comes about simply because each group seems to worship you in all that they appear to adore. No one really wants as his way of worship something that is common practice for all. To want what everyone else wants is imitation. In all those things that man seeks after, that alone is really sought which is the good, and that is You Yourself. What does the person who sees seek other than to see? He who exists, does he not endeavor to continue existing? You, therefore, who are the giver of life and of being, are that one who seems to be sought in the different rites, and who are designated with different names. For since you are Yourself an infinite power, you are something of those things that you have created, nor is any created being able to comprehend the idea of your infinity, since between the finite and the infinite there is no proportion. You can, however, O powerful God, even though you are invisible to all minds, show Yourself in any visible manner you want. Therefore, please do not conceal Yourself any longer. Be kind to us and reveal your face, and all people will be saved, who will desire all the more the artery of life, with a little foretaste of its sweetness. For no one really removes himself from you unless he is ignorant of you.

"If you would only deign to do this then the sword of envy and hatred would cease along with all other evils, and all would recognize that there is, in spite of many varieties of rites, but one religion. If, perchance, this diversity cannot be done away with, or its reduction would not be advisable, since in many cases a particular religion would actually be more vigilant in guarding what it considers to be the noblest way of manifesting its devotion to you as its King, at least just as you are God alone, so also let there be in the same manner one religion and one cult of divine worship. Therefore, O Lord, since your very anger is piety itself and your justice is mercy, be pleased with this suggestion and spare your weak creatures. We, therefore, who are your commissaries, whom you have made the custodians of your people, and, as you already know this situation, we humbly pray and beseech your majesty in the best way we know."

CHAPTER II

At this request of the archangel, since all of the heavenly body has made proper obeissance to the King, He who sat on the throne spoke forth saying that man had been entrusted to His special care, and in this capacity He had created him for His own fellowship. He pointed out that due to the fact that man walked according to the conditions of sensible life, which is nothing else than the world of the Prince of Darkness, his lower nature is detained in ignorance. In this way he acted at variance with the intellectual and interior man whose life is from the region of his origin. He then went on to say that He attempted to recall man to the right path by taking great care and diligence in sending various prophets who were, in comparison with others, His observers. Finally, when not even these prophets were able to sufficiently overcome the Prince of Ignorance, He sent His own Word through whom He created the world. The Word took on human nature so that in this way He could illuminate docile man in accordance with his free will. He wanted to see to it that man would have to walk according to his interior rather than his exterior nature, if he ever hoped to be brought to the sweetness of eternal life; and since the Word took on human nature and gave testimony of His truthfulness through His blood, He showed that man is capable of eternal life and that in attaining this his animal and sensible life is of no avail. He showed also that this eternal life is nothing other than the ultimate desire of the interior man, that is to say, the Truth which alone is sought after, and just as it is eternal it nourishes the mind eternally, and this Truth which feeds the mind is nothing other than the Word Itself, in which all things are contained, through which all things are set forth. This Word took on human nature so that every man, according to the choice of his own will and his own human nature, would not doubt that the everlasting food of Truth could be attained, and that man is also the Word. He added to this that since these things are so, "What is there that could take place and has not taken place?"

CHAPTER III

To that question of the King of Kings the Word made Flesh, Who held first place in this heavenly gathering, had this to say in behalf of all: "Father of Mercies, even though all of your works are most perfect and there is nothing that could be added to make them more complete, yet since in the very beginning you decreed that man must remain in possession of his free will, and since nothing remains unchanged in the sensible world and as from time to time opinions and conjectures change as well as language and interpretations, human nature demands frequent visitations so that the errors which many hold concerning the Word might be eliminated, and thus truth may continually shine forth. Since this Truth is one, and since it can be understood by every free mind, every diversity of religion can be reduced to one orthodox faith." This pleased the King, and summoning the angels who represented all nations and tongues, He ordered each one of them that they bring the most learned to the Word Incarnate. Very soon thereafter there appeared before the Word the more important men of this world, rapt as it were in ecstacy. The Word of God spoke to them in this way: "The Lord of Heaven and Earth has heard the groans of those who have been slaughtered and imprisoned and reduced to slavery, and who suffer because of diversity of religion. And because all of these, who either are the agents of this persecution or suffer the persecution, are motivated in no other way but that they believe that this is necessary for salvation and pleasing to the Creator, He is moved with pity towards His people and will try to reduce all diversity of religion to one that in the opinion of everyone is inviolable in its greater harmony. This task He has given to you chosen individuals by giving you, as assistants, angelic administrators from His own court who will guard you and direct you, and He has pointed out that Jerusalem should be the place most suitable for this."

CHAPTER IV

At this, one who is a little older than the others and, as it appeared, a Greek, making proper adoration, answered: "We give praise to our God whose mercy is above all His works, Who alone is able to bring it about that diversity of religion can be found in one concordant peace, Whose command we His creatures are not able to disobey. We beseech you that you instruct us how this unity of religion may be introduced by us, for a faith other than that which some nations have defended with their very blood will, as we see it, be accepted only with difficulty."

The Word answered: "You will find that it is not another faith but the very same faith which is everywhere presupposed. You who are now present, among those who speak your own language, are called wise, or at least philosophers or the lovers of wisdom."

"This is true," said the Greek, "If everyone loves wisdom, do they not presuppose the same wisdom?"

Everyone answered simultaneously that there was no doubt of this.

The Word then added: "There cannot be but one wisdom. If it were possible to have several wisdoms these would have to be from one; for before there is any plurality there must be a unity."

Greek: Certainly none of us would hesitate in this since there is one wisdom which all of us love, and because of which we are called philosophers, and even though many wise men participate in this, this wisdom remains in itself simple and undivided.

Word: You all agree, therefore, that there is but one most simple wisdom whose power is ineffable, and everyone discovers in explaining the power of this virtue that it is an ineffable and infinite force. Whenever the sight focuses itself on those things that are visible, whatever it sees it attempts to produce by reason of wisdom. The same is true of hearing, and whatever is perceived by the other senses—everything points to the fact that invisible wisdom excels all.

Greek: We who make a profession out of philosophy certainly do not love the sweetness of wisdom in any other way except insofar as we get a foretaste of it through what appeals to the senses. For who would not die to acquire this wisdom from which flows beauty, every sweetness of life, and everything that one can desire? What a great power of wisdom shines forth in the human makeup, in its members, in the coordination of its members, in the infused life and the harmony and motion of its organs, and finally, in the rational soul which is capable of so many marvellous acts, and which is, as it were, the stamp of wisdom. For in the reason eternal wisdom shines forth above all things as a mirror, approaching truth in its closest reflection, and what is even more marvellous than this, this splendor of wisdom by marvellous change enables the soul to move closer and closer to truth, until its living glow moves away from the shadow of the image and grows more in conformity with true wisdom. And even though this wisdom is never perfect, as it is, it can be perceived in another. And thus, that intellectual food might be everlasting and unfailing, we have an eternal and inexhaustible wisdom.

Word: Certainly you are advancing towards the goal we have in mind for all of you, even though you are designated in terms of different religions, yet you presuppose in all this diversity one religion which you call wisdom. But tell me, isn't all that can be expressed contained in one notion of wisdom?

CHAPTER V

The Italian answered: Certainly there is no Word outside of wisdom. The Word is the supreme wisdom and wisdom is in the Word, nor is there anything outside of it. Wisdom embraces everything that is infinite.

Word: If anyone would say that all things are in created wisdom, and if another person would say that all created things are in the Word, would they not say the same thing?

Italian: Even though there appears to be a difference in speech, yet they express the same idea, for the Word of creation, in whom all things were created, can be nothing other than His wisdom.

Word: What does this seem to you? Is this wisdom God Himself or is it a creature?

Italian: Since God as creator creates all things in wisdom, He is through necessity the wisdom of created wisdom. Wisdom must be prior to every creature, through which each creature is what it is.

Word: Thus it is that wisdom is everlasting, since it precedes every beginning and everything made.

Italian: No one can deny that what is understood precedes all beginning and is eternal.

Word: Therefore, it must be the beginning.

Italian: This is certainly true.

Word: It must also be completely uncompounded. Whatever is composite is already begun; component parts cannot exist after they have been brought together.

Italian: I admit this.

Word: Hence it is that wisdom is eternal.

Italian: This could not be otherwise.

Word: Nor is it possible that there be more than one eternal entity, since previous to all plurality there must be unity.

Italian: I don't think anyone would disagree in this.

Word: God, therefore, is wisdom, one, simple, everlasting, and the beginning of all things.

Italian: This has to be so.

Word: Then behold the fact that you as the philosophers of the various sects are in agreement, both insofar as you presuppose a belief in the religion of the one God and insofar as you profess to be the lovers of wisdom.

CHAPTER VI

Here the Arab answered: Nothing clearer or truer can be said.

Word: But just as you, since you are seekers after wisdom, profess absolute wisdom, do you think men active in intellect do not love wisdom?

Arab: I certainly think that all men seek wisdom, since wisdom is the life of the intellect, which cannot be preserved in existence by any nourishment other than the truth and the word of life, or its own intellectual bread-wisdom. Just as every existing thing seeks that without which it cannot live, so too does the intellectual life seek wisdom.

Word: All men, therefore, profess with you one absolute wisdom whose existence they profess; this is the One God.

Arab: Yes—no intelligent person could think otherwise.

Word: Then all who use their reason have one religion and cult which is at the bottom of all the diversity of rites.

Arab: You are wisdom because you are the Word of God. I would ask those who worship many gods how they can reconcile this belief with that of the philosophers in One God. For at no time are philosophers found professing a belief other than that it is impossible for there to be a plurality of gods over whom one God is not exalted; He alone is the principle from which the others have what they possess; He is far greater than simply one amongst many.

Word: All who worship many gods presuppose a divinity. This divinity they adore in all the gods as participants in it. For just as there cannot be things white without presupposing the existence of whiteness, so without the presumption of divinity there can be no gods. So the worship of many gods admits divinity. When they teach a plurality of gods, they teach one antecedent principle of them all; as those who say there are many saints must say there is one Saint of saints, in whose participation all the others are saints. Never was there a race so backward which believed in a plurality of gods and did not admit some first cause, a principle or Creator of the universe.

Arab: I agree. For it is a contradiction that there be a multiplicity of first principles. The first principle cannot be caused because it would be caused of itself and would exist before its existence—this reason cannot accept; the principle, therefore, is eternal. Nor is it possible that there be many external principles, because before all plurality there is unity. Therefore, it is necessary that there be one principle and universal cause. Nor have I yet discovered any race which has slipped from the way of truth in this matter.

Word: If then all who venerate many gods would look at that which they presuppose, namely to the deity which is the cause of everything, and would bring this deity into open adoration as reason would dictate, since they already implicitly adore it in all whom they call gods, there no longer would be any argument.

Arab: Perhaps this point would not be difficult, but to remove the worship of gods will be. For these people certainly believe that help is given them through such veneration, and for this reason they are moved to these divinities for their own salvation.

Word: But if these people were informed about salvation in the way we have mentioned, they would seek salvation in Him who gave existence and who Himself is the saviour and infinite salvation, rather than in those who of themselves have nothing except what is given them by the Saviour Himself. Suppose a people, who reverenced gods, are held in common estimation as holy because they have lived like gods—to these they would turn as intercessors in some sickness or difficulty, or even pay someone the adoration of *dulia,* or reverence his memory as a friend of God or as an example to be followed: provided only that this people would give to God the worship of *latria,* their veneration would not contradict the true religion, and they would in this way be easily reconciled.

CHAPTER VII

Indian: What then of statues and images?

Word: Those images which lead to knowledge of God and which are permitted in the true cult of the One God, these are not condemned. But when they detract from the cult of *latria* due to one God, as though in these stones there were some divinity, then because they deceive and detract from the truth, they rightly should be done away with.

Indian: It is difficult to turn a people from long accustomed idolatry because of responses and answers given to their questions.

Word: Rarely are these answers made up differently by the priests who assert the divinity has thus answered. For once a question is proposed, whether by some art through which they gain information from the universe around them, or by some chance lot, they pretend an answer ascribed to the deity, as though this were the way heaven, Apollo, or the Sun ordered them to answer. So it happens that many of their answers are ambiguous, in order the more easily to escape the charge of falsehood, or else completely false; and if sometimes the answers are true, it is simply a coincidence. When a priest is a talented guesser, he is a better divinator, and his answers are more likely to be true.

Indian: But it is certain that often some spirit of the image actually has given an answer.

Word: This is not the soul of any man, or Apollo, or Esculapius, or of anyone worshipped in place of God—it is the evil spirit, the enemy of man's salvation from the beginning, who has pretended that through human devices (though this is rare) he has been bound to this image and is forced to give answers, that he might thus practice his deceits; but after the falsehood was discovered, he ceased. So today "they have mouths but speak not." Afterwards, by actual experiment, this fallacy was discovered everywhere by intelligent men. Likewise it will not be difficult in the Orient to wipe away the error of idolatry for the invocation of the one God, so that they might conform to the other nations of the world.

Indian: Once these deceptions have been made clear, and the fact that due to such deceptions the Romans, Greeks, and Arabs wisely destroyed these images, it is to be hoped that the Indians will deal in similar fashion with their images, especially since they are an intelligent people and do not hesitate to admit the necessity of worship in the cult of One God. Even if together with this they would venerate idols in their own fashion, these idols would pertain to the adoration of the One God, and they would thus accept this peaceful conclusion. But it will be quite difficult to establish harmony everywhere about the Triune God; the concept of a Trinity without three will seem to all an impossibility. Further, if the trinity is in the divinity, then there will be a plurality in the deity. There is no plurality in an absolute deity, but only in the participants who are gods, not absolutely, but only by participation.

Word: God, as creator, is three-fold and one; as infinite, He is neither three-fold nor one, nor any name that can be offered. For the names which are attributed to God are taken from creatures, since in Himself He is ineffable and above everything which can be named. Therefore, since those who adore God should adore Him as the principle of the universe, in this universe there is found a multiplicity of parts, inequality and separation—the multiplicity of stars, trees, men, rocks, etc., is obvious—unity is the principle of multiplicity: therefore the principle of multiplicity must be eternal unity. There is found in the universe inequality in its parts, since nothing is similar to another, but inequality is a break down from the equality of unity; before an inequality, therefore, there is eternal equality. There is found further in the one universe a distinction or separation between its parts; but before every distinction there is a connection of unity and equality—and consequent to this connection comes separation or distinction; the connection, then, is eternal. Therefore, in one eternity there is unity, equality or union, and a oneness of unity and equality or a "nexus." So the principle of the universe is one and three-fold, since the thing caused derives its complexity from the cause and every caused thing finds in the principle its complexity, and in every caused thing there is found such a three-fold distinction in the unity of its essence. Therefore, the simplest principle of all will be three-fold and one.

CHAPTER VIII

Chaldean: Even if wise men could grasp a bit of this, still they would be far ahead of the common people. For, as I understand it, it is not true that there are three gods, but one, and this One God is a Trinity. Do you mean that this One is a Trinity in his power?

Word: God is the absolute power of all powers, because He is omnipotent. Since, therefore, there must be an absolute power, which is the divine essence, that power can no more be called three-fold than God can be called three-fold. But you would not thus understand power in that it is distinguished from reality, because in God power is reality itself; so too with absolute potency which is itself power. For it would not seem absurd to anyone if it would be said that divine omnipotence, which is God, has in itself a unity, which is being, equality, and a "nexus"; so with the result that the power of unity unifies or gives essence to everything which has existence (insofar as a thing exists, it is one: oneness and existence are interchangeable). The power of equality makes equal or informs everything which exists (insofar as thing is neither greater nor less than that which it is, it has equality; if it were greater or less it would not exist; without equality, therefore, there can be no existence), so the power of "nexus" brings together or joins. So omnipotence in the power of unity summons from nonexistence, so that what was not becomes capable of sharing in its existence; in the power of equality it informs, in the power of the nexus it joins, as in the essence of love you see how loving joins loved one to lover. When man is called from nonexistence through Omnipotence, first in order comes unity, then equality, then the nexus between them. For nothing can exist except it be one; first, then, it must be one. And since man is called from nonexistence, the unity of man comes first in order, then the equality of that unity or thing—for equality is the effect of the form in unity, for 'otherwiseness' does not produce equality, but only unity or identity—then from unity and equality comes love or the nexus between them. Unity and equality cannot be separated from each other. The nexus or love is so constituted that where there is unity there is equality, and no nexus exists except a nexus of unity of equality, so that the nexus is in unity and equality, equality is in the unity and the unity in equality, and unity and equality in the nexus; it is clear that in the Trinity there is no distinction of essence. For those things which differ in essence are so constituted that one can exist without the other. But because the Trinity is such that where there is unity there is equality of unity and vice-versa, and where there is unity and equality there is the nexus between them and vice-versa, so it is that not in essence but in relation are distinguished unity, equality, and the nexus. For a numerical distinction is an essential one. The concept of two differs essentially from that of three; where you have two you do not necessarily have three, and the notion of three does not follow from that of two. So the Trinity in God is not composite or numerical, but is simply unity. Those, therefore, who believe God to be One will not deny He is a Trinity when they understand that that Trinity is not different from simple unity, but is unity itself, so that were He not Trinity in Unity, He would not be the principle omnipotent to create the universe and the things in it. The more unified a power is the stronger it is; the more unified it is, the simpler it is: the more powerful, then, it is, the simpler it is. So since the divine essence is omnipotent, it is most simple and a Trinity; were He not a Trinity He would not be the principle which is at once the simplest, most powerful, and omnipotent.

Chaldean: I would think that no one could disagree with this reasoning. But the fact that God could have a Son and a partaker in His Deity is a point repudiated by the Arabians and many others with them.

Word: Some call the unity the Father, the equality the Son, and the nexus the Holy Spirit; these terms while not proper to them, conveniently signify the Trinity. For from the Father is the Son, and from the unity and equality of the Son is the love or Spirit. For the nature of the Father passes over into some equality of the Son. Therefore, love and the nexus results from unity and equality. Should simpler terms be sought, more apt ones would be unity, 'iddity,' and identity. For these terms seem more to explain the fecund simplicity of the essence. Observe that since in the essence of the rational soul there is a certain fecundity—the mind—wisdom, and love or will, in that the mind exercises the intellect or wisdom from which comes the will or love, it has this three-fold fecundity in the unity of the soul in the likeness of the uncreated Trinity. So every created thing produces an image of the creative power and has in its own way a fecundity in a close or distant likeness to the fecundity of that Trinity which is the creator of all. So the result is that not only does the creature have its being from the divine being, but a productive being in its own way three-fold from the productive being of the Three and One—without this productive being neither the world could exist nor could a creature exist in a way better than it could.

CHAPTER IX

Jew: Well have you explained the Blessed Trinity which cannot be denied. For a prophet opening this up to us briefly said he asked God how He who gave to others the productivity of generation could be Himself sterile. Although the Jews will not admit the Trinity because they think it a plurality, yet once they understand what is meant by productive simplicity, they will readily accept It.

Word: Also the Arabians and all wise men will understand that to deny the Trinity is to deny the divine productivity and creative power; and that to admit the Trinity is to deny plurality and equality of gods. For this productivity, the Trinity, makes it unnecessary that there be many gods who concur in creation, since one infinite productivity suffices to create everything creatable. The Arabians will much better be able to grasp the truth in this way rather in the way in which they assert that God has an essence and a soul and that He has a Verbum and a Spirit. For if God is said to have a soul, 'soul' can be understood only as the 'ratio' or Verbum which is God; for there is no other 'ratio' than the Verbum. And what then is the Holy Spirit but the love which is God? Of the most simple God nothing can be spoken which is not Himself. If it is true that God has a Verbum, it is true that the Verbum is God; if it is true that God has a Spirit, it is true that the Spirit is God. Of course the word 'has' is used improperly of God, because He is everything, so that what God has, He is. Therefore, the Arabians do not deny that God is a mind and from that mind generates a Verbum or Wisdom, and from these proceed a Spirit or Love. This is nothing but the Trinity explained above, and admitted by them, though many of them to not advert to the fact that they are confessing the Trinity. So in your prophets you Jews discover that by the Word of God and His Spirit the heavens were formed. Surely the manner in which the Jews and Arabians deny the Trinity must be rejected; whereas the way we have explained the Trinity should be embraced by all.

CHAPTER X

Scythian: No problem can be found in the adoration of the most simple Trinity which all who adore gods today venerate. For when wise men say that God is the Creator of both sexes and of love, they wish through this to explain in their own fashion the productive Trinity of the Creator. Others assert that the exalted God of Himself exercises intellect or reason; Him they call god of gods, and call Him creator since every created thing demands a cause and reason why it is one thing and not another. The infinite 'ratio' of all things, then, is God. This 'ratio' which is the 'logos' or Verbum, emanates from its source so that when the omnipotent Verbum produces it, there are created in actual existence what was present in the Verbum; so that if omnipotence should say, 'let there be light,' then the light present in the Verbum comes into actual existence. The Verbum of God, then, is intellectual, and insofar as a thing is conceived in the intellect as existing, it exists in reality. Then they say that the Spirit of union proceeds in third order which joins everything to one that it might be unity as the unity of the universe. For they posit a soul of the world or Spirit which joins everything, through which every creature has participation in being part of the universe. But it is necessary that this Spirit in the principle be the principle itself, for love joins. Hence this Spirit whose power is diffused through the universe, God or charity, can be called love; so that the nexus, through which the parts are joined to one or the whole, without which perfection nothing could exist, must have God as its principle. So it can be seen that wise men have touched on the Trinity in Unity; when they hear the explanation we have heard, they will certainly rejoice.

Frenchman: One time I heard this argument discussed among scholars; eternity is either unproduced or produced, or neither unproduced nor produced. Note that the uncreated eternity is reasonably called the Father Almighty, the produced eternity called the Verbum or Son, the neither unproduced nor produced eternity called love or the Holy Spirit, because He proceeds from both. He is not unproduced because He is not the Father, nor produced because He is not the Son, but proceeds from them both. There is, then, one eternity, and that is three-fold and simple; one deity, one essence, one life, one power, one strength—yet all are three-fold. In this discussion things once obscure are now made clearer than light. And since there remain in the world so many disputes, some men saying that the Word was made flesh for the redemption of all, and others with different views, there rests on us the obligation to explain to all how we have in this difficulty achieved harmony.

Word: The Apostle Peter has undertaken the exposition of this part. Listen to him; he will explain to you everything you do now know.

Peter, coming among them, began as follows:

CHAPTER XI

Peter: These are the variations in the different views of the Incarnate Word. First, some say that the Word of God is not God. This has been treated sufficiently, for the Word of God cannot be but God. This Word is reason; for *logos* is the Greek word for reason. That God, who is the creator of all rational souls and spirits, has reason, is beyond doubt. This reason of God is only God, as has been said before, for in God possession and being are the same. For He from whom come all things embraces all things and is all in all, because He is the former of all; therefore, he is form of forms. The form of forms has within himself all formable forms. Therefore the Word, or reason, the infinite cause and measure of all that can exist, is God. Therefore, they who admit that the Word of God is incarnate or made man must admit that that man whom they call the Word of God is also God.

The Persian said: Peter, the Word of God is God. How could God, who is immutable, become not God but man and the creator a creature? Almost all of us, except for a few in Europe, deny this. If there are some among us who are called Christians, they agree with us that this is impossible, that what is infinite is finite and what is eternal is temporal.

Peter: I deny as vigorously as you that the eternal is temporal. But when all of you who follow the law of the Arabs say that Christ is the Word and God—and you say well—you must also admit that He is God.

Persian: We admit that He is the Word and the Spirit of God, for of all who live or have lived no one else had that excellentness of being Word and Spirit of God; but we do not admit therefore that He was God, for God has no co-sharer. Therefore, lest we have a plurality of gods, we deny that He is god but we admit that He is very close to God.

Peter: Do you believe there is human nature in Christ?

Persian: We believe it, and we declare that it was true human nature and remained so in Him.

Peter: Fine! Because this nature was human, it was not divine. And, therefore, in everything which you see in Christ, according to this human nature by which He was like to other men, you see not Christ as God but Christ as man.

Persian: That is correct.

Peter: No one disagrees with you on this point. Human nature was in Christ most perfectly; by it He was true man and also mortal, like other men; according to that nature He was not the Word of God. Now tell me: when you admit that He was the Word of God, what do you mean?

Persian: Not nature but grace; that is, He received the extraordinary grace of having God put His Word in Him.

Peter: Did not God in similar fashion put His Word in other prophets? For all of them spoke with the word of the Lord and were announcers of the Word of God.

Persian: That is true. But Christ was the greatest of the prophets; therefore it more befits Him to be called the Word of God than the other prophets. As an example, many letters can contain the word of a king in regard to particular dealings or in particular provinces; but only one letter has the word of the king that rules the whole kingdom, namely the letter that contains the laws and precepts which all are bound to obey.

Peter: You seem to have given a good example to show this, namely that the word of the king, written in various letters, does not change the letters into other natures, for their nature remains the same after the word was written in them as they were before. This is how you say that human nature remained in Christ.

Persian: That is what we say.

Peter: Alright. But note the difference between letters and the heir of the kingdom. In the heir of the king is properly the living and free and unlimited word of the king, but not at all in letters.

Persian: I admit that. If the king sends his heir into the kingdom, the heir carries the living and unlimited word of the king.

Peter: Is not the heir properly the word and not the messenger or commissariat or a letter or a missive? And are not all the words of letters and messengers in the word of the heir? And, although the heir is not the father but the son, he has the nature of the king, and by this equality is the heir.

Persian: I understand that. But a difficulty is that the king and his son are two, therefore, we do not admit that God has a Son. For the Son would be a different God from the Father, just as the son of a king is a different man than his father.

Peter: Your objection against the similitude is a good one, for it is not an exact one if you look at the persons. But if you remove the numerical diversity of the persons and look at the power which resides in the royal dignity of the Father and His heir, the Son, you see how that royal power is one in the Father and in the Son; in the Father as in one unbegotten, in the Son as in one begotten, or the living Word of the Father.

Persian: Continue.

Peter: Suppose, then, that there is such an absolute unbegotten and begotten royal power, and that such an unbegotten power summons to association in the connatural begotten succession one who is different by nature, so that a different nature in union with his own possesses the kingdom at the same time and undividely. Do not the natural and gratuitous or adoptive successions concur in one heirship?

Persian: That is certain.

Peter: In the same fashion filiation and adoption are united in one succession to one kingship, but the succession by adoption exists not in itself but in the succession of filiation. For if an adoption, which succeeds not in itself, must succeed when there is filiation, then it follows that he who succeeds by nature does so not in himself but in the filiation. Therefore, if adoption, in order to succeed with filiation in the acquiring of a completely simple and indivisible heirship, gets succession not from itself but from filiation, the adoptive and the natural successor will not be different even though the nature of adoption or of nature are different. For if the adopted one were separated and not having the same hypostasis as the natural heir, how would they concur in the succession of an indivisible heirship? Therefore, in Christ it must be held that human nature is so united with the Word or divine nature that the human nature does not pass into the divine but clings so indissolubly with it that it is a distinct person not in itself but in divine nature; so that the human nature, summoned to succeed to eternal life with the divine nature, can acquire immortality in the divine nature.

CHAPTER XII

Persian; I understand that well. But clarify what you have said by another understandable similitude.

Peter: Precise similitudes cannot be given. But try this one: Is wisdom in itself an accident or substance?

Persian: In itself, a substance; as it occurs in another, an accident.

Peter: But all wisdom in all wise persons comes from that wisdom which exists by itself, since it is God.

Persian: This has been set forth.

Peter: Is not one man wiser than another?

Persian: Yes, indeed.

Peter: Therefore, he who is wiser is closer to wisdom-per-se, which is absolutely the greatest; he who is less wise, is farther from it.

Persian: Yes.

Peter: But no man is, according to human nature, so wise that he cannot be wiser, for between received wisdom, that is human wisdom, and wisdom-per-se, which is divine and the greatest and infinite, there is always an infinite distance.

Persian: That, too, is very clear.

Peter: It is similar in regard to absolute and received mastership, for in absolute mastership there is infinite art, in received mastership finite art. Suppose, then, that someone's intellect has such a mastership and such wisdom that it is not possible to have greater wisdom or greater mastership; in that case his intellect is most closely united with wisdom-per-se or mastership-per-se, so that that union could not be greater. Has not that intellect, by virtue of the greatest wisdom and the greatest mastership to which it is united, acquired divine power, and is not the human intellectual nature in a man who has such an intellect most immediately united to divine nature or eternal wisdom, to the Word or omnipotent art?

Persian: I grant all this. But this union, nonetheless, is one of grace.

Peter: When so great a union exists of an inferior nature to a divine one that it could not be greater, then it would be united to it also in personal union. For as long as an inferior nature is not elevated to personal and hypostatic union with the higher nature, it could be greater. Therefore, if it is the greatest, the interior nature subsists by clinging to the higher one; and this occurs not by nature but by grace. This greatest grace, however, which cannot be greater, does not differ by nature but is united with it. Therefore, even if human nature is united with the divine by grace, nevertheless that grace, since it cannot be greater, most immediately terminates in nature.

Persian: In whatever way you say it, since human nature can be elevated by grace to union with the divine in any man, the man-Christ can no more be said to be God than any other man, even though he is the most holy of men.

Peter: If you see in Christ only the loftiest height which cannot be greater, and the greatest grace which cannot be greater, and the greatest holiness, and so on in respect to everything else, you would see that the height cannot be more than one, and similarly with respect to grace and holiness. After this you would see that all loftiness in every prophet, whatever degree it has, differs improportionally from that loftiness which cannot be greater, so that, granted any degree of loftiness, between it and the only highest one there can be an infinite number of degrees higher than the given one, and lower than the highest one. So, too, with regard to grace, holiness, prudence, wisdom, mastership, and everything. Then you would see clearly that Christ can be the only one in whom nature is united in unity of person to the divine nature. This even the Arabs admit, although many do not think it through. For Arabs say that Christ alone is most lofty in this world and the next, and is the Word of God, and they who call Christ God and man say nothing else than that Christ alone is the greatest man and the Word of God.

Persian: It seems that, when that union which is necessary in the highest one is properly considered, that the Arabs can be brought to accept this belief, because by it the oneness of God, which they fight strongly to maintain, is not hurt but preserved. But tell me how it can be that human nature is personified not in itself but by being united with the divine.

Peter: Here is an example, but a farfetched one. A magnet draws iron upwards and by adhering to the metal of the magnet the nature of iron subsists not in its weighty nature—otherwise it would not hang in the air but would, according to its nature fall to the ground—but in virtue of the magnet the iron, by adhering to the magnet, subsists in the air and not by virtue of its own nature, according to which it could not be there. The reason why the nature of the iron is so inclined to the nature of the magnet is that the iron has in itself a likeness to this nature of the magnet, from which it is said to have its origin. In like manner, when human intellectual nature clings closely to divine intellectual nature from which it has received its existence, it clings to it inseparably as to the font of its life.

Persian: I understand.

Peter: The greater number of the Arabs admit that Christ raised the dead to life, and created flying beings from mud, and many other things which they expressly confess that Jesus Christ made like one having power; from which they can easily be led, since it cannot be denied that He did this in virtue of the divine nature to which His human nature was personally united. For the power of Christ, by which He ordered the doing of those things which the Arabs admit He did, could not have been according to human nature unless that human nature had been assumed in union with the divine nature, to the power of which it belongs to give such orders.

Persian: All this and more is affirmed of Christ by the Arabs, and they are written in the Koran. But it will be harder to bring the Jews to believe all this than other persons, because they admit nothing expressly of Christ.

Peter: They have all these statements relative to Christ in their scriptures, but, following the letter, they do not want to understand. But this resistance among the Jews will not hinder concord. For they are not numerous and they cannot by weapons disturb the whole world.

CHAPTER XIII

At this point the Syrian said: "Peter, I heard above that concord can be found in every sect from what is presupposed. Tell us how that statement can be verified in this point."

Peter: I shall tell you. But first tell me: Is not God alone eternal and immortal?

Syrian: I believe this, for everything besides God has a beginning. Hence, since it has a beginning, it will, in accordance with its nature, have an end.

Peter: Does not almost every religion—Jewish, Christian, Arabic, and most other men hold that the human moral nature of every man will, after its temporal death, arise to eternal life?

Syrian: Yes.

Peter: All such persons, therefore, admit that human nature will be united to the divine and immortal one. For how could human nature pass on to immortality if it did not cling to it in an inseparable union?

Syrian: Belief of the resurrection necessarily presupposes this.

Peter: Therefore, if faith holds this, then human nature in some man is previously united to divine nature, in Him, who is the figure of all men and the loftiest Messias and Christus, insofar as the Arabs and Jews call him Christ. He, according to

everyone the closest to God, will be in whom the nature of all
men is priorily united to God. For that reason He is Saviour and
mediator of all men, in whom human nature, which is one and
by which all men are men, is united to the divine and immortal
nature, so that in this way all men of the same nature receive
resurrection from the dead.

Syrian: I understand that you insist that faith in the resurrection from the dead presupposes union of the divine and
human natures, without which this faith would be impossible;
and you say that this union is in Christ; wherefore faith presupposes Christ.

Peter: You've got it. Hence, except that all the promises
made to the Jews are kept in the faith in the Messiah or mediator,
by Whom alone the promises that concern eternal life could and
can be fulfilled.

Syrian: What about other sects?

Peter: In the same way. For all men desire and expect eternal life only in their human nature, and they instituted purgation
of souls and sacred rites so that they may, in better fashion, fit
themselves for eternal life in their own nature; a man wishes only
to be a man, not an angel or another nature; but he wishes to be
a blessed man and to obtain eternal happiness. This happiness is
nothing else than the enjoyment, that is union of human nature
with its font, which flows its life, and this is divine immortal life.
How could this be possible for a man unless it is conceded that
the common nature of all men is elevated to   such a union in
some person, by whom as mediator, all men can acquire the
ultimate of desires? And He is the way because He is the man
by whom every man has access to God, Who is the goal of
desires. Christ, therefore, is the One who is presupposed by all
men who hope to acquire final happiness.

Syrian: This is very welcome. For if human intellect believes
that it can acquire union with wisdom, where it can receive the
eternal food for its life, it presupposes that the intellect of some
lofty man has acquired that union and has received this loftiest
mastership by which it similarly hopes it will at some time arrive
at that wisdom. For if it did not believe it possible in some most
lofty one of men, it would hope in vain, and since the hope of
all men is that they will sometime acquire happiness—for which

reason every religion exists—and since it cannot be deceived in this—for this hope is in everyone from a connate desire and to it every religion, which likewise is in common connate in everyone, aims—I see that this master and mediator, who holds the supremity of human perfection and its principate, is presumed by everyone. But perhaps the Jews say that this prince of nature in whom all defects of all men are made up for, has not yet been born but will sometime be born.

Peter: It is enough that both Arabs and Christians, and others, who have given witness in their blood, testify, by what the prophets have said of Him, and by what He did above the powers of men when He was in the world, that He has come.

CHAPTER XIV

Spaniard: There will, perhaps, be another difficulty regarding the Messiah, whom the greater part of the world admits has come, since Christians and Arabs assert that He was born of the Virgin Mary, while others hold that this is impossible.

Peter: All who believe that Christ has come hold that He was born of a virgin. For, since He is the ultimate of the perfection of nature and alone most high, of what fathers must He be the son? For every father who begets in perfection of nature differs from the ultimateness of perfection in such a fashion that he cannot communicate to his son the ultimate perfection, than which a higher cannot be and which is not possible except for one man. Only that Father can do this Who is Creator of nature. The most high person, therefore, has only Him for Father from Whom is all paternity. By divine power, therefore, was the most lofty One conceived in the womb of a virgin, and in this virgin there went together with virginity the most lofty fecundity. Hence, Christ was so **born** to us that He is almost joined to all men. For He has Him **as** Father from whom every father of a man has it that he is a father; and He has her as mother who is joined carnally to no man; so that thus each man may find by a most close connection in Christ his nature in its ultimate perfection.

Turk: There is still another not small difference, for Christians say that Christ was crucified by the Jews, but others deny this.

Peter: That some deny Christ's crucifixion, but say that He still lives and will come at the time of the Anti-Christ, is because they are ignorant of the mystery of death, and because He will come, as they say, they believe that He will come in mortal flesh, as if otherwise He could not conquer the Anti-Christ. And the denial of Christ's crucifixion by the Jews seems to come for their reverence for Christ, as though such men could not have had power over Christ. But notice that we ought to believe the many accounts of Him and the preaching of the Apostles who died for this truth, that is, that Christ did so die. The prophets, too, told of Christ: how He would die a shameful death, which was the death of the Cross. The reason is this: Christ came, sent by God the Father to preach the good news of the Kingdom of Heaven, and of that Kingdom He said things that could not be proved better than by the witness of His blood. Hence, that He might be most obedient to God the Father and might give all certainty to the truth which He announced, He died. He died a shameful death so that no man might refuse to receive this truth, in witness of which they would know that Christ voluntarily accepted death. For He preached the Kingdom of Heaven, telling how a man, capable of that Kingdom, might come to it. In comparison with that Kingdom this life in this world, which is so tenaciously longed for by all men, is to be regarded as nothing. And that they might know that truth is the life of that Kingdom, He gave the life of this world for truth, that thus He might preach the good tidings of the Kingdom of God and free the world from that ignorance which prefers this life to the life of the future. For this purpose He offered Himself in sacrifice for many, and was lifted up upon the Cross in the sight of all, that He might draw all to believe. He has made clear the message of the Gospel, and comforted the weak of heart. He gave Himself freely in the redemption of many, and all of this He did in the best possible manner, so that mankind would attain the faith of salvation, the hope of acquiring it, and the love necessary for fulfilling the Commandments of God. If, therefore, the Arabs would look to the result of Christ's death, and if they would consider the fact that Christ considered Himself as one sent by God to perform this self-immolation, and in so doing to fulfill the will of the Father, they would not deny the glory of the Cross of Christ.

If they would consider that nothing was more glorious to Christ than to die out of a love of truth and obedience, even a most detestable death, they would not take away this great regard for the Cross of Christ, whereby He merited to be the greatest of men and the most exalted in the splendor of the Father. Finally, if Christ in His preaching proclaimed that man would obtain immortality after death, how could He have more perfectly given proof of this than by Himself undergoing death, and then rising again and appearing as one alive? The world was finally convinced of this when mankind heard the testimony of many witnesses that Christ had died openly on the Cross and had risen from the dead, and was living again. Those who saw this testified with their own death as witnesses to His Resurrection. This, therefore, was the most perfect way of spreading the Gospel, which Christ demonstrated in Himself. Who, therefore, believes that Christ fulfilled the will of the Father in a most perfect manner, must also make a public confession of all these things, without which this spreading of the Gospel would not have been most perfect. Consider the fact that the Kingdom of Heaven was hidden from everyone until the time of Christ. This is the Gospel of Christ, namely to announce this unknown Kingdom to all. For there was no faith, no hope of attaining the Kingdom of Heaven, nor could it have been loved by anyone when it was entirely unknown, nor was it possible that anyone could have obtained this Kingdom, since before this time human nature had not been elevated to a position where it could have been a consort with the divine nature. Christ, therefore, opened the Kingdom of Heaven in every way possible, but the Kingdom of Heaven can be entered by none until they leave the kingdom of this world through death. It is necessary, consequently, that all mortals lay aside mortality, that is, the ability for dying, and this cannot take place unless through death; then and then alone can one put on immortality. Christ, as a mortal man, if He had not died, would never have done away with mortality and, therefore, He would never have entered the Kingdom of Heaven, in which it is impossible for any mortal thing to exist. If, therefore. He who is the foremost and first born of all men had not opened the Kingdom of Heaven, our nature, united with God, would not have been introduced into this Kingdom. Thus it is that no mere human being could be found in this Kingdom, since our human nature united to God had not yet taken place. Everybody admits that the contrary of this is true if they give credence to the existence of this King, for all believe that the holy ones of their particular belief have ascended to happiness; therefore, the belief of all those who hold that their saints enjoy the happiness of heaven presupposes that Christ has died and ascended into heaven.

CHAPTER XV

German: Certainly everything that you say is well said, but I feel that in the matter of happiness not a few discrepancies will be encountered, for it is alleged that the Jews are promised in their law nothing but temporal things which consist in pleasures of the sense. The promises that are made to the Arabs from their law, which is written in their Koran, are nothing other than perpetual carnal pleasures. The Gospel, on the other hand, promises a sort of angelic reward in that men will become as angels, who are certainly not carnal.

Peter: What can possibly be thought of in this world, the desire of which does not decrease but rather continually increases?

German: All temporalities wither away, it is only things of the mind that perdure. These—eating, drinking, and everything that savors of luxury—even though they occasionally are pleasing, are also in themselves unreliable and the cause of displeasure. To know, to comprehend, and to look upon truth with the mind's eye, affords lasting pleasure, and the older a person becomes the more does the lack of these truths grieve him, and the more he acquires of them the greater is his desire for increasing them.

Peter: If, therefore, desire is perpetual and is, as it were, a continuing nourishment, it must be a kind of food for the intellectual life rather than something temporal and sensible, and, therefore, even though there is to be found in the law of the Koran a promise of Paradise, consisting of rivers of wine and honey and a great multitude of damsels, yet there are many even in this world who would not find pleasure in this, so how could they possibly be happy if they acquire in heaven those things that even here below are not the object of their desires? It says,

261

for example, in the Koran, that many beautiful black damsels are to be found, who have large and white eyes. Now certainly no German in this world, even if he were given over to the vices of the flesh, would care for women of this description. Consequently, it ought to be clear that this has to be understood in a kind of allegorical way, for in another place the Koran forbids the presence of concubines in churches and synagogues, or do you suppose that the mosques are more holy places than Paradise? How could these things be prohibited in the mosques and at the same time be allowed in Paradise? In another place we read that heaven will contain all of those things that are required for a complete fulfillment of our pleasures. In this, what is said is tantamount to saying that all these other things will be found, for because these things are generally desired in this world it is presupposed that in the next world there will be an equal desire, and that then they will be found more exquisitely and abundantly, otherwise, without this simile, it would be impossible to explain that this life will be the completion of all desires. The author of the Koran did not wish to instruct the uneducated populace with a lot of hidden meanings, but only with terms that would seem desirable to their senses. He did this since the populace, not being able to really appreciate the things of the spirit, might possibly depreciate all the promises. The chief reason and the main concern of the author of the Koran was to turn the populace away from idolatry, and for this purpose he made these promises, as well as the other things that he wrote. On the other hand, he did not condemn the Gospel, rather he praised it and pointed out that the happiness that is promised in the Gospel is greater than any corporeal happiness. The more intelligent and wise know among themselves that this is true. Avicenna prefers the intellectual happiness of the vision or fruition of God, and incomparably the truth to the happiness, that is described in the law of Abraham, who was under this same law. The same can be said of other wise men. It must be admitted, therefore, that this happiness is beyond whatever can be written or said, since the fulfillment of every desire and the attainment of good is found in its origin, just as fulfillment of life is found in immortality.

German: What about the Jews who do not accept the promise of the Kingdom of Heaven, but rather place their trust only in temporal things.

Peter: The Jews have often undergone death in the observation of their law and its holiness, therefore, if they had not believed that they would secure happiness after death, since they prefer upholding the law to life itself, they would not have died. It is not part of Jewish belief that there is no eternal life, or that it is unattainable, otherwise none of them would have died for the law; rather the happiness that they expect they do not expect from the works of the law, since these works do not promise happiness, but they expect happiness from faith, which as we have already said before, presupposes a belief in Christ.

CHAPTER XVI

Tartar: I have certainly heard many things here that were previously not known to me. Many honest Tartars cherish the one God, as many admire the different rites of others and love the same God along with them, nevertheless, it is true that they ridicule certain of the Christians, and all of the Arabs and circumcised Jews, those who are signed with facial burns as well as those who are Baptised. Finally, in the matter of marriage, there is a great deal of diversity. Some have only one wife, others believe in a single marriage but maintain a number of concubines, while still others have a number of legitimate wives; with regard to sacrifices there are so many different opinions that they cannot be related. Among these various rites that have been mentioned, the sacrifice of the Christians, which involves the offering of bread and wine and which they say is the body and blood of Christ, and which, after they offer it to Him, they eat and drink, this appears the most abominable. They actually devour whom they love. How there could possibly be any kind of union in these things which vary from place to place and from time to time is something that I cannot comprehend. And yet, unless there is some kind of union, persecution will not cease. Diversity of religion produces division and enmities, hatreds and war.

Thereupon Paul, a teacher of the Gentiles, rose up, and by the authority of the Word, spoke the following:

Paul: It is necessary that we show that salvation of the soul is not obtained by works, but rather from faith, for Abraham, the father of the faith of all those who believe, whether Arab, Christian, or Jew, believed in God, and he was considered as being justified. The soul of the just will inherit life everlasting. Once this is admitted, these varieties of ritual will not be a cause of dissension, for as sensible signs of the truth of belief these things that have been instituted and received as signs are capable of change, not so the thing that is signed.

Tartar: Tell us how, then, does faith save?

Paul: If God should promise certain things because of His liberality and generosity, should not He, Who is able to provide all things and Who is truth, be believed?

Tartar: I'll have to admit that. No one can possibly be deceived who believes Him, and if he fails to believe Him he would not be worthy of obtaining any gift.

Paul: What, therefore, justifies him who obtains justice?

Tartar: Not merits, otherwise this would not be something gratuitous, but rather a debt.

Paul: Very well put, but because no living person can be justified through works in the sight of God, but only gratuitously, the Omnipotent gives whatsoever He will to whomsoever He will. Then, if anybody would be worthy to acquire a promise that was purely gratuitous, it is necessary that he believed in God. It is in this, therefore, that he is justified, because from this alone will he obtain the promise, because he believes in God and expects the Word of God to take place.

Tartar: After God has promised something it is certainly just that He keeps His promises. The person who believes Him is justified rather through the promise than through its faith.

Paul: God, Who promised the seed of Abraham, in which all were to be blessed, justified Abraham, that he might acquire the promise. But if Abraham had not believed in God he would have obtained neither justification nor the promise.

Tartar: I agree with that.

Paul: The faith, therefore, in Abraham was only this, that the fulfillment of the promises was just, because otherwise it would not have been just, nor fulfilled.

Tartar: What did God promise?

Nicholas de Cusa

Paul: God promised Abraham that He would give him this one seed in the person of Isaac, in which seed all races would be blessed, and this promise actually took place. Since according to the ordinary laws of nature it was impossible for Sarah, his wife, to conceive or give birth, yet because he believed he acquired a son, Isaac. Later on God tempted Abraham, in that He asked him to offer and slay the boy Isaac, in whom His promise of the seed had been fulfilled. And Abraham obeyed God, believing no less in the future promise, even though it would involve the resucitation of his dead son. When God discovered this faith in Abraham, then he was justified, and the promise was fulfilled in this one seed which descended from him through Isaac.

Tartar: What is this seed?

Paul: It is Christ, for all races have obtained in Him a divine blessing.

Tartar: What is this blessing?

Paul: The divine blessing is that final desire for happiness which we call eternal life, about which you have already heard.

Tartar: Do you desire, therefore, that God should promise us the blessing of eternal life in Christ?

Paul: That is what I wish. For if you believe in this same way you will be justified along with the faithful Abraham, and obtain the promise that was found in the seed of Abraham, Christ Jesus, and that promise is the divine blessing.

Tartar: Do you mean to say, therefore, that this faith alone justifies and enables us to attain of eternal life?

Paul: I do.

Tartar: How can you possibly get this idea across to the simple minded Tartars, so that they can understand that it is Christ in whom they can attain happiness?

Paul: You have already heard that not only Christians but also the Arabians profess that Christ is the very highest of all those who have ever been or ever will be in this world, and that He is the figure of all the races. If, therefore, the blessing of all races is found in one seed, how can it be any other than Christ?

Tartar: Could you give me some kind of proof for this statement?

Paul: As a proof I would rely on the combined testimony of the Arabs and the Christians, that the spirit that brings life to the dead is the spirit of Christ. If, then, the spirit of life is found alone in Christ, Who is able to vivify whom He wishes, He must also be the same spirit without Whom no one is able to raise the dead, and without Whom no spirit can live eternally. For the fullness of divinity and grace dwells in the spirit of Christ, and it is from this same fullness that all who are to be saved receive the grace of salvation.

Tartar: It is pleasing to hear this remark from you, O Teacher of the Nations, for this is in accordance with what has previously been discussed. I see that this belief is necessary for salvation, and that without it no one can be saved. However, I would like to ask now whether this belief is all that is necessary.

Paul: It is quite impossible to please God without faith. It is necessary, however, that this belief be, as it were, activated, for without works it remains dead.

Tartar: What, then, are these works?

Paul: If you believe in God, you will obey His Commandments. For how can you believe that God is really God unless you take care to keep His laws?

Tartar: It is certainly fitting that they should keep the Commandments of God. But it is a fact that the Jews claim that they have received His Commandments from Moses, the Arabs from Mohammed, the Christians through Jesus, and the other various nations venerate their own prophets, from whom they claim to have received the divine precepts. Since this is the case, how can they ever arrive at any concord?

Paul: I think that you will have to agree that the divine mandates are very brief and well known to all, and that they are the common heritage of all nations. In fact, the light that makes them so evident to all of us is created along with the creation of the rational soul. The voice of God speaks forth in all of us, urging that we love Him from Whom we have received our very being, and urging that golden rule, that we do not do unto others what we would not wish them to do to us. Love, therefore, is the fulfillment of divine legislation, and all other laws can be traced to this source.

Tartar: I have no doubt that both the faith of which you speak, as well as the law of mutual charity would be acceptable to the Tartars. However, the question of rites poses many problems. For example, the question of circumcision, a ritual that they ridicule, would hardly be acceptable.

Paul: The acceptance of circumcision is really not pertinent to the truth of salvation. In fact, circumcision does not save any individual, and certainly without it one may attain salvation. Yet whoever does not hold that circumcision is a requisite for reasons of health, but allows it to be performed on his foreskin so that he might be in conformity with Abraham and his followers, will certainly not be condemned for this action, as long as he holds to this basic faith which we are discussing. Thus, for example, Christ was circumcised, as well as many other Christians who lived after Him. The Ethiopians mentioned by St. James and others were not circumcised in the sense that they considered this a sacrament necessary for salvation. The real problem in this matter is how we may preserve peace among the various believers, if some are circumcised and some are not. The fact of the matter is that the great majority of the world's population is not circumcised, and I would contend that circumcision is not a matter of necessity. In my judgment, peace would be better preserved if the minority would conform to the majority with whom they are already united in basic belief. Yet, on the other hand, if for the purpose of maintaining peace the majority should conform to the will of the minority and receive circumcision, it should be done in an arbitrary fashion, so that tranquility might rest on a firmer basis because of this interchange of common practices. In this way, if some nations accepted the basic beliefs of the Christians, and the Christians, on the other hand, allow themselves to be circumcised in order to maintain the peace, its foundation will be better secured. Nonetheless, I think there will be practical difficulties in this. It will suffice that there be unanimity in the matter of belief and the law of charity, and that toleration in the matter of ritual be allowed.

CHAPTER XVII

Armenian: Since you hold that Baptism is a matter of necessity among Christians, how do you propose to explain this?

Paul: Baptism is the sacrament of faith. Whoever believes that it is possible to obtain a certain justification will also believe that through Him there is a taking away of sins. The believer will manifest this in the cleansing that is signified in the Baptismal lotion. For Baptism is nothing other than a profession of his belief in a sacramental sign. He could hardly be called a believer who refused to profess, both verbally and according to the signs instituted by Christ for this purpose, his belief in Him. The idea of religious ablutions, or washings, is common to both the Jews and the Arabs; hence there would be no difficulty in accepting an ablution instituted by Christ as a manifestation of their belief.

Armenian: I can see how it is quite necessary to receive this sacrament, since it is required for salvation.

Paul: Faith is certainly a matter of necessity for adults, who can, nevertheless, be saved without the sacrament when it is impossible to receive it. When, however, they are in a position to receive the sacrament, we can hardly call them believers if they refuse to act as believers in rejecting the sacrament of regeneration.

Armenian: What about the case of children?

Paul: There will be no difficulty in coming to agreement on the matter of infant Baptism. If it was allowed that they undergo circumcision on the eighth day, this practice could be commuted to Baptism, and it would be an optional matter whether they wanted it to be included in the Baptismal rite.

CHAPTER XVIII

Bohemian: I can see that it is quite possible that we can reach agreement in everything that has been discussed up to this point, but I think that there will be a great deal of difficulty in the matter of sacrifices. I know that Christians, holding as they do that the oblation of the bread and wine is held to be the sacrament of the Eucharist, will not be inclined to compromise this belief just to please others. Certain other nations, since they do not hold to this idea of sacrifice, will present difficulties not easily overcome. This situation is further complicated by the fact that they consider the conversion of the bread and wine into the flesh and blood of Christ as something quite insane, especially the eating and drinking of these elements.

Paul: This sacrament of the Eucharist has no other significance than that, as a favor from Christ, we can obtain the nourishment of eternal life, just as in this life we are nourished on bread and wine. Since we believe that Christ is the food of our mind, then we believe also that we receive Him under the appearance of eating. And since it is necessary that we be of one mind in this belief, that we obtain the food of eternal life in Christ, why not demonstrate this by our belief in the sacrament of the Eucharist? It is to be hoped that all who believe will want to taste of this food, through faith, which will in fact, be the food of eternal life in the other world.

Bohemian: How are you going to persuade all these various peoples that the substance of the bread is changed into the body of Christ in the sacrament of the Eucharist?

Paul: Whoever really believes knows that the Word of God in Christ Jesus has transferred us from the misery of this world to adopted sons of God, and to the possession of everlasting life, because for God nothing is impossible. If we believe and hope in this, then we do not hesitate at all to believe that the Word of God, in arrangement with Christ, can change bread into flesh. If nature herself does this in the case of animal life, how should it be impossible to the Word, through which God has created the entire world? It is a matter of faith, then, that we believe this. For if it is impossible that we, as children of Adam, who are made of the slime of the earth, can be transformed in Christ Jesus, the Word of God, into the sons of an immortal God, and if we truly believe and hope in this, that we shall then be like Christ Jesus, the Word of God the Father, then it seems reasonable enough that we, in a similar fashion, give credence to the transubstantiation of bread into flesh and wine into blood through the same Word—the Word through Whom bread is bread, wine is wine, flesh is flesh, blood is blood, and through Whom in nature food is changed into the nourished.

Bohemian: I still find that this changing of the substance of the bread is a difficult thing to handle.

Paul: You will believe this more easily with faith, for this can only be touched upon with the mind. Our reason perceives that something exists, and not what it actually is; the substance preceeds every accident. Hence it is that this substance has neither quality nor quantity, and it alone is changed so that it is no longer the substance of the bread but the substance of the flesh, and this changeover is one of a spiritual nature, which is the farthest removed from what is perceptible to the senses. Consequently, there is no increase in the quantity of the flesh, nor is it numerically multiplied. For this reason there is but one substance of flesh into which the substance of the bread has been changed, although bread be offered in many places, and there be many particles of bread used in the sacrifice.

Bohemian: As far as to the manner in which this sacrament is one of food for eternal life, and as to how, through it, we attain our inheritance as Sons of God in Jesus Christ, Who is the Son of God, I will accept quite willingly. I agree also as to how there is a similitude in this matter to the sacrament of the Eucharist, which is perceptible only to the mind and can be tasted and received through faith. But what will happen if this mystery is not accepted? For the unenlightened will shudder not only at having to believe this, but also will be opposed to taking for granted the other mysteries.

Paul: This sacrament, insofar as it is found in sensible things, arrived as through faith, is not a matter of necessity to the extent that, without it, there is no salvation, for it suffices for salvation to believe, and thus to eat the food of life. And, therefore, regarding its distribution, or to whom and how often it should be given to the faithful, this has not been set down as a matter of obligation, and hence it is that if anyone who believes and yet at the same time judges himself unworthy to approach the table of the great King, I would prefer that this humility be rather praised. Accordingly, with regard to the use and the rite of this sacrament, the Church authorities should be governed by expediency in complying with local conditions. Provided that the faith is preserved, a diversity of rites will not mitigate against a common law.

Englishman: What about the other sacraments, Matrimony, Orders, Confirmation, and Extreme Unction?

Paul: I feel that in this matter, due to the weakness of human nature, a great deal of latitude should be allowed, so long as it does not compromise eternal salvation. Any endeavor to impose exact conformity in everything is bound to disturb the peace. Yet I would hope that in the matter of matrimony and orders a certain agreement can be arrived at. In the question of matrimony it is a common practice among all nations that, following the law of nature, this union should be between one man and one woman. As for the priesthood, all religions have basically the same attitudes towards it. Harmony will be found in stressing these common elements, and the Christian religion will be approved insofar as in its observation it retains in both these sacraments that simplicity that in the estimate of others is most praiseworthy.

Englishman: What about fastings, ecclesiastical duties, abstinence in the matter of food and drink, formulae for prayers, and such matters?

Paul: Where it is impossible to maintain conformity, then, provided that faith and peace are preserved, the various nations should be permitted their own devotions and ceremonies. As a matter of fact, I think that this diversity would bring about an increase in devotion. For each individual nations will endeavor to make its own ritual more splendid, that they might surpass others and, in this way, they will achieve greater praise from both God and man.

After some time, when these matters had been duly considered by the wise men of the various nations, a number of books were produced, culled from among those who wrote on the observances of the ancients. These works were from among the most excellent authors, as for example Marcus Varro representing the Latins, and Eusebius representing the Greeks, who gathered together the varieties of religion. After an examination of these and many others it was ascertained that this diversity was reducible to the worship of one God. It was discovered that from the very beginning there had been but one cult which was everywhere and continually observed in the veneration of the divine. Yet it happened that quite often, due to the simplicity of the people, they were led astray by the power of the Prince of Darkness, and were not aware of what they were doing.

Therefore, it was concluded from reason that in heaven a harmony is somehow permitted. And the King of Kings commanded that these wise men return, and that they lead the various nations to the unity of the true cult; and that in this endeavor they be led and assisted by the spiritual administrators, and finally, that with plenipotentiary power over all they assemble in Jerusalem, as in a common center, and that they accept in the name of all one common faith, and thus secure everlasting peace for themselves, so that the Creator of all men might be praised in peace and blessed for all ages.

The Council of Trent
1566

At the time of the Reformation the printing press had
made it possible for all manner of religious instructional manuals
to be circulated. The Catechisms that resulted, both Catholic
and Protestant, are beyond number. Luther's larger catechism
appeared in 1530, Bucer's in 1534, Calvin's in 1536. The most
famous of the Catholic counterparts was that of Peter Canisius
in 1555. But since the Council of Trent's opening in 1545,
advocates had been calling for an "official" catechism, one that
could be widely circulated with the Council's own responses to
the questions raised by the Reformers. A decree was drafted in
the fourth session in April, 1546, endorsing the idea, but other
matters took precedence for the next sixteen years.

A committee was finally appointed to draw up a catechism
in 1562 during the eighteenth session. Cardinal Seripandi was
its chairman, and its membership was international. They were
instructed by the Council to "avoid particular opinions of individuals and schools, and to express the doctrine of the universal
Church, keeping especially in mind the decrees of the Council
of Trent." When the Council closed in 1565, the committee had
not finished its work, so the pope was directed to take charge of
it and see it through. Meantime Serapandi died and Charles
Borromeo was appointed chairman of the committee.

THE CATHOLIC TRADITION: The Church

Pius V became pope in January, 1566, and late that same year the long-awaited catechism appeared, entitled Catechism of the Council of Trent for Parish Priests, *issued by order of Pope Pius V. Partial and inadequate English translations appeared in 1675, 1687, 1816, 1839, 1852, and 1911. The selection that follows is from the 1923 translation by the American Dominicans Charles Callan and John McHugh.*

This work, also known as The Roman Catechism *or* The Catechism of Pius V, *was intended to provide the basis for pastoral preaching. During the era of the Counter-Reformation it enjoyed considerable prestige. In 1899 Pope Leo XIII, in an encyclical to the French hierarchy and clergy, recommended two books which all seminarians should possess and constantly read and study: the* Summa Theologica *of Thomas Aquinas and "that golden book," the* Roman Catechism, *described as "remarkable for the richness and exactness of its doctrine, and for the elegance of its style." Cardinal Newman said in his* Apologia, *"I rarely preach a sermon but I go to this beautiful and complete Catechism to get both my matter and my doctrine."*

What follows is the Catechism's treatment of Article IX of the Creed: "I believe in the Holy Catholic Church; the Communion of Saints." It gives in compact form the Tridentine view of the Church that prevailed for the four centuries between Trent and Vatican II.

CATECHISM FOR PARISH PRIESTS

With what great diligence pastors ought to explain to the faithful the truth of this ninth Article will be easily seen, if we attend chiefly to two considerations.

First, as St. Augustine observes, the Prophets spoke more plainly and openly of the Church than of Christ, foreseeing that on this a much greater number may err and be deceived than on the mystery of the Incarnation. For in after ages there would not be wanting wicked men who, like the ape that would fain pass for a man, would claim that they alone were Catholics, and with no less impiety than effrontery assert that with them alone is the Catholic Church.

The second consideration is that he whose mind is strongly impressed with the truth taught in this Article, will easily escape the awful danger of heresy. For a person is not to be called a heretic as soon as he shall have offended in matters of faith; but he is a heretic who, having disregarded the authority of the Church, maintains impious opinions with pertinacity. Since, therefore, it is impossible that anyone be infected with the contagion of heresy, so long as he holds what this Article proposes to be believed, let pastors use every diligence that the faithful, having known this mystery and guarded against the wiles of Satan, may persevere in the true faith.

This Article hinges upon the preceding one; for, it having been already shown that the Holy Ghost is the source and giver of all holiness, we here profess our belief that the Church has been endowed by Him with sanctity.

"I Believe in the Holy Catholic Church"

The Latins, having borrowed the word *ecclesia* (church) from the Greeks, having transferred it, since the preaching of the Gospel, to sacred things. It becomes necessary threfore, to explain its meaning.

"Church"

The word *ecclesia* (church) means *a calling forth.* But writers afterward used it to signify a meeting or assembly, whether the people gathered together were members of a true or of a false religion. Thus in the Acts it is written of the people of Ephesus that when the town-clerk had appeased a tumultuous assemblage he said: *And if you inquire after any other matter, it may be decided in a lawful church.* The Ephesians, who were worshippers of Diana, are thus called a lawful church *(ecclesia).* Nor are the Gentiles only, who knew not God, called a church *(ecclesia);* by the same name at times are also designated the councils of wicked and impious men. *I have hated the church (ecclesiam) of the malignant,* says the Prophet, *and with the wicked I will not sit.*

In common Scripture usage, however, the word was subsequently employed to signify the Christian society only, and the assemblies of the faithful; that is, of those who are called by faith to the light of truth and knowledge of God, that, having forsaken the darkness of ignorance and error, they may worship the living and true God piously and holily, and serve Him from their whole heart. In a word, *The Church,* says St. Augustine, *consists of the faithful dispersed throughout the world.*

In this word are contained important mysteries. For, in the *calling forth,* which it signifies, we recognize at once the benignity and splendor of divine grace, and we understand that the Church is very unlike all other societies. Other bodies rest on human reason and prudence, but the Church reposes on the wisdom and counsels of God who has called us inwardly by the inspiration of the Holy Ghost, who opens the hearts of men; and outwardly, through the labor and ministry of pastors and preachers.

Moreover, the end of this vocation, that is, the knowledge and possession of things eternal will be at once understood if we but remember why the faithful of the Old Law were called a Synagogue, that is, *a flock*; for, as St. Augustine teaches, *they were so called, because, like cattle, which are wont to herd together, they looked only to terrestrial and transitory goods.* Wherefore, the Christian people are justly called, not a Synagogue, but a Church, because, despising earthly and passing things, they pursue only things heavenly and eternal.

Many names, moreover, which are replete with mysteries, have been used to designate the Christian body. Thus, by the Apostle, it is called *the house and edifice of God. If*, says he to Timothy, *I tarry long, that thou mayest know how thou oughtest to behave thyself in the house of God, which is the church of the living God, the pillar and ground of truth.* The Church is called a house, because it is, as it were, one family governed by one father of the family, and enjoying a community of all spiritual goods.

It is also called *the flock of the sheep of Christ,* of which He is *the door and the shepherd.* It is called *the spouse of Christ. I have espoused you to one husband,* says the Apostle to the Corinthians, *that I may present you as a chaste virgin to Christ;* and to the Ephesians: *Husbands love your wives, as Christ also loved the church;* and of marriage: *This is a great sacrament, but I speak in Christ and in the church.*

Finally, the Church is called *the body of Christ,* as may be seen in the Epistles to the Ephesians and Colossians. Each of these appellations has very great influence in exciting the faithful to prove themselves worthy of the boundless clemency and goodness of God, who chose them to be the people of God.

The Parts of the Church

These things having been explained, it will be necessary to enumerate the several component parts of the Church, and to point out their difference, in order that the faithful may the better comprehend the nature, properties, gifts, and graces of God's beloved Church, and by reason of them unceasingly praise the most holy name of God.

The Church consists principally of two parts, the one called the Church triumphant; the other, the Church militant. The Church triumphant is that most glorious and happy assemblage of blessed spirits, and of those who have triumphed over the world, the flesh, and the iniquity of Satan, and are now exempt and safe from the troubles of this life and enjoy everlasting bliss. The Church militant is the society of all the faithful still dwelling on earth. It is called militant, because it wages eternal war with those implacable enemies, the world, the flesh and the devil.

277

We are not, however, to infer that there are two Churches. The Church triumphant and the Church militant are two constituent parts of one Church; one part going before, and now in the possession of its heavenly country; the other, following every day, until at length, united with our Saviour, it shall repose in endless felicity.

The Church militant is composed of two classes of persons, the good and the bad, both professing the same faith and partaking of the same Sacraments, yet differing in their manner of life and morality.

The good are those who are linked together not only by the profession of the same faith, and the participation of the same Sacraments, but also by the spirit of grace and the bond of charity. Of these St. Paul says: *The Lord knoweth who are his.* Who they are that compose this class we also may remotely conjecture, but we can by no means pronounce with certainty. Hence Christ the Saviour does not speak of this portion of His Church when He refers us to the Church and commands us to hear and to obey her. As this part of the Church is unknown, how could we ascertain with certainty whose decision to recur to, whose authority to obey?

The Church, therefore, as the Scriptures and the writings of the Saints testify, includes within her fold the good and the bad; and it was in this sense that St. Paul spoke of *one body and one spirit.* Thus understood, the Church is known and is compared to a city built on a mountain, and visible from every side. As all must yield obedience to her authority, it is necessary that she may be known by all.

That the Church is composed of the good and the bad we learn from many parables contained in the Gospel. Thus, the kingdom of heaven, that is, the Church militant, is compared to a net cast into the sea, to a field in which tares were sown with the good grain, to a threshing floor on which the grain is mixed up with the chaff, and also to ten virgins, some of whom were wise, and some foolish. And long before, we trace a figure and resemblance of this Church in the ark of Noah, which contained not only clean, but also unclean animals.

But although the Catholic Faith uniformly and truly teaches that the good and the bad belong to the Church, yet the same faith declares that the condition of both is very different. The wicked are contained in the Church, as the chaff is mingled with the grain on the threshing floor, or as dead members sometimes remain attached to a living body.

Hence there are but three classes of persons excluded from the Church's pale: infidels, heretics and schismatics, and excommunicated persons. Infidels are outside the Church because they never belonged to, and never knew the Church, and were never made partakers of any of her Sacraments. Heretics and schismatics are excluded from the Church, because they have separated from her and belong to her only as deserters belong to the army from which they have deserted. It is not, however, to be denied that they are still subject to the jurisdiction of the Church, inasmuch as they may be called before her tribunals, punished and anathematized. Finally, excommunicated persons are not members of the Church, because they have been cut off by her sentence from the number of her children and belong not to her communion until they repent.

But with regard to the rest, however wicked and evil they may be, it is certain that they still belong to the Church. Of this the faithful are frequently to be reminded, in order to be convinced that, were even the lives of her ministers debased by crime, they are still within the Church, and therefore lose nothing of their power.

Other Uses of the Word "Church"

Portions of the Universal Church are usually called churches, as when the Apostle mentions the Church at Corinth, at Galatia, of the Laodiceans, of the Thessalonians.

The private families of the faithful he also calls churches. The church in the family of Priscilla and Aquila he commands to be saluted; and in another place, he says: *Aquila and Priscilla with the church that is in their house salute you much in the Lord.* Writing to Philemon, he makes use of the same word.

Sometimes, also, the word *church* is used to signify the prelates and pastors of the church. *If he will not hear thee,* says our Lord, *tell the church.* Here the word *church* means the authorities of the Church.

The place in which the faithful assemble to hear the Word of God, or for other religious purposes, is also called a church. But in this Article, the word *church* is specially used to signify both the good and the bad, the governed, as well as the governing.

The Marks of the Church

The distinctive marks of the Church are also to be made known to the faithful, that thus they may be enabled to estimate the extent of the blessing conferred by God on those who have had the happiness to be born and educated within her pale.

The first mark of the true Church is described in the Nicene Creed, and consists in unity: *My dove is one, my beautiful one is one.* So vast a multitude, scattered far and wide, is called one for the reasons mentioned by St. Paul in his Epistle to the Ephesians: *One Lord, one faith, one baptism.*

The Church has but one ruler and one governor, the invisible one, Christ, whom the eternal Father *hath made head over all the Church, which is his body;* the visible one, the Pope, who, as legitimate successor of Peter, the Prince of the Apostles, fills the Apostolic chair.

It is the unanimous teaching of the Fathers that this visible head is necessary to establish and preserve unity in the Church. This St. Jerome clearly perceived and as clearly expressed when, in his work against Jovinian, he wrote: *One is elected that, by the appointment of a head, all occasion of schism may be removed.* In his letter to Pope Damasus the same holy Doctor writes: *Away with envy, let the ambition of Roman grandeur cease! I speak to the successor of the fisherman, and to the disciple of the cross. Following no chief but Christ, I am united in communion with your Holiness, that is, with the chair of Peter. I know that on that rock is built the Church. Whoever will eat the lamb outside this house is profane; whoever is not in the ark of Noah shall perish in the flood.*

The same doctrine was long before established by Saints Irenaeus, and Cyprian. The latter, speaking of the unity of the Church observes: *The Lord said to Peter, I say to thee, Peter! thou art Peter: and upon this rock I will build my Church. He builds His Church on one. And although after His Resurrection He gave equal power to all His Apostles, saying: As the Father*

280

hath sent me, I also send you, receive ye the Holy Ghost; yet to make unity more manifest, He decided by His own authority that it should be derived from one alone, etc.

Again, Optatus of Milevi says: *You cannot be excused on the score of ignorance, knowing as you do that in the city of Rome the episcopal chair was first conferred on Peter, who occupied it as head of the Apostles; in order that in that one chair the unity of the Church might be preserved by all, and that the other Apostles might not claim each a chair for himself; so that now he who erects another in opposition to this single chair is a schismatic and a prevaricator.*

Later on St. Basil wrote: *Peter is made the foundation, because he says: Thou art Christ, the Son of the Living God, and hears in reply that he is a rock. But although a rock, he is not such a rock as Christ; for Christ is truly an immovable rock, but Peter, only by virtue of that rock. For Jesus bestows His dignities on others; He is a priest, and He makes priests; a rock, and He makes a rock; what belongs to Himself, He bestows on His servants.*

Lastly, St. Ambrose says: *Because he alone of all of them professed (Christ) he was place above all.*

Should anyone object that the Church is content with one Head and one Spouse, Jesus Christ, and requires no other, the answer is obvious. For as we deem Christ not only the author of all the Sacraments, but also their invisible minister—He it is who baptizes, He it is who absolves, although men are appointed by Him the external ministers of the Sacraments—so has He placed over His Church, which He governs by His invisible Spirit, a man to be His vicar and the minister of His power. A visible Church requires a visible head; therefore the Saviour appointed Peter head and pastor of all the faithful, when He committed to his care the feeding of all His sheep, in such ample terms that He willed the very same power of ruling and governing the entire Church to descend to Peter's successors.

Moreover, the Apostle, writing to the Corinthians, tells them that there is but one and the same Spirit who imparts grace to the faithful, as the soul communicates life to the members of the body. Exhorting the Ephesians to preserve this unity, he says: *Be careful to keep the unity of the Spirit in the bond of peace; one body and one Spirit.* As the human body consists of many members, animated by one soul, which gives sight to the eyes, hearing to the ears, and to the other senses the power of discharging their respective functions; so the mystical body of Christ, which is the Church, is composed of many faithful. The hope, to which we are called, is also one, as the Apostle tells us in the same place; for we all hope for the same consummation, eternal and happy life. Finally, the faith which all are bound to believe and to profess is one: *Let there be no schisms amongst you,* says the Apostle. And Baptism, which is the seal of our Christian faith, is also one.

The second mark of the Church is holiness, as we learn from these words of the Prince of the Apostles: *You are a chosen generation, a holy nation.*

The Church is called holy because she is consecrated and dedicated to God; for so other things when set apart and dedicated to the worship of God were wont to be called holy, even though they were material. Examples of this in the Old Law were vessels, vestments and altars. In the same sense the first-born who were dedicated to the Most High God were also called holy.

It should not be deemed a matter of surprise that the Church, although numbering among her children many sinners, is called holy. For as those who profess any art, even though they depart from its rules, are still called artists, so in like manner the faithful, although offending in many things and violating the engagements to which they had pledge themselves, are still called holy, because they have been made the people of God and have consecrated themselves to Christ by faith and Baptism. Hence, St. Paul calls the Corinthians sanctified and holy, although it is certain that among them there were some whom he severely rebuked as carnal, and also charged with grosser crimes.

The Church is also to be called holy because she is united to her holy Head, as His body; that is, to Christ the Lord, the fountain of all holiness, from whom flow the graces of the Holy Spirit and the riches of the divine bounty. St. Augustine, interpreting these words of the Prophet: *Preserve my soul, for I am holy,* thus admirably expresses himself: *Let the body of Christ boldly say, let also that one man, exclaiming from the ends of the earth, boldly say, with his Head, and under his Head, I am holy; for he received the grace of holiness, the grace of Baptism and of remission of sins.* And a little further on: *If all Christians and all the faithful, having been baptized in Christ, have put Him on, according to these words of the Apostle: "As many of you as have been baptized in Christ, have put on Christ"; if they are made members of his body, and yet say they are not holy, they do an injury to their Head, whose members are holy.*

Moreover, the Church alone has the legitimate worship of sacrifice, and the salutary use of the Sacraments, which are the efficacious instruments of divine grace, used by God to produce true holiness. Hence, to possess true holiness, we must belong to this Church. The Church therefore it is clear, is holy, and holy because she is the body of Christ, by whom she is sanctified, and in whose blood she is washed.

The third mark of the Church is that she is Catholic; that is, universal. And justly is she called Catholic, because, as St. Augustine says, *she is diffused by the splendor of one faith from the rising to the setting sun.*

Unlike states of human institution, or the sects of heretics, she is not confined to any one country or class of men, but embraces within the amplitude of her love all mankind, whether barbarians or Scythians, slaves or freemen, male or female. Therefore it is written: *Thou . . . hast redeemed us to God, in thy blood, out of every tribe, and tongue, and people, and nation, and hast made us to our God a kingdom.* Speaking of the Church, David says: *Ask of me and I will give thee the Gentiles for thy inheritance, and the utmost parts of the earth for thy possession;* and also, *I will be mindful of Rahab and of Babylon knowing me;* and *man is born in her.*

Moreover to this Church, *built upon the foundation of the apostles and prophets,* belong all the faithful who have existed from Adam to the present day, or who shall exist, in the profession of the true faith, to the end of time; all of whom are founded and raised upon the one corner-stone, Christ, *who made both one,* and announced peace to them that are near and to them that are far.

She is also called universal, because all who desire eternal salvation must cling to and embrace her, like those who entered the ark to escape perishing in the flood. This (note of catholicity), therefore, is to be taught as a most reliable criterion, by which to distinguish the true from a false Church.

The true Church is also to be recognized from her origin, which can be traced back under the law of grace to the Apostles; for her doctrine is the truth not recently given, nor now first heard of, but delivered of old by the Apostles, and disseminated throughout the entire world. Hence no one can doubt that the impious opinions which heresy invents, opposed as they are to the doctrines taught by the Church from the days of the Apostles to the present time, are very different from the faith of the true Church.

That all, therefore, might know which was the Catholic Church, the Fathers, guided by the Spirit of God, added to the Creed the word *Apostolic*. For the Holy Ghost, who presides over the Church, governs her by no other ministers than those of Apostolic succession. Ths Spirit, first imparted to the Apostles, has by the infinite goodness of God always continued in the Church. And just as this one Church cannot err in faith or morals, since it is guided by the Holy Ghost; so, on the contrary, all other societies arrogating to themselves the name of *church*, must necessarily, because guided by the spirit of the devil, be sunk in the most pernicious errors, both doctrinal and moral.

Figures of the Church

The figures of the Old Testament have great power to stimulate the minds of the faithful and to remind them of these most beautiful truths. It was for this reason chiefly that the Apostles made use of these figures. The pastor, therefore, should not overlook so fruitful a source of instruction.

Among these figures the ark of Noah holds a conspicuous place. It was built by the command of God, in order that there might be no doubt that it was a symbol of the Church, which God has so constituted that all who enter therein through Baptism, may be safe from danger of eternal death, while such as are outside the Church, like those who were not in the ark, are overwhelmed by their own crimes.

Another figure presents itself in the great city of Jerusalem, which, in Scripture, often means the Church. In Jerusalem only was it lawful to offer sacrifice to God, and in the Church of

God only are to be found the true worship and true sacrifice which can at all be acceptable to God.

"I Believe the Holy Catholic Church"

Finally, with regard to the Church, the pastor should teach how to believe the Church can constitute an Article of faith. Although reason and the senses are able to ascertain the existence of the Church, that is, of a society of men on earth devoted and consecrated to Jesus Christ, and although faith does not seem necessary in order to understand a truth which even Jews and Turks do not doubt; nevertheless it is from the light of faith only, not from the deductions of reason, that the mind can grasp those mysteries contained in the Church of God which have been partly made known above and will again be treated under the Sacrament of Holy Orders.

Since, therefore, this Article, no less than the others, is placed above the reach, and defies the strength of the human understanding, most justly do we confess that we know not from human reason, but contemplate with the eyes of faith the origin, offices and dignity of the Church.

This Church was founded not by man, but by the immortal God Himself, who built her upon a most solid rock. *The Highest himself,* says the Prophet, *hath founded her.* Hence, she is called *the inheritance of God, the people of God.* The power which she possesses is not from man but from God.

Since this power, therefore, cannot be of human origin, divine faith can alone enable us to understand that the keys of the kingdom of heaven are deposited with the Church, that to her has been confided the power of remitting sins, of denouncing excommunication, and of consecrating the real body of Christ; and that her children have not here a permanent dwelling, but look for one above.

We are, therefore, bound to believe that there is one Holy Catholic Church. With regard to the Three Persons of the Holy Trinity, the Father, the Son, and the Holy Ghost, we not only believe them, but also believe *in* them. But here we make use of a different form of expression, professing to believe the holy, not *in* the holy Catholic Church. By this difference of expression we distinguish God, the author of all things, from His works, and acknowledge that all the exalted benefits bestowed on the Church are due to God's bounty.

"The Communion of Saints"

The Evangelist St. John, writing to the faithful on the divine mysteries, explains as follows why he undertook to instruct them in these truths: *That you may have fellowship with us, and our fellowship may be with the Father, and with his son Jesus Christ.* This fellowship consists in the Communion of Saints, the subject of the present Article.

Would that in its exposition pastors imitated the zeal of Paul and of the other Apostles. For not only is it a development of the preceding Article and a doctrine productive of abundant fruit; it also teaches the use to be made of the mysteries contained in the Creed, because the great end to which we should direct all our study and knowledge of them is that we may be admitted into this most august and blessed society of the Saints, and may steadily persevere therein, *giving thanks with joy to God the Father, who hath made us worthy to be partakers of the lot of the saints in the light.*

The faithful, therefore, in the first place are to be informed that this part of the Article, is, as it were, a sort of explanation of the preceding part which regards the unity, sanctity and catholicity of the Church. For the unity of the Spirit, by which she is governed, brings it about that whatsoever has been given to the Church is held as a common possession by all her members.

The fruit of all the Sacraments is common to all the faithful, and these Sacraments, particularly Baptism, the door, as it were, by which we are admitted into the Church, are so many sacred bonds which bind and unite them to Christ. That this communion of Saints implies a communion of Sacraments, the Fathers declare in these words of the Creed: *I confess one Baptism.* After Baptism, the Eucharist holds the first place in reference to this communion, and after that the other Sacraments; for although this name *(communion)* is applicable to all the Sacraments, inasmuch as they unite us to God, and render us partakers of Him whose grace we receive, yet it belongs in a peculiar manner to the Eucharist which actually produces this communion.

But there is also another communion in the Church which demands attention. Every pious and holy action done by one belongs to and becomes profitable to all through charity, which *seeketh not her own.* This is proved by the testimony of St. Ambrose, who, explaining these words of the Psalmist, *I am a partaker with all them that fear thee,* observes: *As we say that a limb is partaker of the entire body, so are we partakers with all that fear God.* Therefore has Christ taught us that form of prayer in which we say *our,* not *my* bread; and the other Petitions are equally general, not confined to ourselves alone, but directed also to the common interest and the salvation of all.

This communication of goods is often very aptly illustrated in Scripture by a comparison borrowed from the members of the human body. In the human body there are many members, but though many, they yet constitute but one body, in which each performs its own, not all the same, functions. All do not enjoy equal dignity, or discharge functions alike useful or honorable; nor does one propose to itself its own exclusive advantage, but that of the entire body. Besides, they are so well organized and knit together that if one suffers, the rest likewise suffer on account of their affinity and sympathy of nature; and if, on the contrary, one enjoys health, the feeling of pleasure is common to all.

The same may be observed in the Church. She is composed of various members; that is, of different nations, of Jews, Gentiles, freemen and slaves, of rich and poor; when they have been baptized, they constitute one body with Christ, of which He is the Head. To each member of the Church is also assigned his own peculiar office. As some are appointed apostles, some teachers, but all for the common good; so to some it belongs to govern and teach, to others to be subject and to obey.

The advantages of so many and such exalted blessings bestowed by Almighty God are enjoyed by those who lead a Christian life in charity, and are just and beloved of God. As to the dead members; that is, those who are bound in the thraldom of sin and estranged from the grace of God, they are not so deprived of these advantages as to cease to be members of this body; but since they are dead members, they do not share in the spiritual fruit which is communicated to the just and pious. However, as they are in the Church, they are assisted in recovering lost grace and life by those who live by the Spirit; and they also enjoy those benefits which are without doubt denied to those who are entirely cut off from the Church.

Not only the gifts which justify and endear us to God are common. *Graces gratuitously granted*, such as knowledge, prophecy, the gifts of tongues and of miracles, and others of the same sort, are common also, and are granted even to the wicked, not, however, for their own but for the general good, for the edification of the Church. Thus, the gift of healing is given not for the sake of him who heals, but for the sake of him who is healed.

In fine, every true Christian possesses nothing which he should not consider common to all others with himself, and should therefore be prepared promptly to relieve an indigent fellow-creature. For he that is blessed with worldly goods, and sees his brother in want, and will not assist him, is plainly convicted of not having the love of God within him.

Those, therefore, who belong to this holy communion, it is manifest, do now enjoy a certain degree of happiness and can truly say: *How lovely are thy tabernacles, O Lord of hosts! my soul longeth and fainteth for the courts of the Lord. . . . Blessed are they who dwell in thy house, O Lord.*

John Adam Moehler
1796-1838

John Adam Moehler in 1817 went to study at Tübingen for a year, was ordained a priest in 1819, and returned to Tübingen to study from 1820 to 1822. He then took an extended tour of German and Austrian universities, an experience that deeply influenced his whole outlook. Würzburg, Bamberg, Jena, Leipzig, Braunschweig, Magdeburg, then Berlin where he sat in on lectures by the famous Protestant professors, Schleiermacher, Marheineke, and Neander. After three weeks he moved on to Breslau, Prague, Vienna, and Munich, then back to Tübingen. He was a changed person; his ideas had been jolted. Having already a good foundation in Catholic theology, he had then encountered the most vibrant of Protestant theology, and thereupon turned his attention to reading the Church Fathers. The outcome of this combination of factors was a new style for Catholic thinking, leading some to call Moehler "the father of modern theology."

His first important book, The Unity of the Church, *appeared in 1825 amidst high acclaim by some and stinging criticism by others. His driving desire was to resolve the differences between Protestant and Catholic, and eventually reunite the churches. He felt that this would require an accurate and thorough investigation of the points of difference, especially as found in the public formularies or confessions of the Protestant communities. In 1828 he started a series of lectures on this subject and attracted an overflow crowd. Eventually these ideas were put into print in 1832 as* Symbolism, or Exposition of the Doctrinal Differences between Catholics and Protestants, as evidenced by their Symbolical Writings. *The book caused an immediate sensation throughout Germany.*

When Moehler died six years later, only 43 years old, Symbolism *had gone into its fifth edition in German and been translated into Latin, Italian and French, and five years later it appeared in English. If Catholics exulted over its merits, Protestants were greatly dismayed. Schleiermacher, the most celebrated Protestant theologian of the day, who had been so great an influence on young Moehler in Berlin, declared that* Symbolism *was the severest blow ever given to Protestantism.*

What made Moehler's thought both powerful and problematic was the level on which he worked. He tried to draw out the hidden implications in Protestant teachings. He was convinced that there was a latent pantheism in the Reformers' thought that had to be recognized and dealt with. Such contentions, understandably, brought sharp counter-attacks, but that was all to the good, as far as Moehler was concerned. He thought that the calm characterizing Protestant-Catholic relations at the time was a sleep bordering on death, and that renewed controversy, as long as it was conducted at the proper level, would bring new life to both sides.

Symbolism *is thus a product of another age. In the century and a half since its appearance ecumenical relations have changed dramatically. The atmosphere, the concerns, the methods, the hopes, the mutual perceptions of one another by Protestants and Catholics are all quite different today, and yet Moehler must be credited with an important role in the process that has brought about those changes. Considering that the period of his real activity was less than fifteen years, his achievement and impact are both truly astounding. The selection that follows can hardly give more than a taste of his style, but it is enough to convey the intensity and clarity of his approach.*

SYMBOLISM

CHAPTER XXXVIII

THE CHURCH AS TEACHER AND INSTRUCTRESS. TRADITION. THE CHURCH AS JUDGE IN MATTERS OF FAITH.

The main question, which we have now to answer, is this: how doth man attain to possession of the true doctrine of Christ; or, to express ourselves in a more general, and at once more accurate manner, how doth man obtain a clear knowledge of the institute of salvation, proffered in Christ Jesus? The Protestant says, by searching Holy Writ, which is infallible: the Catholic, on the other hand, replies, by the Church, in which alone man arrives at the true understanding of Holy Writ. In a more minute exposition of his views, the Catholic continues: doubtless the sacred Scriptures contain *divine* communications, and, consequently, the pure truth: whether they contain *all* the truths, which, in a religious and ecclesiastical point of view are necessary, or at least very useful to be known, is a question which does not yet come under consideration. Thus, the Scripture is God's unerring word; but however the predicate of inerrability may belong *to it, we ourselves* are not exempt from error; nay, we only become so when we have unerringly received the word, which is in *itself* inerrable. In this reception of the word, human activity, which is fallible, has necessarily a part. But, in order that, in this transit of the divine contents of the Sacred Scriptures into possession of the human intellect, no gross illusion or general misrepresentation may occur, it is taught, that the Divine Spirit, to which are intrusted the guidance and vivification of the Church, becomes, in its union with the human spirit in the Church, a peculiarly Christian tract, a deep sure-guiding feeling, which, as it abideth in truth, leads also into all truth. By a confiding attachment to the perpetuated Apostleship, by education in the Church, by hearing, learning, and living within her pale, by the reception of the higher principle, which renders her eternally fruitful, a deep interior sense is formed that alone is fitted for the perception and acceptance of the written Word, because it entirely coincides with the sense, in which the Sacred Scriptures themselves were composed. If, with such a sense acquired in the Church, the Sacred volume be perused, then its general essential import is conveyed unaltered to the reader's mind. Nay, when instruction through the apostleship, and the ecclesiastical education in the way described, takes place in the individual, the Sacred Scriptures are not even necessary for our acquisition of their general contents.

This is the ordinary and regular course. But errors and misunderstandings, more or less culpable, will never fail to occur; and, as in the times of the apostles, the word of God was combated out of the word of God, so this combat hath been renewed at all times. What, under such circumstances, is the course to be pursued? How is the Divine Word to be secured against the erroneous conceptions that have arisen? The general sense decides against particular opinion—the judgment of the Church against that of the individual: *the Church interprets the Sacred Scriptures.* The Church is the body of the Lord: it is, in its universality, His visible form—His permanent, ever-renovated, humanity—His eternal revelation. He dwells in the community; all His promises, all His gifts are bequeathed to the community—but to no individual, as such, since the time of the apostles. This general sense, this ecclesiastical consciousness is tradition, in the subjective sense of the word. What then is tradition? The peculiar Christian sense existing in the Church, and transmitted by ecclesiastical education; yet this sense is not to be conceived as detached from its subject-matter—nay, it is formed in, and by this matter, so it may be called a full sense. Tradition is the living word, perpetuated in the hearts of believers. To this sense, as the general sense, the interpretation of Holy Writ is entrusted. The declaration, which it pronounces on any controverted subject, is the judgment of the Church; and, therefore, the Church is judge in matters of faith (*judex controversiarum*). Tradition, in the objective sense, is the general faith of the Church through all ages, manifested by outward historical testimonies; in this sense, tradition is

usually termed the norma; the standard of Scriptural interpretation—the rule of faith.

Moreover, the Divine Founder of our Church, when He
constituted the community of believers, as His permanent organ,
had recourse to no other law than that which prevails in every
department of human life. Each nation is endowed with a peculiar character, stamped on the deepest, most hidden parts of its
being, which distinguishes it from all other nations, and manifests
its peculiarity in public and domestic life, in art and science, in
short, in every relation. It is, as it were, the tutelary genius; the
guiding spirit transmitted from its progenitors; the vivifying
breath of the whole community; and, indeed, the nations anterior
to Christianity, personified this their peculiar character, revered
it as their national divinity, deduced from it their civil and religious laws and customs, and placed all things under its protection.

In every general act of a people, the national spirit is infal-
libly expressed; and should contests, should selfish factions
occur, the element destructive to the vital principle of the whole,
will most certainly be detected in them, and the commotion,
excited by an alien spirit, either miscarries, or is expelled, as long
as the community preserves its own self-consciousness, as long
as its peculiar genius yet lives, and works within it. If, on the
other hand, things have come to such an extremity, that the
living bond, which connects the present with the past, is dis-
severed; that no concurrent national effort can be called forth;
that all falls into a state of confusion; that struggle and opposition
totally efface the common characteristics of the community, or
reveal them only in the opposition, which is boasted of as life;
then there is no doubt that such a people is near its downfall,
that its peculiar plastic principle is already paralysed, and its
Divinity has ceased to live.—"Pan is dead," did seamen hear re-
sounded from every quarter, at the period of the birth of Christ.

To confine our attention, more particularly, to religious
communities, we need only look to the Chinese, and the Parsi,
or to the Mohammedans, and we shall be astonished to observe
how consistently, throughout the course of their history, the
principles, established at the outset, were applied to details,
how consistently the latter were conceived and modelled by the
standard of the former. Let us investigate the Hellenic Heathen-

ism also, and the most perfect agreement between the various religious phenomena that have risen up in succession, and the primitive fundamental view, cannot escape observation. Lastly, let us contemplate the religious sect founded by Luther himself. The developed doctrines of his Church, consigned as they are in the symbolical books, retain, on the whole, so much of his spirit, that on the first view, they must be recognized by the observer as genuine productions of Luther. With a sure vital instinct, the opinions of the Majorists, the Synergists and others, were rejected as deadly; and, indeed (from Luther's point of view), as untrue, by that community whose soul, whose living principle he was; and the Church, which the Reformer of Wittenberg established, proved herself the unerring interpretess of his word.

Let us now, for a moment, suppose the case, that the progenitors of nations, and the founders of the above-mentioned religions, had been real envoys from above; then must we consider the movement, that emanated from them, as divine, yet as one which, by its transmission to those attracted by its fundamental principle, had become human; and the later collective actions, whereof we said, that they had retained the spirit of the founder, would then be at once divine and human acts and deeds. They would be divine, because they only worked out what was originally given, and applied it to occurring relations and circumstances; human, because this development was carried on through the agency of men; lastly, an unerring standard of thought and action for all those who follow such a founder; for the breath of life, which proceeded from him, guides, like a natural impulse, the movements of the whole community. According to this type hath the infallibility of the Church also, in its interpretation of the Divine Word, been formed, and by this standard we are to judge it. All the developments of its dogmas and its morality, which can be considered as resulting from formal acts of the whole body, are to be revered as the sentences of Christ himself, and in these his spirit ever recurs. Here, indeed, subsists between the Church and the above-named religious communities the great difference, which must ever be maintained between Jesus Christ and mere men. The institutions of the latter, even after the most consistent expansion of their vital principles, advance to an inevitable end; and their productions, however much they may have worked, according to their original spirit itself, and both, in an equal degree, sink by degrees into nothing.

CHAPTER XXXIX

THE CHURCH AS INTERPRETER OF HOLY WRIT, AND THE DOCTRINE ON TRADITION CONTINUED.

On these subjects, Scripture and tradition, and the relation of the Church to both, we must now enter into fuller and clearer explanations.

Undoubtedly, on this most important matter, the records of ecclesiastical history will serve to throw the clearest light. If we except some Jewish parties, which did not so much spring out of Christianity, as wish to encumber it, in its infancy, with Judæo-national observances, the earliest sect were the Gnostics. Their doctrines on the eternal co-existence of an evil matter with God—on the creation and government of the world, by an inferior spirit, the Demiurgos—their principle of Docetism and the rest, are too well known to be detailed here. However decidedly, in the opinion, perhaps, of all who now profess Christianity, these doctrines are adverse to its nature; did the Gnostics, on that account, suffer themselves to be convinced out of Scripture, of the perversity of their views? So far from it, they preferred to reject the Old Testament, and to declare the Gospels to be falsified! There are certainly few who have studied the Gnostic errors, that are not seized with the deepest astonishment, how their partisans could possibly deem their whimsical opinions, the fantastic forms of their demonoloby, &c. to be *Christian apostolic* doctrines; and many among us perhaps believe, that we could in a single hour confute thousands of them by the Bible, and bring them back to pure Christianity. So confident did they feel in their superiority, that they were even disposed to accuse their then opponents of a want of dexterity, because they did not succeed.

But, when once a peculiar system of moral life hath been called into existence, should it even be composed of the most corrupt elements, no ordinary force of external proofs, no conclusions of ratiocination, no eloquence, are able to destroy it: its roots lie mostly too deep to be pervious to mortal eye: it can only perish of itself, become gradually exhausted, spend its rage, and disappear. But, as long as it flourishes, all around is converted into a demonstration in its favour: the earth speaks for it, and the Heavens are its warranty. Meanwhile, a new age, with another spirit and other elements of life, springs up: this, without any points of internal contact with the past, is often at a loss to comprehend it, and demands with astonishment how its existence had been possible. But, should Divine Grace, which can alone enkindle the opposite *true life*, succeed in delivering one individual from such errors, then he expresses the incomprehensible and inconceivable nature of his former state, by saying, that he had been, as it were, enchanted, and that something, like scales, has fallen from his eyes!

As the impossibility was now manifest of convincing the Gnostics of the truth out of Holy Writ, must the Catholic Church declare, that the questions whether God created the world, whether Christ were a true man, should remain in abeyance, till these doctrines were made evident to them by the testimony of Scripture? By no means. They were directed to tradition—to the living word; they were told that, if even a doubt could arise as to the doctrine of Scripture, the announcement of the word perpetuated in the Church, since her first establishment, and the common faith of believers, decided the question clearly enough; and that to this decision, all who wish to attach themselves to Christ, and choose him for the Shepherd of their souls, ought not to refuse obedience.

The teachers of the Church, indeed, by no means omitted to employ Scripture for the refutation of the Gnostics, and to appeal to its testimony in detailed expositions. But herein, one learned investigation was but opposed to another: man stood against man, and the Bible on both sides. By adherence to Scripture, the individual Christian could undoubtedly convince himself, that the Gnostics were involved in grievous errors. Of this he was subjectively certain: but as the adversary had the like subjective conviction, that the true Christian view of the world was to be found on his side, the objectivity of Christianity would have necessarily disappeared, if, besides the Bible, there had not been a rule of faith, to wit, universal Tradition. Without this rule, it would ever be impossible to determine with positiveness, safety, and general obligation, the peculiar doctrines of Christianity. The individual, at best, could only hazard the assertion, this is *my* view, *my* interpretation of Scripture; or, in other words, without tradition there would be *no doctrine of the Church, and no Church*, but individual Christians only; no certainty and security, but only doubt and probability.

Scarcely had the struggle of the Catholic Church, with Gnosticism, reached its highest point, when, in the most decided contrast with the latter, the one class of Unitarians arose; for these, and not, as Neander thinks, the Montanists, form the contrary extreme to the Gnostics. If the Gnostics saw in Christianity *nothing but* what was divine, and in Christ recognized *merely* the divine reason, so that they attributed to the Redeemer only an apparent body, represented him as merely putting on an illusive form of man, but not taking the real nature of man, and regarded moreover the visible world as thoroughly evil; these Unitarians on the other hand, discovered in the Saviour a mere man, enlightened by Heaven; and consistently with this doctrine, denied the descent of the Divine Spirit upon the apostles and the Church, and the high supernatural aids of grace; which they the less needed, as they acknowledged the existence of no deeply implanted corruption in human nature. Did the former look upon the Gospel as a plastic impulse, a divine germ of life, a celestial energy; so the latter regarded it as a law of formation, a dead rule, an abstract notion, a pure ethical system, by application whereof the defects to be found in our otherwise excellent moral nature, may be totally eradicated. The Unitarians of this class (after falsifying Holy Writ), appealed to the same, and by the rejection of tradition, relied exclusively on its authority. What course, under these circumstances, was the Church to be advised? Was she to declare that every one was provisionally to follow his own views, until results, satisfactory to each individual, could be more surely obtained from the study of Holy Writ? More undoubtedly, if the Church had been a mere historico-antiquarian association; if she had had no conception of herself, of her foundation, of her essence, and of her task, and no sense of the power of faith. But, as she enjoyed the possession of these, she acted otherwise, and from her conduct clearly resound the words: "eternally certain is the doctrine of the Redeemer to his disciples—the written word is one with the living—that which is inscribed on paper and parchment, with that which is engraven on hearts by the power of the Holy Spirit; and the doubts, which may arise out of the former, are dispelled by the latter." The faith existing in the Church, from the beginning throughout all ages, is the infallible standard to determine the true sense of Scripture; and accordingly it is certain, beyond the shadow of doubt, that the Redeemer is God, and hath filled us even with divine power. In fact, he who grounds his faith on Scripture only, that is, on the result of his exegetical studies, has no faith, can have none, and understands not its very nature. Must he not be always ready to receive better information; must he not admit the possibility, that by mature study of Scripture, another result may be obtained, than that which has already been arrived at? The thought of this very possibility precludes the establishment of any decided, perfectly undoubting, and unshaken faith, which, after all, is alone deserving of the name. He who says, "this is my faith," hath no faith. Faith, unity of faith, universality of faith, are one and the same; they are but different expressions of the same notion. He who, if even he should not believe the truth, yet believes truly, believes at the same time that he holds fast the doctrine of Christ, that he shares the faith with the Apostles, and with the Church founded by the Redeemer, that there is but one faith in all ages, and one only true one. This faith is alone rational, and alone worthy of man: every other should be called a mere opinion, and, in a practical point of view, is an utter impotency.

Ages passed by, and with them the ancient sects: new times arose, bringing along with them new schisms in the Church. The formal principles of all these productions of egotism were the same; all asserted that Holy Writ, abstracted from Tradition and from the Church, is at once the sole source of religious truth, and the sole standard of its knowledge for the individual. This formal principle, common to all parties, separated from the Church; to the Gnostic of the second century, and the Albigensian and Vaudois of the twelfth, to the Sabellian of the third, the Arian of the fourth, and the Nestorian of the fifth century—this principle, we say, led to the most contradictory belief. What indeed can be more opposite to each other, than Gnosticism and Pelagianism, than Sabellianism and Arianism? The very circumstance, indeed, that one and the same formal principle can be applied to every possible mode of belief; or rather that this belief, however contradictory it may be in itself, can still make use of that formal principle, should alone convince every one, that grievous errors must here lie concealed, and that between the individual and the Bible a mediating principle is wanting.

What is indeed more striking than the fact, that every later religious sect doth not deny that the Catholic Church, in respect to the parties that had previously seceded from her, has in substance right on her side, and even recognizes in these cases her dogmatic decisions; while on the other hand, it disputes her formal principles? Would this ecclesiastical doctrine, so formed and so approved of, have been possible, without the peculiar view the Church entertained of herself? Doth not the one determine the other? With joy the Arian recognizes what has been decided by the Church against the Gnostics; but he does not keep in view the manner in which she proceeded against them; and he will not consider that those dogmas on which he agrees with the Church, she would not have saved and handed down to his time, had she acted according to those formal principles which he requires of her, and on which he stands.The Pelagian and the Nestorian, embrace also, with the undoubting faith, the decisions of the Church against the Arians. But as soon as the turn comes to either, he becomes as it were stupified, and is inconsiderate enough to desire the matter of Christian doctrine without the appropriate ecclesiastical form—without that form, consequently, by the very neglect whereof those parties, to which he is most heartily opposed, have fallen on the adoption of their articles of belief. It was the same with Luther and Calvin. The pure Christian dogmas, in opposition to the errors of the Gnostics, Paulicians, Arians, Pelagians, Nestorians, Monophysites and others, they received with the most praiseworthy firmness and fervency of faith. But, when they took a fancy to deliver their theses on the relations between faith and works, between free will and grace, or however else they may be called, they trod (as to form) quite in the footsteps of those whom they execrated, and when they were able to obtain possession of their persons, even burned them.

This accordingly is the doctrine of Catholics. Thou wilt obtain the knowledge full and entire of the Christian religion, only in connection with its essential form, which is the Church. Look at the Scripture in an ecclesiastical spirit, and it will present thee an image perfectly resembling the Church. Contemplate Christ in, and with his creation—the Church; the only adequate authority; the only authority representing Him, and thou wilt then stamp His image on thy soul. Should it, however, be stated, in ridicule of this principle, that it were the same as to say—"Look at the Bible through the spectacles of the Church," be not disturbed, for it is better for thee to contemplate the star by the aid of a glass, than to let it escape thy dull organ of vision, and be lost in mist and darkness. Spectacles, besides, thou must always use, but only beware lest thou get them constructed by the first casual glass-grinder, and fixed upon thy nose.

CHAPTER XL

FORMAL DISTINCTION BETWEEN SCRIPTURAL AND ECCLESIASTICAL DOCTRINE.

If we have hitherto shown that, conformably to the principles of Catholics, the doctrine of Scripture is one and the same with the doctrine of the Church, since the Church hath to interpret the Scripture, and in this interpretation cannot err; so this unity applies to the substance only, and not to the form. In respect to the latter, a diversity is found inherent in the very essence and object of the Church; so that, indeed, if the divine truth must be preserved and propagated by human organs, the diversity we speak of could not possibly be avoided, as will appear from the following observations. The conduct of the Redeemer, in the announcement of His Word, was corresponded to by that of the apostles, and the Word became immediately in them faith—a human possession—and after his ascension, existed for the world in no other form than in this faith of the Lord's disciples, whose kernel in Peter he therefore called the rock, whereon his Church was, in such a way, to be built, that the powers of hell should never prevail against it. But, after the

Divine Word had become human faith, it must be subject to all mere human destinies. It must be constantly received by all the energies of the human mind, and imbibed by the same. The preservation and communication of the Word were, in like manner, attached to a human method. Even with the evangelists, who only wished to recount what Christ had spoken, wrought, and suffered, the Divine Word appears subject to the law here described; a law which manifests itself in the choice and arrangement of the matter, as well as in the special plan, which each proposed to himself, and in the general conception, and execution of his task.

But, the Divine Word became still more subject to this law, when the apostles were fulfilling their mission—executing the divine charge, which they had received; for, various questions of dispute arose, the settlement whereof could not be avoided, and on that account claimed human reflection, and required the formation of notions, judgments, and conclusions—things which were not possible to be effected, without tasking the reason and the understanding. The application of the energies of the human mind to the subject matter, received from the Lord, necessarily caused the Divine Word, on one hand, to be analyzed, and, on the other hand, to be reduced to certain leading points; and the multiplicity of objects to be contemplated in their mutual bearings, and resolved into a higher unity, whereby the human mind obtained, on these matters, greater clearness and definiteness of conception. For, every thing, that the human mind hath received from an external source, and which is destined to become its property, wherein it must find itself perfectly at home, must be first reproduced by the human mind itself. The original doctrine, as the human mind had variously elaborated it, exhibited itself in a much altered form: it remained the original, and yet did not; it was the same in substance, and yet differed as to form. In this process of the developement of the Divine Word, during the apostolic age, we may exalt as high, and extend as wide as we please the divine guidance, given to the disciples of Christ; yet certainly, without human co-operation, without the peculiar activity of man, it did not advance of itself. As in the good work of the Christian, free-will and grace pervade each other, and one and the same undivided deed is at once divine and human, so we find this to be the case here.

The same could not fail to hold good, even after the death of the apostles, even after the Gospels and the Epistles, were written and whatever else we include in the canon of the New Testament, were already in the hands of the faithful. When, in the manner described, the Church explains and secures the original doctrine of faith against misrepresentations; the apostolic expression is necessarily changed for another, which is the most fitted alike clearly to set forth and reject the particular error of the time. As little as the apostles themselves, in the course of their polemics, could retain the form, wherein the Saviour expounded his divine doctrine; so little was the Church enabled to adhere to the same. If the evangelical doctrine be assailed, by a definite theological system, and a terminology peculiar to itself; the false notions cannot by any means be repelled in a clear, distinct, evident, and intelligible manner, unless the Church have regard to the form of the error, and exhibit its thesis in a shape, qualified by the garb, wherein the adverse doctrine is invested, and thus render itself intelligible to all contemporaries. The origin of the Nicene formula, furnishes the best solution to this question. This form is in itself the human, the temporal, the perishable element, and might be exchanged for a hundred others. Accordingly, tradition often hands down to later generations, the original deposit in another form, because that deposit hath been entrusted to the care of men, whose conduct must be guided by the circumstances, wherein they are placed.

Lastly, in the same manner as in the Apostolic writings, the truths of salvation are laid open with greater clearness, and in all their mutual organic connexion; so, in the doctrine of the Church, the doctrine of Scripture is ever progressively unfolded to our view. Dull, therefore, as it is, to find any other than a mere *formal* distinction, between the doctrine of Christ and that of his apostles; no less senseless is it, to discover any other difference, between the primitive and the later tradition of the Church. The blame of this formal difference arises from overlooking the fact, that Christ was a God-Man, and wished to continue working in a manner, conformable to his two-fold nature.

302

Moreover, the deeper insight of the human mind into the divine revelations in Christ, seems determined by the struggles of error against Christian truth. It is to the unenlightened zeal of the Jewish Christians for the law, we owe the expositions of Paul touching faith and the power of the Gospel: and to the schisms in Corinth we are indebted for his explanation of principles, in respect to the Church. The Gnostic and Manichean errors, led to a clearer insight into the character of evil, destitute of, and opposed to, all existence as it is, as well as to a maturer knowledge of the value of God's *original* creation (nature and freedom), and its relation to the *new* creation in Christ Jesus. Out of the Pelagian contest arose a fuller and more conscious recognition of human infirmity, in the sphere of true virtue; and so have matters gone on down to our days. It would be ridiculous, on the part of Catholics, to deny as a foolish boast of Protestants (should the latter be inclined to claim any merit in the case), that the former had gained much from the controversy with them. By the fall of the Protestants, the Catholics necessarily rose; and from the obscurity, which overclouded the minds of the reformers, a new light was cast upon the truth; and such indeed had ever been the case in all earlier schisms in the Church. Assuredly, in Christian knowledge we stand one degree higher than the period prior to the reformation; and all the dogmas that were called in question, received such an elucidation and confirmation, that it would require no very diligent or long-continued comparison between the modern theological works, and those written prior to the Council of Trent, to see the important difference which, in this respect, exists between the two epochs.

The fact that the deeper consciousness of Christian truth (in itself eternally one and unchangeable), is the result of contest and struggle, and consequently matter of history, is of too much importance not to detain our attention for some moments. It explains the necessity of a living, visible authority which, in every dispute, can, with certainty, discern the truth, and separate it from error. Otherwise, we should have *only* the variable—the disputed—and at last Nichilism itself. Hence it happens (and this we may venture to premise) that where Holy Writ, without tradition and the authority of the Church, is declared to be the sole source and rule for the knowledge of Gospel truth, all more precise explanations and developements of Christian dogmas are willingly left in utter ignorance, nay, are even absolutely rejected. Guided by this principle, men can find no rational object to connect with the history of believing intelligence in the Christian Church, and must necessarily evince hostility towards every thing of this tendency, which hath occurred in the Church. Or, when they lose all confidence and all hope of freeing themselves from the turmoil of opinions, and of seeing a bright, steady light arise out of the dark chaos, they cast, in their despair, upon the Bible the whole mass of opinions, that ages have thrown up; and of that which is, boldly assert it could not have been otherwise, consequently exists of necessity, and is inherent in the very essence of Christianity. They do not see that, with that complaisance to acknowledge every variety of opinion, which, in the course of time, may have gradually been founded on Scripture, a destructive principle, for the solution of all the enigmas of Christian history, is laid down:—to wit, the principle that its object is to show, that the Scripture, as it includes *every* sense, hath consequently none. But all charges against the Catholic Church are reduced to this, that she has been so absurd, as to suppose the Scriptures to contain one sense, and consequently only one, and that definite, whereof the faithful, in the course of history, must ever obtain a clearer and more intuitive knowledge; while, on the other hand, the refutation of the above-mentioned prejudice, which manifested itself soon after the origin of the Church, hath been, in the succession of ages, the peculiar task of Christian science.

CHAPTER XLI

TRADITION IN A MORE LIMITED SENSE. THE CANON OF THE SCRIPTURES.

From that notion of tradition, which we have hitherto expounded, another is to be distinguished, although both are intimately united with each other. Tradition we have hitherto described as the consciousness of the Church, as the living word of faith, according to which the Scriptures are to be interpreted, and to be understood. The doctrine of tradition contains, in this sense, nothing else than the doctrine of Scripture; both, as to their contents, are one and the same. But, moreover, it is asserted by the Catholic Church, that many things have been delivered to her by the apostles, which Holy Writ either doth not at all comprise, or, at most, but alludes to. This assertion of the Church is of the greatest moment, and partially, indeed, includes the foundations of the whole system. Among these oral traditions must be included the doctrine of the canonicity, and the inspiration of the Sacred Scriptures; for, in no part of the Bible do we find the books belonging to it designated; and were such a catalogue contained in it, its authority must first be made matter of inquiry. In like manner, the testimony as to the inspiration of the biblical writings is obtained only through the Church. It is from this point we first discern, in all its magnitude, the vast importance of the doctrine of Church authority, and can form a notion of the infinite multitude of things, involved in that doctrine. He can scarcely be a sincere Christian, who will not attribute to a special protection of Divine Providence, the preservation of the works of those apostles, and of such of their disciples, who have made a contribution to the biblical canon. But, in taking into consideration this special protection, he cannot set aside the Catholic Church, and must, even in despite of deliberate repugnance, admit that it was that Church, which the Saviour employed as a medium for preserving to all ages the writings, that had been penned under his peculiar assistance. Every learned theologian is aware, that the Gnostics, as well as one class of anti-Trinitarians, in the second and third centuries, rejected sometimes this or that gospel, sometimes the Acts of the Apostles, and sometimes the apostolic epistles; nay, even brought forward spurious gospels and acts of the apostles, and mutilated, in the most criminal manner, the genuine apostolic works, which they retained. And yet no one can refuse to acknowledge, that the visible Church, which these heretics assailed, in the same manner as is usual with Protestants,—the Church that the former, like the latter, continually denounced as the corruptress of pure doctrine, as exerting a tyranny over minds, as wicked beyond conception—that this Church, we say, was selected and deemed worthy by Almighty God, to preserve the most precious jewel of Christians! What conclusions may not hence be immediately deduced! On Luther himself, as we shall have occasion later to see, this fact made a deep impression; and he brought it forward at times, in a train of ideas, that can scarcely be reconciled with the position which, in other respects, he had taken up against the Catholic Church.

Moreover, in reference to the canon of the sacred writings, some difference exists between Catholics and Protestants. Originally, indeed, it seemed probable as if in this department very important differences would have arisen; as if the melancholy spectacle of the first ages would have been renewed, in which, according to the suggestions of caprice, or the interest of mere individual opinions, sometimes one, sometimes another portion of the Bible was rejected. It is generally known (and indeed in Berthold's and De Wette's Introductions to the Sacred Books, the reader may in part see the passages on this matter cited from Luther), that the Reformer called the Epistle of St. James, an epistle of straw, and was not disposed to acknowledge it as an apostolic production: judged not more favourably of the Revelations of St. John, and was wont to say of the first three Gospels, that in them the Gospel was not to be found; whereas, the Gospel of St. John, the Acts of the Apostles, and the Epistles of St. Paul, he exalted in peculiar strains of eulogy. In this matter, the opposition between St. James's doctrine, on the relation between faith and works, and Luther's exposition of the same subject, exerted an undeniable influence. Luther preferred the rejection of **this** valuable portion of Holy Writ, to the amendment of his **own opi**nions, and chose rather to question the genuineness of a canonical Scripture, than to doubt the truth of his own theory. Assuredly, if in the otherwise obscure apocalypse, there had not been found passages of extreme clearness, like the following: "Happy are they who sleep in the Lord, *for their works follow them;*" Luther would have found less to offend him in this book. The remarkable expression, "that in the Gospels the Gospel is not contained," may be explained from what has been said above, respecting the signification, which the old Lutherans attached to the word *Gospel*. Luther's prejudices, however, were not able to obscure the sounder sense of his followers; and so it came to pass, that they, as well as the Calvinists, admitted with the Catholic Church, the entire books of the New

Testament to be canonical. But, in regard to the Old Testament, doctrinal prejudices prevailed; and those Scriptures, which the Catholics call the deutero-canonical, were gradually expunged from the Canon, yet more decidedly on the part of the Calvinists, than of the Lutherans. Among the modern Protestants, Clausen, at least, has not denied, that in this matter regard was paid to other considerations, than those of a merely historical and critical kind.

CHAPTER XLII

ON THE RELATION OF THE ECCLESIASTICAL INTERPRETATION OF HOLY
WRIT TO THE LEARNED AND SCIENTIFIC EXEGESIS. PATRISTIC
AUTHORITY AND FREE INVESTIGATION.

As the notion of doctrinal tradition, and of the ecclesiastical interpretation of Holy Writ, has been now fully unfolded, it is necessary, in order to obviate some singular misconceptions, to state, in a few words, the relation between the learned exegesis as applied to the sacred writings, and that interpretation which emanates from the Church. The interpretation of the Church does not descend to the details, which must claim the attention of the scientific exegetist. Thus, for example, it does not hold it for a duty, nor include it in the compass of its rights, to determine when, by whom, and for what object the Book of Job was written; or what particular inducement engaged St. John to publish his gospel, or the Apostle Paul to address an epistle to the Romans; in what order of time the epistles of this messenger of the Lord followed each other, &c. &c. As little doth the Church explain particular words and verses, their bearings one to the other, or the connexion existing between larger portions of a sacred book. Antiquities, in the widest sense of the word, fall not within the domain of her interpretation; in short, that interpretation extends only to doctrines of faith and morals. Thus much as to the extent of her interpretation.

But now as to the nature and mode of the Church's interpretation; this is not conducted according to the rules and well-known aids of an historical and grammatical exegesis, whereby the individual seeks to obtain scientific insight into the sense of

Holy Writ. On the contrary, the doctrinal contents of Scripture she designates in the general spirit of Scripture. Hence, the earliest œcumenical councils did not even adduce any particular scriptural texts, in support of their dogmatic decrees; and Catholic theologians teach with general concurrence, and quite in the spirit of the Church, that even a Scriptural proof in favour of a decree held to be infallible, is not itself infallible, but only the dogma as defined. The deepest reason for this conduct of the Church, lies in the indisputable truth, that she was not founded by Holy Writ, but already existed before its several parts appeared. The certainty which she has of the truth of her own doctrines, is an immediate one, for she received her dogmas from the lips of Christ and the apostles; and by the power of the Divine Spirit, they are indelibly stamped on her consciousness, or as Irenæus expresses it, on her heart. If the Church were to endeavour, by learned investigation, to seek her doctrines, she would fall into the most absurd inconsistency, and annihilate her very self. For, as it would be the Church that should institute the enquiry, her existence would be presupposed; and yet, as she would have first to find out her own being, the thing whereby and wherein she absolutely consists, namely, Divine Truth, her non-existence must at the same time be presupposed! She would have to go in search of herself, and this a madman only could do: she would be like the man, that would examine the papers written by himself, in order to discover whether he really existed! The essential matter of Holy Writ, is eternally present in the Church, because it is her heart's-blood—her breath—her soul—her all. She exists only by Christ, and yet she must have to find him out! Whoever seriously reflects on the signification of those words of Chrsit, "I am with ye even to the consummation of the world," will be able to conceive at least the view, which the Catholic Church takes of herself.

What we have said involves the limits prescribed to the freedom of the Catholic scholar, in the interpretation of Holy Writ. It is evident, of course, that we speak not here of that general freedom possessed by every man, at the peril of his own soul, like the Jew and the Heathen, to hold the Bible as the work of impostors or dupes, as a medley of truth and error, wisdom and folly. This freedom the Catholic possesses, like the Protestant;

but we speak of that freedom only which the Catholic enjoys, when he will not renounce his character as Catholic; for were he to entertain the above-mentioned view of the Sacred Scriptures, he would thereby renounce all connexion with our Church. As a Catholic, he is freely convinced, that the Church is a divine institution, upheld by supernal aid, "which leads her into all truth;" that, consequently, no doctrine rejected by her is contained in Scripture; that with the latter, on the contrary, her dogmas perfectly coincide, though many particulars may not be verbally set forth in Holy Writ. Accordingly he has the conviction, that the Scripture, for example, doth not teach that Christ is a mere man; nay, he is certain, that it represents him also as God. Inasmuch as he professes this belief, he is not free to profess the contrary, for he would contradict himself; in the same way as a man, who has resolved to remain chaste, cannot be unchaste, without violating his resolution. To this restriction, which every one most probably will consider rational, the Catholic Church subjects her members, and consequently, also, the learned exegetists of Scripture. A Church which would authorize any one to find what he pleased in Scripture, and without any foundation to declare it as unecclesiastical, such a Church would thereby declare, that it believed in nothing, and was devoid of all doctrines; for the mere possession of the Bible no more constitutes a Church, than the possession of the faculty of reason renders any one really rational. Such a Church would in fact, as a moral entity, exhibit the contradiction just adverted to, which a physical being could not be guilty of. The individual cannot at one and the same time believe, and not believe, a particular point of doctrine. But if a Church, which consists of a union of many individuals, permitted every member, as such, to receive or to reject at his pleasure, any article of faith, it would fall into this very contradiction, and would be a monster of unbelief, indifferent to the most opposite doctrines, which we might, indeed, on our behalf, honour with the finest epithets, but certainly not denominate a Church. The Church must train up souls for the kingdom of God, which is founded on definite facts and truths, that are eternally unchangeable: and so a Church, that knows no such immutable dogmas, is like to a teacher, that knows not what he should teach. The Church has to stamp the image of

Christ on humanity; but Christ is not sometimes this, and sometimes that, but eternally the same. She has to breathe into the hearts of men the word of God, that came down from heaven: but this word is no vague, empty sound, whereof we can make what we will.

That, accordingly, the principles of the Catholic Church agree with the idea of a positive Church, and the claim is but natural, which she exacts of her members, to recognize in the Bible, when they make it the subject of a learned exegesis, those doctrines of faith and morality, which they themselves acknowledge to be biblical, we trust we have now made sufficiently evident. In other respects, no one belonging to the Catholic Church professes aught else, than her doctrines of faith and morality. For, in this respect only, she expresses the sense of Holy Writ, and indeed only in a general way; so that the learned expositor, by the laws of his religious community, is bound to nothing more; and a wide field is ever open to him, whereon he may exert his talents, his hermeneutical skill, his philological and archæological learning, and employ them usefully for the advancement of science.

But, if we should be reminded of the decree of the Council of Trent, which directs the Catholic to interpret the Scripture, according to the unanimous testimony of the holy fathers, how can we escape the reproach, that an *absolutely* sacred exegesis hath existed for centuries, and that consequently all idea of progress in the understanding of the Bible must be given up? Before we lay down the Catholic view of this subject, it may be proper to state, with the utmost succinctness, the relation of patristic authority to learned investigation. Whoever takes the pains to study the writings of the holy fathers, may without much penetration discover, that while agreeing perfectly on all ecclesiastical dogmas, they yet expatiate most variously on the doctrines of Christian faith and morality. The mode and form, wherein they appropriate the one Gospel to themselves, demonstrate its truth to others, develop it in their own interior, and philosophize and speculate upon its doctrines, most strikingly evince the individuality of each writer. One manifests a deeper, the other a clearer and acuter view of his subject; one turns this, the other that talent to profit. While now all Catholics gladly profess the same dogmas with the fathers of the Church, the individual opinions, the mere human views of the latter, possess in their estimation no further value, but as they present reasonable grounds for acceptance, or as any peculiar affinity of mind may exist between one father of the Church, and a Catholic of a subsequent age. These principles, at all periods of the Church, were openly professed, and brought into practice. Never did any father, not even the most revered, succeed in imposing his own peculiar opinions on the Church; as of this fact, St. Augustine furnishes a remarkable proof. What writer ever acquired greater authority than he? Yet, his theory respecting original sin and grace, never became the doctrine of the Church; and herein precisely he showed himself a good Catholic, that he gave us the permission to examine his private opinions, and to retain only what was sound. Moreover, the expression, "doctrine of the fathers," is frequently synonimous with tradition: in this sense they are considered as representatives of *the faith* of antiquity— as channels and witnesses of transmitted doctrine; but by no means so when, upon a thousand subjects, they lay before us their own peculiar views and speculations. From this point of view, where they do not speak, *but through them the belief of the universal Church is made known*, they possess, undoubtedly, a decisive authority:—an authority, however, which belongs not to their persons, but to the tradition, whereby they themselves were regulated, and which they only reflect. In this respect, we must needs agree with them, because one doctrine of faith hath subsisted, and must subsist, through the whole history of the Church. We will not and cannot believe otherwise, than as our fathers have believed; but as to their peculiarities of opinion, we may adopt them or not, as we please. Besides, the truth, which we possess in common with them, has, as we have already elsewhere had occasion to observe, by means of the splendid intellects, which devoted their undivided energy to its defence, been often more deeply investigated, or contemplated in all its bearings, and viewed in a more general connexion; so that Christian science makes continual progress, and the mysteries of God are ever more clearly unfolded. For, this subjective insight into the doctrines of salvation, eternally immutable in themselves, the fathers of the Church have by no means laid down the standard, nor prescribed any pause in the progress of inquiry.

The same principle holds good, with regard to their interpretation of Scripture. Except in the explanation of a very few classical passages, we know not where we shall meet with a general uniformity of Scriptural interpretation among the fathers, further than that all deduce from the sacred writings, the same doctrines of faith and morality, yet each in his own peculiar manner; so that some remain for all times distinguished models of Scriptural exposition, others rise not above mediocrity, while others again are, merely by their good intentions and their love for the Saviour, entitled to veneration. As in this manner, among the fathers themselves, one is superior to the other, and by his exegetical tact, by the acuteness and delicacy of his perceptions, by an intellectual affinity with the writer expounded, by the extent of the philological and historical knowledge brought to the task of interpretation, holds a higher place; so this may and will be the case in all ages. The same dogmas, the same morality, all like the fathers, will find in Holy Writ; yet in another way: we will bring forward the same things, but often not in the same manner. More extensive philological acquirements, and the more abundant aids of every kind, which modern times furnish, enable us, without in the least degree deviating from the unanimous interpretation of the fathers, to explain many things in a better and more solid manner than they did. The better Catholic exegists since the reformation, from Thomas de Vio, Contareni, Sadoletus, Masius, Maldonado, Justinian, Estius, Cornelius à Lapide, down to our own days, furnish a proof of what is here asserted; and the Biblical researches of several critics, such as Richard Simon, Hug, Jahn, Feilmoser, and others, will certainly not show, that the earlier theologians have left nothing to the later ones, but to edit their works anew. Accordingly, wherein consists the impropriety that we should still revere in the Holy Scriptures, the same miracles of divine wisdom and compassion, which our fathers revered fourteen and eighteen hundred years ago? Doth the impropriety lie in the short-sightedness of our understanding, which is unable to discover, that such simple writings as the Sacred Books, should not have been understood as to their essential import in the times wherein they were published, and in the communities to which they were addressed? Must we thus look for this impropriety, in our inability to conceive how an age, which was nearest to the composition of the Bible, should have been the furthest removed from the true understanding thereof? Or, doth it consist in our regarding the opinion as singular, that the Christian Church had not penetrated into the sense of her own sacred records at a time, when she exerted a truly renovating influence over the world, when she conquered Judaism, destroyed Heathenism, and overcame all the powers of darkness? Or, that we should not be able to convince ourselves, that the night is dispersed by darkness, and illusions by error? Or, doth the impropriety consist in the opinion, that Holy Writ could not possibly have been destined in the course of every fifteen years, and even under the hand of each of its expositors, to receive, as if by a divine miracle, an essentially different import than in former times.

Lastly (and this is the principal point), since the Catholic Church regards herself as that institution of the Lord, wherein His doctrines of salvation and the knowledge of the same, have, by the immediate instruction of the apostles, and the power of the Divine Spirit, been deposited; her claim to interpret, according to her rule of faith, the sacred writings, in which the same doctrines of salvation, under the guidance of the same Spirit, have been laid down, perfectly agrees with the claims of a genuine historical and grammatical exegesis; and it is precisely the most successful interpretation of this kind, that would, of necessity, most faithfully reflect her doctrines. From her point of view, it appears accordingly quite unintelligible, how her claim should not be consistent with the laws of a true exegesis, alone deserving of the name; or, how the, in other respects able interpreter, when supported by her rule, should not be precisely the most distinguished. The Protestants, on the other hand, starting from the prejudice, that the peculiar doctrines of the Catholic Church are not conformable to Scripture, must consequently regard her principle of interpretation as one outwardly imposed, and therefore arbitrary and unnatural; but this prejudice the Catholic repels as idle, and totally devoid of foundation.

Matthias Joseph Scheeben

1835-1888

Matthias Scheeben was born near Bonn, Germany, in 1835. He studied at the Gregorian University in Rome (1852-1859) and was ordained a priest in 1858. For the rest of his life he taught theology at the seminary in Cologne.

In the controversy over papal infallibility at the time of the First Vatican Council, Scheeben staunchly defended that doctrine against the attacks of Döllinger. His influence extended far beyond his own diocese, especially through the three volume manual of dogmatic theology which he wrote and which was widely adopted in the seminaries of the time. He was admired for his exceptional familiarity with the Fathers, the Scholastics, and his contemporaries.

It was not, however, only the clergy or the learned who profited from his contributions. He held the conviction that theology was important for all believers, and early in his teaching career he began work on a book that in large part accounts for his subsequent reputation, The Mysteries of Christianity, *two chapters of which are found in the following selection.*

The first edition of The Mysteries of Christianity *came out in 1865. It enjoyed lasting success, so that the publisher in 1887 asked him to prepare a revised edition. Scheeben was working on this revision at the time of his unexpected death the next year. He had completed reworking seven of the ten parts of the* book. *A number of circumstances kept this revised edition from being published in full until 1941, and five years later it was expertly translated into English by Cyril Vollert, S.J.*

Few books of theology have received the acclaim that this one has. It has been called "the most original, the most profound, and the most brilliant work which recent theology has produced." Vollert saw it as "a work unique in the literature of theology . . . It aims to present a unified view of the whole vast panorama of revealed truth in terms of the nine key mysteries of Christianity, and to relate them to modern life."

The nine key mysteries according to which Christian theology was organized by Scheeben are: Trinity, Creation, Sin, Incarnation, Eucharist, Church, Justification, Glorification, and Predestination. They constitute the first nine parts of the work, which is then concluded with Part Ten on Theology as the Science of the Mysteries. The ten parts are in turn divided into 29 chapters.

The selection that follows consists of chapter one (Introduction), called "The Mystery of Christianity in General" where Scheeben lays the groundwork for his whole approach; and chapter 19 (Part VI) on "The Mystery of the Church," where we see how his approach affects his understanding of the Church. Keeping in mind that the chapter was originally written a few years before Vatican I but revised a decade and a half after it, and recalling also Scheeben's role in the controversy with Döllinger, his treatment of papal infallibility takes on a special interest.

All in all, it is easy to see how Scheeben was both a man of his time and a man ahead of his time, for much of his perspective anticipates developments in the theology of the Church in our own century.

THE MYSTERIES
OF CHRISTIANITY

CHAPTER I

THE MYSTERY OF CHRISTIANITY IN GENERAL

1. INTEREST OF THE SUBJECT

C hristianity entered the world as a religion replete with mysteries. It was proclaimed as the mystery of Christ, as the "mystery of the kingdom of God." Its ideas and doctrines were unknown, unprecedented; and they were to remain inscrutable and unfathomable.

The mysterious character of Christianity, which was sufficiently intelligible in its simplest fundamentals, was foolishness to the Gentiles and a stumbling block to the Jews; and since Christianity in the course of time never relinquished and could never relinquish this character of mystery without belying its nature, it remained ever a foolishness, a stumbling block to all those who, like the Gentiles, looked upon it with unconsecrated eyes or, like the Jews, encountered it with uncircumcised hearts. With bitter scorn they would ever scoff at its mysterious nature as obscurantism, superstition, fanaticism, and absurdity.

After the mystery of Christianity had, in spite of all this, succeeded in making its way and became firmly entrenched in the belief of the nations, it found other and less malevolent adversaries. Many souls were too noble to disdain the lofty and beneficent force of Christianity, or too respectful of the faith of their childhood and the heritage of their fathers to turn from it in arrogance, but still not humble enough to surrender themselves to it with childlike trust. They sought to snatch the veil from the sanctuary of Christianity, to cleave the mystery so as to liberate the kernel of truth from the dark prison of its shell and bring it to light.

Even friends and zealous defenders of Christianity could not always suppress a certain dread when they stood in the obscurity of its mysteries. To buttress belief in Christian truth and to defend it, they desired to resolve it into a rational science, to demonstrate articles of faith by arguments drawn from reason, and so to reshape them that nothing would remain of the obscure, the incomprehensible, the impenetrable. They did not realize that by such a procedure they were betraying Christianity into the hands of her enemies and wresting the fairest jewel from her crown.

The greater, the more sublime, and the more divine Christianity is, the more inexhaustible, inscrutable, unfathomable, and mysterious its subject matter must be. If its teaching is worthy of the only-begotten Son of God, if the Son of God had to descend from the bosom of His Father to initiate us into this teaching, could we expect anything else than the revelation of the deepest mysteries locked up in God's heart? Could we expect anything else than disclosures concerning a higher, invisible world, about divine and heavenly things, which "eye hath not seen, nor ear heard," and which could not enter into the heart of any man? And if God has sent us His own Spirit to teach us all truth, the Spirit of His truth, who dwells in God and there searches the deep things of God, should this Spirit reveal nothing new, great, and wondrous, should He teach us no sublime secrets?

Far from repudiating Christianity or regarding it with suspicious eyes because of its mysteries, we ought to recognize its divine grandeur in these very mysteries. So essential to Christianity are its mysteries that in its character of truth revealed by the Son of God and the Holy Spirit it would stand convicted of intrinsic contradiction if it brought forward no mysteries. Its Author would carry with Him a poor recommendation for His divinity if He taught us only such truths as in the last analysis we could have learned from a mere man, or could have perceived and adequately grasped by our own unaided powers.

I would go even further: the truths of Christianity would not stir us as they do, nor would they draw us or hearten us, and they would not be embraced by us with such love and joy, if they contained no mysteries. What makes many a man recoil from the Christian mysteries as from sinister specters is neither the voice of nature nor the inner impulse of the heart nor the yearning for light and truth, but the arrogance of a wanton and overweening pride. When the heart thirsts after truth, when the

318

knowledge of the truth is its purest delight and highest joy, the sublime, the exalted, the extraordinary, the incomprehensible all exercise an especial attraction. A truth that is easily discovered and quickly grasped can neither enchant nor hold. To enchant and hold us it must surprise us by its novelty, it must overpower us with its magnificence; its wealth and profundity must exhibit ever new splendors, ever deeper abysses to the exploring eye. We find but slight stimulation and pleasure in studies whose subject matter is soon exhausted and so leaves nothing further for our wonderment. But how powerfully sciences enthrall us when every glance into them suggests new marvels to divine, and every facet of the object imprisons new and greater splendors!

The greatest charm in knowledge is astonishment, surprise, wonderment. The less we previously knew of a thing, especially the less we dared hope to learn about it by ourselves and the more we marvel at its existence, the more fortunate we regard ourselves when at length we come to know it. The more exalted an object is, the more its beauty and greatness impress us and the more it compels our admiration, the more even the slightest glance that we dare fix on it captivates us. In a word, the charm of truth is proportionate to its abstruseness and mystery. Must not Christianity, too, be especially valuable and dear to us because of the mysteries it involves? And indeed is it not all the more precious the greater are the mysteries which it harbors within itself? Does not Christianity impress us so powerfully just because it is one vast mystery, because it is the greatest of mysteries, the mystery of God?

Fundamentally, of course, it is not exactly the obscurity engulfing an object that makes the mystery so highly prized and attractive for us. Our souls, born of Light and destined for Light, flee darkness and long for light; darkness as such has no enticement for them. Why does the dawn exercise so enchanting an influence over us, why does it charm us more than the full light of day? Not because the light is mixed with darkness, but rather because it disperses the darkness that surrounded us, and brings in its train the light we have yearned for so long and so earnestly, and because our anxious hearts are cheered by the ever-growing glories of the sun.

What captivates us is the emergence of a light that had been hidden from us. Mysteries must in themselves be lucid, glorious truths. The darkness can be only on our side, so far as our eyes are turned away from the mysteries, or at any rate are not keen enough to confront them and see through them. There must be truths that baffle our scrutiny not because of their intrinsic darkness and confusion, but because of their excessive brilliance, sublimity, and beauty, which not even the sturdiest human eye can encounter without going blind.

When truths which had been entirely inaccessible to us become manifest, when God by His grace makes it possible for us, if only from afar, to cast a timid glance into their depths, a wondrous light dawns in us and the rosy morning glow of a heavenly world breaks over us; and although the darkness that surrounded us and still surrounds us strikes our consciousness only when we have such an experience, a single ray of the higher light that shines upon us is powerful enough to fill us with unutterable rapture.

The fascination of mystery is so strong that almost all religious and social organizations that exercise or have exercised an inspiring and lasting influence on mankind have wrapped themselves up in the obscurity of mystery, and have even gloried in the mysteries which they were aware of, although they disdained Christianity because of its mysteries. Their mysteries, products of human invention, are of course mere caricatures of the divine mysteries. Either they are plain mystifications with which to dupe the uninitiate, or they are in part genuine, in part spurious truths which lose the noble character of mystery by the very fact that they are proposed to the initiate as evident. The Christian, on the other hand, is really initiated into the mysteries of God. He rightly regards this initiation as an illumination replete with wonder and grace; but for this very reason he is filled with the deepest reverence for the sublimity of his mysteries. He acknowledges the grace of God with holy gratitude, but without despising the uninitated. He earnestly desires that they too may participate in this same tremendous grace; and if in former ages Christians kept their mysteries hidden from unbelievers, it was only because of their solicitude that what was sacred should not be profaned and defiled in the eyes and hands of the unclean.

But when the Christian humbly receives the revelation of God's mysteries as a great grace, he is entitled to a holy pride. With holy pride he can and ought to glory in the exalted mysteries that he possesses by the grace of God; he can and should regard himself as the object of an extraordinary illumination, as an initiate into the great mysteries, which are hidden from the mighty and wise of this world. Today especially, when a superficial enlightenment with its deceptive glimmer is intent on supplanting the mysteries of our faith, the Christian must be conscious of his sublime illumination and proud of the dawn of a higher, fairer, supernatural world that has risen over him in the faith. How can we call forth and strengthen this lofty consciousness, this holy pride? Not by denying the darkness which still shrouds the mysteries from the eyes of the initiate, but by pointing out that even the feeble ray gleaming forth from the darkness is strong enough at least to herald the incredible magnificence of the mysteries. Such demonstration is what we have desired to furnish in the present work, and thus we hope to make a contribution to the advancement of Christian knowledge and Christian life.

In order at the very outset to disclose the plan that we are following in this book, and the principles that guide us, we must first of all, by a careful analysis, come to an understanding about the notion of mystery.

2. THE NOTION OF MYSTERY IN GENERAL AND OF CHRISTIAN MYSTERY IN PARTICULAR

What do we mean by mystery in general? We mean all that is secret, hidden from us; consequently everything that is not seen or known by us, and that cannot be either seen or known by us.

But if this is the case, does it not follow that as soon as a thing comes to our actual knowledge, as soon as it becomes manifest to us, it ceases to be a mystery? To be sure, so far as it becomes really known by us and becomes really manifest to us, it can no longer remain hidden from us, can no longer be a secret, and hence can no longer be a mystery. But cannot a thing which is manifest to us still present obscurity in some respects, and thus remain hidden from us? In fact, is it not usually the case that we know things only according to some aspect, or in general have only a superficial acquaintance with them, without comprehending them from all angles or penetrating into their innermost nature? Indeed, is it not usually true that even what we know of a thing remains obscure and perplexing for the very reason that we cannot reach down into its innermost depths and hence cannot conceive and explain it in terms of its ultimate essence? And in particular, when we have to sketch a composite picture of a thing's nature from the various properties which it displays, is not this picture ordinarily as dark and enigmatic as a silhouette, because we lack an intimate and thorough understanding of the relationships among its various properties?

Nearly all the objects of our knowledge, even the simplest, the most natural, and the most familiar, continue to remain mysteries for us in some respect. The light that falls upon them cannot dispel all darkness from them. Everything remains to some extent inconceivable to us, because our concepts and representations do not embrace all the knowable details of an object; likewise, everything is unfathomable, because the more deeply our gaze penetrates into an object the weaker and less certain it becomes. Further, an essential characteristic of the knowledge we have of a thing is an awareness of the imperfection, deficiency, and obscurity of that knowledge; we do not deceive ourselves that the little we perceive is all that can be perceived. If we were thus to deceive ourselves, we should be regarding darkness itself as light, and we should betray the fact that the light does not shine for us even where its rays actually fall. All true philosophers have quite rightly considered the consciousness of lack of knowledge as an essential factor of true knowledge. Conscious lack of knowledge was for them a "learned ignorance" and enabled them to mark off light from shadow, and thus to bring out in sharper prominence the clear lines of their system of philosophy.

But the basic reason why our cognition does not perfectly and thoroughly illuminate its objects is the feebleness and limitation of the inner light from which it proceeds. Only God's cognition excludes all mysteries, because it springs from an infinite Light which with infinite power penetrates and illuminates the innermost depths of everything that exists. But the created intellect, no matter how pure and perfect it may be, will never with its finite power comprehend and conceive everything that is; its eye is impeded by its very nature from reaching into the deepest foundations of things, and so it cannot perfectly fathom all objects. Much less can the human intellect do so, because it is not a pure spirit but is shackled to matter. Angels have an immediate perception at least of themselves. But man, whether we consider him in himself or with regard to objects outside of himself, has an immediate perception only of the phenomena, the external appearances, the accidents proper to things, from which he may grope toward some knowledge of essences. His reason makes it possible for him, even demands of him, that he pass beyond the phenomenon so that he may perceive not only the phenomenon itself, but also the essence which externalizes and expresses itself in the phenomenon, and thereby to some extent explain and understand the phenomena themselves. His intelligence not only perceives the signs and manifestations that strike the eye, but from them reasons to the cause without which they cannot exist and endure. He reads beneath the surface into the essence which the external appearances disclose to him, and into the cause which confronts him in its effects and which lies concealed behind the effects. But since no essence is entirely revealed in its phenomena, and no cause in its effect, the ray of light with which we penetrate the shell cannot expose the kernel. Knowledge of an essence gained from its phenomena will never equal knowledge gained from immediate intuition, and therefore even the understanding of the phenomena will never be perfect. The former as well as the latter will never equal knowledge gained from immediate intuition, and therefore even the understanding of the phenomena will never be perfect. The former as well as the latter will always remain obscure and full of mystery.

If by mystery we mean nothing more than an object which is not entirely conceivable and fathomable in its innermost essence, we need not seek very far to find mysteries. Such mysteries are found not only above us, but all around us, in us, under us. The real essence of all things is concealed from our eyes. The physicist will never fully plumb the laws of forces in the physico-chemical world and perfectly comprehend their effects; and the same is true of the physiologist with regard to the laws of organic nature, of the psychologist with regard to the soul, of the metaphysician with regard to the ultimate basis of all being.

Christianity is not alone in exhibiting mysteries in the above, mentioned sense. If its truths are inconceivable and unfathomable, so in greater part are the truths of reason. This by itself does not imply anything against Christianity, nor does it imply much in its favor. As will be shown, however, the truths that are specifically proper to Christianity are inconceivable and unfathomable in an exclusively special sense. To appreciate this fact, we must go on to consider another aspect of the notion of mystery.

When a person understands a truth, it is no longer a mystery for him but is clear to him, to the extent that he understands it. But do we not ordinarily say that he who understands a truth which he had not previously been aware of and did not suspect, or which others are not yet aware of, knows a secret or mystery? That is so; still, the truth is no longer a mystery for him. Well then, what if he were of himself utterly incapable of discovering the truth which he now knows, and which even now, after it has become manifest to him, is known only because another to whom he lends credence has communicated it to him, and which, finally, even now he does not grasp by the light of his own intellect but only by faith? In this case the truth, in spite of such revelation, still remains hidden, because it does not lie open to our scrutiny and is not perceived in itself. If, in addition, the truth which has been revealed by another has absolutely no similarity, or but very slight similarity, with anything which we ourselves have ever seen or experienced, then naturally we are much less capable of forming a clear idea of it than we are of other things which do not extend beyond our experience. Thus in a double respect it will be obscure in its own way even after it has been revealed, and accordingly will be and will remain a mystery in a quite special sense.

Mysteries of this sort are, to some extent, found even in the natural order. Let us suppose, for instance, that a traveler from a foreign country, to which we cannot go, gives us an account of a plant whose color, blossom, and fragrance have practically no similarity with any we have seen; or that someone should discourse on light and its effects to a man born blind. In such cases, of course, the mystery is not absolute, and does not obtain for all men, since it is not at all obscure for some, or even for a large number. But let us take a truth to which no men, no creatures at all can attain by the natural means of cognition at their disposal, which they can perceive only by a supernatural illumination, which can be grasped only by belief in God's word, and which is remote from everything that the creature naturally knows, as remote as heaven is from earth. Then we have a mystery in its absolute form as a truth whose existence the creature cannot ascertain without belief in God's word, and whose subject matter he cannot represent and conceive directly, but only indirectly by comparison with dissimilar things.

Mystery in its absolute form, as we have just described it, is Christian mystery, that is, mystery which divine revelation in the person of the incarnate Word proposes to the world for belief.

In accordance with our description, two elements are essential to a mystery: first, that the existence of the proposed truth is attainable by no natural means of cognition, that it lies beyond the range of the created intellect; secondly, that its content is capable of apprehension only by analogous concepts. If either one of these two elements is lacking, a truth cannot be called a mystery of Christianity in the strict sense, even if it has actually been proposed by Christian revelation. Owing to the absence of the first element, the doctrine of the existence of God and His essential attributes, for example, is not a mystery in this sense. For, although we apprehend all this only by analogous concepts, so that our notion must always remain obscure, reason can know that the objects apprehended really exist. Conversely, we are aware of many of God's works only through divine revelation (for example, the establishment of the Church as a juridical society pertaining to divine right, prescinding from its interior, supernatural character), the abstract notion of which, however, presents no special difficulty, because such things are similiar to objects of our natural perception. Hence they are not mysteries in the narrower sense.

Mystery is generally defined as a truth concerning which we know that it is, but not how it is; that is, according to the usual explanation, we know that the subject and the predicate are really connected, but we are unable to determine and perceive the manner of the association.

This definition, if rightly explained, agrees in essentials with ours as given above. But it requires a detailed clarification, which is explicitly contained in our definition, and is not sufficiently expressed in the customary explanation.

Hence we shall do well to adhere to our definition, which is in no need of all these explanations and supplementary qualifications. In simpler form we can phrase it thus: Christian mystery is a truth communicated to us by Christian revelation, a truth to which we cannot attain by our unaided reason, and which, even after we have attained to it by faith, we cannot adequately represent with our rational concepts.

3. THE PLACE OF MYSTERIES IN THE SYSTEM OF CHRISTIAN REVELATION

That Christianity contains mysteries of this kind is beyond question. It is likewise clear that not all its truths, but only those to which our definition applies, in contrast to the rest to which it does not apply, deserve to be called mysteries in the full and proper sense of the term. Accordingly we are entitled to detach the mysteries from the rest of the truths, and to consider them under a special category.

I am well aware that difficulties are raised in some quarters against such a division, partly out of zeal for the mysteries, partly in the interests of reason, according as it is argued that the truths of Christianity are all either equally remote from the reason, or are equally proximate to it.

Obviously there can be no question of a like remoteness or proximity in every respect. Who would undertake to maintain that all truths are equally hard or equally easy to learn? Even if such an undertaking should occur to anyone, we have no need to waste words in arguing with him. Those whom we have in mind do not take such a stand. The only contention, with reference to the boundaries set up by our definition, is either that all the truths of Christianity lie without the horizon of the reason, or that all lie within it.

The first of these two contentions is found in the article "Mysterien" of the first edition of the *Freiburger Kirchen-Lexikon,* which in other respects is very stimulating, and is especially good in its criticism of the usual definition of mystery. The article insists that the whole of Christianity is a single great mystery, because it can be known as a whole only through divine revelation; and although its incomprehensibility does not equally pertain to all parts of the whole, it cannot by itself alone yield any definite norm for singling out individual parts of the whole, particularly since there is no special basis for such selection.

Unlike the superficial, inconsistent view of mysteries which occupied the author of the article mentioned above, and which received a sharp criticism from him, this theory is in part quite correct. It is true, and we ourselves have pointed it out above, that inconceivability alone, taken in general, can furnish no definite norm for the distinction; only later, after the necessity of revelation for the knowledge of the existence of the mystery has become apparent, does it prove decisive. Likewise it is perfectly true that Christianity, or rather the content of Christianity taken as a whole, and particularly its specific content, is a mystery in the sense that it can be known only through divine revelation. Lastly it is true that even if the only non-mysterious elements were subordinate truths regarded individually in themselves, we could not rightly consider the primary truths as the sole mysterious section of the whole, since such subordinate truths, which have no meaning apart from the whole, merge with the whole and hence participate in its mysterious character.

But here our ways part. Without doubt Christianity comprises many truths knowable by reason. To such belongs all that concerns the nature of man, man's utter dependence on God, and the existence of this personal God Himself (apart from the precision of His personality in the Trinity). These truths constitute a definite system in themselves; and they are related to the truths that lie beyond the reach of the reason not as secondary truths to primary truths, but as the body to the soul

327

which is above it but at the same time dwells in it, or as the foundation to the edifice constructed thereon, or as the vestibule to the interior of the temple, or as two juxtaposed but subordinate parts of the same whole.

The mysterious part, as the superior, is at once the soul and the proper essence of the whole, gives its name to the whole, and renders the latter specifically distinct from any other whole. So when I say that Christianity as a whole is mysterious, and is a single vast mystery, I do not mean that everything in Christianity is a mystery, but only that the higher and nobler part of it, that part which renders it specifically distinct from every other system of religious truths, even from true and uncontaminated natural religion, is mysterious and a mystery throughout; in the same way as we should say that man, although visible in body, is invisible in his essential form, his soul. And as I should say that the body itself is invisible so far as it belongs to the whole, that is, in its conjunction and union with the soul, so I might say of Christianity likewise, that its naturally known truths are themselves mysterious when considered in their conjunction and relation with the mysterious part. But in this case they are not taken by themselves alone; only their conjunction with the mysterious is designated as a mystery, and the mysterious character of this relationship can be perceived in the very fact that we single out and study the mysterious character of the one part in opposition to the non-mysterious character of the other.

That the relationship of rational truths to mysterious truths is such as we have just described, will be found to be one of the first fruits of our work, which will definitely show that Christianity is essentially a tremendous mystery at every point. That the learned author of the above-mentioned article does not share this view, is owing to the fact, if we understand him aright, that objectively and subjectively he establishes too close a connection between genuinely mysterious truths and the truths which we have designated as rational truths, that he excessively confuses both, and hence notably defrauds reason in its own domain. Thus, for example, he maintains that without a knowledge of the Trinity in God we can have no true notion of God at all, and consequently that any teaching about

God is true only in terms of a mystery that comes to our knowledge through revelation. We can admit neither of these propositions, the first if only for the reason that the second would thereupon follow. In the second proposition we discern a decided encroachment on reason in its own realm, and in the first a confusion between a false notion and a one-sided, inadequate notion. I shall later have more to say about this.

Zeal for the mysterious character of the whole of Christianity dictated this protest against the elimination of mysteries from the sum total of Christian truths. At the other extreme is the error, still frequently proclaimed, that all the truths of Christianity lie as close to the reason as any part of them.

No one, to be sure, would deny that to attain to some of the truths of Christianity reason stands in greater need of revelation than in the case of other truths. The view is even put forward that reason by itself could not have discovered them, that they were hidden from reason prior to revelation. But, this view adds, subsequently to revelation, and guided by revelation, reason can direct its gaze toward such truths and by concentrated contemplation can actually perceive them. And in fact there can be no controversy that Christianity makes known in this sense many a truth which had been hidden from us before. But such truths must lie within the range of our natural vision. Hence they are not absolute mysteries, because reason, though not without external assistance, can attain to them by its own inner light, and because, consequent upon revelation, they stand out clearly within the horizon of reason. There is no essential difference between them and the truths discovered by us prior to revelation; they are rational truths just as much as are these latter. Revelation of such truths would not open up the prospect of an entirely new and unknown domain, but would merely guide the reason and assist it in the mastery of its own province.

No, we may not have so mean an estimate of the riches and grandeur of divine revelation. We must certainly be grateful that revelation has pointed out the right path leading to the reason's richest development; but we should prove ungrateful were we to be thankful only for this, were we, enamored of the fancied greatness of our reason, to restrict the inestimable wealth of Christ to so narrow a compass. Incomparably greater is the call upon our gratitude for the communication of truths lying entirely beyond the sphere of investigation possible for our natural reason, truths to which reason itself, in spite of the greatest endeavor and the most competent guidance, can never attain. Our gratitude to revelation for such truths must be all the greater inasmuch as they lie absolutely beyond the reach of reason, and inasmuch as these suprarational truths are more sublime, more precious, more valuable than purely rational truths, so that even the slightest knowledge of them calls for the greatest esteem and appreciation on our part.

In fact, it is precisely the objective sublimity and grandeur of certain truths of Christianity that place them above the horizon of our reason. Whatever the finite reason, precisely because it is finite, cannot reach and grasp, must of necessity lie beyond all that it can reach and grasp. Suprarationality is a consequence, and hence the best sign, of the greatness and sublimity of a truth. It coincides with the supernaturality in which the objective sublimity of a thing is expressed. Deny the suprarationality of a part of Christian truth, and you destroy its supernatural grandeur and sublimity, its intrinsic excellence and wealth. Vice versa, if you deny the supernaturalness of these truths, they cease automatically to transcend reason, and so the absolute necessity and the highest value of revelation itself vanish.

4. GUIDING PRINCIPLES AND METHOD OF OUR DISCUSSION OF MYSTERIES

Thus far we have seen that we may classify the mysteries of Christianity as a special category of the truths which it teaches; and we have also fixed upon the reason why such a classification and a special consideration of them are useful and profitable, if not necessary.

Our purpose in isolating the mysteries from the other truths of Christianity is to understand and present them in their supernatural grandeur and sublimity, so as to bring together in one comprehensive view all that Christianity possesses beyond anything that the human mind and heart can discover or contrive in the realm of beauty and greatness, and thus to unveil its proper, intrinsic nature in all its wealth. This we undertake in the hope of being able to show that precisely those doctrines which appear to the proud mind as horrible wraiths, as senseless, impossible enigmas, infinitely surpass in beauty and clarity all that reason in its loftiest flights can achieve. And we hope further that, considered precisely as mysteries, whether singly or in their mutual relationships, they will stand forth in as clear a light as possible here on earth.

We trust that we shall be able to bring together the mysteries of Christianity into an independent, well-ordered system in which they will appear to be a great, mystic cosmos erected, out of the depths of the divinity, upon the world of nature which is visible to the bodily eye, and upon the world of spirit which is visible only to the mind. Lastly, we believe that for the scientific understanding of Christianity, for theology, nothing is more important and rich in blessings, and today in particular nothing is more seasonable, than this specialized and systematic treatment of the doctrine of mysteries.

There is in our day a pronounced tendency toward the strict separation of the various branches of knowledge. The supposition is that each science will come to full and distinct self-consciousness if it is studied in its opposition to other sciences. But how can theology build up a science of its own, and especially how can it detach itself objectively from philosophy, unless it becomes conscious of its own proper domain in which alone it is at home, and into which philosophy cannot follow? And where is its most proper domain situated if not in its doctrine of mysteries?

Such clear self-consciousness is necessary for theology if it is to be quite at home in its own sphere and is to be brought to a genuinely scientific form.

The treatment of those doctrines of Christianity which are really mysteries in the sense explained cannot be fruitful and successful unless we clearly determine and keep before our eyes the position of the reason and its natural objects with respect to these suprarational and supernatural objects. If this is not done, there is a proximate danger of confusing the higher objects with the lower, of drawing the higher down within the orbit of the reason, and of treating them in the same manner as the lower. The result is that these higher objects are viewed obliquely and in a false light by the contemplating eye. Instead of appearing in their extraordinary greatness and harmony, they become disarranged and distorted, if not actually deformed. Thus, instead of gaining in clarity they become darker, even though to a diseased or unfocused eye they seem distinct and beautiful.

Mysteries become luminous and appear in their true nature, their entire grandeur and beauty, only when we definitely recognize that they are mysteries, and clearly perceive how high they stand above our own orbit, how completely they are distinct from all objects within our natural ken. And when, supported by the all-powerful word of divine revelation, we soar upon the wings of faith over the chasm dividing us from them and mount up to them, they temper themselves to our eyes in the light of faith which is supernatural, as they themselves are; then they display themselves to us in their true form, in their heavenly, divine nature. The moment we perceive the depth of the darkness with which heaven veils its mysteries from our minds, they will shine over us in the light of faith like brilliant stars mutually illuminating, supporting, and emphasizing one another; like stars that form themselves into a marvelous system and that can be known in their full power and magnificence only in this system. Lastly, the more we bring ourselves to a realization of the supernaturality in the suprarationality, and of the suprarationality in the supernaturality of these mysteries, the less will the darkness of the incomprehensibility enveloping them trouble and bewilder us. Yet we can never forget that this incomprehensibility is part of their sublimity. Any confusion or apparent contradiction involved in this incomprehensibility will tend to vanish the more we recall the sublimity of these objects and guard against mixing them up with the objects of our natural perception or measuring them with the norm of the latter, and the more careful we are, under the guidance of faith, to refer the natural to them only as an analogy.

Guided by such reflections, we desired to make the attempt to present the higher Christian truths, so far as they are intelligible, in their supernatural magnificence and consummate harmony. To accomplish this task, we must specify the mysterious character of these truths. We believe that, as correct perspective is indispensable to astronomy and the graphic arts, an accurate determination of the mysterious character of the higher Christian truths is indispensable to an understanding and presentation of the mysteries themselves. For thousands of years astronomy had judged the magnitude and relations of the heavenly bodies according to their superficial appearance, and came to a correct appreciation of these matters only when man had learned to determine the distance of the stars from our eye and terrestrial objects by means of the parallax. Similarly theology will understand its exalted objects with greater accuracy and clarity the more exactly we learn to determine their distance from our natural intellect and from the latter's near-by natural objects. Sculpture and painting could achieve their perfection only after man had learned to apply the right perspective to pictorial presentation. In like manner theology will be able to display faithful and lifelike pictures to its disciples only when it succeeds in drawing its designs according to all the laws of correct perspective.

In all departments of experimental science and the graphic arts perspective has in our day come into its full importance. We have studied its laws with zeal and success, and have applied it universally with happy results. In the field of theology the great doctors of the Church, and especially the princes of medieval Scholasticism, investigated and applied its laws with nice judgment, at a time when those laws were scarcely known and but slightly esteemed in the sphere of physical observation and technical works. Far from neglecting them, theology must devote its attention to them more than ever at the present time, when it is apparently being summoned to a new and noble resurgence, so that the sacred sciences may keep pace with the secular sciences, and Christian learning with the renewal of Christian life and the revival of sacred art.

Rationalism, which believes that it alone possesses the philosopher's stone and pretends to be the sole representative of science even in the domain of faith, is the only tendency that will object to the fundamental postulate of theological science. It is not so long ago that a Catholic philosopher in the name of science raised a protest against the withdrawal of the mysteries from the natural purview of the reason, as though theological science would be rendered radically impossible unless confined to the domain of reason. Concerning the validity and necessity of such segregation, the head of the Church has instructed him; concerning the havoc wrought upon science not by the withdrawal, but by the denial of mysteries, science itself will instruct him.

The following studies on the mysteries of Christianity are worked out in line with the procedure explained above. We have selected nine of the mysteries as being the most important; all the others are reducible to these nine. We have taken pains to indicate and determine the supernatural, mysterious character of each of them, so as to pave the way for as clear and lucid an exposition of its subject matter as is possible, in view of the obscurity which shrouds it and of our own feeble powers. The light derived from the consideration of each separate mystery spreads automatically far and wide over the inner relationship and the wonderful harmony pervading them all, and thus the individual pictures take their places in an orderly gallery, which comprises everything magnificent and sublime that theology possesses far in excess of all the other sciences, including even philosophy.

CHAPTER XIX

THE MYSTERY OF THE CHURCH

77. GENERAL NOTION OF THE MYSTERY

By becoming man the Son of God has called the whole human race to fellowship in His body. That which was remote, that which was far from God and vastly below Him, He has brought near in His person, and has joined in one body, His own body. Upon Himself and in Himself He has established a great community and society of men. He is at once the head and the foundation of this society. In it He wills to continue His activity and His reign. Through it He wishes to unite men to Himself and to His heavenly Father. This society is the Church.

The Church is a great and stupendous mystery. It is a mystery in its very being, a mystery in its organization, a mystery in the power and activity it exercises. Let us endeavor first of all to determine the perspective according to which it is to be viewed.

When we assert that the Church is a mystery, do we intend to do away with its natural visibility? By no means; the Church is visible in its members, in its external organization, and in the relations existing between its superiors and subjects. It is as visible as any other human society.

I venture to make an even greater claim: the Church is visible not only as it actually stands at present, but in its divine foundation and institution.

The astonishing origin and the no less astonishing continuance and growth of this society, the numberless moral and physical miracles marking its course throughout the centuries and in every quarter of the globe, prove that it is no mere work of man. They proves that it is a work of God, that God has instituted it and continues still to acknowledge and uphold it as an organization that He Himself has founded.

The Church is visible in the very way that its historical founder and head, the God-man Himself, was visible. The God-man was visible both as a real man, and as a man sent by God and standing in a unique relationship to God. Similarly the Church is visible both as a society of men, and as a society founded and sustained by God.

The likeness of the Church to Christ is carried out even in its invisibility and its mysterious character. Despite the visibility of His humanity and its unique relationship to God, the proper character of Christ as true God and true man lay hidden beneath the visible veil in the depths of the Godhead. So too, the inner nature of the Church, the sacred bond which envelops its members and links them together, the marvelous power which holds sway in it and energizes it with life, the heavenly goal which it pursues—all this, notwithstanding the visibility of its external organization and its divine origin, is simply impenetrable to the natural eye of man, and hence is incomprehensible and inconceivable. It is only by belief in divine revelation that we can conceive and know the true nature of the God-man, head of the Church. Likewise it is only by acceptance of this same revelation that we are able to grasp the true inner greatness which marks the Church because of the divine-human character of its head.

The inner nature of the Church is absolutely supernatural, as is that of the God-man. This is the reason why it is so hidden and mysterious; this is the reason why the Church, although conformable to other human societies in its outward organization, differs essentially from these in its innermost character; and this is the reason why its unity, its power, and its organization are so matchless, sublime, and inconceivable.

Concerning the nature of the Church, the temptation might arise to form a notion that has regard only to externals, on the analogy of other societies that exist among men, and to account for its radical difference from these only by the fact that it is a religious community founded by God. Such it is, no doubt; but this alone would not place it so high beyond the range of our minds. In the same way that men organize themselves for other purposes, they could also band together for common worship; there is nothing supernatural in this. Indeed, by a positive ordination God Himself could decree the formation of such a society, assign laws to it, bestow special rights and privileges on it, and, on the other hand, bind men to it and refer them to it for the fulfillment of their religious obligations, as was done through the Mosaic institutions of the Old Testament. A society of this kind would not come into existence without a supernatural, extraordinary intervention on God's part. But this circumstance would not make it supernatural and mysterious in its very nature. The worship of God would be purely natural, except that it would be regulated and conducted according to fixed norms. And if God were to attach a special efficacy to the priestly and jurisdictional functions of this society, so that remission of sins and other graces would be guided with full certitude in the conduct of their religious life by the latter, this indeed would be quite extraordinary. It would be the effect of a special, gratuitous Providence, but it would not be genuinely mysterious and supernatural. If such were the case, the entire Church as an institution would be reduced to a mere system of education and guidance directed by God, and a legal code regulating man's dealings with God;

its unity and activity would be only something moral, after the analogy of other human societies.

Faith shows us that there is vastly more to the Church than this. Faith enables us to see in the Church not merely an institution established for the education and guidance of natural man, but one that confers on man a new existence and a new life, a wholly new, supernatural rank and destiny, and that is designed to support, strengthen, and direct him in his striving for this destiny. To the eyes of faith the Church is not merely a society founded and approved by God or a divine legate; but it is built upon the God-man, it is made an organic part of Him, it is raised to His level, it is upheld by His divine power and is filled with His divine excellence. The Church is the body of the God-man; and all who enter it become members of the God-man so that, linked together in Him and through Him, they may share in the divine life and the divine glory of their head. Lastly, as seen by faith, the Church is more than a handmaid of God or of the God-man, a servant who would aid in bringing about a certain limited intimacy between God and man. As the mystical body of Christ, the Church is His true bride who, made fruitful by His divine power, has the destiny of bearing heavenly children to Him and His heavenly Father, of nourishing these children with the substance and light of her bridegroom, and of conducting them beyond the whole range of created nature up to the very bosom of His heavenly Father.

In brief, the Church is a most intimate and real fellowship of men with the God-man, a fellowship that achieves its truest and most perfect expression in the Eucharist. If the God-man dwells in the Church in so wonderful a manner as to associate Himself with all its members to form one body, then evidently the unity in which He joins them is so august and mysterious that no human mind can conjecture or understand it. And if through the agency of this unity He draws the members of the Church up to and into Himself in order to permeate them with His divine power and glory, to offer them in Himself and with Himself as an infinitely pleasing sacrifice to God, this also is a mystery surpassing all human understanding and all human notions. This mystery induces in us the realization that we can never think too highly of the nature and importance of the Church.

78. THE MYSTERY OF THE CHURCH IN THE FELLOWSHIP OF ITS MEMBERS WITH CHRIST AS HEAD AND BRIDEGROOM

If the mystical nature of the Church, as the fellowship of men with the God-man, culminates and receives its fullest expression in the Eucharist, we cannot better study the Church than by regarding it from the standpoint of the Eucharist, its very heart. Let us begin with a consideration of that fellowship with Christ which is common to all the members of the Church.

The Eucharist, whether regarded as sacrament or as sacrifice, is the sacred and mysterious bond encircling all the members of the Church. Fellowship in the Church attains its full perfection in the actual partaking of the Eucharist, and in actual participation in the Eucharistic sacrifice. The right to participate in the Eucharist as sacrifice and sacrament is the chief factor that determines membership in the Church. Faith and baptism truly initiate us into the Church, but only for the reason that they qualify us for participation in the Eucharist. Indeed, by faith and baptism we spiritually anticipate the power conferred by the Eucharist, and are made members of Christ's body in proportion to our dignity. But this membership looks forward to a closer, substantial fellowship in His body that is to be effected later.

Hence to be a member of the Church is to be a member of Christ's body. In a wider sense man is a member of Christ's body by the very fact that he belongs to the human race, but only so far as he is thereby called actually to attach himself to Christ and to enter into the organism of His body.

On the one hand man is to move toward his head by faith in His dignity and power, and on the other hand he is to appropriate to himself the signature and the seal of his head, so as to belong to His body in the stricter sense, to become a member that will be responsive to the influence emanating from the head and will stand in organic connection with the head. The first step is made by faith, the second by baptism. Faith and baptism together make man a member of Christ in the organism of the Church instituted by Christ Himself.

338

Matthias Joseph Scheeben

What high, supernatural dignity is attained by man when he becomes a member of the Church, how astounding the union into which he enters with Christ, and through Christ with God, and at the same time with all his fellow members in the Church! What a tremendous mystery lies even in simple membership in the Church! It is a mystery as great as the mystery of the mystical body of Christ, as the mystery of the Eucharist in which it culminates, as the mystery of the Incarnation upon which it is based, as the mystery of grace which is its fruit.

To conceive of the integration of all members of the Church in Christ under the notion of a mystical marriage with the God-man, as the Apostle does, is merely to express the truth in another way. By the Incarnation Christ has assumed our nature in order to yoke Himself with us. The Fathers view Incarnation itself as a marriage with the human race, inasmuch as it virtually contains everything that can lead to the full union of the Son of God with men. But the relationship of unity it sets up comes to full fruition only in the Church. Man is to attach himself to his divine bridegroom by faith; and the bridegroom seals His union with man in baptism, as with a wedding ring. But both faith and baptism are mere preliminaries for the coming together of man and the God-man in one flesh by a real Communion of flesh and blood in the Eucharist, and hence for the perfect fructifying of man with the energizing grace of his head. By entering the Church every soul becomes a real bride of God's Son, so truly that the Son of God is able, in the Apostle's words, not only to compare His love and union with the Church and her members with the unity achieved in matrimony, but can even propose it as the ideal and model of the latter. Is not such unity an ineffable, stupendous mystery, which infinitely transcends all the notions of natural man?

If the Church in all its members is thus the body of Christ and the bride of Christ, the power of its divine head, the Spirit of its divine bridegroom, must be gloriously operative in it. In all its members the Church is a temple of the Holy Spirit, who dwells in it as the soul in its own body, and manifests His divine and divinizing power in it. He is active in the Church not only in the way in which, as the Spirit of eternal wisdom and order,

He guides and directs all well-regulated societies, not merely by sustaining with special assistance individuals and the entire community in its religious pursuits, by granting the remission of sins, and by helping to heal our moral weaknesses and informities. No, He must be active in the members of Christ's body as He is in the real body of Christ, namely, by filling them with the plenitude of the divinity. He must overshadow the bride of Christ as once He overshadowed Mary's womb, so that in her the Son of God may be reborn in His divine holiness and majesty. With His divine fire He must gloriously change Christ's bride into the image of the divine nature, transform her whole being by adding splendor to splendor, and pervade her with His own divine life. All this He must do so radically and powerfully that it may be said of her that she does not herself live, but God lives in her. He must make her so like her divine head and bridegroom that she seems to be Christ Himself.

When it is asserted of other societies that the member joining it becomes like a plant that is transplanted in a new soil, or grafted onto a new trunk, the figure is to be taken in a very diluted and weakened sense. For in such cases the soil and the trunk of the society can do no more than give a new bent to the member's growth, and aid him in the developing of existing aptitudes. These societies cannot transform the new member's innermost being and nature, or the root of his life. All that is possible is a moral suasion by moral influence. But when a person becomes a member of the Church, he is taken up to the bosom of God in Christ and through Christ; he is planted in a heavenly soil, and grafted on a divine trunk; he enters into a new, supernatural sphere where his nature is transformed and transfigured. A wholly new life is infused into him, and this new life is nourished and cultivated under the sun and dew of a new heaven. The Holy Spirit, it is true, reigns in the members of the Church by guiding, assisting, and healing them. But such aid is granted only on the basis of that elevation and transfiguration of man beyond his nature which is effected by the Holy Spirit. Its purpose is to inaugurate and foster the divine life which must first be implanted in human nature by Him, and to furnish and adorn the divine temple which must first be built by Him.

We shall see later how the Holy Spirit gradually unfolds His activity in the individual members of the Church. Here our object is to make clear that the presence and activity of the Holy Spirit in the members of the Church, as the members of Christ, must be intimate and mysterious to a high degree, inasmuch as it is the emanation and the continuation of that presence and activity with which He dwells in the humanity of the Son of God. Since the Holy Spirit Himself proceeds from the Son of God and as such belongs to Him, He necessarily enters into the Son's humanity and into His whole mystical body, and belongs also to the latter. This is true all the more inasmuch as in the Eucharist the Son of God dwells bodily and essentially, with all the plenitude of His divinity, among His members in the bosom of the Church. In the Son and through the Son the Holy Spirit dwells there also, personally and essentially. He is the very Spirit and, as it were, the soul of the Church.

Thus the great mystery of the Eucharistic Christ is the center around which is grouped the noble community of Christ's faithful. This community we call the Church. It is a fellowship that is a great mystery in its own right, because it elevates all its members in a mysterious way, and operates in them in a mysterious way.

79. THE MYSTERY OF THE CHURCH IN ITS MATERNAL ORGANIZATION

With all this we are still far from appreciating the mystery of the Church in all its greatness. The God-man had no intention of making the members of the ecclesiastical community His members simply in order to act in them as their head. He willed further to appoint some of them as representatives and organs of His own activity, so that His mystical body might be equipped with an internal organization, which would, however, find expression in external signs. As bridegroom He had a higher object in view than merely to be yoked with all the members of the Church so that they might benefit their own persons by sharing in His dignity and honor. In a part of its members the Church, as His bride, was meant to be a true mother to the children who were to be reborn to Him as bridegroom, so that the heavenly rebirth of the human race might correspond to its natural generation, and the organization of the God-man's family might conform to the family of earthly man. To this end He weds a part of the members of the Church in a special way, entrusts to their keeping the mystical resources belonging to the Church in common, and overshadows them beyond all others with the power of the Holy Spirit, so that they may bear Him children and bring them into closest fellowship with Himself.

This is the great mystery of the maternity of the Church in her priesthood. In general the priesthood of the Church functions as intermediary between Christ and His children, much as the mother does between father and children. But the similarity between this twofold intermediacy must be adequately understood.

In accordance with its office the priesthood must bring Christ to birth anew in the bosom of the Church, both in the Eucharist and in the hearts of the faithful, by the power of Christ's Spirit reigning in the Church. Priests must build up the organism of Christ's mystical body, as Mary, by the power of the same Holy Spirit, brought forth the Word in His own humanity, and gave Him His physical body. The miraculous conception of Christ and His birth from the womb of the Virgin is the model and also the basis of the further spiritual conception and birth of Christ in the Church through the priesthood. And this priesthood stands in a relationship to the God-man similar to that of Mary to the Son of God who descended into her and was born of her. The two mysteries are complementary; they illuminate and set off each other.

As Mary conceived the Son of God in her womb by the overshadowing of the Holy Spirit, drew Him down from heaven by her consent, and gave Him, the Invisible, to the world in visible form, so the priest conceives the Incarnate Son of God by the power of the same Spirit in order to establish Him in the bosom of the Church under the Eucharistic forms. Thus Christ is born anew through the priesthood by a continuation, as it were, of His miraculous birth from Mary; and the priesthood itself is an imitation and extension of the mysterious maternity that Mary possessed with regard to the God-man. The priesthood is for the Eucharistic Christ what Mary was for the Son of God about to become man.

With this maternity which the Church in her priesthood exercises over Christ who is to be received into her bosom, is connected, or rather from it proceeds, her mysterious motherhood over her individual members. Christ is brought into the Church in the Eucharist because the Church is to be joined with Him in one body, because He is to be reborn in her members. For this reason also the priesthood has the power, through the overshadowing of the Holy Spirit, to bring forth Christ anew in the hearts of the faithful, and the faithful in Christ, in order to effect a substantial union between them and Christ in His real body, and to nourish them with His own flesh and blood in their new, supernatural life. As the priesthood gives rebirth to Christ, the head of the Church, so it must also impart new birth to the members of the head.

The underlying idea and the essential functions of the sublime motherhood that we must ascribe to the Church in her priesthood consist in making the real body of Christ present in the Eucharist for union with His mystical body, and in building up this mystical body itself. Hence this maternity is no empty formula, it is not a weak analogue of natural motherhood. It implies more than the fact that the Church has the attitude of a loving mother toward her members by caring for them, nourishing them, instructing them, and rearing them like children. All such activity exercised by the Church and its priesthood has its basis and receives its true meaning and character from the fact that the priesthood is supernaturally related to the children of the Church with a relationship no less real and true than that of a natural mother to the children she has borne. In its own way this relationship is as real and objective as the real presence of the God-man in the Eucharist which is effected through the co-operation of the priesthood, or as the new, supernatural existence and life of the children of God which is brought into being through the agency of the same priesthood.

Hence the priesthood itself is as great and mysterious as the two effects with which it is associated. Inexpressibly sublime is the dignity imparted to the priesthood, and in it to the Church: to be the mother of the God-man in His sacramental existence, and of men in their higher, divine existence. Incomprehensible is the fruitfulness which the Church reveals in this maternity, unspeakable the union with the overshadowing Holy Spirit, who in her bosom and through her brings about marvels similar to those that took place in the most pure womb of Mary. This supernatural motherhood is the central mystery of the Church as an organically constructed society. For it is this motherhood by which the ecclesiastical fellowship is made a soundly constituted society, wherein the children are linked to the Father through the mother. By it the body of the Church, the mystical body of Christ, is developed and extended by a process of growth from within; by it the real presence and the real union of the head with His members is sustained and perfected. Finally, this maternity is the basis of all the other social relations and activities which regulate and shape the Church in the unfolding of its life. It imparts to these a supernatural, mysterious stamp which they would lack apart from union with the Church.

The activity of the priesthood in the Church, to use the Apostle's words, amounts to this: to fashion Christ in its members, to unite them to Christ, to conform them to Him, to build them up to the full measure of the stature of Christ. Because of this end the activity of the priesthood receives, to a greater or less extent, a higher, supernatural significance wherever it is exercised. The sublime motherhood of the Church leaves its mark upon all the functions of the priesthood.

As a heavenly mother, the Church nourishes her children with heavenly bread, the flesh of the Son of God. With this same flesh and blood of God's Son she places in their hands a gift by the oblation of which they can offer a perfect sacrifice to their heavenly Father. In this oblation they can also offer themselves to Him in a fitting manner, so as to honor Him as He deserves, to thank Him, to make satisfaction to Him for all their sins, and to obtain abundant gifts from Him. As heavenly mother she stamps on their forehead the seal of the Holy Spirit in the sacrament of confirmation, to equip and strengthen them for strife and battle. As heavenly mother she washes her children clean from the filth of sin, and after the disastrous separation from their heavenly Father leads them back into His arms. As heavenly mother she cures and heartens them in their illnesses of body and soul, particularly at that decisive hour when in the midst of harsh conflict their very entrance into the joys of their heavenly Father is at issue. As heavenly mother she reproduces herself in the persons of the priests who bear her maternal dignity, and with her blessing accompanies those of her children who, animated with her dispositions and by virtue of the Holy Spirit's consecration imparted to them, join in wedlock for the bodily propagation and multiplication of her members.

In all these activities the Church operates on the basis of her motherhood, with an ever-growing manifestation of the marvelous fertility she possesses by reason of her union with the Holy Spirit. But, since she is a mother, she must do more than prove herself fruitful in her children by the communication or renovation of an increasingly intimate fellowship with Christ and His heavenly Father. She must also guide and regulate the activity which her children are to undertake for the purpose of entering into that fellowship; or, when in it, of making it known and further developing it. She must teach and educate them. She must instruct her children especially concerning those supernatural, mysterious truths which the Son of God has brought down to her from His heavenly Father. She must initiate her children into the mysteries of God and of their own supernatural nobility and destiny. She must teach them with an authority and infallibility which correspond to the dignity of Christ's bride who occupies the place of God, and to the sublimity of the faith which is to be engendered in them. And she must so guide and rule her children that, led by her hand, they may with certainty and confidence set out toward the mysterious, supernatural goal which, in the person of her divine head, she has long since anticipated and taken into possession.

The power to teach and educate, even when exercised with a certain infallibility, may perhaps not seem to be a very great mystery. But at any rate there is a great mystery in the teaching and educating power which the Church possesses as the heavenly mother of the human race, and which is inseparably bound up with that motherhood. For this power supposes that the priesthood of the Church is truly the bride of Christ and the organ of the Holy Spirit. This Holy Spirit, by the glorious presence and union whereby He imparts to the priesthood its sublime fruitfulness, enables Christ's bride to keep alive and cultivate her fruit in the faithful, and to make that fruit beneficial and salutary to the faithful through their obedience in matters of faith and conduct.

80. RELATION OF THE SACRAMENTAL MATERNITY TO THE JURISDICTIONAL ORGANIZATION OF THE CHURCH

The maternity of the Church, which is represented by a specially favored number of its members, comprises two functions: the power to confer grace, and the power to direct the use or acquisition of grace. A clearer understanding of the relationship between these two functions is indispensable for a deeper insight into the mystical organization of the Church.

This distinction coincides with the distinction familiar to theologians of a former age, between the power of orders and the power of jurisdiction, as two powers essentially different and even separable in those who possess them. In more recent times the distinction has repeatedly been assailed; the contention has been advanced that it is inadequate because it excludes the teaching authority, and that it sets up too great a cleavage between the powers which it distinguishes. It may well be that many theologians have given occasion for such strictures, owing to a superficial appreciation of the purport of the distinction. But at bottom it is a profound concept, and is rich in most weighty consequences.

By the power of jurisdiction we must here understand not only external legislative power in the ordinary sense, as it is found in other societies, but especially the power by which the Church authoritatively directs and regulates the activity of its subjects, and by which it establishes and enforces the norms for that activity. But the Church does precisely this and nothing else even in the exercise of its teaching power, since in virtue of its divine authority it rules and regulates outward actions and also their inner principle, and the inner attitude of those who perform them. By jurisdiction we usually mean no more than disciplinary power over external actions and over the external order prevailing in a society, since it is only in such cases that an external code of laws, or jurisdiction in the narrower sense, can be administered. But the Church has judicial competency even in matters of faith; although it can pass no judgment concerning the fact of interior belief, it can at least determine the obligation of believing. Were it not for this competency, we could well forego the expression "power of jurisdiction," and substitute "pastoral office" for it. This is the term used by the Savior Himself; it implies the competence which the Church possesses with regard to the guidance and education of its children, an office to be discharged by feeding and leading them. The Church feeds its children by setting up norms for their belief, and guides them by setting up norms for their conduct. At the same time this term tones down the opposition of this power to the power of orders, that is, the priesthood, and clears the way for an understanding of the connection between them.

Despite such connection, we must hold fast to the truth that the pastoral power is not formally bound up with the power of orders, since there can be priests and bishops without actual jurisdiction. In virtue of its higher "order," the priesthood constitutes, so to speak, the nobility in the Church, a nobility whose higher dignity and control of the society's supernatural goods in the realm of grace set it apart from the other members. On account of its rank it is called upon, as a body, to wield the pastoral power in the Church. As the spiritual mother of the rest of the faithful, the priesthood is also the natural custodian of the educational authority over them. Moreover, since the priesthood is so closely related to the God-man, and since the Holy Spirit resides in the sacerdotal order with the rich fruitfulness of His graces, it is the organ by which the same Holy Spirit wills to lead the Church to all truth and to guide it to all good.

This is not to say that the pastoral office is entrusted wholly or in part to any individual simply because of his priestly rank. Nor do we assert that any individual has, without further consideration, even the right to exercise his sacerdotal fruitfulness, or to dispose of the treasures of grace contained therein, either for himself or in behalf of the faithful; for this disposal does not belong to the sacerdotal power as such, but to the pastoral power. In virtue of the title by which the pastoral power has the exclusive right to guide and to regulate the ecclesiastical activity of the rest of the faithful, it has the right to govern and to regulate those activities by which the Holy Spirit distributes His graces. In general, of course, the Holy Spirit entrusts the guidance and government of His Church to His priestly organs, as is in keeping with their position. But if the great number of these organs is to prove no detriment to the union and order of the Church, He must regulate the exercise of their sacerdotal power and the transmission of the pastoral office to them according to a definite hierarchy, and place it under undivided control. Hence the organism of the Church, which is based on the segregation of Christ's priestly organs from the lay members, must be carried on and be brought to perfection by the organization of its governing power.

Therefore the unity of the Church in its social life depends in a special way on the unity of the pastoral power. This unity of the pastoral power must be a clear sign that the Spirit of the Church operating in many organs is a single Spirit, who brings all these organs together in one whole, and causes them to exercise their activity in an orderly manner conformable with the unity of the whole. The members and organs of the Church form one body of Christ and assemble around the Eucharist as the source of their common life, and they are called to image forth the highest unity of all, that of the Trinity. In the unfolding of their life and activity, these members and organs constitute a closely knit whole, in which the unity and harmony of external social life is the faithful reflection of its true, internal, mysterious unity. This fact must be manifested by the unity of the pastoral power.

This unity of pastoral power in the Church is guaranteed by the revealed doctrine that the entire plenitude of such power is in one supreme pontiff. Moreover, this power is so vested that the whole flock of the Church and even the priests and high priests are entrusted to his care and are subject to him, and that all these high priests and priests can obtain and exercise their pastoral office in the Church only in dependence on him and in union with him. The entire social structure of the Church rests on him as its foundation. The pastoral power passes from him to the other pastors of the Church as rays proceed from the sun, brooks from their source, branches from the tree. Owing to the fact that the plenitude of the pastoral power resides in him, and that no such power can be envisaged in the Church as independent of his, the Church is made truly and perfectly one, not only in its summit, but in its deepest base—and from the base up; not only in its topmost branch, but in its root—and from the root up. Any other, lesser unity in the Church is unthinkable, unless the structure of its social organization is to be quite at odds with its inner nature.

Prior to the Vatican Council many theologians could not rise to this lofty idea of the position of the papacy in the Church. One of the reasons for this failure, and not the least, is the fact that they did not sufficiently know or view the Church in terms of its supernatural, mysterious nature which is reflected and expressed precisely in the papacy. The Church, although founded by God, was made to conform too much to the pattern of natural societies. In natural societies the undivided ruling power, even when the form of government is monarchical, is never more than representative of the common interest; the unification of power in one hand does not pertain to the essence of such societies, but constitutes only a special mode of their existence and structure. Hence the monarch is the pinnacle of the society rather than its base or an essential condition of its existence. The Church, on the contrary, is formed around an already existing, supernatural center, namely, Christ and His Holy Spirit, and this center must, by intrinsic necessity, manifest itself in the social organism in the person of a single representative, a single organ. The Church does not project this central point from itself; nor is the center set up by God merely for the purpose of completing the Church as an undivided whole. Rather it is intended to be the foundation upon which the Church is constructed, by which the Church rests upon the God-man and the Holy Spirit, and by which the unity of the Church is not incidentally brought about or crowned, but is essentially procured. The Church, as a society, is held together in this central point, as it is in Christ; through it the Church is in Christ, because it is only through it that Christ Himself, as the supreme head of the Church, is in the Church with His pastoral power.

If such is the true notion of the unity of the pastoral power in the Church, and of the unity of the Church which stands or falls with the unity of the pastoral power, the infallibility which is associated with it or, rather, is intrinsic to it, must evidently reside in him who possesses the pastoral power in its plenitude. The pastoral office must involve infallibility, at least with regard to the regulation of faith and morals, since otherwise it could not with absolute reliability guide those who are subject to it. It is so in fact, because they who possess it administer it as representatives of Christ and organs of the Holy Spirit. Consequently he who has this power in its plenitude, who therefore is the fully qualified representative of Christ and the spokesman of the Holy Spirit, must possess infallibility, so far, of course, as he acts in virtue of his full power and asserts the full range of his authority. Through him Christ wills to bring all the members of the Church together in unity of faith and love; through him and in him all the faithful are to attach themselves to their supernatural head and permit themselves to be guided by the Holy Spirit.

This supernatural infallibility of the pastoral power in the pope is, like the radical unity of the same power in his person, the reflection of the inner, mysterious character of the Church. Hence it is itself a supernatural mystery, which the Church in its divine greatness offers for our contemplation. A mere infallibility of the whole—that is, of the whole Church, or even of the entire episcopate, as resulting from the agreement of individuals—would be only an imperfect, deliberately planned measure of expediency, unworthy of the sublime activity which the Holy Spirit unfolds in the Church. On the other hand, its center of gravity would be withdrawn from the direct influence of the Holy Spirit, and would be shifted to a natural basis. If none other than the Holy Spirit is to gather the many together, why should He not group them organically, by assigning them to a common center? Surely, where such agreement in matters of faith actually exists among the faithful or their pastors, it must be referred to the Holy Spirit, who operates in all. But their infallible certitude would at the same time have a predominantly natural cause and warrant in the fact that the constant agreement of so many men could not otherwise be procured than by the objective truth of the matter agreed upon.

An explanation thus based on natural causality obviously weakens the mystery of infallibility. Those who acknowledge the root of the Church's infallibility only in such accord, show only too clearly that they shy away from whatever is supernatural or mysterious in the Church, and cannot reconcile themselves to these qualities of the Church. Indeed, they undermine even the external organization of the Church, which rests essentially upon supernatural foundations. If this view is justified, the Church is lacking in an organ to produce such accord among the faithful, when it is not already present; the pronouncement of the pope is no more than an official witness of the existing agreement, and the pope himself is but the spokeman of the community, and only in this sense is also the spokesman of the Holy Spirit who abides in the community. His faith, therefore, would not be the basis of the faith of the community; and instead of upholding the community, in accord with the words of the Savior, his faith would be upheld by the community.

But why should we be reluctant to admit a mysterious foundation for the external organization of this structure, whose entire being is a mystery? Why should not the Holy Spirit, who dwells in the priesthood with His marvelous fruitfulness in order to distribute His graces in the Church through its agency, be able so to dwell, and why should He not actually dwell, in the central point of the Church's social structure, in the bearer of His pastoral power? Why should He not bring the whole flock together in faith and love from that point, and through it impart unity and stability to the structure? Such union of the Holy Spirit with the head of the Church would be a tremendous wonder; but it ought to be precisely that. The Church is throughout an awe-inspiring, divine edifice. What wonder that its foundation should be so remarkable? The Church is the bride of the God-man. What wonder that it should be so closely united to Him through its head, and be so marvelously guided by Him through its head?

Only in terms of the mystery of the fullness of the pastoral office in the head of the bishops, can we form an adequate notion of the mystery of the sublime maternity of the Church, as it has been described above.

The motherhood of the Church in the strict sense pertains not to the whole community, but to those persons endowed with the fruitfulness and the pastoral power by which the children of the Church are begotten, reared, and guided. In a word, it belongs to the fathers of the Church. We call them "fathers" because of their natural sex character, which in conformity with propriety is demanded by Christ for the carrying out of the higher offices in the Church. But if their function in the Church is considered formally according to its supernatural side, and if attention is focused on their dignity rather than on their persons, they obviously have a maternal character. Thus viewed, their persons are seen in a special way to be wedded to the God-man in His Holy Spirit: they are persons through whom the God-man begets, rears, and educates His children, as the father of the family does through the mother. In this particular respect the multiplicity of their persons does not enter into consideration, but rather the unity of their relationship to Christ and to the Holy Spirit; and even in the external organism this unity is represented by the dependence of them all on him who possesses the pastoral power in its fullness.

In virtue of this double union (internally with Christ and the Holy Spirit, and externally with the representative of both), the priests constitute the one bride of Christ. Christ Himself renders them fruitful for the purpose of begetting and nourishing the children of the Church, and He crowns their head with His pastoral power. Thereby they are likewise made the one mother of the faithful. They possess this dignity when all of them are taken together as a unit, whereas their head, the pope, possesses it by himself alone. So far as they proceed and act in virtue of their double connection, the qualities of their individual personalities do not enter into consideration. Whether such personality is good or evil, Christ acts through them as through His organs. This activity is ever fruitful, or infallible according to the nature of the case; no account is taken of the personal condition of the organs. They are fruitful in the exercise of the sacerdotal power, and infallible in the exercise of the complete pastoral office, with regard to faith and morals. This is the concrete sense of the words that are often understood but vaguely: the Church as such cannot err; the errors of her members and of him who holds authority do not touch the Church herself. Her womb remains ever undefiled and immaculate, for it is the abode and vehicle of the fructifying and ruling power of the Holy Spirit. And so, too, the children of the Church, so far as they are begotten of her and are reared and guided by her in the power of the Holy Spirit, are unstained and holy: they are children of God in their very being and in their life.

But since even those who are endowed with the glorious maternity of the Church do not always personally measure up to their dignity, and since the children of the Church do not always conduct themselves as such, but thwart the fruitfulness of their mother and withdraw from her guidance, the outer countenance of this heavenly bride is often stained and disfigured. In her womb, but not from her womb, rankly grows many a weed that casts a shade over her heavenly blossoms. And although often enough her inner majesty and greatness are manifested in luminous rays, these brilliant signs are not sufficient to disclose the entire wealth of her grandeur. The true glory of the King's daughter is from within; it lies hidden within the wonderful power with which the Holy Spirit acts in her and through her. That glory will be completely unveiled only when it will have completely purified, sanctified, transfigured, and deified all her true children. The less that glory can be perceived and grasped from without, the greater and more sublime it is; and the less the sordidness clinging even to the Church can tarnish or destroy her inner glory, the more divine must that glory be. These reasons show the august mystery that is the Church; a mystery calling forth a vigorous divine faith that will soar above whatever is visible and natural, but also providing that faith with an inconceivably lofty object.

John Henry Newman

1801-1890

John Henry Newman was born in London and attended
Trinity College, Oxford. In 1822 he became a fellow of Oriel
College, Oxford, then in 1828 he was made vicar of St. Mary's,
Oxford. He was at the heart of the Oxford Movement, which
began in 1833 with the aim of reforming the Church of England
after the pattern of the Church of the first five centuries. His
Parochial and Plain Sermons (1834–1842) took the principles
of the movement into the country at large. The controversy he
found himself involved in caused him to withdraw into isolation.
He left Oxford for Littlemore where with a few friends he
established a virtual monastery. He preached his last Anglican
sermon in 1843 and undertook a long period of meditation to
resolve the obstacles that prevented him from accepting Roman
Catholicism. The idea of development was the crucial notion
that had to be explored and applied.

In 1845 Newman was received into the Roman Catholic
Church at Littlemore. A few weeks later he published his Essay
on the Development of Christian Doctrine, one of the most
original theological works ever written in English. He went
to Rome to be ordained a priest and in 1848 founded the
Birmingham Oratory. In 1852 he went to Ireland to establish
the new Catholic University in Dublin. It was a frustrating

experience, but out of it came another of his lasting works,
The Idea of a University.

*In 1864 Charles Kingsley challenged him to show that his
conversion had been honest. His reply was one of the most
famous religious autobiographies since Augustine's* Confessions,
Newman's great Apologia Pro Vita Sua. *It won for him new
national recognition. In 1870 he produced another masterful
theological work,* The Grammar of Assent, *an intriguing treatment of faith and certainty. In 1879 the new Pope Leo XIII
made him a cardinal, an honor that was particularly gratifying
to him because of the suspicion of his orthodoxy which some
conservative theologians voiced.*

*The selection found here is an example of Newman's
"religious journalism." His uncanny simplicity and clarity of
thought and language enabled him to reach people at every level.
This particular essay was written in 1866, two years after his*
Apologia. *A book called* Ecce Homo *by J. R. Seeley was the
sensation of the season. Newman starts out by entering into
Seeley's viewpoint, doing him full justice insofar as possible.
But then he turns and lets his razor-sharp mind play devastatingly
on Seeley's shortcomings. He is appalled at the author's "bad
logic," "rash and gratuitous assumptions," and "half-digested
thought," but even more by his arbitrary selections of those
portions of Christianity which happen to appeal to his mind.*

*When it came to arguing Christianity, Newman was no one
to fool around with. The struggle had been too hard, the cost
too high, for him to let any second-rate fabrications carry the
day. Seldom has the dialectic of faith and understanding been
more fruitful than in the mind of Newman. For him the Church
was always a matter of life and death.*

AN INTERNAL ARGUMENT
FOR CHRISTIANITY

T he word "remarkable" has been so hacked of late in theological criticism—nearly as much so as "earnest" and "thoughtful"—that we do not like to apply it without an apology to the instance of a recent work, called *Ecce Homo*, which we propose now to bring before the reader. In truth, it presents itself as a very convenient epithet, whenever we do not like to commit ourselves to any definite judgment on any subject before us, and prefer to spread over it a broad neutral tint to painting it distinctly white, red, or black. A man, or his work, or his deed, is "remarkable" when he produces an effect; be he effective for good or for evil, for truth or for falsehood—a point which, as far as that expression goes, we by adopting it, leave it for others or for the future to determine. Accordingly it is just the word to use in the instance of a Volume in which what is trite and what is novel, what is striking and what is startling, what is sound and what is untrustworthy, what is deep and what is shallow, are so mixed up together, or at least so vaguely suggested, or so perplexingly confessed,— which has so much of occasional force and circumambient glitter, of pretence and of seriousness,—as to make it impossible either with a good conscience to praise it, or without harshness and unfairness to condemn. Such a book is at least likely to be effective, whatever else it is or is not; it may be safely called remarkable; and therefore we apply the epithet "remarkable" to this *Ecce Homo*.

It is remarkable, then, on account of the sensation which it has made in religious circles. In the course of a few months it has reached a third edition, though it is a fair-sized octavo, and not an over-cheap one. And it has received the praise of critics and reviewers of very distinct shades of opinion. Such a reception must be owing either to the book itself, or to the circumstances of the day in which it has appeared, or to both of these causes together. Or, as seems to be the case, the needs of the day have become a call for some such work; and the work, on its appearance, has been thankfully welcomed, on account of its professed object, by those whose needs called for it. The author includes himself in the number of these; and while providing for his own wants he has ministered to theirs. This is what we especially mean by calling his book "remarkable." It deserves remark, because it has excited it.

CHAPTER 1

Disputants may maintain, if they please, that religious doubt is our appropriate, our normal state; that to cherish doubts is our duty; that to complain of them is impatience; that to dread them is cowardice; that to overcome them is inveracity; that it is even a happy state, a state of calm philosophic enjoyment, to be conscious of them;—but after all, unavoidable or not, such a state is not natural, and not happy, if the voice of mankind is to decide the question. English minds, in particular, have too much of a religious temper in them, as a natural gift, to acquiesce for any long time in positive, active doubt. For doubt and devotion are incompatible with each other; every doubt, be it greater or less, stronger or weaker, involuntary as well as voluntary, acts upon devotion, so far forth, as water sprinkled, or dashed, or poured out upon a flame. Real and proper doubt kills faith, and devotion with it; and even involuntary or half-deliberate doubt, though it does not actually kill faith, goes far to kill devotion; and religion without devotion is little better than a burden, and soon becomes a superstition. Since, then, this is a day of objection and of doubt about the intellectual basis of Revealed Truth, it follows that there is a great deal of secret discomfort and distress in the religious portion of the community, the result of that general curiosity in speculation and inquiry which has been the growth among us of the last twenty or thirty years.

The people of this country, being Protestants, appeal to Scripture, when a religious question arises, as their ultimate informant and decisive authority in all such matters; but who is to decide for them the previous question, that Scripture is really such an authority? When, then, as at this time, its divine authority is the very point to be determined, that is, the character and extent of its inspiration and its component parts, then they find themselves at sea, without the means of directing their course. Doubting about the authority of Scripture, they doubt about its substantial truth; doubting about its truth, they have doubts concerning the Object which it sets before their faith, about the historical accuracy and objective reality of the picture which it presents to us of our Lord. We are not speaking of wilful doubting, but of those painful misgivings, greater or less, to which we have already referred. Religious Protestants, when they think calmly on the subject, can hardly conceal from themselves that they have a house without logical foundations, which contrives indeed for the present to stand, but which may go any day,—and where are they then?

Of course Catholics will bid them receive the canon of Scripture on the authority of the Church, in the spirit of St. Augustine's well-known words: "I should not believe the Gospel, were I not moved by the authority of the Catholic Church." But who, they ask, is to be voucher in turn for the Church, and for St. Augustine?—is it not as difficult to prove the authority of the Church and her doctors as the authority of the Scriptures? We Catholics answer, and with reason, in the negative; but, since they cannot be brought to agree with us here, what argumentative ground is open to them? Thus they seem drifting, slowly perhaps, but surely, in the direction of scepticism.

CHAPTER 2

It is under these circumstances that they are invited, in the Volume of which we have spoken, to betake themselves to the contemplation of our Lord's character, as it is recorded by the Evangelists, as carrying with it its own evidence, dispensing with extrinsic proof, and claiming authoritatively by itself the faith and devotion of all to whom it is presented. Such an argument, of course, is as old as Christianity itself; the young man in the Gospel calls our Lord "Good Master," and St. Peter introduces Him to the first Gentile converts as one who "went about doing good;" and in these last times we can refer to the testimony even of unbelievers in behalf of an argument which is as simple as it is constraining. *"Si la vie et la mort de Socrate sont d'un sage,"* says Rousseau, *"la vie et la mort de Jésus sont d'un Dieu."* And he clenches the argument by observing, that were the picture a mere conception of the sacred writers, *"l'inventeur en serait plus étonnant que le héros."* The force of this argument lies in its directness; it comes to the point at once, and concentrates in itself evidence, doctrine, and devotion. In theological language, it is the *motivum credibilitatis,* the *objectum materiale,* and the *formale,* all in one; it unites human reason and supernatural faith in one complex act; and it comes home to all men, educated and ignorant, young and old. And it is the point to which, after all and in fact, all religious minds tend, and in which they ultimately rest, even if they do not start from it. Without an intimate apprehension of the personal character of our Saviour, what professes to be faith is little more than an act of ratiocination. If faith is to live, it must love; it must lovingly live in the Author of faith as a true and living Being, *in Deo vivo et vero;* according to the saying of the Samaritans to their townswoman: "We now believe, not for thy saying, for we ourselves have heard Him." Many doctrines may be held implicitly; but to see Him as if intuitively is the very promise and gift of Him who is the object of the intuition. We are constrained to believe when it is He that speaks to us about Himself.

Such undeniably is the characteristic of divine faith viewed in itself: but here we are concerned, not simply with faith, but with its logical antecedents; and the question returns on which we have already touched, as a difficulty with Protestants,—how can our Lord's Life, as recorded in the Gospels, be a logical ground of faith, unless we set out with assuming the truth of those Gospels; that is, without assuming, as proved, the original matter of doubt? And Protestant apologists, it may be urged—Paley, for instance—show their sense of this difficulty when they place the argument drawn from our Lord's character only among the auxiliary Evidences of Christianity. Now the following answer may fairly be made to this objection; nor need we grudge Protestants the use of it, for, as will appear in the sequel, it proves too much for their purpose, as being an argument for the divinity not only of Christ's mission, but of that of His Church also. However, we say this by the way.

It may be maintained then, that, making as large an allowance as the most sceptical mind, when pressed to state its demands in full, would desire, we are at least safe in asserting that the books of the New Testament, taken as a whole, were existing about the middle of the second century, and were then received by Christians, or were in the way of being received, and nothing else but they were received, as the authoritative record of the origin and rise of their Religion. In that first age they were the only account of the mode in which Christianity was introduced to the world. Internal as well as external evidence sanctions us in so speaking. Four Gospels, the book of the Acts of the Apostles, various Apostolic writings, made up then, as now, our sacred books. Whether there was a book more or less, say even an important book, does not affect the general character of the Religion as those books set it forth. Omit one or other of the Gospels, and three or four Epistles, and the outline and nature of its objects and its teaching remain what they were before the omission. The moral peculiarities, in particular, of its Founder are, on the whole, identical, whether we learn them from St. Matthew, St. John, St. Peter, or St. Paul. He is not in one book a Socrates, in another a Zeno, and in a third an Epicurus. Much less is the religion changed or obscured by the loss of particular chapters or verses, or even by inaccuracy in fact, or by error in opinion, (supposing *per impossibile* such a charge could be made good,) in particular portions of a book. For argument's sake, suppose that the three first Gospels are an accidental collection of traditions or legends, for which no one is responsible, and in which Christians had faith because there was nothing else to put faith in. This is the limit to which extreme scepticism can proceed, and we are willing to commence our argument by granting it. Still, starting at this disadvantage, we should be prepared to argue, that if, in spite of this, and after all, there be shadowed out in these anonymous and fortuitous documents a Teacher *sui generis*, distinct, consistent, and original, then does that picture, thus accidentally resulting, for the very reason of its accidental composition, only become more marvellous; then is He an historical fact, and again a supernatural or divine fact;—historical from the consistency of the representation, and because the time cannot be assigned when it was not received as a reality; and supernatural, in proportion as the qualities with which He is invested in those writings are incompatible with what it is reasonable or possible to ascribe to human nature viewed simply in itself. Let these writings be as open to criticism, whether as to their origin or their text, as sceptics can maintain; nevertheless the representation in question is there, and forces upon the mind a conviction that it records a fact, and a superhuman fact, just as the reflection of an object in a stream remains in its general form, however rapid the current, and however many the ripples, and is a sure warrant to us of the presence of the object on the bank, though that object be out of sight.

CHAPTER 3

Such, we conceive, though stated in our own words, is the argument drawn out in the pages before us, or rather such is the ground on which the argument is raised; and the interest which it has excited lies, not in its novelty, but in the particular mode in which it is brought before the reader, in the originality and precision of certain strokes by which is traced out for us the outline of the Divine Teacher. These strokes are not always correct; they are sometimes gratuitous, sometimes derogatory to their object; but they are always determinate; and, being such, they present an old argument before us with a certain freshness, which, because it is old, is necessary for its being effective.

We do not wonder at all, then, at the sensation which the Volume is said to have caused at Oxford, and among Anglicans of the Oxford school, after the wearisome doubt and disquiet of the last ten years; for it has opened the prospect of a successful issue of inquiries in an all-important province of thought, where there seemed to be no thoroughfare. Distinct as are the liberal and Catholicizing parties in the Anglican Church both in their principles and their policy, it must not be supposed that they are also as distinct in the members that compose them. No line of demarcation can be drawn between the one collection of men and the other, in fact; for no two minds are altogether alike; and individually, Anglicans have each his own shade of opinion, and belong partly to this school, partly to that. Or rather, there is a large body of men who are neither the one nor the other; they cannot be called an intermediate party, for they have no discriminating watchwords; they range from those who are almost Catholic to those who are almost Liberals. They are not Liberals, because they do not glory in a state of doubt; they cannot profess to be "Anglo-Catholics," because they are not prepared to give an internal assent to all that is put forth by the Church as truth of revelation. These are the men who, if they could, would unite old ideas with new; who cannot give up tradition, yet are loth to shut the door to progress; who look for a more exact adjustment of faith with reason than has hitherto been attained; who love the conclusions of Catholic theology better than the proofs, and the methods of modern thought better than its results; and who, in the present wide unsettlement of religious opinion, believe indeed, or wish to believe, Scripture and orthodox doctrine, taken as a whole, and cannot get themselves to avow any deliberate dissent from any part of either, but still, not knowing how to defend their belief with logical exactness, or at least feeling that there are large unsatisfied objections lying against parts of it, or having misgivings lest there should be such, acquiesce in what is called a practical belief, that is, accept revealed truths, only because such acceptance of them is the safest course, because they are probable, and because to hold them in consequence is a duty, not as if they felt absolutely certain, though they will not allow themselves to be actually in doubt. Such is about the description to be given of them as a class; though, as we have said, they so materially differ from each other, that no general account of them will apply strictly to any individual in their body.

Now, it is to this large class which we have been describing that such a work as that before us, in spite of the serious errors which they will not be slow to recognize in it, comes as a friend in need. They do not stumble at the author's inconsistencies or shortcomings; they are arrested by his professed purpose, and are profoundly moved by his successful hits (as they may be called) towards fulfilling it. Remarks on the Gospel history, such as Paley's, they feel to be casual and superficial; such as Rousseau's to be vague and declamatory; they wish to justify with their intellect all that they believe with their heart; they cannot separate their ideas of religion from its revealed Object; but they have an aching dissatisfaction within them, that they should be apprehending Him so feebly, when they should fain (as it were) see and touch Him as well as hear. When, then, they have logical grounds presented to them for holding that the recorded picture of our Lord is its own evidence, that it carries with it its own reality and authority, that His *revelatio* is *revelata* in the very act of being a *revelatio*, it is as if He Himself said to them, as He once said to His disciples, "It is I, be not afraid"; and the clouds at once clear off, and the waters subside, and the land is gained for which they are looking out.

The author before us, then, has the merit of promising what, if he could fulfil it, would entitle him to the gratitude of thousands. We do not say, we are very far from thinking that he has actually accomplished so high an enterprise, though he seems to be ambitious enough to hope that he has not come far short of it. He somewhere calls his book a treatise; he would have done better to call it an essay; nor need he have been ashamed of a word which Locke has used in his work on the Human Understanding. Before concluding, we shall take occasion to express our serious sense, how very much his execution falls below his purpose; but certainly it is a great purpose which he sets before him, and for that he is to be praised. And there is at least this singular merit in his performance, as he has given it to the public, that he is clear-sighted and fair enough to view our Lord's work in its true light, as including in it the establishment of a visible Kingdom or Church. In proportion, then, as we shall presently find it our duty to pass some severe remarks upon his Volume, as it comes before us, so do we feel bound, before doing so, to give some specimens of it in that point of view in which we consider it really to subserve the cause of Revealed Truth. And in the sketch which we are now about to give of the first steps of his investigation, we must not be understood to make him responsible for the language in which we shall exhibit them to our readers, and which will unavoidably involve our own corrections of his argument, and our own colouring.

CHAPTER 4

Among a people, then, accustomed by the most sacred traditions of their Religion to a belief in the appearance, from time to time, of divine messengers for their instruction and reformation, and to the expectation of One such messenger still to come, the last and greatest of all, who should also be their king and deliverer as well as their teacher, suddenly is found, after a long break in the succession, and a period of national degradation, a prophet of the old stamp, in one of the deserts of the country—John, the son of Zachary. He announces the promised kingdom as close at hand, calls his countrymen to repentance, and institutes a rite symbolical of it. The people seem disposed to take him for the destined Saviour; but, instead, he points out to them a private person in the crowd which is flocking about him; and henceforth the interest which his own preaching has excited centres in that Other. Thus our Lord is introduced to the notice of His countrymen.

Thus brought before the world, He opens His mission. What is the first impression it makes upon us? Admiration of its singular simplicity and directness, both as to object and work. Such of course ought to be its character, if it was to be the fulfilment of the ancient, long-expected promise; and such it was, as our Lord proclaimed it. Other men, who do a work, do not at once set about it as their object; they make several failures; they are led on to it by circumstances; they miscalculate their powers; or they are drifted from the first in a different direction from that which they had chosen; they do most where they are expected to do least. But our Lord said and did. "He formed one plan and executed it."

In the next place, what was that plan? Let us consider the force of the words in which, as the Baptist before Him, He introduced His ministry: "The kingdom of God is at hand." What was meant by the kingdom of God? "The conception was no new one, but familiar to every Jew" (p. 19). At the first formation of the nation and state of the Israelites, the Almighty had been their King; when a line of earthly kings was introduced, then God spoke by the prophets. The existence of the theocracy was the very constitution and boast of Israel, as limited monarchy, liberty, and equality are the boast respectively of certain modern nations. Moreover, the Gospel proclamation ran, *"Pœnitentiam agite*; for the kingdom of heaven is at hand;"* here again was another and recognized token of a theophany; for the mission of a prophet, as we have said above, was commonly a call to reformation and expiation of sin.

A divine mission, then, was a falling back upon the original covenant between God and His people; but again, while it was an event of old and familiar occurrence, it ever had carried with it in its past instances something new in connexion with the circumstances under which it took place. The prophets were accustomed to give interpretations, or to introduce modifications of the letter of the Law, to add to its conditions and to enlarge its application. It was to be expected, then, that now, when the new Prophet to whom the Baptist pointed, opened His Commission, He too, in like manner, would be found to be engaged in a restoration, but in a restoration which should be a religious advance; and that the more, if He really was the special, final Prophet of the theocracy, to whom all former prophets had looked forward, and in whom their long and august line was to be summed up and perfected. In proportion as His work was to be more signal, so would His new revelations be wider and more wonderful.

Did our Lord fulfil these expectations? Yes; there was this peculiarity in His mission, that He came, not only as one of the prophets in the kingdom of God, but as the King Himself of that kingdom. Thus His mission involves the most exact return to the original polity of Israel, which the appointment of Saul had disarranged, while it recognizes also the line of Prophets, and infuses a new spirit into the Law. Throughout His ministry our Lord claimed and received the title of King, which no prophet ever had done before. On His birth, the wise men came to worship "the King of the Jews." "Thou art the Son of God, Thou art the King of Israel," cried Nathaniel after His baptism; and on His cross the charge recorded against Him was that He professed to be "King of the Jews." "During His whole public life," says the author, "He is distinguished from the other prominent characters of Jewish history by His unbounded personal pretensions. He claims expressly the character of the Divine Messiah for which the ancient prophets had directed the nation to look."—P. 25.

He is, then, a King, as well as a Prophet; but is He as one of the old heroic kings, David or Solomon? Had such been His pretension, He had not, in His own words, "discerned the signs of the times." It would have been a false step in Him, into which other would-be champions of Israel, before and after Him, actually fell, and in consequence failed. But here this young Prophet is from the first distinct, decided, and original. His contemporaries, indeed, the wisest, the most experienced, were wedded to the notion of a revival of the barbaric kingdom. "Their heads were full of the languid dreams of commentators, the unpracticable pedantries of men who live in the past" (p. 27). But He gave to the old prophetic promises an interpretation which they could undeniably bear, but which they did not immediately suggest; which we can maintain to be true, while we can deny it to be imperative. He had His own prompt, definite conception of the restored theocracy; it was His own, and not another's; it was suited to the new age; it was triumphantly carried out in the event.

CHAPTER 5

In what, then, did He consider His royalty to consist? First, what was it not? It did not consist in the ordinary functions of royalty; it did not prevent His payment of tribute to Cæsar; it did not make Him a judge in questions of criminal or of civil law, in a question of adultery, or in the adjudication of an inheritance; nor did it give Him the command of armies. Then perhaps, after all, it was but a figurative royalty, as when the Eridanus is called "*fluviorum rex*," or Aristotle "the prince of philosophers." No; it was not a figurative royalty either. To call oneself a king, without being one, is playing with edged tools—as in the story of the innkeeper's son, who was put to death for calling himself "heir to the crown." Christ certainly knew what He was saying. "He had provoked the accusation of rebellion against the Roman government: He must have known that the language He used would be interpreted so. Was there then nothing substantial in the royalty He claimed? Did He die for a metaphor?" (p. 28). He meant what He said, and therefore His kingdom was literal and real; it was visible; but what were its visible prerogatives, if they were not those in which earthly royalty commonly consists? In truth, He passed by the lesser powers of royalty to claim the higher. He claimed certain divine and transcendent functions of the original theocracy, which had been in abeyance since that theocracy had been infringed, which even to David had not been delegated, which had never been exercised except by the Almighty. God had created, first the people, next the state, which He deigned to govern. "The origin of other nations is lost in antiquity" (p. 33); but "this people," runs the sacred word, "have I formed for Myself." And "He who first called the nation did for it the second work of a king: He gave it a law" (p. 34). Now it is very striking to observe that these two incommunicable attributes of divine royalty, as exemplified in the history of the Israelites, are the very two which our Lord assumed. He was the Maker and the Law-giver of His subjects. He said in the commencement of His ministry, "*Follow* Me;" and He added, "and I will make you"—you in turn—"fishers of men." And the next we read of Him is, that His disciples came to Him on the Mount, and He opened His mouth and *taught* them. And so again, at the end of it, "Go ye, make *disciples* of all nations, *teaching* them." "Thus the very works for which the [Jewish] nation chiefly hymned their Jehovah, He undertook in His name to do. He undertook to be the Father of an everlasting state, and the Legislator of a world-wide society" (p. 36); that is, showing Himself, according to the prophetic announcement, to *Admirabilis, consiliarius, pater futuri sæculi, princeps pacis.*

To these two claims He added a third: first, He chooses the subjects of His kingdom; next, He gives them a law; but thirdly, He judges them—judges them in a far truer and fuller sense than in the old kingdom even the Almighty judged His people. The God of Israel ordained national rewards and punishments for national obedience or transgression; He did not judge His subjects one by one; but our Lord takes upon Himself the supreme and final judgment of every one of His subjects, not to speak of the whole human race (though, from the nature of the case, this function cannot belong to His present visible kingdom). "He considered, in short, heaven and hell to be in His hand" (p. 40).

We shall mention one further function of the new King and His new kingdom: its benefits are even bound up with the maintenance of this law of political unity. "To organize a society, and to bind the members of it together by the closest ties, were the business of His life. For this reason it was that He called men away from their homes, imposed upon some a wandering life, upon others the sacrifice of their property, and endeavoured by all means to divorce them from their former connexions, in order that they might find a new home in the Church. For this reason He instituted a solemn initiation, and for this reason He refused absolutely to any one a dispensation from it. For this reason, too . . . He established a common feast, which was through all ages to remind Christians of their indissoluble union" (p. 92). But *cui bono* is visible kingdom, when the great end of our Lord's ministry is moral advancement and preparation for a future state? It is easy to understand, for instance, how a sermon may benefit, or personal example, or religious friends, or household piety. We can learn to imitate a saint or a martyr, we can cherish a lesson, we can study a treatise, we can obey a rule; but what is the definite advantage to a preacher or a moralist of an external organization, of a visible kingdom? Yet Christ says, "Seek ye *first* the kingdom of God," as well as "His justice." Socrates wished to improve man, but he laid not stress on their acting in concert in order to secure that improvement; on the contrary, the Christian law is political, as certainly as it is moral.

Why is this? It arises out of the intimate relation between Him and His subjects, which, in bringing them all to Him as their common Father, necessarily brings them to each other. Our Lord says, "Where two or three are gathered together in My name, I am in the midst of them." Fellowship between His followers is made a distinct object and duty, because it is a means, according to the provisions of His system, by which in some special way they are brought near to Him. This is declared, still more strikingly than in the text we have just quoted, in the parable of the Vine and its Branches, and in that (if it is to be

called a parable) of the Bread of Life. The almighty King of
Israel was ever, indeed, invisibly present in the glory above the
Ark, but He did not manifest Himself there or anywhere else as
a present cause of spiritual strength to His people; but the new
King is not only ever present, but to every one of His subjects
individually is He a first element and perennial source of life.
He is not only the head of His kingdom, but also its animating
principle and its centre of power. The author whom we are
reviewing does not quite reach the great doctrine here suggested, but he goes near it in the following passage: "Some men
have appeared who have been 'as levers to uplift the earth and
roll it in another course.' Homer by creating literature, Socrates
by creating science, Cæsar by carrying civilization inland from
the shores of the Mediterranean, Newton by starting science
upon a career of steady progress, may be said to have attained
this eminence. But these men gave a single impact like that
which is conceived to have first set the planets in motion. Christ
claims to be a perpetual attractive power, like the sun, which
determines their orbit. They contributed to men some discovery,
and passed away; Christ's discovery is Himself. To humanity
struggling with its passions and its destiny He says, Cling to Me;—
cling ever closer to Me. If we believe St. John, He represented
Himself as the Light of the world, as the Shepherd of the souls
of men, as the Way to immortality, as the Vine of Life-tree of
humanity" (p. 177). He ends this beautiful passage, of which we
have quoted as much as our limits allow, by saying that "He
instructed His followers to hope for life from feeding on His
Body and Blood."

CHAPTER 6

Osi sic omnia! Is it not hard, that, after following with
pleasure a train of thought so calculated to warm all Christian
hearts, and to create in them both admiration and sympathy for
the writer, we must end our notice of him in a different tone,
and express as much dissent from him and as serious blame of
him as we have hitherto been showing satisfaction with his
object, his intention, and the general outline of his argument?
But so it is. In what remains to be said we are obliged to speak
of his work in terms so sharp that they may seem to be out of

keeping with what has gone before. With whatever abruptness, we must suddenly shift the scene, and manifest our disapprobation of portions of his book as plainly as we have shown an interest in it. We have praised it in various points of view. It has stirred the hearts of many; it has recognized a need, and gone in the right direction for supplying it. It serves as a token, and a hopeful token, of what is going on in the minds of numbers of men external to the Church. It is so far a good book, and, we trust, will work for good. Especially as we have seen, is it interesting to the Catholic, as acknowledging the visible Church to be our Lord's own creation, as the direct fruit of His teaching, and the destined instrument of His purposes. We do not know how to speak in an unfriendly tone of an author who has done so much as this; but at the same time, when we come to examine his argument in its details, and study his chapters one by one, we find, in spite of, and mixed up with, what is true and original, and even putting aside his patent theological errors, so much bad logic, so much of rash and gratuitous assumption, so much of half-digested thought, that we are obliged to conclude that it would have been much wiser in him, instead of publishing what he seems to confess, or rather to proclaim, to be the jottings of his first researches upon sacred territory, to have waited till he had carefully traversed and surveyed and mapped the whole of it. We now proceed to give a few instances of the faults of which we complain.

His opening remarks will serve as an illustration. In p. 41 he says, "We have not rested upon *single* passages, nor drawn from the *fourth Gospel*." This, we suppose, must be his reason for ignoring the passage in Luke ii. 49: "Did you not know that I must be about My Father's business?" for he directly contradicts it, by gratuitously imagining that our Lord came for St. John's baptism with the same intention as the penitents around Him; and that, in spite of His own words, which we suppose are to be taken as another "single passage," "So it becometh us to fulfil all justice" (Matt. iii. 15). It must be on this principle of ignoring single passages such as these, even though they admit of combination, that he goes on to say of our Lord, that "in the agitation of mind caused by His baptism, and by the Baptist's designation of Him as the future Prophet,

He retired into the wilderness," and there "He matured the plan of action which we see Him executing from the moment of His return into society" (p. 9); and that not till then was He "conscious of miraculous power" (p. 12). This neglect of the sacred text, we repeat, must be allowed him, we suppose, under cover of his acting out his rule of abstaining from single passages and from the fourth Gospel. Let us allow it; but at least he ought to adduce passages, single or many, for what he actually does assert. He must not be allowed arbitrarily to add to the history, as well as cautiously to take from it. Where, then, we ask, did he learn that our Lord's baptism caused Him "agitation of mind," that He "matured His plan of action in the wilderness," and that He then first was "conscious of miraculous power"?

But again: it seems he is not to refer to "single passages or the fourth Gospel"; yet, wonderful to say, he actually does open his formal discussion of the sacred history by referring to a passage from that very Gospel,—nay, to a particular text, which is not to be called "single," only because it is not so much as a single text, but an unfair half text, and half a text such, that, had he taken the whole of it, he would have been obliged to admit that the part which he puts aside just runs counter to his interpretation of the part which he recognizes. The words are these, as they stand in the Protestant version: "Behold the Lamb of God, which taketh away the sin of the world." Now, it is impossible to deny that "which taketh away," etc., fixes and limits the sense of "the Lamb of God"; but our author notices the latter half of the sentence, only in order to put aside the light which it throws upon the former half; and instead of the Baptists's own interpretation of the title which he gives to our Lord, he substitutes another, radically different, which he selects for himself out of one of the Psalms. He explains "the Lamb" by the well-known image, which represents the Almighty as a shepherd and His earthly servants as sheep—innocent, safe, and happy under His protection. "The Baptist's opinion of Christ's character, then," he says, "is summed up for us in the title he gives Him—the Lamb of God, taking away the sins of the world. There *seems* to be, in the last part of this description, an allusion to the usages

372

of the Jewish sacrificial system; and, in order to explain it fully, it would be necessary to anticipate much which will come more conveniently later in this treatise. *But* when we remember that the Baptist's mind was *doubtless* full of imagery drawn from the Old Testament, and that the conception of a lamb of God makes the subject of one of the most striking of the Psalms, *we shall perceive what he meant to convey by this phrase*" (pp. 5,6). This is like saying, to take a parallel instance, "Isaiah declares, 'Mine eyes have seen the King, the Lord of hosts;' *but*, considering that doubtless the prophet was well acquainted with the first and second books of Samuel, and that Saul, David, and Solomon are the three great kings there represented, we shall easily perceive that, by 'seeing the King,' he meant to say that he saw Uzziah, King of Judah, in the last year of whose reign he had the vision. As to the phrase 'the Lord of hosts,' which seems to refer to the Almighty, we will consider its meaning by-and-by";—but, in truth, it is difficult to invent a paralogism, in its gratuitous inconsecutiveness parallel to his own.

CHAPTER 7

We must own that, with every wish to be fair to this author, we never recovered from the perplexity of mind which this passage, in the very threshold of his book inflicted on us. It needed not the various passages, constructed on the same argumentative model, which follow it in his work, to prove to us that he was not only an *incognito*, but an enigma. "Ergo," is the symbol of the logician:—what is the scientific method of a writer whose symbols, profusely scattered through his pages are "probably," "it must be," "doubtless," "on this hypothesis," "we may suppose," and "it is natural to think," and that at the very time that he pointedly discards the comments of school theologians? Is it possible that he can mean us to set aside, in his own favour, the glosses of all that went before him, and to exchange our old lamps for his new ones? Men have been at fault, when trying to determine whether he was an orthodox believer on his road to liberalism, or a liberal on his road to orthodoxy: this doubtless may be to some a perplexity; but our own difficulty is, whether he comes to us as an investigator or rather as a prophet, as one unequal or superior to the art of reasoning. Undoubtedly he is an able man; but what can he possibly mean by startling us with such eccentricities of argumentation as are quite familiar with him? Addison somewhere bids his readers bear in mind, that if he is ever especially dull, he always has a special reason for being so; and it is difficult to reconcile one's imagination to the supposition that this anonymous writer, with so much religious thought as he certainly evidences, is without some recondite reason for seeming so inconsequent, and does not move by some deep subterraneous process of investigation, which, if once brought to light, would clear him of the imputation of castle-building.

There is always a danger of misconceiving an author who has no antecedents by which we may measure him. Taking his work as it lies, we can but wish that he had kept his imagination under control; and that he had more of the hard head of a lawyer, and the patience of a philosopher. He writes like a man who cannot keep from telling the world his first thoughts, especially if they are clever or graceful; he has come for the first time upon a strange world, and his remarks upon it are too often obvious rather than striking, and crude rather than fresh. What can be more paradoxical than to interpret our Lord's words to Nicodemus, "Unless a man be born again," etc., as the necessity of external religion, and as a lesson to him to profess his faith openly and not to visit Him in secret? (p. 86). What can be more pretentious, not to say vulgar, than his paraphrase of St. John's passage about the woman taken in adultery? "In His burning embarrassment and confusion," he says, "He stooped down so as to hide His face . . . They had a glimpse perhaps of the glowing blush upon His face," etc. (p. 104).

We should be very sorry to use a severe word concerning an honest inquirer after truth, as we believe this anonymous writer to be; but we will confess that Catholics, kindly as they may wish to feel towards him, are scarcely even able, from their very position, to give his work the enthusiastic reception which it has received from some other critics. The reason is plain; those alone can speak of it from a full heart, who feel a need, and recognize in it a supply of that need. We are not in the number of such; for they who have found, have no need

374

to seek. Far be it from us to use language savouring of the
leaven of the Pharisees. We are not assuming a high place,
because we thus speak, or boasting of our security. Catholics
are both deeper and shallower than Protestants; but in neither
case have they any call for a treatise such as this *Ecce Homo*.
If they live to the world and the flesh, then the faith which
they profess, though it is true and distinct, is dead; and their
certainty about religious truth, however firm and unclouded,
is but shallow in its character, and flippant in its manifestations. And in proportion as they are worldly and sensual, will
they be flippant and shallow. But their faith is as indelible as
the pigment which colours the skin, even though it is skin-
deep. This class of Catholics is not likely to take interest in a
pictorial *Ecce Homo*. On the other hand, where the heart is
alive with divine love, faith is as deep as it is vigorous and
joyous; and, as far as Catholics are in this condition, they will
feel no drawing towards a work which is after all but an arbitrary and unsatisfactory dissection of the Object of their
devotion. Faith, be it deep or shallow, does not need Evidences.
That individual Catholics may be harassed with doubts, particularly in a day like this, we are not denying; but, viewed as a
body, Catholics, from their religious condition, are either too
deep or too shallow to suffer from those elementary difficulties,
or that distress of mind, and need of argument, which serious
Protestants so often experience.

We confess, then, as Catholics, to some unavoidable absence
of cordial feeling in following the remarks of this author,
though not to any want of real sympathy; and we seem to be
justified in our indisposition by his manifest want of sympathy
with us. If we feel distant towards him, his own language about
Catholicity, and (what may be called) old Christianity, seems
to show that that distance is one of fact, one of mental position, not any fault in ourselves. Is it not undeniable, that the
very life of personal religion among Catholics lies in a knowledge of the Gospels? It is the character and conduct of our
Lord, His words, His deeds, His sufferings, His work, which are
the very food of our devotion and rule of our life. "Behold the
Man," which this author feels to be an object novel enough
to write a book about, has been the contemplation of Catholics

from the first age when St. Paul said, "The life that I now live in the flesh, I live in the faith of the Son of God, who loved me, and delivered Himself for me." As the Psalms have ever been the manual of our prayer, so have the Gospels been the subject-matter of our meditation. In these latter times especially, since St. Ignatius, they have been divided into portions, and arranged in a scientific order, not unlike that which the Psalms have received in the Breviary. To contemplate our Lord in His person and His history is with us the exercise of every retreat, and the devotion of every morning. All this is certainly simple matter of fact; but the writer we are reviewing lives and thinks at so great a distance from us, as not to be cognizant of what is so patent and so notorious a truth. He seems to imagine that the faith of a Catholic is the mere profession of a formula. He deems it important to disclaim, in the outset of his work, all reference to the theology of the Church. He eschews with much precision, as something almost profane, the dogmatism of former ages. He wishes "to trace" our Lord's "biography from point to point, and accept those conclusions—not which Church doctors or even Apostles have sealed with their authority—but which the facts themselves critically weighed, appear to warrant."—(Preface.) Now, what Catholics, what Church doctors, as well as Apostles, have ever lived on, is not any number of theological canons or decrees, but, we repeat, the Christ Himself, as He is represented in concrete existence in the Gospels. Theological determinations about our Lord are far more of the nature of landmarks or buoys to guide a discursive mind in its reasonings, than to assist a devotional mind in its worship. Common sense, for instance, tells us what is meant by the words, "My Lord and my God;" and a religious man, upon his knees, requires no commentator; but against irreligious speculators, Arius or Nestorius, a denunciation has been passed, in Ecumenical Council, when "science falsely so-called" encroached upon devotion. Has not this been insisted on by all dogmatic Christians over and over again? Is it not a representation as absolutely true as it is trite? We had fancied that Protestants generally allowed the touching beauty of Catholic humns and meditations; and after all is there not That in all Catholic churches which goes beyond any written devotion, whatever its force or its pathos? Do we not believe in a Presence in the sacred Tabernacle, not as a form of words, or as a notion, but as an Object as real as we are real? And if before that Presence we need neither profession of faith nor even manual of devotion, what appetite can we have for the teaching of a writer who not only exalts his first thoughts about our Lord into professional lectures, but implies that the Catholic Church has never known how to point Him out to her children?

CHAPTER 8

It may be objected, that we are making too much of so accidental a slight as is contained in his allusion to "Church doctors," especially as he mentions Apostles in connexion with them; but it would be affectation not to recognize in other places of his book an undercurrent of antagonism to us, of which the passage already quoted is but a first indication. Of course he has quite as much right as another to take up an anti-Catholic position, if he will; but we understand him to be putting forth an investigation, not a polemical argument: and if, instead of keeping his eyes directed towards his own proper subject, he looks to the right or left, hitting at those who view things differently from himself, he is damaging the ethical force of a composition which claims to be, and mainly is, a serious and manly search after religious truth. Why cannot he let us alone? Of course he cannot avoid seeing that the lines of his own investigation diverge from those drawn by others; but he will have enough to do in defending himself, without making others the object of his attack. He is virtually opposing Voltaire, Strauss, Renan, Calvin, Wesley, Chalmers, Erskine, and a host of other writers, but he does not denouce *them*; why then does he single out, misrepresent, and anathematize a main principle of Catholic orthodoxy. It is as if he could not keep his hand off us, when we crossed his path. We are alluding to the following magisterial passage:

"If He (our Lord) meant anything by His constant denunciation of hypocrites, there is nothing which He could have visited with sterner censure than that *short cut to belief* which many persons take, when, overwhelmed with difficulties which beset their minds, and afraid of damnation, they *suddenly* resolve to strive no longer, but, giving their minds a holiday, to rest content with *saying* that they believe, and acting *as if* they did. A melancholy end of Christianity indeed! Can there be such a disfranchised pauper class among the citizens of the New Jerusalem?" (p. 79).

He adds shortly afterwards:

"Assuredly, those who represent Christ as presenting to man an abstruse theology, and saying to them peremptorily, 'Believe or be damned,' have the coarsest conception of the Saviour of the world" (p. 80).

Thus he delivers himself: Believe or be damned is so detestable a doctrine, that if any man denies that it *is* detestable, I pronounce him to be a hypocrite; to be without any true knowledge of the Saviour of the world; to be the object of His sternest censure; and to have no part or place in the Holy City, the New Jerusalem, the eternal Heaven above.—Pretty well for a virtuous hater of dogmatism! We hope we shall show less dictatorial arrogance than his in the answer which we proceed to make to him.

Whether or not there are persons such as he describes, Catholics, or, Protestant converts to Catholicism,—men who profess a faith which they do not believe, under the notion that they shall be eternally damned if they do not profess it without believing,—we really do not know—we never met with such; but since facts do not concern us here so much as principles, let us, for argument's sake, grant that there are such men. Our author believes they are not only "many," but enough to form a "class;" and he considers that they act in this preposterous manner under the sanction, and in accordance with the teaching, of the religious bodies to which they belong. Especially there is a marked allusion in his words to the Athanasian Creed and the Catholic Church. Now we answer him thus:

It is his charge against the teachers of dogma that they impose on men as a duty, instead of believing, to "act as if they did" believe:—now in fact this is the very kind of profession which, if it is all that a candidate has to offer, absolutely shuts him out from admission into Catholic communion. We suppose, that by belief of a thing this writer understands an inward conviction of its truth;—this being supposed, we plainly say that no priest is at liberty to receive a man into the Church who has not a real internal belief, and cannot say from his heart, that the things taught by the Church are true. On the other hand, as we have said above, it is the very characteristic of the profession of faith made by numbers of educated Protestants, and it is the utmost extent to which they are able to go in believing, to hold, not that Christian doctrine is certainly true, but that it has such a semblance of truth, it has such considerable marks of probability upon it, that it is their duty to accept and act upon it as if it were true beyond all question or doubt: and they justify themselves, and with much reason, by the authority of Bishop Butler. Undoubtedly, a religious man will be led to go as far as this, if he cannot go farther; but unless he can go farther, he is no catechumen of the Catholic Church. We wish all men to believe that her creed is true; but till they do so believe, we do not wish, we have no permission, to make them her members. Such a faith as this author speaks of to condemn—(our books call it *"practical* certitude")—does not rise to the level of the *sine qua non*, which is the condition prescribed for becoming a Catholic. Unless a convert so believes that he can sincerely say, "After all, in spite of all difficulties, objections, obscurities, mysteries, the creed of the Church undoubtedly comes from God, and is true, because He who gave it is the Truth," such a man, though he be outwardly received into her fold, will receive no grace from the sacraments, no sanctification in baptism, no pardon in penance, no life in communion. We are more consistently dogmatic than this author imagines; we do not enforce a principle by halves; if our doctrine is true, it must be received as such; if a man cannot so receive it, he must wait till he can. It would be better, indeed, if he now believed; but since he does not as yet, to wait is the best he can do under the circumstances. If we said anything else than this, certainly we should be, as the author thinks we are, encouraging hypocrisy. Nor let him turn round on us and say that by thus proceeding we are laying a burden on souls, and blocking up the entrance into that fold which was intended for all men, by imposing hard conditions on candidates for admission; for, as we shall now show, we have already implied a great principle, which is an answer to this objection, and which the Gospels exhibit and sanction, but which he absolutely ignores.

CHAPTER 9

Let us avail ourselves of his own quotation. The Baptist said, "Behold the Lamb of God." Again he says, "This is the Son of God." "Two of his disciples heard him speak, and they followed Jesus." They believed John to be "a man sent from God" to teach them, and therefore they believed his word to be true. We suppose it was not hypocrisy in them to believe in John's word; rather they would have been guilty of gross inconsistency or hypocrisy, had they professed to believe that he was a divine messenger, and yet had refused to take his word concerning the Stranger whom he pointed out to their veneration. It would have been "saying that they believed," and *not* "acting as if they did;" which at least is not better than saying and acting. Now was not the announcement which John made to them "a short cut to belief"? and what the harm of it? They believed that our Lord was the promised Prophet, without making direct inquiry about Him, without a new inquiry, on the ground of a previous inquiry into the claims of John himself to be accounted a messenger from God. They had already accepted it as truth that John was a prophet; but again, what a prophet said must be true; else he would not be a prophet; now, John said that our Lord was the Lamb of God; this, then, certainly was a sacred truth.

Now it might happen, that they knew exactly and for certain what the Baptist meant in calling our Lord "a Lamb;" in that case they would believe Him to be that which they knew the figurative word meant, as used by the Baptist. But, as our author reminds us, the word has different senses; and though the Baptist explained his own sense of it on the first occasion of using it, by adding "that taketh away the sin of the world," yet when he spoke to the two disciples he did not thus explain it. Now let us suppose that they went off, taking the word each in his own sense, the one understanding by it a sacrificial lamb, the other a lamb of the fold; and let us suppose that, as they were on their way to our Lord's home, they became aware of this difference between their several impressions, and disputed with each other which was the right interpretation. It is clear that they would agree so far as this, viz., that, in saying that the proposition was true, they meant that it was true in that sense in which the Baptist spoke it, whatever that was; moreover, if it be worth noticing, they did after all even agree, in some vague way, about the meaning of the word, understanding that it denoted some high characteristic, or office, or ministry. Anyhow, it was absolutely true, they would say, that our Lord was a Lamb, whatever it meant; the word conveyed a great and momentous fact, and if they did not know what that fact was, the Baptist did, and they would accept it in its one right sense, as soon as he or our Lord told them what that was.

Again, as to that other title which the Baptist gave our Lord, "the Son of God," it admitted of half a dozen meanings. Wisdom was "the only begotten;" the Angels were the sons of God; Adam was a son of God; the descendants of Seth were sons of God; Solomon was a son of God; and so is "the just man." In which of these senses, or in what sense, was our Lord the Son of God? St. Peter, as the after-history shows us, knew, but there were those who did not know; the centurion who attended the crucifixion did not know, and yet he confessed that our Lord was the Son of God. He knew that our Lord had been condemned by the Jews for calling Himself the Son of God, and therefore he cried out, on seeing the miracles which attended his death, "Indeed this *was* the Son of God." His words evidently imply, "I do not know precisely what He meant by so calling Himself; but this I do know,—what He said He was, that He is; whatever He meant, I believe Him; I believe that His word about Himself is true, though I cannot prove it to be so, though I do not even understand it; I believe His word, for I believe *Him*."

Now to return to the accusation which has led to these remarks. Our author says that certain persons are hypocrites, because they "take a short cut to belief, suddenly resolving to strive no longer, but to rest content with saying they believe." Does he mean by "a short cut," believing on the word of another? As far as we see, he can mean nothing else; yet how *can* he really mean this and mean to blame this, with the Gospels before him? He cannot mean it, if he pays any deference to the Gospels, because the very staple of the sacred narrative, from beginning to end, is a call on all men to believe what is not proved, not plain, to them, on the warrant of divine messengers; because the very form of our Lord's teaching is to substitute authority for argument; because the very principle of His grave earnestness, the very key to His regenerative mission, is the intimate connexion of faith with salvation. Faith is not simply trust in His legislation, as the writer says; it is definitely trust in His word, whether that word be about heavenly things or earthly; whether it is spoken by His own mouth, or through His ministers. The Angel who announced the Baptist's birth, said, "Thou shalt be dumb, because thou believest not my words." The Baptist's mother said of Mary, "Blessed is she that believed." The Baptist himself said, "He that believeth on the Son hath everlasting life; and he that believeth not the Son shall not see life, but the wrath of God abideth on him." Our Lord, in turn said to Nicodemus, "We speak that we do know, and ye receive not our witness; he that believeth not is condemned already, because he hath not believed in the Name of the Only-begotten Son of God." To the Jews, "He that heareth My word, and believeth on Him that sent Me, shall not come into condemnation." To the Capharnaites, "He that believeth on Me hath everlasting life." To St. Thomas, "Blessed are they that have not seen, and yet have believed." And to the Apostles, "Preach the Gospel to every creature; he that believeth not shall be damned."

How is it possible to deny that our Lord, both in the text and in the context of these and other passages, made faith in a message, on the warrant of the messenger, to be a condition of salvation, and enforced it by the great grant of power which He emphatically conferred on His representatives? "Whosoever shall not receive you," He says, "nor hear your words, when ye depart, shake off the dust of your feet." "It is not ye that speak, but the Spirit of your Father." "He that heareth you, heareth Me; he that despiseth you, despiseth Me; and he that despiseth Me, despiseth Him that sent me." "I pray for

them that shall believe on Me through their word." "Whose
sins ye remit, they are remitted unto them; and whose sins ye
retain, they are retained." "Whatsoever ye shall bind on earth
shall be bound in heaven." "I will give unto thee the keys of
the kingdom of heaven; and whatsoever thou shalt bind on
earth shall be bound in heaven, and whatsoever thou shalt
loose on earth shall be loosed in heaven." These characteristic
and critical announcements have no place in this author's
gospel; and let it be understood, that we are not asking why
he does not determine the exact doctrines contained in them—
for that is a question which he has reserved (if we understand
him) for a future Volume—but why he does not recognize the
principle they involve—for that is a matter which falls within
his present subject.

CHAPTER 10

It is not well to exhibit some sides of Christianity, and
not others; this we think is the main fault of the author we
have been reviewing. It does not pay to be eclectic in so serious
a matter of fact. He does not overlook, he boldly confesses,
that a visible organized Church was a main part of our Lord's
plan for the regeneration of mankind. "As with Socrates,"
he says, "argument is everything, and personal authority nothing; so with Christ, personal authority is all in all, an argument
altogether unemployed" (p. 94). Our Lord rested His teaching,
not on the concurrence and testimony of His hearers, but on
His own authority. He imposed upon them the declarations of
a Divine Voice. Why does this author stop short in the delinea-
tion of principles which he has so admirably begun? Why does
he denounce "short cuts," as a mental disfranchisement, when
no cut can be shorter than to "believe and be saved"? Why does
he denounce religious fear as hypocritical, when it is written,
"He that believeth not shall be damned"? Why does he call it
dishonest in a man to sacrifice his own judgment to the word of
God, when, unless he did so, he would be avowing that the
Creator knew less than the creature? Let him recollect that no
two thinkers, philosophers, writers, ever did, ever will agree,
in all things with each other. No system of opinions, ever given
to the world, approved itself in all its parts to the reason of any

one individual by whom it was mastered. No revelation then is conceivable, which does not involve, almost in its very idea as being something new, a collision with human intellect, and demands accordingly, if it is to be accepted, a sacrifice of private judgment of the part of those to whom it is addressed. If a revelation be necessary, then also in consequence is that sacrifice necessary. One man will have to make a sacrifice in one respect, another in another, all men in some.

We say, then, to men of the day, Take Christianity, or leave it; do not practise upon it; to do so is as unphilosophical as it is dangerous. Do not attempt to halve a spiritual unit. You are apt to call it a dishonesty in us to refuse to follow out our reasonings, when faith stands in the way; is there no intellectual dishonesty in your self-trust? First, your very accusation of us is dishonest; for you keep in the background the circumstance, of which you are well aware, that such a refusal on our part to back Reason against Faith, is the necessary consequence of our accepting an authoritative Revelation; and next you profess to accept that Revelation yourselves, whilst you dishonestly pick and choose, and take as much or as little of it as you please. You either accept Christianity, or you do not: if you do, do not garble and patch it; if you do not, suffer others to submit to it ungarbled.

James Gibbons
1834-1921

James Gibbons was born in Baltimore and baptized in the cathedral there where he was to be buried 87 years later. When he was three years old, his family returned to Ireland due to his father's poor health. His father died in 1847 and in 1853 his mother decided to bring the family back to the United States, this time to New Orleans. Two years later James returned to Baltimore to enter St. Charles College to study for the priesthood. Ordained a priest in 1861, he was selected as secretary by Archbishop Spalding in 1865 and in that capacity organized much of the Second Plenary Council of Baltimore in 1866.

Named bishop in 1868, Gibbons was assigned as Vicar Apostolic of North Carolina. The next year he sailed for Rome, the youngest bishop in the Catholic world, to take part in Vatican I. He was appointed Bishop of Richmond in 1872, then Archbishop of Baltimore in 1877. In 1884 he presided over the Third Plenary Council of Baltimore which set the tone for most aspects of church life in America for decades to come. In 1887 he went to Rome to defend the Knights of Labor, to get the Catholic University chartered, and to receive the red hat of cardinal.

When Pope Leo XIII died in 1903, Gibbons went to Rome as the first American to take part in a papal election. Eleven years later when Pius X died, Gibbons sailed with

Cardinal O'Connell of Boston, but due to several scares from German U-boats that lengthened the journey, they arrived in Rome too late. Benedict XV had been elected the very morning of the day of their arrival.

Gibbons held an exceptional place in American public life. When he came out in favor of the controversial Draft Law in 1916, Teddy Roosevelt assured him, "taking your life as a whole, I think you now occupy the position of being the most respected, and venerated, and useful citizen of our country." And when he died on Holy Thursday, March 24, 1921, the New York Times proclaimed: "He was one of the wisest men in the world," while the New York Herald said: "In the sense that Francis of Assisi is everybody's saint, James Gibbons was everybody's cardinal. No matter what their religious beliefs, Americans who knew him held him in the highest respect and esteem."

Despite the busy career just outlined, demanding so much of his time in administrative tasks, Gibbons had a gift for simple expression, both in speaking and in writing. While in Wilmington, North Carolina (1868-1872), he was urged by a colleague to put his many instructions and discourses on the Catholic faith into book form. It was not until 1876 that he finally managed to complete the manuscript and get it published as The Faith of Our Fathers. It turned out to be the most popular religious work ever published by an American. It went through 110 editions with over two million copies sold, and was translated into all the major languages.

The book consists of 31 chapters, and the following selection contains two of them: 8—"The Church and the Bible" and 9—"The Primacy of Peter." They serve to illustrate "popularized Vatican I at its best." Much has changed in the meantime, especially in ecumenical relations and understanding. But the integrity of intention and outlook that are reflected in these straightforward pages still have something of value to convey.

THE FAITH OF OUR FATHERS

CHAPTER VIII

THE CHURCH AND THE BIBLE

The Church, as we have just seen, is the only Divinely constituted teacher of Revelation.

Now, the Scripture is the great depository of the Word of God. Therefore, the Church is the divinely appointed Custodian and Interpreter of the Bible. For, her office of infallible Guide were superfluous if each individual could interpret the Bible for himself.

That God never intended the Bible to be the Christian's rule of faith, independently of the living authority of the Church, will be the subject of this chapter.

No nation ever had a greater veneration for the Bible than the Jewish people. The Holy Scripture was their pride and their glory. It was their national song in time of peace; it was their meditation and solace in time of tribulation and exile. And yet the Jews never dreamed of settling their religious controversies by a private appeal to the Word of God.

Whenever any religious dispute arose among the people it was decided by the High Priest and the Sanhedrim, which was a council consisting of seventy-two civil and ecclesiastical judges. The sentence of the High Priest and of his associate judges was to be obeyed under penalty of death. "If thou perceive," says the Book of Deuteronomy, "that there be among you a hard and doubtful matter in judgment, . . . thou shalt come to the Priests of the Levitical race and to the judge, . . . and they shall show thee the truth of the judgment . . . . And thou shalt follow their sentence; neither shalt thou decline to the right hand, nor to the left . . . . But he that will . . . . refuse to obey the commandment of the Priest, . . . that man shall die, and thou shalt take away the evil from Israel."

From this clear sentence you perceive that God does not refer the Jews for the settlement of their controversies to the letter of the law, but to the living authority of the ecclesiastical tribunal which He had expressly established for that purpose.

Hence, the Priests were required to be intimately acquainted with the Sacred Scripture, because they were the depositaries of God's law, and were its expounders to the people. "The lips of the Priest shall keep knowledge, and they (the people) shall seek the law at his mouth, because he is the angel (or messenger) of the Lord of hosts."

And, in fact, very few of the children of Israel, except the Priests, were in possession of the Divine Books. The holy manuscript was rare and precious. And what provision did God make that all the people might have an opportunity of hearing the Scriptures? Did He command the sacred volume to be multiplied? No; but He ordered the *Priests* and the *Levites* to be distributed through the different tribes, that they might always be at hand to instruct the people in the knowledge of the law. The Jews were even forbidden to read certain portions of the Scripture till they had reached the age of thirty years.

Does our Savior reverse this state of things when He comes on earth? Does He tell the Jews to be their own guides in the study of the Scriptures? By no means; but He commands them to obey their constituted teachers, no matter how disedifying might be their private lives. "Then said Jesus to the multitudes and to His disciples: The Scribes and Pharisees sit upon the chair of Moses. All things therefore whatsoever they shall say to you, observe and do."

It is true our Lord said on one occasion: "Search the Scriptures, for you *think* in them to have life everlasting, and the same are they that give testimony to Me." This passage is triumphantly quoted as an argument in favor of private interpretation. But it proves nothing of the kind. Many learned commentators, ancient and modern, express the verb in the indicative mood: "Ye search the Scriptures." At all events, our Savior speaks here only of the Old Testament because the New Testament was not yet written. He addresses not the multitude, but the Pharisees, who were the teachers of the law, and reproaches them for not admitting His Divinity. "You have,"

He says, "the Scriptures in your hands; why then do you not recognize Me as the Messiah, since they give testimony that I am the Son of God?" He refers them to the Scriptures for a proof of His Divinity, not as to a source from which they were to derive all knowledge in regard to the truths of revelation.

Besides, He did not rest the proof of His Divinity upon the *sole* testimony of Scripture. For He showed it:

First—By the testimony of John the Baptist (v. 33), who had said, "Behold the Lamb of God; behold Him who taketh away the sins of the world." See also John i. 34.

Second—By the miracles which He wrought (v.36).

Third—By the testimony of the Father (v. 37), when He said: "This is my beloved Son, in whom I am well pleased; hear ye Him." Matt. iii. 16; Luke ix. 35.

Fourth—By the Scriptures of the Old Testament; as if He were to say, "If you are unwilling to receive these three proofs, though they are most cogent, at least you cannot reject the testimony of the Scriptures, of which you boast so much."

Finally, in this very passage our Lord is explaining the sense of Holy Writ; therefore, its true meaning is not left to the private interpretation of every chance reader. It is, therefore, a grave perversion of the sacred text to adduce these words in vindication of private interpretation of the Scriptures.

But when our Redeemer abolished the Old Law and established His Church, did He intend that His Gospel should be disseminated by the circulation of the Bible, or by the living voice of His disciples? This is a vital question. I answer most emphatically, that it was by preaching alone that He intended to convert the nations, and by preaching alone they were converted. No nation has ever yet been converted by the agency of Bible Associations.

Jesus Himself never wrote a line of Scripture. He never once commanded His Apostles to write a word, or even to circulate the Scriptures already existing. When He sends them on their Apostolic errand, He says: "Go *teach* all nations." *"Preach* the Gospel to every creature." "He that heareth you heareth Me." And we find that Apostles acting in strict accordance with these instructions.

Of the twelve Apostles, the seventy-two disciples, and early followers of our Lord only eight have left us any of their sacred writings. And the Gospels and Epistles were addressed to particular persons or particular churches. They were written on the occasion of some emergency, just as Bishops issue Pastoral letters to correct abuses which may spring up in the Church, or to lay down some rules of conduct for the faithful. The Apostles are never reported to have circulated a single volume of the Holy Scripture, but "they going forth, *preached* everywhere, the Lord co-operating with them."

Thus we see that in the Old and the New Dispensation the people were to be guided by a living authority, and not by their private interpretation of the Scriptures.

Indeed, until the religious revolution of the sixteenth century, it was a thing unheard of from the beginning of the world, that people should be governed by the dead letter of the law either in civil or ecclesiastical affairs. How are your civil affairs regulated in this State, for instance? Certainly not in accordance with your personal interpretation of the laws of Virginia, but in accordance with decisions which are rendered by the constituted judges of the State.

Now what the civil code is to the citizen, the Scripture is to the Christian. The Word of God, as well as the civil law, must have an interpreter, by whose decision we are obliged to abide.

We often hear the shibboleth: "The Bible, and the Bible only, must be your guide." Why, then, do you go to the useless expense of building fine churches and Sabbath-schools? What is the use of your preaching sermons and catechizing the young, if the Bible at home is a sufficient guide for your people? The fact is, you reverend gentlemen contradict in practice what you so vehemently advance in theory. Do not tell me that the Bible is all-sufficient; or, if you believe it is self-sufficient, cease your instructions. Stand not between the people and the Scriptures.

I will address myself now in a friendly spirit to a non-Catholic, and will proceed to show him that he cannot consistently accept the silent Book of Scripture as his sufficient guide.

A copy of the sacred volume is handed to you by your minister, who says: "Take this book; you will find it all-sufficient for your salvation." But here a serious difficulty awaits you at the very threshold of your investigations. What assurance have you that the book he hands you is the *inspired* Word of God; for every part of the Bible is far from possessing intrinsic evidences of inspiration? It may, for ought you know, contain more than the Word of God, or it may not contain all the Word of God. We must not suppose that the Bible was always, as it is now, a compact book, bound in a neat form. It was for several centuries in scattered fragments, spread over different parts of Christendom. Meanwhile, many spurious books, under the name of Scripture, were circulated among the faithful. There was, for instance, the spurious Gospel of St. Peter; there was also the Gospel of St. James and of St. Matthias.

The Catholic Church, in the plenitude of her authority, in the third Council of Carthage, (A. D. 397,) separated the chaff from the wheat, and declared what Books were Canonical, and what were apocryphal. Even to this day the Christian sects do not agree among themselves as to what books are to be accepted as genuine. Some Christians of continental Europe do not recognize the Gospels of St. Mark and St. Luke because these Evangelists were not among the Apostles. Luther used to call the Epistle of St. James a letter of straw.

But even when you are assured that the Bible contains the Word of God, and nothing but the Word of God, how do you know that the translation is faithful? The Book of Scripture were originally written in Hebrew and Greek, and you have only the translation. Before you are certain that the translation is faithful you must study the Hebrew and Greek languages, and then compare the translation with the original. How few are capable of this gigantic undertaking!

Indeed, when you accept the Bible as the Word of God, you are obliged to receive it on the authority of the Catholic Church, who was the sole Guardian of the Scriptures for fifteen hundred years.

But after having ascertained to your satisfaction that the translation is faithful, still the Scriptures can never serve as a complete Rule of Faith and a complete guide to heaven independently of an authorized, living interpreter.

A competent guide, such as our Lord intended for us, must have three characteristics. It must be within the reach of everyone; it must be clear and intelligible; it must be able to satisfy us on all questions relating to faith and morals.

First—A complete guide of salvation must be within the reach of every inquirer after truth; for, God "wishes all men to be saved, and to come to the knowledge of the truth;" and therefore He must have placed within the reach of everyone the means of arriving at the truth. Now, it is clear that the Scriptures could not at any period have been accessible to everyone.

They could not have been accessible *to the primitive Christians,* because they were not all written for a long time after the establishment of Christianity. The Christian religion was founded in the year 33. St. Matthew's Gospel, the first part of the New Testament ever written, did not appear till eight years after. The Church was established about twenty years when St. Luke wrote his Gospel. And St. John's Gospel did not come to light till toward the end of the first century. For many years after the Gospels and Epistles were written the knowledge of them was confined to the churches to which they were addressed. It was not till the close of the fourth century that the Church framed her Canon of Scripture and declared the Bible, as we now possess it, to be the genuine Word of God. And this was the golden age of Christianity! The most perfect Christians lived and died and went to heaven before the most important parts of the Scriptures were written. And what would have become of them if the Bible alone had been their guide?

The art of printing was not invented till the fifteenth century (1440). How utterly impossible it was to supply everyone with a copy of the Scriptures *from the fourth to the fifteenth century!* During that long period Bibles had to be copied with the pen. There were but a few hundred of them in the Christian world, and these were in the hands of the clergy and the learned. "According to the Protestant system, the art of printing would have been much more necessary to the Apostles than the gift of tongues. It was well for Luther that he did not come into the world until a century after the immortal invention of Guttenberg. A hundred years earlier his idea of directing two hundred and fifty million men to read the Bible would have been received with shouts of laughter, and would inevitably have caused his removal from the pulpit of Wittenberg to a hospital for the insane."

And even *at the present day,* with all the aid of steam printing presses, with all the Bible Associations extending through this country and England, and supported at enormous expense, it taxes all their energies to supply every missionary country with Bibles printed in the languages of the tribes and peoples for whom they are intended.

But even if the Bible were at all times accessible to everyone, how many millions exist in every age and country, not excepting our own age of boasted enlightenment, who are not accessible to the Bible because they are incapable of reading the Word of God! Hence, the doctrine of private interpretation would render many men's salvation not only difficult, but impossible.

Second—A competent religious guide must be clear and intelligible to all, so that everyone may fully understand the true meaning of the instructions it contains. Is the Bible a book intelligible to all? Far from it; it is full of obscurities and difficulties not only for the illiterate, but even for the learned. St. Peter himself informs us that in the Epistles of St. Paul there are "certain things hard to be understood, which the unlearned and the unstable wrest, as they do also the other Scriptures, to their own destruction." And consequently he tells us elsewhere "that no prophecy of Scripture is made by private interpretation."

We read in the Acts of the Apostles that a certain man was riding in his chariot, reading the Book of Isaiah, and being asked by St. Philip whether he understood the meaning of the prophecy he replied: "How can I understand unless some man show me?" admitting, by these modest words, that he did not pretend of himself to interpret the Scriptures.

The Fathers of the Church, though many of them spent in pronouncing the Bible a book full of knotty difficulties. And yet we find in our days pedants, with a mere smattering of Biblical knowledge, who see no obscurity at all in the Word of

God, and who presume to expound it from Genesis to Revelation. "Fools rush in where angels fear to tread."

Does not the conduct of the Reformers conclusively show
the utter folly of interpreting the Scriptures by private judgment? As soon as they rejected the oracle of the Church, and
set up their own private judgment as the highest standard of
authority, they could hardly agree among themselves on the
meaning of a single important text. The Bible became in their
hands a complete Babel. The sons of Noe attempted in their
pride to ascend to heaven by building the tower of Babel, and
their scheme ended in the confusion and multiplication of
tongues. The children of the Reformation endeavored in their
conceit to lead men to heaven by the private interpretation of
the Bible, and their efforts led to the confusion and the multiplication of religions. Let me give you one example out of a
thousand. These words of the Gospel, "This is My Body,"
were understood only in one sense before the Reformation. The
new lights of the sixteenth century gave no fewer than eighty
different meanings to these four simple words, and since their
time the number of interpretations has increased to over a
hundred.

No one will deny that in our days there exists a vast
multitude of sects, which are daily multiplying. No one will
deny that this multiplying of creeds is a crying scandal, and a
great stumbling-block in the way of the conversion of heathen
nations. No one can deny that these divisions in the Christian
family are traceable to the assumption of the right of private judgment. Every new-fledged divine, with a superficial
education, imagines that he has received a call from heaven to
inaugurate a new religion, and he is ambitious of handing down
his fame to posterity by stamping his name on a new sect. And
every one of these champions of modern creeds appeals to the
unchanging Bible in support of his ever-changing doctrines.

Thus, one body of Christians will prove from the Bible
that there is but one Person in God, while the rest will prove
from the same source that a Trinity of Persons is a clear article
of Divine Revelation. One will prove from the Holy Book that
Jesus Christ is not God. Others will appeal to the same text to
attest His Divinity. One denomination will assert on the author-

ity of Scripture that infant baptism is not necessary for salvation, while others will hold that it is. Some Christians, with Bible in hand, will teach that there are no sacraments. Others will say that there are only two. Some will declare that the inspired Word does not preach the eternity of punishments. Others will say that the Bible distinctly vindicates that dogma. Do not clergymen appear every day in the pulpit, and on the authority of the Book of Revelation point out to us with painful accuracy the year and the day on which this world is to come to an end? And when their prophecy fails of execution they coolly put off our destruction to another time.

Very recently several hundred Mormon women presented a petition to the government at Washington protesting against any interference with their abominable polygamy and they insist that their cherished system is sustained by the Word of God.

Such is the legitimate fruit of private interpretation! Our civil government is run not by private judgment, but by the constituted authorities. No one in his senses would allow our laws to be interpreted, and war to be declared by sensational journals, or by any private individuals. Why not apply the same principle to the interpretation of the Bible and the government of the Church?

Would it not be extremely hazardous to make a long voyage in a ship in which the officers and crew are fiercely contending among themselves about the manner of explaining the compass and of steering their course? How much more dangerous is it to trust to contending captains in the journey to heaven! Nothing short of an infallible authority should satisfy you when it is a question of steering your course to eternity. On this vital point there should be no conflict of opinion among those that guide you. There should be no conjecture. But there must be always someone at the helm whose voice gives assurance amid the fiercest storms that *all is well.*

Third—A rule of faith, or a competent guide to heaven, must be able to instruct in all the truths necessary for salvation. Now the Scriptures alone do not contain all the truths which a Christian is bound to believe, nor do they explicitly enjoin all the duties which he is obliged to practice. Not to mention other examples, is not every Christian obliged to sanctify

Sunday and to abstain on that day from unnecessary servile work? Is not the observance of this law among the most prominent of our sacred duties? But you may read the Bible from Genesis to Revelation, and you will not find a single line authorizing the sanctification of Sunday. The Scriptures enforce the religious observance of Saturday, a day which we never sanctify.

The Catholic Church correctly teaches that our Lord and His Apostles inculcated certain important duties of religion which are not recorded by the inspired writers. For instance, most Christians pray to the Holy Ghost, a practice which is nowhere found in the Bible.

We must, therefore, conclude that the Scriptures *alone* cannot be a sufficient guide and rule of faith because they cannot, at any time, be within the reach of every inquirer; because they are not of themselves clear and intelligible even in matters of the highest importance, and because they do not contain all the truths necessary for salvation.

God forbid that any of my readers should be tempted to conclude from what I have said that the Catholic Church is opposed to the reading of the Scriptures, or that she is the enemy of the Bible. The Catholic Church the enemy of the Bible! Good God! What monstrous ingratitude! What base calumny is contained in that assertion! As well might you accuse the Virgin Mother of trying to crush the infant Savior at her breast as to accuse the Church, our Mother, of attempting to crush out of existence the Word of God. As well might you charge the patriotic statesman with attempting to destroy the constitution of his country, while he strove to protect it from being mutilated by unprincipled demagogues.

For fifteen centuries the Church was the sole guardian and depository of the Bible, and if she really feared that sacred Book, who was to prevent her, during that long period, from tearing it in shreds and scattering it to the winds? She could have thrown it into the sea, as the unnatural mother would have thrown away her offspring, and who would have been the wiser?

What has become of those millions of once famous books written in past ages? They have nearly all perished. But amid this wreck of ancient literature, the Bible stands almost a solitary monument like the Pyramids of Egypt amid the surrounding wastes. That venerable Volume has survived the wars and revolutions and the barbaric invasions of fifteen centuries. Who rescued it from destruction? The Catholic Church. Without her fostering care the New Testament would probably be as little known today as "the Book of the days of the kings of Israel."

Little do we imagine, in our age of steam printing, how much labor it cost the Church to preserve and perpetuate the Sacred Scriptures. Learned monks, who are now abused in their graves by thoughtless men, were constantly employed in copying with the pen the Holy Bible. When one monk died at his post another took his place, watching like a faithful sentinel over the treasure of God's Word.

Let me give you a few plain facts to show the pains which the Church has taken to perpetuate the Scriptures.

The Canon of the Bible, as we have seen, was framed in the fourth century. In that same century Pope Damascus commanded a new and complete translation of the Scriptures to be made into the Latin language, which was then the living tongue not only of Rome and Italy, but of the civilized world.

If the Popes were afraid that the Bible should see the light, this was a singular way of manifesting their fear.

The task of preparing a new edition of the Scriptures was assigned to St. Jerome, the most learned Hebrew scholar of his time. This new translation was disseminated throughout Christendom, and on that account was called the *Vulgate,* or popular edition.

In the sixth and seventh centuries the modern languages of Europe began to spring up like so many shoots from the parent Latin stock. The Scriptures, also, soon found their way into these languages. The Venerable Bede, who lived in England in the eighth century, and whose name is profoundly reverenced in that country, translated the Sacred Scriptures into Saxon, which was then the language of England. He died while dictating the last verses of St. John's Gospel.

Thomas Arundel, Archbishop of Canterbury, in a funeral discourse on Queen Anne, consort of Richard II., pronounced

397

in 1394, praises her for her diligence in reading the four Gospels. The Head of the Church of England could not condemn in others what he commended in the queen.

Sir Thomas More affirms that, before the days of Wycliffe, there was an English version of the Scriptures, "by good and godly people with devotion and soberness well and reverently read."

If partial restrictions began to be placed on the circulation of the Bible in England in the fifteenth century, these restrictions were occasioned by the conduct of Wycliffe and his followers, who not only issued a new translation, on which they engrafted their novelties of doctrine, but also sought to explain the sacred text in a sense foreign to the received interpretation of tradition.

While laboring to diffuse the Word of God it is the duty, as well as the right of the Church, as the guardian of faith, to see that the faithful are not misled by unsound editions.

Printing was invented in the fifteenth century, and almost a hundred years later came the Reformation. It is often triumphantly said, and I suppose there are some who, even at the present day, are ignorant enough to believe the assertion, that the first edition of the Bible ever published after the invention of printing was the edition of Martin Luther. The fact is, that before Luther put his pen to paper, no fewer than fifty-six editions of the Scriptures had appeared on the continent of Europe, not to speak of those printed in Great Britain. Of those editions, twenty-one were published in German, one in Spanish, four in French, twenty-one in Italian, five in Flemish and four in Bohemian.

Coming down to our own times, if you open an English Catholic Bible you will find in the preface a letter of Pope Pius VI., in which he strongly recommends the pious reading of the Holy Scriptures. A Pope's letter is the most weighty authority in the Church. You will also find in Haydock's Bible the letters of the Bishops of the United States, in which they express the hope that this splendid edition would have a wide circulation among their flocks.

These facts ought, I think, to convince every candid mind that the Church, far from being opposed to the reading of the Scriptures, does all she can to encourage their perusal.

A gentleman of North Carolina lately informed me that the first time he entered a Catholic bookstore he was surprised at witnessing on the shelves an imposing array of Bibles for sale. Up to that moment he had believed the unfounded charge that Catholics were forbidden to read the Scriptures. He has since embraced the Catholic faith.

And perhaps I may be permitted here to record my personal experiences during a long course of study. I speak of myself, not because my case is exceptional, but, on the contrary, because my example will serve to illustrate the system pursued toward ecclesiastical students in all colleges throughout the Catholic world in reference to the Holy Scriptures.

In our course of Humanities we listened every day to the reading of the Bible. When we were advanced to the higher branches of Philosophy and Theology the study of the Sacred Scriptures formed an important part of our education. We read, besides, every day a chapter of the New Testament, not standing or sitting, but on our knees, and then reverently kissed the inspired page. We listened at our meals each day to selections from the Bible, and we always carried about with us a copy of the New Testament.

So familiar, indeed, were the students with the sacred Volume that many of them, on listening to a few verses, could tell from what portion of the Scriptures you were reading. The only dread we were taught to have of the Scriptures was that of reading them without fear and reverence.

And after his ordination every Priest is obliged in conscience to devote upwards of an hour each day to the perusal of the Word of God. I am not aware that clergymen of other denominations are bound by the same duty.

What is good for the clergy must be good, also, for the laity. Be assured that if you become a Catholic you will never be forbidden to read the Bible. It is our earnest wish that every word of the Gospel may be imprinted on your memory and on your heart.

CHAPTER IX

THE PRIMACY OF PETER

The Catholic Church teaches also, that our Lord conferred on St. Peter the first place of honor and jurisdiction in the government of His whole Church, and that the same spiritual supremacy has always resided in the Popes, or Bishops of Rome, as being the successors of St. Peter. Consequently, to be true followers of Christ all Christians, both among the clergy and the laity, must be in communion with the See of Rome, where Peter rules in the person of his successor.

Before coming to any direct proofs on this subject I may state that, in the Old Law, the High Priest appointed by Almighty God filled an office analogous to that of Pope in the New Law. In the Jewish Church there were Priests and Levites ordained to minister at the altar; and there was, also, a supreme ecclesiastical tribunal, with the High Priest at its head. All matters of religious controversy were referred to this tribunal and in the last resort to the High Priest, whose decision was enforced under pain of death. "If there be a hard matter in judgment between blood and blood, cause and cause, leprosy and leprosy, . . . thou shalt come to the Priest of the Levitical race and to the judge, . . . and they shall show thee true judgment. And thou shalt do whatever they say who preside in the place which the Lord shall choose, and thou shalt follow their sentence. And thou shalt not decline to the right hand, or to the left . . . . But he that . . . . will refuse to obey the commandment of the Priest, who ministereth at the time, . . . that man shall die, and thou shalt take away the evil from Israel."

From this passage it is evident that in the Hebrew Church the High Priest had the highest jurisdiction in religious matters. By this means unity of faith and worship was preserved among the people of God.

Now the Jewish synagogue, as St. Paul testifies, was the type and figure of the Christian Church; for "all these things happened to them (the Jews) in figure." We must, therefore, find in the Church of Christ a spiritual judge, exercising the same supreme authority as the High Priest wielded in the Old

Law. For if a supreme Pontiff was necessary, in the Mosaic dispensation, to maintain purity and uniformity of worship, the same dignitary is equally necessary now to preserve unity of faith.

Every well-regulated civil government has an acknowledged head. The President is the head of the United States Government. Queen Victoria is the ruler of Great Britain. The Sultan sways the Turkish Empire. If these nations had no authorized leader to govern them they would be reduced to the condition of a mere mob, and anarchy, confusion and civil way would inevitably follow, as recently happened to France after the fall of Napoleon III.

Even in every well-ordered family, domestic peace requires that someone preside.

Now, the Church of Christ is a visible society—that is, a society composed of human beings. She has, it is true, a spiritual end in view; but having to deal with men, she must have a government as well as every other organized society. This government, at least in its essential elements, our Lord must have established for His Church. For was He not as wise as human legislators? And shall we suppose that, of all lawgivers, the Wisdom Incarnate alone left His Kingdom on earth to be governed without a head?

But someone will tell me: "We do not deny that the Church has a head. God himself is its Ruler." This is evading the real question. Is not God the Ruler of all governments? "By Me," He says, "kings reign, and lawgivers decree just things." He is the recognized Head of our Republic, and of every Christian family in the land; but, nevertheless, there is always presiding over the country a visible chief, who represents God on earth.

In like manner the Church, besides an invisible Head in heaven, must have a visible head on earth. The body and members of the Church are visible; why not also the Head? The Church without a supreme Ruler would be like an army without a general, a navy without an admiral, a sheepfold without a shepherd, or like a human body without a head.

The Christian communities separated from the Catholic Church deny that Peter received any authority over the other Apostles, and hence they reject the supremacy of the Pope.

401

The absence from the Protestant communions of a Divinely appointed, visible Head is to them an endless source of weakness and dissension. It is an insuperable barrier against any hope of a permanent reunion among themselves, because they are left without a common rallying centre or basis of union and are placed in an unhappy state of schism.

The existence, on the contrary, of a supreme judge of controversy in the Catholic Church is the secret of her admirable unity. This is the keystone that binds together and strengthens the imperishable arch of faith.

From the very fact, then, of the existence of a supreme Head in the Jewish Church; from the fact that a Head is always necessary for civil government, for families and corporations; from the fact, especially, that a visible Head is essential to the maintenance of unity **in** the Church, while the absence of a Head necessarily leads **to** anarchy, we are forced to conclude, even though positive evidence were wanting, that, in the establishment of His Church, it must have entered into the mind of the Divine Lawgiver to place over it a primate invested with superior judicial powers.

But have we any positive proof that Christ did appoint a supreme Ruler over His Church? To those, indeed, who read the Scriptures with the single eye of pure intention the most abundant evidence of this fact is furnished. To my mind the New Testament establishes no doctrine, unless it satisfies every candid reader that our Lord gave plenipotentiary powers to Peter to govern the whole Church. In this chapter I shall speak of the Promise, the Institution, and the exercise of Peter's Primacy, as recorded in the New Testament. The next chapter shall be devoted to its perpetuity in the Popes.

Promise of the Primacy. Our Savior, on a certain occasion, asked His disciples, saying: "Whom do men say that the Son of Man is? And they said: Some say that Thou art John the Baptist; and others, Elias; and others, Jeremiah, or one of the Prophets. Jesus said to them: But whom do ye say that I am?" Peter, as usual, is the leader and spokesman. "Simon Peter answering, said: Thou art Christ, the Son of the living God. And Jesus answering said to him: Blessed art thou, Simon Bar-Jona: because flesh and blood hath not revealed it to thee, but My

Father who is in heaven. And I say to thee: that thou art Peter, and upon this rock I will build My Church, and the gates of hell shall not prevail against it. And I will give to thee the keys of the Kingdom of Heaven: and whatsoever thou shalt bind on earth shall be bound also in heaven; and whatsoever thou shalt loose on earth shall be loosed also in heaven." Here we find Peter confessing the Divinity of Christ, and in reward for that confession he is honored with the promise of the Primacy.

Our Savior, by the words "thou art Peter," clearly alludes to the new name which He Himself had conferred upon Simon, when He received him into the number of His followers (John i. 42); and He now reveals the reason for the change of name, which was to insinuate the honor He was to confer on him, by appointing him President of the Christian Republic; just as God, in the Old Law, changed Abram's name to Abraham, when He chose him to be the father of a mighty nation.

The word *Peter*, in the Syro-Chaldaic tongue, which our Savior spoke, means *a rock*. The sentence runs thus in that language: *"Thou art a rock, and on this rock I will build My Church."* Indeed, all respectable Protestant commentators have now abandoned, and even ridicule, the absurdity of applying the word *rock* to anyone but to Peter; as the sentence can bear no other construction, unless our Lord's good grammar and common sense are called in question.

Jesus, our Lord, founded but one Church, which He was pleased to build on Peter. Therefore, any church that does not recognize Peter as its foundation stone is not the Church of Christ, and therefore cannot stand, for it is not the work of God. This is plain. Would to God that all would see it aright and with eyes free from prejudice.

He continues: "And I will give to thee the keys of the Kingdom of Heaven," etc. In ancient times, and particularly among the Hebrew people, keys were an emblem of jurisdiction. To affirm that a man had received the keys of a city was equivalent to the assertion that he had been appointed its governor. In the Book of Revelation our Savior says that He has "the keys of death and of hell," which means that He is endowed with power over death and hell. In fact, even to this day does not the presentation of keys convey among ourselves the idea of authority? If the proprietor of a house, on leaving it for the summer, says to any friend: "Here are the keys of my house," would not this simple declaration, without a word of explanation, convey the idea, "I give you full control of my house; you may admit or exclude whom you please; you represent me in my absence?" Let us now apply this interpretation to our Redeemer's words. When He says to Peter: "I will give to thee the keys," etc., He evidently means: I will give the supreme authority over My Church, which is the citadel of faith, My earthly Jerusalem. Thou and thy successors shall be My visible representatives to the end of time. And be it remembered that to Peter alone, and to no other Apostle, were these solemn words addressed.

Fulfillment of the Promise. The promise which our Redeemer made of creating Peter the supreme Ruler of His Church is fulfilled in the following passage: "Jesus saith to Simon Peter: Simon, son of John, lovest thou Me more than these? He saith to Him: Yea, Lord, Thou knowest that I love Thee. He saith to him: Feed My lambs. He saith to him again: Simon, son of John, lovest thou Me? He saith to Him: Yea, Lord, Thou knowest that I love Thee. He saith to him: Feed My lambs. He saith to him the third time: Simon, son of John, lovest thou Me? Peter was grieved because He had said to him the third time: Lovest thou Me? And he said to Him: Lord, Thou knowest all things. Thou knowest that I love Thee. He said to him: Feed My sheep."

These words were addressed by our Lord to Peter after His resurrection. The whole sheepfold of Christ is confided to him, without any exception or limitation. Peter has jurisdiction not only over the lambs—the weak and tender portion of the flock— by which are understood the faithful; but also over the sheep, *i. e.,* the Pastors themselves, who hold the same relations to their congregations that the sheep hold to the lambs, because they bring forth unto Jesus Christ, and nourish the spiritual lambs of the fold. To other Pastors a certain portion of the flock is assigned; to Peter the entire fold; for, never did Jesus say to any other Apostle or Bishop what He said to Peter: Feed My whole flock.

Candid reader, do you not profess to be a member of Christ's flock? Yes, you answer. Do you take your spiritual food from Peter and his successor, and do you hear the voice of Peter, or have you wandered into the fold of strangers who spurn Peter's voice? Ponder well this momentous question. For if Peter is authorized to feed the lambs of Christ's flock, the lambs should hear Peter's voice.

Exercise of the Primacy. In the Acts of the Apostles, which contain almost the only Scripture narrative that exists of the Apostles subsequent to our Lord's ascension, St. Peter appears before us, like Saul among the tribes, standing head and shoulders over his brethren by the prominent part he takes in every ministerial duty.

The first twelve chapters of the Acts are devoted to Peter and to some of the other Apostles, the remaining chapters being chiefly occupied with the labors of the Apostles of the Gentiles. In that brief historical fragment, as well as in the Gospels, the name of Peter is everywhere pre-eminent.

Peter's name always stands first in the list of the Apostles, while Judas Iscariot is invariably mentioned last. Peter is even called by St. Matthew *the first Apostle.* Now Peter was first neither in age nor in priority of election, his elder brother Andrew having been chosen before him. The meaning, therefore, of the expression must be that Peter was first not only in rank and honor, but also in authority.

Peter is the first Apostle who performed a miracle. He is the first to address the Jews in Jerusalem while his Apostolic brethren stand respectfully around him, upon which occasion he converts three thousand souls.

Peter is the first to make converts from the Gentile world in the persons of Cornelius and his friends.

When there is question of electing a successor to Judas Peter *alone speaks.* He points out to the Apostles and disciples the duty of choosing another to succeed the traitor. The Apostles silently acquiesce in the instructions of their leader.

In the Apostolic Council of Jerusalem Peter is the first whose sentiments are recorded. Before his discourse "there was much disputing." But when he had ceased to speak "all the multitude held their peace."

St. James and the other Apostles concur in the sentiments of Peter without a single dissenting voice.

St. James is cast into prison by Herod and afterward beheaded. He was one of the three most favored Apostles. He was the cousin of our Lord and brother of St. John. He was most dear to the faithful. Yet no extraordinary efforts are made by the faithful to rescue him from death.

Peter is imprisoned about the same time. The whole Church is aroused. Prayers for his deliverance ascend to heaven, not only from Jerusalem but also from every Christian family in the land.

The army of the Lord can afford to lose a chieftain in the person of James, but it cannot yet spare the commander-in-chief. The enemies of the Church had hoped that the destruction of the chief shepherd would involve the dispersion of the whole flock; therefore they redoubled their fury against the Prince of the Apostles, just as her modern enemies concentrate their shafts against the Pope, his successor. Does not this incident eloquently proclaim Peter's superior authority? In fact Peter figures so conspicuously in every page that his Primacy is not only admissible, but is forced on the judgment of the impartial reader.

What are the principal objections advanced against the Primacy of Peter? They are chiefly, I may say exclusively, confined to the three following: First—That our Lord rebuked Peter. Second—That St. Paul criticised his conduct on a point not affecting doctrine, but discipline. The Apostle of the Gentiles blames St. Peter because he withdrew for a time from the society of the Gentile converts, for fear of scandalizing the newly-converted Jews. Third—That the supremacy of Peter conflicts with the supreme dominion of Christ.

For my part I cannot see how these objections can invalidate the claims of Peter. Was not Jesus Peter's superior? May not a superior rebuke his servant without infringing on the servant's prerogatives?

And why could not St. Paul censure the conduct of St. Peter without questioning that superior's authority? It is not a very uncommon thing for ecclesiastics occupying an inferior position in the Church to admonish even the Pope. St. Bernard, though only a monk, wrote a work in which, with Apostolic freedom, he administers counsel to Pope Eugenius III., and cautions him against the dangers to which his eminent position exposes him. Yet no man had more reverence for any Pope than Bernard had for this great Pontiff. Cannot our Governor animadvert upon the President's conduct without impairing the President's jurisdiction?

Nay, from this very circumstance, I draw a confirming evidence of Peter's supremacy. St. Paul mentions it as a fact worthy of record that he actually *withstood Peter to his face.* Do you think it would be worth recording if Paul had rebuked James or John or Barnabas? By no means. If one brother rebukes another, the matter excites no special attention. But if a son rebukes his father, or if a Priest rebukes his Bishop to his face, we understand why he would consider it a fact worth relating. Hence, when St. Paul goes to the trouble of telling us that he took exception to Peter's conduct, he mentions it as an extraordinary exercise of Apostolic freedom, and leaves on our mind the obvious inference that Peter was his superior.

In the very same Epistle to the Galatians St. Paul plainly insinuates St. Peter's superior rank. "I went," he says, "to Jerusalem to see Peter, and I tarried with him fifteen days." Saints Chrysostom and Ambrose tell us that this was not an idle visit of ceremony, but that the object of St. Paul in making the journey was to testify his respect and honor for the chief of the Apostles. St. Jerome observes in a humorous vein that "Paul went not to behold Peter's eyes, his cheeks or his countenance, whether he was thin or stout, with nose straight or twisted, covered with hair or bald, not to observe the outward man, *but to show honor to the first Apostle.*"

There are others who pretend, in spite of our Lord's declaration to the contrary, that loyalty to Peter is disloyalty to Christ, and that, by acknowledging Peter as the rock on which the Church is built, we set our Savior aside. So far from this being the case, we acknowledge Jesus Christ as the "chief cornerstone," as well as the Divine Architect of the building.

The true test of loyalty to Jesus is not only to worship Him, but to venerate even the representatives whom He has chosen. Will anyone pretend to say that my obedience to the

Governor's appointee is a mark of disrespect to the Governor himself? I think our State Executive would have little faith in the allegiance of any citizen who would say to him: "Governor, I honor you personally, but your official's order I shall disregard."

St. Peter is called the first Bishop of Rome because he transferred his see from Antioch to Rome, where he suffered martyrdom with St. Paul.

We are not surprised that modern skepticism, which rejects the Divinity of Christ and denies even the existence of God, should call in question the fact that St. Peter lived and died in Rome.

The reason commonly alleged for disputing this well-attested event is that the Acts of the Apostles make no mention of Peter's labors and martyrdom in Rome. For the same reason we might deny that St. Paul was beheaded in Rome; that St. John died in Ephesus, and that St. Andrew was crucified. The Scripture is silent regarding these historical records, and yet they are denied by no one.

The intrinsic evidence of St. Peter's first Epistle, the testimony of his immediate successors in the ministry, as well as the avowal of eminent Protestant commentators, all concur in fixing the See of Peter in Rome.

"Babylon," from which Peter addresses his first Epistle, is understood by learned annotators, Protestant and Catholic, to refer to Rome—the word Babylon being symbolical of the corruption then prevailing in the city of the Cæsars.

Clement, the fourth Bishop of Rome, who is mentioned in terms of praise by St. Paul; St. Ignatius, Bishop of Antioch, who died in 105; Irenæus, Origen, St. Jerome, Eusebius, the great historian, and other eminent writers testify to St. Peter's residence in Rome, while no ancient ecclesiastical writer has ever contradicted the statement.

John Calvin; a witness above suspicion; Cave, an able Anglican critic; Grotius and other distinguished Protestant writers, do not hesitate to re-echo the unanimous voice of Catholic tradition.

Indeed, no historical fact will escape the shafts of incredulity, if St. Peter's residence and glorious martyrdom in Rome are called in question.